The Collected Works of Paddy Chayefsky
THE STAGE PLAYS

APPLAUSE
BOOKS
NEW YORK • LONDON

An Applause Original

The Stage Plays

Library of Congress Cataloging-in-Publication Data

Chayefsky, Paddy, 1923-1981
    The stage plays / Paddy Chayefsky
      p. cm. -- (The collected works of Paddy Chayefsky ; 1)
      Contents: Middle of the night -- The tenth man -- Gideon -- The passion of Josef D. -- The latent heterosexual.
      ISBN 1-55783-192-0 : $12.95
    I. Title. II. Series: Chayefsky, Paddy, 1923-1981   Works. 1994 ; 1.
PS3505.H632A19 1994 vol. 1
812'.54--dc20

94-23040
CIP

British Library Cataloging-in-Publication Data

A catalogue record for this book is available from the British Library.

Applause Books
211 West 71st Street
New York, NY 10023
Phone (212) 496-7511
Fax: (212) 721-2856
First Applause Printing 1995

406 Vale Road
Tonbridge Kent TN9 1XR
Phone 073 235-7755
Fax 073 207-7219

Printed in Canada

This collection is dedicated to the memory of its author, Paddy Chayefsky, and to the enormous gift of his talent and insight which fills these pages.

—Susan Chayefsky

An enormous debt of gratitude is owed to Karen Jaehne, who provided invaluable help on this publication. With care and uncommon dedication, she edited the screenplays and contributed greatly to compiling this work. She has our great thanks.

The following people were of special assistance in the preparation of these volumes, and their help is gratefully acknowledged: Susan Brown, Dan Chayefsky, David Cleaver, Barbara Cramer, Herb Gardner, Howard Gottfried, Arthur Hiller, Andrew Pontious, Arthur Schlesinger, Jr., J. Stephen Sheppard, Paul Sugarman, Ken Swezey, and all the staff at Applause.

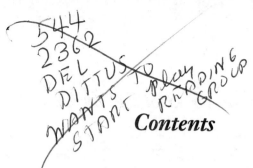

Contents

The Collected Works of Paddy Chayefsky

The Stage Plays

•

The Television Plays

•

The Screenplays Volume I
Marty, The Goddess, The Americanization of Emily

•

The Screenplays Volume II
The Hospital, Network, Altered States

PADDY

He was a small, compact, tidy man, with a trim beard and a glint in his eye —a glint of mischief, a glint of passion; for, though he was wildly funny, his humor sprang from an exasperated sense of the lunacy of life; he laughed in order to save himself from sounding like an Old Testament prophet. His wit was elegant and irrepressible and gathered momentum as he seized on an idea and launched into a scintillating cascade of comic improvisation. He was a cultivated man, widely if erratically read in literature, history, science. His curiosity was endless. At bottom, he was a profoundly serious man who despised hypocrisy, injustice and humanity's addiction to inhumanity.

We met first in 1959. Through an inscrutable but benign decision by the Eisenhower State Department, we were both selected as members of the first American writers' delegation to go to the Soviet Union. Our fellow travelers were the critic Alfred Kazin and Edward Weeks, the patrician editor of the *Atlantic Monthly*. It was an oddly assorted group, but we had a highly entertaining time with each other and a highly contentious, irritable and irritating time with our hosts from the Soviet Writers' Union, a collection of dogmatic and humorless bureaucrats. I fear that we set back Soviet-American cultural relations by twenty years or so.

We did have a fascinating afternoon with the weary and cynical Ilya Ehrenburg and some interesting exchanges with a couple of literary editors. But most of the time we were lectured at by people telling us how communism was solving all the problems of humanity. In retrospect, I suppose they were trying to convince themselves. "The Soviet Union," Paddy said after a while, "is like a husband and wife who keep telling everyone all the time how happy they are."

When they weren't lecturing at us, they were lying to us. One expected to be lied to on large issues—that Soviet writers were free to write as they pleased or that South Korea had invaded North Korea. These were high-policy lies, and comparable lies would probably be told to foreigners touring the United States. But we were lied to, casually, contemptuously and persistently—on trivial issues.

Paddy had come with a specific sentimental objective—one he had communicated to the Soviet Embassy in Washington and again to the Writers' Union in Moscow. He wanted above all to visit the village in the Ukraine from which his parents had emigrated to America. In due course, a trip was scheduled to Kiev. There the rest of us would meet local writers while Paddy would go by automobile to his ancestral home. But the day before we were to leave Moscow, the trip was cancelled. The Writers' Union blandly explained that no hotel rooms were available in Kiev.

Kiev was a large city, and it seemed improbable that the Writers' Union could not commandeer a few hotel rooms. Paddy walked over to the INtourist office and was told there were plenty of hotel rooms available in Kiev. A man of iron determination, he booked passage to New York and announced that he would depart the next day unless the Kiev trip were reinstated by five o'clock that afternoon. A few moments before the deadline, hotel rooms were found.

So we went on to Kiev. For Paddy to make his pilgrimage and rejoin the party in time to make what we were repeatedly told was "the last plane that evening to Moscow," he would have to leave the hotel at eight in the morning. He would then be driven five hours to the village, stay an hour and drive back in time for the evening plane. But no car appeared that morning at eight, or at nine, or at ten, or at eleven. Paddy sat fuming in the hotel lobby, extemporizing in picturesque language about our hosts and the Soviet system.

The car arrived around noon. They told Paddy that, if he went now, he could not catch up with the rest of us that evening. He glared at them and said he had come all this distance to see his parents' birthplace. After consultation, they discovered a later plane to Moscow; if he hurried, he was told, he could still get back to Moscow that night. Then they drove him with deliberate and painful slowness through the Ukrainian countryside.

After several hours, he reached his destination. The villagers had never before seen an American. They greeted Paddy with enthusiasm. Older folk who remembered his parents appeared. Preparations were under way for a banquet. But after seven minutes, his driver told him that, if he wanted to make the last plane, he must leave at once. Tearing himself away, he got sadly into the car. They drove furiously back to the Kiev airport—and found that there was no late plane to Moscow and hence no reason to rush from the village. When Paddy finally rejoined us in another twenty-four hours, he had already shaped this saga of manipulation, mendacity and frustration into a marvelous story, at once hilarious, wrathful and touching. I had admired the writer, and now I loved the man.

When I moved to New York a few years later, I began seeing Paddy with some regularity. He had made his early success as a dramatist of the inarticulate. His writing for television and the movies was distinctive in its wry and compassionate social observation. Paddy had an instinctive sweet understanding of forlorn people in the big city, bravely living lives of quiet desperation. *Marty*, *The Bachelor Party*, *Middle of the Night* all had the impact of acrid realism in the 1950s when television and movies were salesmen for the glossy consumer society.

By the 1960s, Paddy was well embarked on what became the dominating theme of his later plays and films. His concern was still the fate of the individual in modern society, but now it was the individual at the mercy of the corrupt and crazy energies secreted by our great organizations, whether television (*Network*), medicine (*The Hospital*), the army (*The Americanization of Emily*), the church (*The Tenth Man*), the laboratory (*Altered States*), the Hollywood studio (*The Goddess*), the Maoist underground (*Network*).

He had an exact and stinging satiric gift. But he did not use that gift for purely destructive purposes. The *Network* cry — "I'm mad as hell, and I'm not going to take this anymore" — was preceded by the messianic commentator's impassioned plea: "You've got to say, 'I'm a human being, god damn it, my life has some value!'" Paddy was sardonic, not cynical. He believed, god damn it, that everyone's life has some value — if we can only clear our minds of cant and hypocrisy that we can get on with the business, at once serious and joyous, of living. His wit was devastating but liberating. He thought life absurd, but also thought it glorious. For all his relish in human folly, he never abandoned hope in humanity.

At some point, Paddy fell out with New York's commercial theater and swore up and down that he would never permit a play of his to be staged on Broadway again. His last completed play, *The Latent Heterosexual*, had its premiere in Texas. Movies, oddly, were generally more amenable to Paddy's blazing style — though he hated what Ken Russell did to *Altered States*.

He was a dear and generous friend. One day we had an etymological argument. The next day there arrived, with his card, the compact edition of *The Oxford English Dictionary*, complete with magnifying glass. He was only fifty-eight when he died in 1981, and he was then, as always, overflowing with notions for plays, films and novels — enough to keep him, and us, going for the rest of the century.

During his long and anguishing sickness, he was darkly funny about his misadventures in the hospital. "The doctors have never forgiven that movie," he would say, referring to the George C. Scott/Diana Rigg film. "Now they are paying me back." The gallows humor was combined with an unquenchable optimism that seemed to exclude the idea of death. He was a very gallant man.

In squalid times, he was a man of passion, and his work and life had the lucidity of his passion. He had a rage against pomposity, a rage against stupidity, a rage against injustice, and his rage sprang from love for the beleaguered, distraught but indomitable individual. Should there be a hereafter, I should like to end up in the same place with Paddy. I cannot wait to hear his commentary on the state of things up there.

Arthur Schlesinger, Jr.

Middle of the Night

To Sue

MIDDLE OF THE NIGHT *was first presented by Joshua Logan at the ANTA Theatre, New York City, on February 8, 1956, with the following cast:*

(In Order of Appearance)

THE GIRL	Gena Rowlands
THE MOTHER	June Walker
THE KID SISTER	Joan Chambers
THE MANUFACTURER	Edward G. Robinson
THE SISTER	Nancy R. Pollock
THE WIDOW	Betty Walker
THE DAUGHTER	Patricia Benoit
THE CANASTA PLAYER	Ruth Masters
THE NEIGHBOR	Effie Afton
THE FRIEND	Janet Ward
THE SON-IN-LAW	Martin Balsam
THE HUSBAND	Lee Philips

Directed by Joshua Logan
Settings and Lighting by Jo Mielziner
Costumes by Motley

The action of the play takes place in the West Eighties, New York City, between November and February of the present year.

There are three acts.

ACT I

SCENE 1

The living room, a bedroom, and a foyer of a four and a half room apartment in the West Eighties. Furnished in lower-middle-class, not much above shabby. We also see the tiled landing outside the apartment, with its iron railing and stairway leading from the floor below to the floor above.

It is eight-thirty in the morning. The apartment is dark, however, almost murky, as if all the shades were drawn—which they are. For a moment, the thick silence of sleep fills the stage. There is a figure sleeping on the bed in the bedroom, and another figure sleeping on the couch in the living room. We know they are girls from the articles of clothing lying about in each room.

After a long moment, THE GIRL *on the couch in the living room sits up, slowly moving her legs till they dangle over the side of the couch. We see now that she is a pretty, blond girl of twenty-five. She is wearing a slip. Her face is swollen and sodden, and she sits heavily, her shoulders slumped. Suddenly she begins to cry. We cannot hear her at first, but we can see the shivering of her shoulders. She stands up and pads aimlessly around the living room, her eyes open, crying more audibly now. Then, as quickly as it began, the abrupt flush of tears stops, and she sits in the sofa chair of the room, her breath coming out in long, shuddering sighs, which eventually stop. She sits quietly now, her hands folded slackly in her lap.*

Now she rises, goes to the end table at the side of the couch, picks up her wrist watch and looks at the time. She stands frowning as if it were difficult to concentrate on the reality of the moment, and then she shuffles to the soft chair again, perches on the edge of it, picks up the telephone receiver at her elbow and dials a number. She waits.

There is some movement upstage in the foyer, and then a woman in her late forties—tall, angular, wearing a blue kimono over her slip and with her hair still early-morning awry—comes into the bedroom and moves down to the figure of the girl sleeping on the bed.

THE GIRL
(On phone, in living room)

Hello, who's this—Caroline? Caroline, this is Betty—Betty Preiss. I just called in to say I won't be in to work today.... No, no, it's nothing like that,

5

it's a personal matter....

THE MOTHER
(Shaking the blanketed hip on the bed)
Come on, get up because it's half-past eight.
(THE MOTHER disappears back into the foyer.)

THE GIRL
(On phone)
The only thing is, I just remembered I took some sales slips home with me yesterday.... I don't know. I think these are the sales slips Mr. Ellman sent down from the factory in Brooklyn yesterday.... No, I don't have them on me, Caroline. I left them home. Wait a minute. Yes, I do. I have them in my purse.
(THE MOTHER appears in the living-room doorway, pauses to listen for a moment, then disappears again back into the foyer. In the bedroom, THE KID SISTER slowly crawls out from under her blankets during THE GIRL's phone call. THE KID SISTER is an amiable, if still sluggish, girl of seventeen, wearing rumpled blue pajamas. THE GIRL sits huddled on the soft chair in the living room, her eyes closed, the effort of speaking an enormous one.)

THE GIRL
No, I'm at my mother's house, 120 West Eighty-First Street, apartment 6E. E like in easy. It's on the top floor.... All right, you'd better tell Mr. Kingsley about the sales slips.... That's really very sweet of you but I'll be in tomorrow.... All right, I'll see you. Thank you, Caroline. Good-bye.
(She seems terribly weary. She rests her head on the palm of her free hand. THE MOTHER comes padding into the living room.)

THE MOTHER
Did you just call in to say you wasn't going to work today? I think you should go in to work, keep your mind occupied. I'm getting dressed, I'm going in to work myself. And Alice'll be in school all day because I'm not up at the Seventy-ninth Street Hanscom's any more. They switched me down to the Fifty-seventh Street bakery, and you'll be here all alone. *(To THE KID SISTER, who has appeared in the bedroom doorway)* Will you get dressed and go to school!
(THE KID SISTER promptly disappears back into her bedroom.)

THE GIRL
Ma, stay with me a couple of minutes because I feel lousy.

THE MOTHER
Betty, I have a seventeen-year-old daughter still in high school I have to support—

(THE MOTHER scowls at her fingers, and a silence falls between the two women. THE GIRL finds the silence unbearable.)

THE GIRL

George and I are not getting along. Listen, I wouldn't have come over here and bothered you with my problems, but I was in a panic last night about two o'clock in the morning. When I got down into the street there were a couple of tough-looking kids hanging on the corner, so I didn't know where to go so I just came up here. Ma, stay with me for about half an hour. I feel lousy.

THE MOTHER

Well, what do you want to say, Betty?

THE GIRL

(Sits on the edge of the bed)

George and I, I think our marriage is through. Ma, we have a physical marriage, and that's it. That's the only time he wants me. The rest of the day he's always trying to get away from me. He's got this job with a band in Las Vegas. He's leaving Monday. He came in yesterday and he said, "Listen, want to go out to Las Vegas with me?" The next minute he said, "Maybe you better not come because you won't have any fun out there, it's just a desert. You'll be by yourself all the time. I'll be playing with the band all day." Do you understand what I mean, Ma? He asked me to go because he felt it was his duty as my husband, but he really didn't want me to. He really doesn't like to be with me. Then around eight o'clock I asked him if we could stay home alone that evening. So about five minutes later he said, "Let's go to a movie." That's his idea of being alone with me. You see, we can sit in a movie and he doesn't have to deal with me. He avoids me all the time. So we didn't go to a movie. We watched TV the whole night. I don't think we said a word. Ma, it's not just last night. It's every night. Then I went to bed. Then he came in around one o'clock. He got undressed and got in bed. I turned over to him and I said, "George, just hold me in your arms a little," and he reached over and began feeling my leg. I just wanted him to hold me and talk to me. You know what he was thinking? He just wanted to get me to sleep so I wouldn't bother him any more. So I waited until he was asleep, and I got up and came over here.

THE MOTHER

(After a moment)

You get along in bed all right?

THE GIRL

Ma, I just told you. We get along fine that way.

THE MOTHER

Because that's the whole thing, how you get along in bed.
(Having shown this maternal concern, THE MOTHER *pauses.)*

THE GIRL

I think I want a divorce.

THE MOTHER

Oh, for God's sakes.

THE GIRL

I've been thinking about it for a couple of months.

THE MOTHER

You had a fight with your husband, for heaven's sakes. You'll be kissing and making up before— How long you been married, one year, for heaven's sakes? Stop acting like a baby, will you? Divorce! *(She starts to go, but some suspicion of inadequacy holds her)* Well, Betty, I've got a seventeen-year-old daughter still in high school I've got to support. Your father abandoned me with two little girls on my hands, one of them one year old. I had no source of income. I have scrubbed floors for my two daughters. As heaven is my witness, I have gone down on my knees and scrubbed floors so my two children could eat. I can say now that my two girls are decent girls who have never been in any trouble.

THE GIRL
(Muttering)

I'm in trouble now, Ma.

THE MOTHER

Well, as long as you get along in bed, that's the whole thing.
*(*THE GIRL *turns, and, for lack of anything better to do, she looks on the end table for her cigarettes.)*

THE GIRL

Well, you better get to work, Ma.

THE MOTHER

Yeah, I'd better get to work because I'm not working up at the Seventy-Ninth Street Hanscom's any more. They switched me down to the Fifty-Seventh Street bakery. I'm working mornings now. *(Stands, looks at her daughter, aware that something more is expected of her)* How do you feel? Do you feel all right?

THE GIRL

I'm fine, Ma. You go to work.

THE MOTHER

All right, so I'm going to get dressed.

(She shuffles out of the room, turns left at the foyer and exits. THE GIRL *sits on the couch, frowning down at the floor. The scene is held for a moment.)*

The lights fade quickly

SCENE 2

The lights come up instantly on a room in another apartment. This is a considerably posher living room—what might be described as West End Avenue elegance. It is one of those dropped living rooms, separated from the anteroom by two steps and a wrought-iron railing. Wall-to-wall carpeting, French Provincial furniture. We can see the front door of the apartment, leading upstage. The sun streams boldly in through the windows.

The lights are no sooner on than the door to the apartment opens, and a middle-aged man in his early fifties comes in. He is warmly bundled up in a winter overcoat and wears a gray fedora. He is given a little to portliness but is not an unhandsome man. He puts away the key he has just used to open the door. He lets the door close behind him, and, unbuttoning his coat, he moves across the small anteroom, down the two steps into the living room, and goes to the telephone, which rests on a small telephone table beside a straight-back French Provincial chair. He picks up the receiver, dials, his face expressionless, his mind occupied with his thoughts. He pushes his hat back a little as he waits for someone to answer.

THE MANUFACTURER
(On phone)

Hello, Sylvia, this is Mr. Kingsley. I want you to go into my office, you'll find a piece of paper on my desk with Betty Preiss's name on it, and an address.... No, no, she's at her mother's house, Eighty-fifth Street somewheres. Somebody died in her family or something.... Ask Caroline. She knows where it is. No, don't send the boy. I'll pick them up on the way to the factory. It's right in the neighborhood.

(He looks up at the entrance of two middle-aged women, who have come in from an unseen recess of the apartment. They are West End Avenue women, well dressed but somehow vaguely new-rich. The handsomer of the two is THE SISTER. *The shorter, stouter and more amiable is* THE WOMAN.*)*

THE SISTER

What are you doing home so early ?

THE MANUFACTURER
(Still holding the phone, waiting)

I just stopped in for a minute. I'm going out to the factory. I want to change my shirt. I got some dye on it.

THE SISTER

(*To* THE WOMAN)

Rosalind, you know my brother Jerry?

THE WOMAN

Sure, sure, how are you there?

THE MANUFACTURER

How do you do? (*To his sister, indicating the rest of the apartment with his head*) What's going on in there, the card players?

THE SISTER

(*Stepping down into the living room*)

Yeah, we're playing a little cards. Your daughter Lillian is here with the baby.

THE MANUFACTURER

(*Smiling*)

Oh, yeah? With the baby?

THE SISTER

She dropped in about an hour ago. She drove in to shop a little, so she dropped up here. She wants us to come out to New Rochelle tonight for dinner.

THE MANUFACTURER

Well, I'll tell you, Evelyn, I'm a little tired, and I got to go to Brooklyn yet, and...

THE WOMAN

(*Stepping down into the living room*)

Mr. Kingsley, I just want to tell you, you have a lovely apartment here. I was away in Europe, my married daughter and myself, for three months, we had a wonderful time, so this is my first time in this apartment, and as I was telling your sister, it's just beautiful. How much rent do you pay, if I may ask?

THE MANUFACTURER

Two hundred and forty.

THE WOMAN

I was in your other apartment once when you lived on Central Park West. I don't know whether you recall me or not. My name is Mrs. Nieman.

THE MANUFACTURER

How do you do?

THE WOMAN

I knew your wife casually. She was a lovely woman, and I was distressed at the news. We were in Bermuda at the time, we had a wonderful time, and Mrs. Hillman, I don't know if you knew her but she was a close friend of your wife's, called me on the phone and told me of her passing, and I wondered whether I should send some kind of greeting, but I felt we were not that well acquainted, so I would like to take this opportunity, belated as it is—it's more than a year now, isn't it?—to express my sympathy and condolences.

THE MANUFACTURER

Thank you. Well, listen, don't let me hold you from your game.

THE SISTER

I just got up to make coffee, anyway. Would you like a cup?

THE MANUFACTURER

Yeah, make me a cup. (*His attention is called back to the phone*) Yeah, that's right, yeah.... All right, let me get a pencil.... (*He fishes in his jacket pocket and extracts a pencil and an envelope.*)

THE SISTER
(To THE WOMAN)

Stay here, it'll take me a minute.

  (THE WOMAN *looks at her, undecided for a moment, but* THE SISTER *turns and moves out up through the anteroom and disappears into the recesses of the apartment.*)

THE MANUFACTURER
(On phone)

All right, so listen, Sylvia. I'm going out to the factory from here. I'll be there about half-past three. If Lockman calls, tell him I went out to the factory, I'm getting the samples, I'll have the boy bring them down the shop, he can pick them up around half-past four.... All right. So I won't be in the rest of the day.... All right. (*He hangs up, looks up, a little surprised at Mrs. Nieman's presence. He slips out of his coat*) Nieman. I used to know a Nieman, used to supply us with embroideries about seven, eight years ago.

THE WOMAN

That's my brother-in-law, used to be in embroideries.

THE MANUFACTURER

Is that right? A very nice fellow. Whatever happened to him?

THE WOMAN

He moved to Los Angeles.

THE MANUFACTURER

Oh, yeah, that's right.

THE WOMAN

He's in the hospital now. Gall bladder. Nothing serious. We thought for a while he had to have an operation, but he's responding to treatment beautifully.

THE MANUFACTURER

Well, listen, you get to our age, you figure a couple of weeks in the hospital every year.

THE WOMAN

Absolutely.

THE MANUFACTURER

These are the years, you know. Everybody starts dropping dead around you. A man I know for twenty years, I played cards with him every Wednesday for years—he died last week in the hospital. Cancer.

THE WOMAN

Perhaps you know Roger Benedict. He used to live in this neighborhood. His wife was president of the PTA here in Public School 9 for many years.

THE MANUFACTURER

I'm afraid I don't know him.

THE WOMAN

He died last month. A cerebral hemorrhage. A relatively young man. Fifty-eight. Far from old.

THE MANUFACTURER

My wife was only forty-eight when she died.

THE WOMAN

My own husband passed away only last July.

THE MANUFACTURER

(Glances quickly at THE WOMAN, *suddenly wary)*
I'm very sorry to hear that.

THE WOMAN

I have a twenty-eight-year-old son. I live with him, and my married daughter is very solicitous. They took me, she and her husband, for three months in Europe, we had a wonderful time. He works for a chemical concern, very successful. But it's very difficult to give up a companionship of so many years.

THE MANUFACTURER

Well, it's a very lonely business. There's no doubt about it. But you get used to it.

THE WOMAN

Well, I must admit I'm very lonely.

THE MANUFACTURER

Well, if you'll excuse me, Mrs. Nieman, I have to change my shirt.

(THE MANUFACTURER *goes up into the anteroom to greet a young woman who has just entered. She is twenty-five, big-boned but handsome, amiable and smiling, and carries a blanketed baby. She is followed by* THE SISTER, *who is carrying a cup and saucer.*)

THE DAUGHTER

Hello, Pa, how are you?

THE MANUFACTURER

(*With open-armed welcome*)

Well, for God's sakes, what did you do, drive all the way in with the baby?

(THE SISTER *steps into the living room and sets the coffee on the telephone table.*)

THE SISTER

Jerry, I'm putting your coffee here.

THE MANUFACTURER

(*To his daughter*)

How are you, sweetheart? What did you do, just feed him? Look how he's sleeping.

THE SISTER

(*To* THE WOMAN)

Rosalind, do me a favor. The coffee is all ready. Pour in the cups and take it in on the tray there where the cake is...

THE MANUFACTURER

(*To his daughter*)

Let me hold him....

THE SISTER

(*To* THE WOMAN)

Also, there's some petit fours in the refrigerator...

THE DAUGHTER

(*Giving the baby to her father*)

So how's everything, Pa? Put the cigar down, Pa....

THE MANUFACTURER

Fine...

THE SISTER
(To THE WOMAN*)*
...and you know where I put the serving plate with the doily on it...

THE WOMAN
...Sure, sure...

THE MANUFACTURER
(Moving back into the living room with the baby)
...Boy, you're getting heavy, kid. You're going to weigh like a bolt of cloth pretty soon....

THE WOMAN
(To THE SISTER*)*
...You want me to serve the coffee?

THE SISTER
...Would you, please, Rosalind? I'll be right in.

THE MANUFACTURER
(Sitting down with the baby)
...So what's new, Lillian?

THE DAUGHTER
(Moving down into the living room)
...Nothing. Same old story....

THE SISTER
So, Rosalind, would you take it in because the coffee is perked all ready.

THE WOMAN
Sure. So, Mr. Kingsley, it was wonderful to have made your acquaintance.

THE MANUFACTURER
Very nice to have met you, Mrs. Nieman.

THE WOMAN
Some time, when your sister drops over for a visit, why don't you come along?

THE MANUFACTURER
Absolutely, Mrs. Nieman. Very nice of you to invite me.
*(*THE WOMAN *steps into the anteroom, smiling at* THE DAUGHTER, *who smiles back pleasantly.)*

THE SISTER
I'll be in in a minute, Rosalind. Pour six cups. *(*THE WOMAN *nods, smiles and exits)* A very nice woman, really. Her husband died just about a half-year ago, left her quite an estate. A well-educated woman and very sweet, really.

THE MANUFACTURER
(*Rather brusquely*)

Don't matchmake, Evelyn. I don't like it.

THE SISTER

What are you talking about? Did I know you were coming home three
o'clock in the afternoon?

THE MANUFACTURER

No, you didn't know, but, if I had come home at the regular time, she
would have been here just the same.

THE DAUGHTER

Is she trying to marry you off, Pa?

THE SISTER

He sits around the house, for God's sakes, every night. He comes home,
he eats dinner, he goes to sleep.

THE MANUFACTURER

I work hard, and I'm tired, and I come home, and I...

THE SISTER

Helen died, it's almost two years now. It's time to stop mourning, Jerry.

THE MANUFACTURER

I'm not mourning. Stop making a soap opera out of this. Now, I want an
end to this business, Evelyn. Is that clear? I'm very annoyed by this.
(*He frowns angrily down at the baby in his arms. His sister and daughter
stand a moment in silent discomfort.*)

THE SISTER

So, do you want to go up to Lillian's tonight or not?

THE MANUFACTURER
(*Angrily*)

I said no, didn't I?

THE SISTER
(*Looks down at the floor, shrugs*)

I can see you're in a bad temper.
(*She turns and goes up the steps into the anteroom.*)

THE DAUGHTER

I'll be in in a little while, Evelyn. I just want to put the baby to sleep. I'll
put him on your bed, all right?

THE SISTER

Sure, nobody will bother him.
(*She exits off into the apartment.* THE MANUFACTURER *turns back to the
baby, regaining his usual good humor.*)

THE MANUFACTURER
(Without looking up)
I'll tell you something, Lillian. I think I'm going through a change of life.

THE DAUGHTER
Yeah?

THE MANUFACTURER
(Looks up, smiling)
Yeah. I've become very touchy lately. I lose my temper any little thing. You should have seen me screaming at a salesman this morning. Listen, men go through a change of life too. *(Apparently the baby stirs in his arms, because he hastens to quiet it with tender solicitude, standing as he does.)* Stevie, Stevie boy, we woke you up. Oh, he's a sweetheart. (THE DAUGHTER *sits comfortably back into a soft chair.)* A friend of mine named Louie Sherman, you know him, he used to come up when we used to live on Central Park West, play cards all the time.

THE DAUGHTER
Sure, I know Mr. Sherman.

THE MANUFACTURER
Well, he's retiring from his business. He was up the office today, his doctor told him he has very low blood pressure. If you remember, he once fainted in our house. Anyway, he's retiring. It seems to me everybody's dying, everybody's in the hospital, everybody's retiring. Listen, when you get to fifty, fifty-five, believe me...I'll be sitting in the shop there, cutting a pattern, when suddenly, for no reason, I'll think, "My God, I'm fifty-three years old. I'll be an old man with white hair soon. My life is coming to an end." Listen, I know it sounds very irrational, but listen...

THE DAUGHTER
No, Pa, I can understand how you feel.

THE MANUFACTURER
You're a good kid, Lillian. I look at you, and I say to myself, "I didn't do so bad if I have a couple of mature, grown-up kids like you and Paul."

THE DAUGHTER
Pa, why don't you come up to dinner tonight?

THE MANUFACTURER
Well, we was up to your house Monday, and we was there Thursday before. *(He suddenly concerns himself with the baby in his arms.)* Listen, you better take him. He's getting restless.

THE DAUGHTER

Just put him on the couch, Pa. He'll fall asleep.

(THE MANUFACTURER *lays the blanketed baby down on the couch.*)

THE MANUFACTURER

I better get a shirt, it's getting late. I got to go out to Brooklyn. Lockman is taking out a buyer tonight, and the samples are still out in the factory, and I better get out there.

THE DAUGHTER

Sit down a minute, Pa. Let's talk a minute.

THE MANUFACTURER
(*Frowning*)

Well, Lillian, I'm going through a kind of period—a change of life, it's the best way I can describe it— It's a transitional thing. I've seen my friends go through it. Listen, you met Walter Lockman, one of my partners. He's going through hell. He's a man fifty-nine, going to be sixty, and, in the last couple of years, he has become absolutely obsessed with women. That's all he talks about. He comes in the office, the first thing he says, he's got a story about some girl he was out with. It's always a beautiful girl, and it always winds up the girl tells him that he's a better lover than all the young men she knows. And he sees doctors. Pills, everything. If it wasn't so sad, it would be comic. And listen, this is a man with four grown children, a grandfather three times. Walter, I'll tell you quite frankly, I'm worried about. But with me, it's a sort of vaguely depressed state. Your mother went through the same thing. In fact, I recognize many symptoms about myself. Look, don't let me bother you with all this, because you don't understand it, and you'll make more out of it than it really is.

THE DAUGHTER

Evelyn tells me that you sit sometimes in the living room like a corpse.

THE MANUFACTURER

Evelyn. You don't know by now not to listen to Evelyn.

THE DAUGHTER

Pa, how's your sex life?

(THE MANUFACTURER *regards his daughter for a moment. Then laughs gently.*)

THE MANUFACTURER
(*Ruffling his daughter's hair*)

You're all right, Lillian.

THE DAUGHTER

I'm serious, Pa. You're a vigorous man with normal appetites.

THE MANUFACTURER
(Smiling at her)
You're funny. All right, my sex life is not so hot.

THE DAUGHTER
I meant it very seriously.

THE MANUFACTURER
I know you did, sweetheart. I know a woman. I go up to see her every now and then. A nice woman. A widow. She's a buyer for a department store. Lord and Taylor's, if you want to know. She's a very tasteful woman, quite attractive, her early forties. *(He turns away, somehow disturbed by this confession)* Actually, I haven't seen her in a couple of months now. If you want to know, I asked her to marry me, and she said no, and I was very hurt, actually. *(He turns back to his daughter)* For God's sakes, what am I telling you all this nonsense for?

THE DAUGHTER
Don't be silly, Pa. You got to pour out your heart to somebody.

THE MANUFACTURER
No, no, I'm putting you in a terrible position. You're not my wife. I'm going through a kind of temporary depression. It'll pass in time—a month, two months. Don't worry about it.
(THE SISTER appears in the anteroom. She is carrying a man's white shirt.)

THE SISTER
Lillian, don't you want some coffee?

THE MANUFACTURER
Go ahead, Lillian, go have your coffee.

THE SISTER
(Coming down into the living room)
I brought you a new shirt, Jerry. Mrs. Mason feels a little sick, she's lying down on your bed, so you change in here. Nobody'll come in.

THE MANUFACTURER
All right.
(He unbuttons his double-breasted jacket.)

THE DAUGHTER
(Picking up the baby)
All right, Pa, so when'll we see you?

THE MANUFACTURER
We'll be up some time next week.

THE DAUGHTER
(Moving to the anteroom)

Listen, Evelyn, I'll put him on your bed.

THE SISTER

Fine.

THE DAUGHTER

All right, Pa, come in and say goodby before you go.

THE MANUFACTURER
(Now unbuttoning a noticeably stained shirt)

I'll come in.

(THE DAUGHTER *exits.* THE SISTER *moves down into the living room, puts the shirt on a chair. She looks briefly at her brother, who is expressionlessly taking off his shirt. Then she looks out the window.)*

THE SISTER

You want to eat in a restaurant tonight, because I really haven't got anything in the house?

THE MANUFACTURER

Fine.

THE SISTER

I was going to go shopping this morning, but I woke up with a headache and before I knew it the girls were here for canasta, and I never had a chance even to phone down an order.

THE MANUFACTURER

Fine, we'll eat out.

(He picks up the fresh shirt, removes the cardboard and collar bracing.)

THE SISTER

You want to go to a movie tonight?

THE MANUFACTURER
(Unbuttoning the fresh shirt)

I'm a little tired. Why don't you call one of your friends, go to a movie with her?

THE SISTER
(Makes a wry face)

Tell you the truth, I got a little headache. Maybe we'll take a little walk after dinner. *(She looks at him quickly, a little apprehensively)* Well, listen, maybe, if you don't want to see Lillian, maybe we'll drive down and see Paul and his...

THE MANUFACTURER
(Whirls on her in a fury, crying out)

Evelyn, I don't want to visit my children! I hope to God I haven't reached that point where I don't know what to do with myself, I have to go visit my children!

THE SISTER
(Sensitive to the presence of her friends in the other room)

All right, all right...

THE MANUFACTURER
(Walking around the room furiously)

God Almighty, you can drive somebody right out of their minds! How many times...

THE SISTER

All right, all right...

THE MANUFACTURER

...do I have to tell you I don't want to visit my children! I'm tired, for God's sakes! I'm fifty-three years old! Will you get that in your mind, God Almighty! I do a hard day's work! I come home! I want to watch a little TV, go to sleep! Stop trying to marry me off! Stop trying to fix me up with all your friends! I'm fifty-three years old!

(Another middle-aged woman, obviously attracted by the loud voices, suddenly pokes her head into the anteroom. THE SISTER *looks quickly at her and embarrassedly back. The woman promptly disappears.* THE MANU-FACTURER *angrily puts on his fresh shirt, buttons it, breathing heavily. After a moment, he mutters)*

THE MANUFACTURER

Evelyn, I'm a little depressed and angry today. It would be a good policy for you to stay away from me.

THE SISTER

All right, I'll leave you alone. *(She stands a moment, then turns and goes up the steps to the anteroom, where she pauses)* So you'll be home around six?

THE MANUFACTURER

Yeah.

*(*THE SISTER *nods involuntarily, exits off into the apartment.* THE MAN-UFACTURER *finishes buttoning his shirt, his face a dark scowl, his mind tumbling with dark thoughts. He sits down on the soft chair, with his shirt tails still out. He sits for a moment, his face set and troubled. Then, pulling himself together, he stands, stuffs his shirt into his trousers, takes his tie, adjusts it into his collar. He pauses abruptly and stands rigidly as some troubled thoughts lurch through his mind. He moves to the telephone, sits*

down on the straight-back French Provincial chair, picks up the receiver,
dials Information, waits, fixing his tie as he sits. Then, on phone)

THE MANUFACTURER

Can you give me the telephone number of Lord and Taylor Department
Store?…Yes, thank you…. *(He waits again, cradling the receiver on his shoul-*
der so that his two hands are left free to tie his necktie knot. In the middle of tying
it, his attention is called back to the phone) Yes…Yes, thank you…. *(He pushes*
the receiver holder down, then dials again, his face assuming a determined,
expressionless cast. He finishes tying his necktie knot as he waits) Hello, Lord
and Taylor's? Infants' wear department, please…. *(He just sits now, waiting)*
Hello, is Miss Herbert there?…Miss Herbert, the buyer?…Could you
switch me, please? *(The tension of the phone call is beginning to tell on him*
now. Apparently he is sweating, for he wipes his brow quickly with his fingers.
Then he adjusts a smile onto his face and nails it there) Hello, Grace? This is
Jerry Kingsley, how are you, for God's sakes?…Yeah, Jerry Kingsley.
Listen, are you busy or can you spare me a few minutes?…No, no, nothing important. I just called, it's been how many months now? Frankly, I'd
like to see you…. *(He moves the receiver quickly away from his mouth and*
takes a deep, shuddering breath) Oh, is that right, when are you leaving?…Well, listen, there's a whole week end. How about tonight? We'll
have a little dinner, maybe we'll take in a show…. *(The hearty smile remains*
plastered on his face, but he has closed his eyes, and the pain of the call is evident)
Are you angry with me, Grace, because you seem so unfriendly?…Oh,
really? Well, I didn't know that, of course. Congratulations. Do I know the
man?…Well, that's wonderful, Grace. I hope from the bottom of my heart
that you'll be very happy because you're a good woman…. Well, he's a
very lucky fellow, whoever he is…. Of course, dear…. No, no, don't let me
hold you up from your work. You must be terribly busy with the season
starting and…Of course. My very best wishes to you and your future husband…. Of course, good-bye…. *(He hangs up. For a moment, he sits. Then*
he stands. A sort of pensiveness has come over him. He looks absently around the
room for his jacket, finds it on a chair, picks it up, puts it on, buttons it, adjusts
it. He picks up his coat, drapes it over his arm, picks up his gray fedora. He moves
up the steps into the anteroom, turns to look down the foyer leading to the unseen
parts of the apartment. Apparently he sees someone. A vague, tenuous smile slips
onto his lips, and he calls down the foyer) Lillian…. *(He moves a step toward the*
foyer) Lillian, sweetheart…no, no, stay there. Listen, sweetheart, I'll tell
you what. It's a little after three now. Why don't you stick around? I'll be
back around six, and, what the hell, we'll drive out to New Rochelle, have
dinner with you.

THE DAUGHTER
(Off stage)

That's wonderful, Pa.

THE MANUFACTURER

All right, then? So I'll be back as soon as I can. So tell Evelyn.

(He turns abruptly, puts his hat on, moves quickly to the front door, putting on his coat as he goes. He opens the door, and exits, still slipping into his coat. The door closes with a soft click.)

The lights fade quickly

SCENE 3

The lights come up in THE GIRL's *apartment. It is three-thirty in the after-noon. The Venetian blinds in* THE KID SISTER's *bedroom have been opened, and fierce sunlight streams into that room. Indeed, although none of the beds have been made, and the clothes are still strewn about as they were in Scene 1, the whole apartment is bright with the light of the afternoon sun.*

A young girl comes hurrying down the stairs from the floor above and disap-pears down to the floor below. Then, for a moment, the stage is silent. There is a movement in the foyer now, and THE GIRL *strides nervously into the living room. She is wearing the black dress that had been draped over the back of a chair in Scene 1, and she has combed her blond hair. She is a strikingly pretty girl. She seems, however, to be governed by an enormous restlessness. Frowning, she moves around the living room, holding a glass ash tray in one hand, into which she con-tinuously flicks the cigarette she is smoking. With a deep sigh, she sits down on the soft chair by the telephone, and then, cigarette in mouth, lifts the telephone receiv-er as if she is going to dial but changes her mind, and sets the phone down again. She rises, and, still carrying the ash tray, goes to the unmade couch, lies down, set-ting the ash tray on the floor beside her, tapping her cigarette nervously into it. A moment later she gets up again, crosses to the phone, lifts the receiver and starts to dial, standing beside the telephone table. She waits for an answer. Apparently somebody finally does answer. Her eyes suddenly close, and she almost cries at her success.*

THE GIRL
(On phone)
Where have you been, for God's sakes, Marilyn? This is Betty. I must have called you twenty times.... Betty Preiss, for God's sakes.... Yes, yes. I called you around eleven. I called you every half-hour on the half-hour. It's twenty minutes after three now.... Well, you couldn't have been taking a shower all that time.... Well, how's Frank and the kids?...No, I'm at my mother's house.... Well, who told you?...Oh, really, when was this?...You mean, he called you four o'clock in the morning?...Well, then you know all about it.... No, he finally got me. He called here about half-past eight this morning. Listen, Marilyn, can I come over and stay with you for a couple of nights? I'll sleep on the couch. I'm over here at my mother's ⸺ouse, and...Well, when will Frank get home?...I'm not blaming George, ⸺lyn. He's a nice guy, but...Marilyn, can I come over and see you,

because I'm going crazy all alone here? My kid sister called about twenty minutes ago. She won't be home till dinner, and...I don't know, Marilyn. I don't want to talk about this over the phone. Can I come over and see you?...(*She sinks slowly into the soft chair, her eyes closed, exhausted again*) Can I come over after dinner then?...Well, do you have to go see your mother tonight? I need to talk to somebody because...Well, how seriously sick is she?...Well, give Frank my best...No, no, no, it's all right, Marilyn.... No, I'm all right, Marilyn. No, it's...No, I'll call you late tonight.... Sure...Okay, I'll see you. (*She hangs up, crushes out her cigarette. Her attention falls on the television set. She pads to the set, turns it on, waits expressionlessly. After the usual moment of station adjustment, the program comes on. It is "The Ted Mack Matinee," a program perhaps best described as a variety show. She stands in front of the set, watching the show with no expression. Then, with sudden shrill fury*) For God's sakes! For God's sakes!...(*She walks around, feverishly restless, her arms moving jerkily as she paces. She looks up at the ceiling again and screams out*) Oh, my God, my God!

(THE MANUFACTURER *appears now, coming up the stairs to the landing. In the living room,* THE GIRL *continues to move restlessly, almost bursting with frustration.* THE MANUFACTURER *locates the apartment easily enough, rings the bell. The sound of the bell, which is a raucous buzz, startles* THE GIRL *She goes out into the foyer, turning to her left, and reappears a moment later, coming down the foyer to answer the door. She opens it, sees her employer.*)

THE GIRL
(*Trying to control herself*)

Hello, Mr. Kingsley, how are you? I didn't expect you personally. I thought they were going to send the boy up.

THE MANUFACTURER

It was on my way. I live right in the neighborhood.

THE GIRL

Come in for a minute, Mr. Kingsley.

THE MANUFACTURER

Perhaps it would be better if I waited out here.

THE GIRL

There's nobody home, Mr. Kingsley.

THE MANUFACTURER

I was under the impression someone was sick in your family.

THE GIRL

No. Please come in.

(THE MANUFACTURER *moves tentatively into the foyer.* THE GIRL *has*

*already turned on her heel and is moving with nervous quickness down the
foyer.* THE MANUFACTURER *closes the door and follows her slowly.* THE
GIRL *reappears in the living room, coming quickly to the telephone table,
where her purse is lying. She opens it, takes out a stapled pile of papers,
turns toward the living-room door, through which* THE MANUFACTURER
is just now coming)

THE GIRL

Please excuse the condition of the room, Mr. Kingsley. Here are the
slips, Mr. Kingsley. I hope they're the ones.

THE MANUFACTURER
(Taking the papers)

You seem very distraught. Is there something I can do?

THE GIRL

No, no, Mr. Kingsley, no, that's all right. I'm all right. Well, I'll tell you
what it is. I had a fight with my husband, and we're breaking up, and I
don't know. *(The thin veneer of her control begins to crack. She turns nervously away, trying not to cry)* Oh, I don't know. *(A hoarse, racking sob escapes her
now, and she begins to cry with painful and deep agony. The tears stream down
her cheeks, and she walks quickly away from her boss, horribly embarrassed. She
mumbles)* Excuse me, Mr. Kingsley...

THE MANUFACTURER
(A little ill at ease)

Don't be silly.

THE GIRL

Excuse me...*(She sits down on the soft chair and bends forward so that her
face is buried in her knees. She sits, hunched into a ball, as if she were in physical pain, unsuccessfully trying not to cry, mumbling between sobs)* I'm sorry, Mr.
Kingsley...

THE MANUFACTURER

Isn't there somebody home with you here? Your mother or somebody?
*(*THE GIRL *abruptly stands up again, and, shielding her face with her
hand, she walks around the living room.* THE MANUFACTURER *stands, not
quite sure what to do.)*

THE GIRL
(As she walks, mumbling)

Stay with me a minute, please, Mr. Kingsley.

THE MANUFACTURER

I'm sorry, dear. I didn't hear what you said.

THE GIRL

⁻tay with me a minute, please. I'm sorry about this, Mr. Kingsley.

THE MANUFACTURER

Don't be so embarrassed. Sometimes life gets so complicated, the only thing you can do is scream.

THE GIRL
(In confusion)

It just burst out of me. I've been calling my friends all day, but none of them are home. It's just one of those days. He's a nice guy, really, my husband. Everybody likes him. He's a piano player. No, he's more than that. He's a pianist. He plays classical as well as jazz. He's very good-looking, by the way. He flirts a lot, but I don't think he ever did anything. That's just one of his little vanities, that he's so attractive, and I don't mind it, really. No, that's not true. I do mind it a lot. But that isn't it, his flirting, I mean. Oh, Mr. Kingsley, you'd better grab those sales slips and escape. Don't let me take advantage of you like this.

THE MANUFACTURER

Please, Betty, don't worry about me.

THE GIRL

You know what my husband would do if he came in like you just did and found me breaking down like I just did, do you know what he'd do? He'd turn on the television set, do you know what I mean, Mr. Kingsley? Or else he'd invite the neighbors in. Anything except sit down with me and talk things out. Oh, I'm not being fair to him. He tried, he really tried. You just can't imagine how naïve I was about marriage, Mr. Kingsley. I really thought you lived happily ever after. Look, Mr. Kingsley, if I sound like I'm blaming my husband, I don't want to sound that way. This is me. I wanted poor George to make up for everything I never had in my life. My father ran away when I was six years old. Oh, Mr. Kingsley, here I go again. You'd better get out of here because I've been building up all day like a volcano.

THE MANUFACTURER

Please don't worry about me.

THE GIRL
(Suddenly)

Did you ever go downtown in the afternoon by the Paramount Theatre? Did you ever see those fourteen- and fifteen-year-old kids hanging around, cutting school? They're the loneliest-looking kids in the world. Well, that's just what I was like when I was a kid. I used to go to the Paramount three or four times a week. I didn't cut school, though. I was always very good in school. Can I get you something to eat or drink, Mr. Kingsley? I don't know what we have in the house. I haven't eaten all day, but do you know what I mean by lonely kids, Mr. Kingsley? *(She begins to cry; she wanders around the room, distracted)*

I'm sorry, Mr. Kingsley, but just seeing you sitting there, listening to me...Boy, you came here just to pick up a couple of sales slips. Oh, Mr. Kingsley, I'm so glad you came. My husband, George, the last couple of months we've hardly talked to each other. He comes home and I ask him what happened during the day. He always says, "Nothing." We never eat home any more. We go to a restaurant and we just sit there, eating. He doesn't know what to do with me, do you know what I mean? There's no love or anything. Well, I can't stand that. I want him to love me. I want him to be pleased to see me. I want him to come home and tell me all that's happened to him and how he feels about things. And I want to tell him how I feel. I want something. I mean, is this what marriage is? Is this what life is? Boy, life isn't much if that's what it is. The other night we had this big fight and he came in the next morning...

(The lights dim quickly. THE GIRL's *voice fades into inaudibility. There is a moment of silence and the stage is completely dark. Then the living-room lamp is turned on, casting a sharp cone of light in the dark room. Through the window of* THE KID SISTER's *room, we can see it is nighttime.* THE MANUFACTURER, *who has just turned on the lamp, has taken his coat off.* THE GIRL *is lying on the couch now, her head propped up against one arm of the couch. She is still talking, as if she had been talking throughout the passage of hours. Now, however, there is a noticeable increase of energy and animation. She is almost gay, exhilarated by her patient, cigar-smoking audience.)*

THE GIRL

...So any time we have a fight, that's just what happens. So one time, you know what happened?...

(She sits up quickly, leaning across to her boss, eager to tell another incident. She notices he is looking at his watch.)

THE MANUFACTURER
(Smiling)

You know what time it is?

THE GIRL

Boy, I've been talking your head off.

THE MANUFACTURER

It's half-past six. Do you mind if I use your phone?

THE GIRL

ᵣ. Kingsley, I'm terribly sorry I used up your afternoon like this.

THE MANUFACTURER

Don't be sorry. Do you feel better?

THE GIRL

Oh, I feel much better. *(She stands)* I really do, got this all off my chest. Gee, half-past six. I don't know where my mother and my sister are. My mother's on a new shift now. I don't know what time she gets home. Would you like to stay for dinner, Mr. Kingsley?

THE MANUFACTURER

No, I don't think so, dear. I have to make a call though.

THE GIRL

The phone's right there. *(He reaches for the phone, but before he can pick up the receiver,* THE GIRL *is talking again)* So, what do you think I ought to do? I've been considering a divorce for a couple of months now, but it seems so complicated. I don't know anybody who's divorced, so I don't know how you go about it. My mother, she won't hear about divorce. My grandmother was Catholic. My mother's a Lutheran, but even so. My husband, it would just kill him. His vanity would be so hurt.

(She sits and stares at the middle-aged, cigar-smoking man in the soft chair.)

THE MANUFACTURER

Betty, tell me something. How old are you?

THE GIRL

I'll be twenty-four in March.

THE MANUFACTURER

Twenty-four years old. I have a daughter of my own, twenty-five years old, lives out in New Rochelle, she's married now with two fine children, and you make me think of her when she was ten years old. So I'm going to talk to you like I was your father. About twenty times tonight, you've asked me, "What should I do about my husband?" Betty, this is a decision you have to make for yourself. Don't expect your mother to make it for you, or your husband's mother, and don't worry so much about hurting your husband.

THE GIRL

Because I know this would hurt him.

THE. MANUFACTURER

The only person you have to worry about hurting is yourself. You have to do what you want to do, not what other people want you to do; otherwise you and everyone else concerned will be miserable. You have to say to yourself, "Do I want to go back to him or do I think I can find something better for my life?"

THE GIRL

I don't want to go back to him.

THE MANUFACTURER

All right, there's your decision. (THE GIRL *looks at him, a little confused at the sudden clarity of her situation*) If it means a divorce, then you go ahead and get one. You go to a lawyer, and he'll tell you what you'll have to do. It may be a little complicated, but nothing is too complicated. Then you start going out on dates again, and take my word for it, you'll run across some young fellow who will understand that you need a lot of kindness. There are plenty of nice young fellows around, believe me.

THE GIRL

You know something? I really feel much better now...

THE MANUFACTURER

Sure, you do...

THE GIRL

...talking it out like this.

THE MANUFACTURER

Well, you made a decision, and suddenly there's not such big, black clouds in the sky, and it isn't going to rain, and life isn't so terrible. Life, believe me, can be a beautiful business. And you're a young kid, and you got plenty of joy ahead of you. So go wash your face. I want to make a phone call.

THE GIRL

(Stands)

I want to thank you very much, Mr. Kingsley, for letting me pour my heart out.

THE MANUFACTURER

There's nothing to thank, sweetheart.

(THE MANUFACTURER *reaches over for the phone and begins to dial.*)

THE GIRL

Your wife must have had a wonderful life with you.

(THE MANUFACTURER *pauses in his dialing to look up at* THE GIRL.)

THE MANUFACTURER

(Touched)

That's a very sweet thing for you to say, my dear.

THE GIRL

Well, I'll go wash my face.

She turns and goes out into the foyer, disappearing to her right. We see

her passing the open doorway of her sister's room. THE MANUFACTURER
returns to his dialing. He waits, then gets an answer.)

THE MANUFACTURER
(On phone)

Hello, Evelyn, this is Jerry.... No, I'll tell you what happened. Is Lillian
still there?...Well, I see it's half-past six. I tell you, I'm very, very tired
right now. Why don't you drive out with Lillian, and I'll catch a bite
around the corner, and you can take the train in from New Rochelle
tomorrow.... Well, I'll tell you. I never got out to Brooklyn. Remember I
told about this girl in the office who was sick?...I didn't tell you?...No,
Betty Preiss, the very pretty one. She sits by the reception window.... You
know her. The very pretty one. So I had to stop off at her house, pick up
some papers she had, she didn't come in today. So I come up here, I tell
you, this girl was in an emotional state. So, to cut a long story short,
I talked to her, it turns out, she's leaving her husband, that's why she
couldn't come in today, and it poured out of her, the whole story.... No,
no, no, the blond girl, the very pretty one. The fat one is Elaine.... The
exceptionally attractive one. I used to look at her, I used to think, "A beautiful girl like that, what problems could she have? The young men must
fall all over themselves." This girl is a real beauty. I've seen lots of girls on
television who aren't so beautiful. An intelligent girl, a good worker, but
emotionally very immature.... *(Annoyed)* Oh, don't be foolish. What did
you mean, I'm showing a marked interest in how beautiful she is? It happens that she's a very pretty girl.... All right, so you go out to New
Rochelle if you want to and...I'll tell you the truth, I think I'll just come
home and go to bed....

(THE GIRL *returns to the living-room doorway, where she pauses.* THE
MANUFACTURER *darts a look at her)*

No, I'll be fine.... Apologize to Lillian for me.... Absolutely, why should
you stay in the house?...Fine, give my regards to Jack and the kids.... All
right, I'll see you.

(He hangs up, stands, frowning for some unaccountable reason.)

THE GIRL

I don't know what happened to my family.

(THE MANUFACTURER *has found his coat and is putting it on.)*

THE MANUFACTURER

I'll take the slips here with me.

THE GIRL

I hope I didn't inconvenience you too much, Mr. Kingsley.

THE MANUFACTURER

It was no inconvenience. I was supposed to go out to the factory, but, I tell you, I was grateful to get out of it. I had the boy deliver the stuff. *(He puts on his hat)* I have the feeling you didn't eat anything at all today.

THE GIRL

You know, I really don't think I did.

THE MANUFACTURER

Well, eat something now. *(He starts for the door to the foyer, pauses on the threshold, looks at his watch)* It's almost seven o'clock. *(He frowns)* Listen, you want a bite to eat? Come on, I'll buy you a bite to eat.

*(*THE GIRL *considers this suggestion with no particular expression.)*

THE GIRL

I'd like to very much, Mr. Kingsley. I have to put some make-up on.

THE MANUFACTURER

Hurry up, put some make-up on.

*(*THE GIRL *smiles briefly, turns and heads for the foyer door.)*

THE GIRL

(As she goes)

I'll just be a minute, Mr. Kingsley.

(She disappears into the foyer, carrying her purse, which she has picked up on her way out. THE MANUFACTURER *moves slowly downstage into the living room. He puts his hands into his coat pockets and walks slowly around the room.)*

THE MANUFACTURER

(Suddenly calling out)

You like Italian food? Very good restaurant here on Seventy-ninth Street. *(Apparently* THE GIRL *doesn't hear him, for there is no answer. He moves around the room aimlessly. He pauses by a wall, pokes it with his fist. Then he moves downstage again, almost up to the footlights. He punches his head lightly, self-admonishingly. He mutters)* Jerk. Jerk. What are you doing? Jerk.

(He continues to move around the room.)

Curtain

ACT II

SCENE 1

Three months have passed since the preceding act. The curtain rises on THE GIRL's *apartment. It is nighttime, about eight o'clock. There are lights in every room, even in the foyer. Some changes have been made in the apartment. There is now a day bed in* THE KID SISTER's *room, in addition to the bed that was there before.* THE GIRL *apparently shares the bedroom; it has the look of a room shared by two girls.*

In the living room THE KID SISTER *sits at the table, hunched over her text-books. A middle-aged woman in a housecoat with a flowered pattern on it, whom we shall call* THE NEIGHBOR, *perches on the soft chair. A young woman in her late twenties, carrying a small parcel as well as her purse, is leaning against the doorjamb of the living-room doorway. We shall call her* THE FRIEND.

THE NEIGHBOR
Oh, the whole neighborhood has gone to pot. It's practically Harlem. The whole block is Puerto Rican.

*(*THE MOTHER *appears, coming up the stairs. She wears a hat, a black winter coat with a fur collar, wet with snow, and carries a purse.)*

THE FRIEND
Well, I used to live on Ninety-Eighth Street, just off the park, you know.

THE NEIGHBOR
Oh, sure. What the hell.

THE FRIEND
That used to be a very nice neighborhood.

THE NEIGHBOR
Oh, sure, absolutely.

*(*THE MOTHER *inserts her key into the lock. The sound of the door being opened attracts* THE FRIEND's *attention. She looks casually down the foyer to the front door.)*

THE FRIEND
I live up in Washington Heights now with my husband, there's a lot of Puerto Ricans up there.

THE NEIGHBOR

Well, that's the way it is, sure.

THE FRIEND

(*To* THE MOTHER, *as she enters the apartment*)

Hello, Mrs. Mueller, how are you?

THE MOTHER

(*She can't quite make out who is greeting her from her position in the apartment doorway*)

Who's that?

THE KID SISTER

(*Looking up from her texts*)

Who's that, my mother?

THE FRIEND

(*To* THE MOTHER, *who is closing the front door now*)

This is Marilyn, Mrs. Mueller.

THE MOTHER

Hello, Marilyn, how are you, dear? Oh, it's really snowing out.

(THE KID SISTER *gets up, joins* THE FRIEND *at the living-room doorway, waiting for* THE MOTHER *to come up the foyer.*)

THE FRIEND

(*To* THE MOTHER)

I was downtown, so my husband took the kids over to his mother's, so I thought I'd just drop up, see if Betty wants to go to a movie.

THE KID SISTER

(*To* THE MOTHER, *now visible at the living-room doorway—conspiratorially*)

Ma, you better get dressed because he's coming over here. I came home, and Betty was just going in to take a shower—she's in the shower now— so she says, "Don't start walking around the house in your underwear, because Mr. Kingsley's coming over tonight."

THE MOTHER

What do you mean, Mr. Kingsley is coming over here tonight?

THE KID SISTER

I came home, Betty was getting undressed, and she told me....

THE MOTHER

What time's he coming over?

THE KID SISTER

I don't know. She went in to take a shower, so then Mrs. Carroll rang the bell, so...

THE NEIGHBOR

Hello, Mrs. Mueller, how are you?

THE MOTHER

I'm fine, Mrs. Carroll, how are you?

THE KID SISTER

So I thought it was him.

THE NEIGHBOR

The whole neighborhood is turning Puerto Rican, I'll tell you that. I was just talking about that with this young lady here.

THE MOTHER

(*To* THE KID SISTER)

Where is she, in the shower?

THE KID SISTER

She went in about fifteen minutes ago.

THE MOTHER

(*To* THE FRIEND)

Do you know who we're talking about?

THE FRIEND

Yes, I know, because...

THE MOTHER

(*To* THE KID SISTER)

What did she say exactly? He's coming over tonight? She didn't tell me nothing about his coming over. Well, I'd like to get a look at him. (*She has unbuttoned her coat, and we see now that she is wearing the white uniform of the bakery clerk.*)

THE FRIEND

Mrs. Mueller, I talked to Betty about this at length, and she is absolutely infatuated with this man, and my advice to you is just let the affair run its course.

THE MOTHER

Well, I'll tell you, I'm worried sick about it. I was thinking about it all day, and I had no appetite at all. (*She moves to a chair and sits down, addressing most of her comments to* THE NEIGHBOR) Because she sees him three and four times a week. He's fifty-two, you know. She told me that just yesterday. I had no idea he was that old. I thought he was in his late thirties, and that was bad enough. Because I told her, you know, "There's plenty of young fellows your own age." Because a man, fifty-two, what the hell does he want with a kid like her except for you-know-what? Oh, God knows what she does with him.

THE FRIEND

Mrs. Mueller, I wouldn't interfere with her.

THE MOTHER

Oh, my God, I live in a living terror she's going to come in some night while I'm in bed and tell me she's pregnant.

THE FRIEND

She can take care of herself, Mrs. Mueller.

THE MOTHER

She's only a kid, for God's sakes. She ain't got much more sense than Alice here. I always favored Alice. The living truth is, I didn't want Betty when she was born. She came almost a month early. I had a terrible fight with my husband, that's what brought her on. I didn't even want to see her after she was born. That old Irish lady that was living next door took care of her.

(She stares, quite pained, at the others in the room.)

THE FRIEND

Mrs. Mueller, a lot of girls find older men attractive because they're debonair and know a lot of tricks. I have a girl friend who went with a married man for eight years, and she finally had a nervous breakdown.

THE MOTHER

(Not exactly heartened by this piece of news, turns to THE NEIGHBOR*)*

When she was born, there was an Irish lady lived next door, gave her the formula and diapered her and everything. I didn't do a thing for a month.

THE NEIGHBOR

Oh, sure, what the hell.

THE MOTHER

(Turns to her younger daughter, whose attention is far more with the talk than with her texts)

You're not supposed to be listening to any of this.

THE FRIEND

I knew a girl in my neighborhood who was running around with a man in his forties. She had to have an abortion, but everything turned out all right.

THE MOTHER

(Stands, mutters)

You're full of cheerful anecdotes today, Marilyn.

THE FRIEND

Mrs. Mueller, I know Betty for six years now, and she's got a good head on her shoulders.

THE MOTHER
(Taking off her coat, frowns)
Well, I won't say nothing to her no more.

THE FRIEND
She's having a big romance right now. She thinks she's going out with Spencer Tracy. But in the bottom of her heart, she's still crazy about George.

THE MOTHER
(Moving to the living-room door)
Well, I won't interfere because she doesn't listen to anything I say anyway. She's always had her own way, and I gave up long ago trying to tell her anything. *(Apparently* THE GIRL *is coming out of the bathroom because* THE MOTHER *abruptly looks down the foyer toward the bathroom and cries out)* This is the last time you're going out with that man, do you hear me, Betty! *(To the others)* This is the last time she's going out with that man.

> *(*THE GIRL *now appears in the bedroom, closing the door behind her. She has obviously just finished taking a shower. She is wearing a pink peignoir and is vigorously toweling her hair. She reacts expressionlessly to her mother's outburst.* THE MOTHER *scowls and disappears off into her own room.)*

THE NEIGHBOR
Well, I suppose I ought to get up and go, but, to tell you the truth, I'd like to get a look at the fellow myself.

> *(She exits off after* THE MOTHER. THE FRIEND, *standing in the foyer but still visible through the open doorway, now decides to go to* THE GIRL. *She turns and disappears behind the wall of the living room, knocks on the bedroom door, and* THE GIRL, *who is perched on the edge of her bed, toweling her hair, looks up.)*

THE GIRL
What?

THE FRIEND
(Through the closed door)
Can I come in a minute, Betty?

THE GIRL
Sure, come on in. *(The door opens and* THE FRIEND *comes in. She closes the door carefully behind her)* I didn't know you were here, Marilyn.

THE FRIEND
I yelled at you through the shower, but I guess you didn't hear me.

THE GIRL
How long you been here?

THE FRIEND

I just came in about fifteen minutes ago. I was downtown at Macy's, so I called Frank, and he said he was going to take the kids over to his mother's house, so, you know, I can't stand her, so I told him I'd probably go to a downtown movie here.

THE GIRL

Well, I got a date tonight.

THE FRIEND

Oh, I know. (THE FRIEND *sits down on* THE KID SISTER's *bed. There is a short pause*) Well, how you feel?

THE GIRL

Fine.
(She stands, the towel draped over her head, goes to the chest of drawers, opens a drawer and searches around for something.)

THE FRIEND

You hear anything from George?

THE GIRL
(Fiddling around in the drawer)

Oh, he called three times last week all the way from Las Vegas. Three o'clock in the morning he called once.

THE FRIEND

What did he have to say?
*(*THE GIRL *finally finds what she has been looking for—several nylon stockings, which she holds up and examines for runs.)*

THE GIRL
(After a moment)

Well, I wrote him a letter about a week ago. I asked him for a divorce. *(She has found two matching stockings with no runs and returns to the bed and begins to put on her stockings. After she has put the first one on, she pauses)* I finally went up to see this lawyer last week. You remember Carol McKeever? Her brother, he's a lawyer. So he told me the cheapest way to get a divorce is to go to Mexico. So I said, "Oh, boy." So it really isn't so complicated. It costs about seven hundred and fifty dollars, the plane tickets and everything. So I wrote George, and I asked him for a divorce, I sent the letter registered, airmail, special delivery. The next night, I swear to God, George was on the phone from Las Vegas. So we must have talked about twenty minutes. Oh, boy, I wonder what he paid for that call. He called from his hotel room. He was calling between shows. Frank Sinatra is out there now. So, anyway, he called again about three o'clock in the morning after the last show. Of course, it's only twelve o'clock out there, but he should have realized there's a time difference. He woke up the whole house. My mother got on the phone. She doesn't know I wrote this letter to him. So I couldn't really talk to him with my mother hanging all over me. So I told him to call me the next day at six o'clock because my mother don't get home till around seven-thirty. So he called me, and we had a long talk, and he was all broken up. He was saying all kinds of wild things like he was going to take the next plane. So I told him, my mind was made up. So he finally said he wouldn't contest the divorce. So that's the last I heard from him. That was last Thursday. No, Friday.

(She starts on the second stocking.)

THE FRIEND

Are you really going to go through with this divorce?

THE GIRL

Don't tell my mother, because she doesn't know about it.

(She stands now, back to the audience, and garters her stockings.)

THE FRIEND

I'm your friend, Betty, and I'm going to tell you something right from the shoulder. You're making a big mistake.

(THE GIRL rises again, goes to the open closet, fishes around in the incredibly crowded rack of clothes for a skirt, finds the one she wants.)

THE GIRL

I know you feel that way, Marilyn.

THE FRIEND

What do you figure, to marry this man?

THE GIRL

If he asks me. I think I'm happy, Marilyn. I can't tell you how I feel in so many words, but life seems very pleasant to me right now. I even get along with my mother. I think I'm in love. Seriously in love. I feel so full sometimes it just wells up in me, my feelings for him. He went away for three days on a business trip to Detroit, I thought I'd die before he came back.

(She has taken off her peignoir and is in her slip and stockinged feet. She quickly slips the skirt over her head and adjusts it.)

THE FRIEND

Boy, he must be some operator, this guy.

(THE GIRL frowns, regards her friend with some irritation.)

THE GIRL

You want to know something? In the whole three months, he hasn't touched me once. I know what my mother thinks. She thinks I walk out of this door, I head straight for a hotel somewheres. Do you know where we go? We go dancing. We go driving. We go to a restaurant, we sit and talk for five hours. He hasn't put a hand on me in the whole three months.

THE FRIEND

Is that good?

THE GIRL

No, it isn't good. I think he's afraid of getting too involved with me.
(*She picks up a blouse that has been lying on* THE KID SISTER's *bed.*)

THE FRIEND

What I mean is, do you think he's going to be able to satisfy you sexually?

THE GIRL

(*Putting on her blouse. She is disturbed by the question*)
All I know is I can't wait to see him all the time.

THE FRIEND

Betty, you're jumping into a marriage, and you have to be a little realistic too. In ten years he's going to be sixty-three and you're going to be thirty-four. Do you think you're going to be happy with a sixty-three-year-old husband in ten years? Think about that a minute. A sixty-three-year-old husband with white hair. You're a kid, you know that? You really are. What do you think life is, a Street and Smith love story magazine? You had a good marriage with George. You paid the rent and you went to bed. What are you looking for?

THE GIRL

Well, I'm looking for more than that.
(*She is quite disturbed now. She buttons her blouse, stands before the mirror on the chest of drawers, surveys herself.* THE FRIEND *scowls down at her feet.* THE GIRL *now begins to apply make-up.* THE FRIEND *extracts a pack of cigarettes from* THE GIRL's *purse, lights one.*
THE MANUFACTURER *now appears, coming up the stairs to the landing. He wears his winter coat and his hat, both marked by what must be a fairly heavy snow outside. He stands before the door of the apartment but makes no move to ring the bell.*)

THE FRIEND

You want to know what life is? You live, that's all. That's life. You get married, you have kids—you get up in the morning and you go to sleep at night. Frank goes bowling every Thursday, and I manage to get down to Macy's once a week, and that's it, and it's not so bad. I don't know what you mean by happiness. You had a good marriage with George. At least he was hungry for you all the time. It was all over his face. That's more than most of us can say about our husbands.

THE GIRL

Are you having trouble with Frank, Marilyn?

THE FRIEND

Frank and me? We get along fine. We're perfectly happy. He stays out of my way and I stay out of his. You know, I envy you George, you know that? You have a husband who's crazy about you. Sure, he has his faults. He's a little selfish. He's a little conceited. But he doesn't go bowling on Thursday nights or stay up reading a magazine all night long. And one thing you know for sure, he isn't going to be sixty-three in ten years. You're going to want to have children, Betty. How do you know he's going to be able to give you kids? Because after a couple of years, that's all there really is, the kids.

(THE MANUFACTURER *has decided to ring the doorbell. It buzzes raucously, interrupting* THE FRIEND'*s speech.* THE GIRL *looks up nervously. In the living room, the ringing of the doorbell has galvanized everybody into action.* THE NEIGHBOR *pops into the room, straightens out her housedress, and sits.* THE KID SISTER *stands at her table, not quite knowing what to do.* THE MOTHER *now appears in the living-room doorway, having changed into her black church dress.*)

THE MOTHER
(Calling to THE GIRL's room)

Betty, you going to answer the door?

THE GIRL
(Calling back)

I'll be right out.

THE FRIEND
(To THE GIRL)

You want me to answer the door?

THE GIRL

Please, Marilyn, would you? (*She is hurriedly applying her make-up. She looks anxiously at her friend*) Now don't expect anything special.

(THE FRIEND *opens the door and starts down the foyer.*)

THE KID SISTER
(In the living room)

Where should I go, should I stay here!

THE NEIGHBOR
(In the living room, to THE MOTHER)

I'll just stay back here out of the way.

THE FRIEND

(Now passing THE MOTHER, *who is still standing in the living-room doorway)*
I'll let him in, Mrs. Mueller.

> *(She reappears a moment later, coming down the foyer to the front door.*
> THE MOTHER *looks down the foyer, blatantly curious about* THE MANU-
> FACTURER's *appearance. In the bedroom,* THE GIRL *is not as in control of*
> *herself as she would like to be. She was considerably disturbed by the scene*
> *with her friend. She has to pause now in her hurried application of cos-*
> *metics to allow a deep sigh. She closes her eyes and tries to regain the com-*
> *posure she showed at first. In the foyer* THE FRIEND *opens the door to*
> *admit* THE MANUFACTURER.)

THE FRIEND

How do you do?

THE MANUFACTURER

How do you do? My name is Kingsley.

THE FRIEND

How do you do? I'm Betty's friend Marilyn. Won't you come in, please?

THE MANUFACTURER

Well, I'll tell you, I'm soaking wet with snow here, and I wouldn't want
to dirty up your carpets.

> (THE MOTHER *edges onto the landing.)*

THE MOTHER

How do you do there?

THE MANUFACTURER

How do you do?

THE MOTHER

Come in the house, for heaven's sakes.

THE MANUFACTURER

Well, I'll tell you, we're a little late as it is, and I have tickets here for a
play, so just to come in for a couple of minutes, it really isn't worth the
trouble.

THE MOTHER

Well, give me your coat, I'll hang it up in the bathroom.

THE MANUFACTURER

Thank you, I'm fine.

THE MOTHER

Well, I'm Betty's mother, how do you do?

THE MANUFACTURER

How do you do, Mrs. Mueller?

THE MOTHER

Would you excuse me a minute?

THE MANUFACTURER

Yes, certainly.

THE MOTHER

(Going into the living room)

He don't look like no Spencer Tracy to me. *(At the bedroom door, to* THE GIRL*)* He's waiting outside.

THE GIRL

(From the bedroom)

I'll be right out.

*(*THE MOTHER *goes back to the landing, followed by* THE KID SISTER *and* THE NEIGHBOR, *so that the landing suddenly seems embarrassingly crowded.)*

THE FRIEND

(To THE MANUFACTURER*)*

I happen to be here because my husband is taking the kids to my mother-in-law's and I don't happen to get along with her, so I thought I'd go to a downtown movie. It's really snowing out, isn't it?

THE MANUFACTURER

Yes, it's coming down quite heavily.

THE MOTHER

I told her you was here. This is my younger daughter, Alice. She's seventeen. She goes to George Washington High School. And this is my neighbor, Mrs. Carroll.

THE NEIGHBOR

(Mumbling)

Neighbor Mrs. Carroll...

THE MOTHER

She always comes in when I have dinner, to pass the time of day.

THE NEIGHBOR

(Mumbling)

Pass the time of day.

THE MANUFACTURER

Well, I'm very pleased to meet you all. *(An uncomfortable silence falls over the group)* Really, you don't have to stand here on my account. I'd come in, believe me, except I would leave pools of water everywhere.

(Again the silence.)

THE NEIGHBOR

We was just talking about the deterioration of the neighborhood. It's practically Harlem. There's nothing but colored people and Puerto Ricans living here now.

(*She seems to have said everything that needed to be said. Again the silence.*)

THE MOTHER

Well, Betty'll be right out.

(*THE FRIEND abruptly detaches herself from the group and disappears down the foyer in the direction of THE GIRL's room.*)

THE MANUFACTURER

Well, the Puerto Ricans, after all, they have to have a place to live, too. In my business, which is the garment business, the operators are paid a thirty-two dollar a week minimum, and nowadays the young women don't care to work for such a salary. And, of course, we were faced with a serious competitive threat from the southern garment manufacturers. There's no unions down there, you understand. And frankly we have found that the Puerto Rican women are fine workers, very intelligent, very industrious. So that's the situation.

THE NEIGHBOR

(*After considering this address for a moment*)

He's absolutely right. The whole neighborhood's gone to pot.

(*THE FRIEND knocks on THE GIRL's door and walks right in. THE GIRL, examining herself in front of the mirror, looks up quickly.*)

THE GIRL

(*Nervously*)

What do you think of him?

THE FRIEND

(*Who really didn't think too much of him*)

He seems very nice.

THE MOTHER

(*On the landing, suddenly, to THE MANUFACTURER*)

Would you like me to hang your coat in the shower?

THE MANUFACTURER

No, no, I'm fine.

(*THE MOTHER nods and goes quickly to the bedroom.*)

THE MOTHER

(*Enters, more confused than anything else*)

Is he a Jewish man, for God's sakes?

(THE GIRL *whirls on her mother, her composure completely shattered.*)

THE GIRL
(Crying out)

So what?!

THE MOTHER

Well, I just asked, that's all.

THE FRIEND
(To THE MOTHER*)*

Maybe we better get out and leave Betty finish up.

THE GIRL
(Looking in the closet for a coat)

I'm all finished.

THE MOTHER
(To THE GIRL*)*

Where are you going tonight?

(THE GIRL *rips her coat off the hanger and faces her mother furiously.*)

THE GIRL

We're not going to a hotel, if that's what you want to know! In the whole three months, he hasn't put a hand on me! Is that what you want to know?

THE MOTHER

All right, all right, he can hear every word you're saying.

(THE GIRL *pulls the door open and strides out into the foyer. A moment later, she is on the landing.*)

THE GIRL
(To THE MANUFACTURER*)*

All right, I'm ready, Jerry, let's go.

(THE MANUFACTURER *nods, turns to* THE NEIGHBOR *and* THE KID SIS-TER.*)

THE MANUFACTURER

Well, goodby, it was nice to have met you.

THE NEIGHBOR

Goodby, sir.

(THE KID SISTER *nods.* THE MANUFACTURER *looks quickly at* THE GIRL.*)

THE MANUFACTURER
(To THE MOTHER, *who is now on the landing)*

Well, goodby, Mrs. Mueller.

THE MOTHER

Goodby, Mr. Kingsley.

THE FRIEND

Goodby, Mr. Kingsley.

(*THE MANUFACTURER looks at* THE GIRL, *who is slipping into her coat. She is obviously disturbed. The others all go into the living room.*)

THE MOTHER

(*In a heavy whisper, to* THE NEIGHBOR)

He's a Jewish man, you know.

THE NEIGHBOR

Oh, sure, what the hell.

(*On the landing,* THE MANUFACTURER *has started for the stairs, but pauses when he sees* THE GIRL *is making no move to follow him.*)

THE MANUFACTURER

Is something wrong, Betty?

THE GIRL

(*Turns to* THE MANUFACTURER, *keeping her eyes down*)

I want to go somewheres with you tonight, you know what I mean? (*THE MANUFACTURER looks at her, not quite knowing what she means*) I want to go to a hotel. I think it's time we went to a hotel.

THE MANUFACTURER

(*After a moment*)

We can go to my house. I don't want to go to a hotel.

(*THE MANUFACTURER turns and starts down the stairs. She follows him. They both disappear from view.*)

THE MOTHER

(*In the living room*)

I never was much of a mother to her. She keeps throwing that up to me. I want to do the right thing this time. You know what I mean?

THE NEIGHBOR

Oh, sure, what the hell.

The lights fade slowly

Scene 2

THE MANUFACTURER's *apartment, later that night. The only light on is the dim one in the anteroom, which casts just enough light for us to see into the darkened living room. After a moment,* THE GIRL *appears in the anteroom, entering from another part of the apartment. She is wearing the dress she wore in the preceding scene, but is adjusting it as though she has just put it on. She is in her stockinged feet. The light in the anteroom is so inadequate that we can barely make out more than her silhouette. Her hair is disheveled, and she begins to straighten it. As she does, she steps down into the living room, finds a lamp and turns it on. A soft cone of light spreads across much of the room. We can see now that her coat and* THE MANUFACTURER's *have been dropped on the davenport and on a chair, that her purse is on the floor, and that her shoes lie tumbled on their sides in the middle of the room.*

She moves to her shoes, straightens them with her toes, and squeezes her feet into them. Throughout all this, she has been soddenly expressionless. Now she closes her eyes and just stands, letting a sigh escape. Then she shakes her head and picks up her purse and puts it on the end table.

THE MANUFACTURER *now appears in the anteroom. He is in his shirt sleeves and does not wear a tie. He stands in the anteroom, watching* THE GIRL, *who is aware of his presence but does not turn to him.*

The entire scene is shadowed and silhouetted.

THE MANUFACTURER
(Gently)
Would you like something, a cup of coffee or anything like that? (THE GIRL *shakes her head, does not turn to him.* THE MANUFACTURER *moves down into the living room, to the window, touches the radiator cover under the window)* One thing I can say about this building, there's always steam. This is something from my childhood. I don't care what I have to pay in rent as long as I got steam in the winter. (THE GIRL *opens her purse, takes out her lipstick, sits on the davenport and begins to apply it.* THE MANUFACTURER *regards her with a slight, almost hurt smile)* It wasn't such a good idea, after all.

THE GIRL
(Looks briefly up and then back to her lipstick)
Oh, I'm all right.
(THE MANUFACTURER *turns away, apparently disturbed.* THE GIRL

pauses in the application of her lipstick, lets her hands fall to her lap. THE
MANUFACTURER *looks back at her, almost angrily.)*

THE MANUFACTURER

Please, Betty, don't put on lipstick. To jump out of bed and put on lipstick, it's like a whore. *(He turns away again, edgy, angry with himself for
being irritable.* THE GIRL *sits miserably, her hands in her lap.* THE MANUFAC-
TURER *sits down several chairs away from her)* Listen, did you know
Lockman tried to commit suicide yesterday?

THE GIRL
(Looks up, startled)

Mr. Lockman?

THE MANUFACTURER

He called his wife from a hotel, and he said he was going to take fifty
sleeping pills. So she called me, so I called the police. That's what all the
fuss in the office was about yesterday. That's why I had to run out. We
broke down the door, and they took him to Bellevue. Oh, my God, what
a time that was. *(He stands again, shaken a little)* I know what you think
about Walter Lockman. He's always pinching you and flirting. He wasn't
that way till the last couple of years. He's a kind, generous man. *(He turns
to* THE GIRL, *almost pleading)* I told the psychiatrist there, I said, "This
man, my partner, whom I know for twenty-odd years," I told the psychiatrist, I said, "He's getting old, and he's so terrified of being impotent."
That's why he flirts so much. That's why he runs around with buyers and
prostitutes from hotels. You have to understand the torture and the doubts
that a man has when he reaches middle age.

THE GIRL

I'm not angry with him, Jerry.

*(*THE MANUFACTURER *straightens up, walks away a few paces. He sits
down, his mind heavy with his thoughts. He looks across to* THE GIRL.*)*

THE MANUFACTURER

There was a hundred times in the last couple of months when it would
have been better than tonight. At least a hundred times, where I looked at
you and I had tears in my eyes, I had such a gentleness for you. Love is a
gentle business, Betty. Because this way, this way...I'll tell you what it was
like this way. About five, six months ago, Walter Lockman came to me, he
says, "Listen, I'm taking out a buyer tonight. We'll go to the Copa. We'll
go to the Bon Soir down in the Village. We'll get a couple of girls. Come
on. We'll have a good time." This is the wheels of industry operating.
Some of these buyers come in, you don't get them a girl, they won't order
fifty dozen blouses. All right, so I was lonely, so I said all right. *(He stands,*

angry with the memory of the incident. He moves around as he tells the story) So I came home and took a shave. I put on a new suit. I went with them down the Bon Soir. They had three girls. Nice-looking girls. You be surprised how nice-looking some of these girls are. So I got a little drunk there. I made a lot of jokes. Listen, sometimes, I can be pretty witty. Everybody was laughing. We got in a cab, and we went to a hotel on Thirty-Second Street. Lockman had a suite of rooms there. Oh, I'm telling you. We were laughing in the cab, and we were laughing in the elevator. Everything I said, my girl would fall over from laughter. So we got in the room, this girl with me keeps pulling me by the arm into the bedroom.

THE GIRL
(Mumbling)
I don't want to hear about it, Jerry.

THE MANUFACTURER
So let me tell you. So we got in the bedroom, and my girl kept hanging all over me. So we closed the door, so she turned to me, she said, "You'll have to pay the fifty dollars first." At the risk of being a little dramatic, I was sick. *(He sits down again on still another chair)* I thought she liked me, you know what I mean? *(With his hand he kneads his brow nervously and absently)* Well, to make a long story short, as soon as it was over, she got right up, she began putting on lipstick.

THE GIRL
(With deep tenderness)
I love you, Jerry, from the bottom of my heart.
(For a brief moment, they regard each other with a strange, delicate pain.)

THE MANUFACTURER
(Turning away, feeling tears)
I wasn't pleading for Lockman before, sweetheart. I was pleading for myself.

THE GIRL
I know. I want to marry you, Jerry.

THE MANUFACTURER
I'm afraid to. I'm afraid. I knew tonight was going to happen sooner or later. I kept pushing it off. I didn't want to touch what we had. It meant so much to me. I had a new life with you. I didn't want to think about marriage. I'm afraid of such a marriage. I'm afraid of myself. At my age, you become afraid of things. You begin to be conscious of your fingers, that they're not as clever as they used to be. Your legs get tired from standing fifteen minutes. Your whole body resists you. I don't know what I'll be like in five years, Betty. I don't want a five-year marriage.

(He turns away again, shielding his eyes, the tears flooding up in him again.)

THE GIRL

Let's not make problems. I'm not worried about what's going to happen in five years.

THE MANUFACTURER
(Sits)

I told my sister today I've been seeing a lot of you.

THE GIRL

What did she say?

THE MANUFACTURER

Well, she suspected, of course, that I was seeing somebody, but she was a little upset when I told her it was you and how young you were.

THE GIRL

I'm the big scandal of my family. All my aunts and uncles and my cousin Loretta were over the house the other night, and she called you my sugar daddy. And my mother picked it up, and that's all I've been hearing the last couple of days, all about my sugar daddy. *(He says nothing; he is still troubled by deep, anxious thoughts. She senses this)*
Don't break up with me, Jerry.

(For a moment, THE MANUFACTURER looks at her, somewhat distracted.)

THE MANUFACTURER

You know what I did tonight?

THE GIRL

What?

THE MANUFACTURER

I came out of the office, I was going to take a cab to go to the garage to get the car. So it was just starting to snow and the air was so clear. So you know what I did?

THE GIRL

What?

THE MANUFACTURER

I walked all the way up from the office to the garage.

THE GIRL

Oh, for Pete's sake.

THE MANUFACTURER

That's forty blocks. That's a good two miles.

THE GIRL

That's wonderful. *(Pause)* Please ask me to marry you, Jerry.

THE MANUFACTURER

I'll tell you what honest to God bothers me. I love you, Betty. My whole life has been a pleasure since I know you. A pleasure to wake up, a pleasure to go to work. I cherish you. I cherish you like you were a diamond, but I'm afraid in a couple of years I'll be like Lockman. I'll be running around with prostitutes. It won't matter any more if they like me.

THE GIRL

Jerry...

THE MANUFACTURER

Pay them the fifty dollars already!

THE GIRL

I don't know what to do when you're this way.

THE MANUFACTURER

(Mounting panic)

I'll tell you what I'm really afraid of. I'm afraid in a couple of years you'll start looking around for a younger man!

THE GIRL

I would never do that.

THE MANUFACTURER

What do you see in me, Betty? I'm like a father to you!

THE GIRL

No!

THE MANUFACTURER

You never had a father. I'm like a father to you!

THE GIRL

It's more than that! You know that! I'll make you happy, I promise you I'll make you happy. What do you want me to do?

(He turns away from her, and the two of them sit, afraid to look at each other.)

THE MANUFACTURER

(Muttering)

If any of my friends told me he was going to marry a young girl, I would say, "Don't be a fool. It's not a healthy relationship."

(THE GIRL looks at him now, her eyes wide and wet with tears.)

THE GIRL

I love you, Jerry. I love you from the bottom of my heart.

(They regard each other in a sudden stillness.)

THE MANUFACTURER

Will you marry me, Betty?

(She moves to him, and they suddenly clutch at each other, embracing with an abrupt, fierce desperation. After a long moment, they release each other, and THE MANUFACTURER *stands, deeply stirred. He shuffles a few paces away.* THE GIRL *stands, and he turns to look at her, and then he goes to her again, and they cling to each other, both crying quietly now in each other's arms)*

THE MANUFACTURER

Oh, my sweet girl, I love you so much, you don't know. *(They release each other again, and then* THE MANUFACTURER *sits down in one of the chairs, strangely exhilarated, yet confused and not quite understanding his own immense emotions. He seems a little abstracted. He looks up at* THE GIRL, *who stands, profoundly moved. Quietly)* If you change your mind tomorrow, I won't be angry with you. I want you to think about everything. I won't lie to you, Betty. I'm afraid.

(THE GIRL nods absently, then goes to the davenport and sits down again. They each sit now, quietly, touched a little with terror at the decisive step they have just taken.)

The lights fade slowly

SCENE 3

The same night, later. THE MANUFACTURER's *living room. One of the lamps is on, and there is another light on somewhere deeper in the apartment. No one is on stage at the moment.*

The front door opens and THE SISTER, THE DAUGHTER *and* THE SON-IN-LAW *enter. They are wearing winter coats.* THE SON-IN-LAW *is a tall, lean fellow in his early thirties. He wears a hat. He is an amiable, good-natured nebbisch sort of fellow.* THE SISTER *seems disturbed about something.*

THE SISTER
(Turning on the anteroom light)
There's a light on. I told you there was a light on. His jacket's on the chair there.

*(*THE DAUGHTER *moves into the living room, unbuttoning her coat, and, with a small sigh, sinks down into a chair. Her husband follows her a few steps.)*

THE DAUGHTER
(To her husband)
Maybe you better call home, tell the baby sitter we'll be a little late.

THE SON-IN-LAW
(Moving to the phone)
We going to be here that long?

*(*THE DAUGHTER *frowns.* THE SON-IN-LAW *dials.)*

THE SISTER
(Peering nervously down into the apartment)
Jerry, are you in the bathroom? I think there's a light on in the bathroom. Sit down a minute. I'll bring you some fruit.

(She disappears into the apartment.)

THE SON-IN-LAW
(On phone)
Hello, Bernice? This is Mr. Englander. How's the baby?...

*(*THE SISTER *comes back into the anteroom, taking off her coat.)*

THE SISTER
(Heading for the hall closet)
He's in the bathroom. He'll be right out. I told him you was here.

THE DAUGHTER
(To her aunt)
I don't know what you want us to say to him, Evelyn.

THE SISTER
(Hanging her coat in the closet)
Don't say nothing. I wasn't supposed to tell you about this girl.

THE SON-IN-LAW
(On phone)
Listen, Bernice dear, we're going to be a little late, about one or one-thirty...*(He looks at his wife for confirmation, and she nods)* Sure, call your mother. I'll drive you home, so don't worry...

(THE SISTER moves into the living room now, a little distraught, her hands twisting restlessly.)

THE SISTER
We're sitting down to dinner, he says to me, "I've been going out with a girl." So I thought a forty-five-year-old girl, a fifty-year-old girl. It comes out later it's a twenty-four-year-old girl. I couldn't eat. I didn't say nothing. I kept my mouth shut. But I was sick.

(She sits down, her fingers moving restlessly on the arms of the chair. She sighs nervously.)

THE DAUGHTER
Evelyn, why are you so worked up? My father is having a middle-aged fling.

THE SISTER
It's not a fling. If it was a fling, would he tell me? Your father doesn't make flings.

THE DAUGHTER
Do you feel he intends to marry the girl?

THE SISTER
I don't know. *(Stands suddenly)* I forgot the fruit.
(She starts off for the kitchen again.)

THE DAUGHTER
What exactly did he say to you, Evelyn?

THE SISTER
Look, he's coming out in a minute, so let's drop the subject. I didn't tell you nothing. You don't know nothing about it.

THE DAUGHTER
We don't know nothing.

(THE SISTER disappears into the apartment. THE DAUGHTER stares at

her shoes with a vague scowl. THE SON-IN-LAW *finds a chair, sits down, his opened coat falling to his sides.)*

THE SON-IN-LAW
(After a moment)

So what do you say, Lillian, about Monday? *(His wife looks up at him, not quite knowing what he's talking about)* We always wind up my vacations sitting in the backyard. I was talking to Paul there, as I was telling you, before Evelyn started this whole business, and he said, and Elizabeth said, they'd take the kid off our hands for the two weeks. What the hell, we took their Richard when they went to the Poconos last summer.

THE DAUGHTER

Do you remember any blonde up in my father's office, Jack?

THE SON-IN-LAW

I haven't been up there in a couple of years.

THE DAUGHTER

Oh, wait a minute. Yes, I do. There's a blonde up there. Sits in front of Caroline. A very sweet-looking girl.
(She frowns slightly.)

THE SON-IN-LAW

So, what'll I tell my boss? Shall I tell him I'll take the vacation Monday? I'll tell you, Lillian. I'd like to get away. I'm tired, and the snow and the slush. The tax season starts in a couple of weeks, and I'll be working nights. I'd like to get away, I think.

THE DAUGHTER
(Not really interested)

Elizabeth said she'd take the baby?

THE SON-IN-LAW

Sure. We took their Richard when they went to the Poconos. *(He stands, feeling in his coat pockets for cigarettes. He sends a brief look over to his wife, who is sitting, apparently concerned with her own thoughts)* I don't know. It seems to me it wouldn't hurt us to get away somewheres and relax. I feel there's a tenseness between us. I don't know. It seems that...I don't know...
(He lights his cigarette, wishing he hadn't brought up the matter.)

THE DAUGHTER

What do you mean, tenseness?

THE SON-IN-LAW

I don't know. It seems we never talk or go out. It seems...

THE DAUGHTER

We went out tonight.

THE SON-IN-LAW

I don't know what I mean. I come home, and we have dinner, and you tell me about the baby, or your father comes over, or...

THE DAUGHTER

My father hasn't been up the house in three weeks.

THE SON-IN-LAW

Listen, I like your father. I wasn't objecting to his coming over.

THE DAUGHTER

I don't know what you mean by tenseness.

THE SON-IN-LAW

Well, maybe that's the wrong word, I just feel that...

THE DAUGHTER

We've been married more than three years, Jack.

THE SON-IN-LAW

No! No! It's not that. Listen, I like your father. He's a prince of a man. *(THE DAUGHTER crosses to the end table, on which her purse lies.)*

THE DAUGHTER

(Fishing in her purse, apparently for her cigarettes. She smiles)
She's so funny, Evelyn. She's so upset about this girl.

THE SON-IN-LAW

(Proffering his pack of cigarettes)
Have one of mine, Lillian.

THE DAUGHTER

(Shakes her head, gets one of her own out, continues to smile)
She was in a state when we went in to get our coats. She comes over to me, she says, "I got something terrible to tell you." I thought she was going to tell me she had cancer. So she says, "Your father is seeing a girl, twenty-four years old." So I looked at her, I said, "So?" *(She sits down, leans across to her husband)* You know what it is with her, Jack? Subconsciously, she thinks of herself as my father's wife. She resents any woman who gets close to him. She never got along with my mother. I didn't get along with my mother either, but that was an entirely different matter. So now she lives here in the house with him, and...I was against it, you know. When my mother died, and my father told me that Evelyn wanted to move in with him, I said, "Pop, you're just feeding her neurotic attachment for you." I wanted him to move in with us.

THE SON-IN-LAW

Listen, I was perfectly willing.

THE DAUGHTER

She resents me a great deal. Every time my father and I sit down for one of our little talks, she always finds some way of breaking in. She resents any woman my father likes. It's frankly a little incest, that's what it is.

(THE SON-IN-LAW *gestures with his head to remind her of* THE SISTER's *off-stage presence. They lower their voices.*)

THE SON-IN-LAW

Well, she's a lonely old woman, and...

THE DAUGHTER

So my father is going to bed with some girl, what's so terrible about it? (*She stands, moves nervously a few paces, puffs on her cigarette. She turns back to her husband*) I can see how a girl could go for my father. He's a damned attractive man. For a man with no formal education, he is amazingly literate. I wonder if he actually goes to bed with this little tramp.

THE SON-IN-LAW

Well, I assume...

THE DAUGHTER

He's got a lot of charm, my old man. (*She sits down again, smoking.* THE SON-IN-LAW *interests himself in the needlework of the doily on his chair.* THE DAUGHTER *leans toward him, lowers her voice, smiles, shakes her head*) What surprises me is my father didn't mention a word about this little affair of his to me. He usually tells me everything.

THE SON-IN-LAW
(*Smiles tentatively*)
Well, it's hardly something a father would tell his daughter.

THE DAUGHTER

It so happens we're pretty damn close, Jack. I'm probably closer to my father than to any other person I know.

(*Her husband looks quickly down, and* THE DAUGHTER, *aware that this was something of a slight to her husband, flushes.*)

THE SON-IN-LAW

Listen, he's a prince of a man, your father. I'm the first one to admit it.

(THE DAUGHTER *stands, looks around for an ash tray, sees one across the room, crosses to it. A moment of silence.*)

THE DAUGHTER

What I meant was, in many ways, he's a remarkable man, and I respect him very much. (*She looks at her husband for a moment*) Jack, we'll go to Florida Monday. I could do with a vacation myself, and you've been looking very tired recently.

THE SON-IN-LAW

Listen, why take the train down, and waste a whole day? We'll fly.

THE DAUGHTER

Elizabeth said she'd take the baby?

THE SON-IN-LAW

We got a couple of hotels down there for accounts, and I can get a room or a suite if you like, cheap.

THE DAUGHTER

I'll call Elizabeth tomorrow, see just how serious she is. Otherwise, we could leave the baby with your mother.

(*She breaks off as* THE SISTER *returns with a tray, on which there is a bowl of fruit.*)

THE SISTER

(*As she comes down into the room*)

You see, why should he tell me about it? I don't know what he does with his nights. I don't want to know. He calls up, he says he's not coming home for dinner. All right. That's his business. So why should he bother to tell me about this girl if it wasn't a serious business? I don't want him to do something he'll regret the rest of his life.

(THE DAUGHTER *whirls on* THE SISTER *as she sets the tray down on an end table.*)

THE DAUGHTER

(*Angrily*)

Evelyn! Leave him alone, you hear me! He's having a little fun for himself! Don't destroy it for him!

THE SISTER

(*Looking up, a little startled*)

What's the matter with you?

THE DAUGHTER

You're jealous of this girl! Any woman that gets close to my father, I resent...I mean you resent! He's having an affair! What are you so upset about?

THE SISTER

You seem more upset than me.

(THE DAUGHTER *turns angrily away, sits heavily down on a chair.*)

THE DAUGHTER

I don't want any fruit!

(THE SISTER *looks at* THE SON-IN-LAW.)

THE SISTER

What's the matter with her? I just don't want my brother to do something he'll regret the rest of his life.

(THE MANUFACTURER *suddenly calls out from deeper in the apartment.*)

THE MANUFACTURER
(Off)

Hello! I'll be right there!

THE SISTER
(Calling back)

All right, we got fruit. (*To* THE SON-IN-LAW) What did I say? I don't even know what I said that she suddenly starts yelling at me like that.

(THE MANUFACTURER *appears now, coming into the anteroom. He is in his shirt sleeves but wears a tie. He seems to be in excellent and hearty spirits.*)

THE MANUFACTURER

Hello, Jack boy, how are you there?

THE SON-IN-LAW

Hello, Jerry, how are you?

THE MANUFACTURER
(Coming down into the living room)

I just got in about half an hour ago myself. I was soaking wet. I was walking in the snow there. I took a hot shower, and I feel wonderful. Hello, Lillian sweetheart, how are you? Where were you all tonight, at Paul's? (*He has started for the fruit bowl but he is intercepted by his daughter, who stops him to give him a sudden embrace. He regards her with mild surprise*) Why such a big hug?

THE DAUGHTER
(Still holding him)

I haven't seen you in a couple of weeks, I missed you. I called every night last week, you wasn't in. What have you been doing with yourself?

THE MANUFACTURER
(Releasing himself)

Well, listen, give me some fruit, I'll tell you all about it.

THE SON-IN-LAW

We're going down to Florida Monday, Jerry. Lillian and me.

THE MANUFACTURER
(Taking an apple)

Hey, you lucky bums, you. But I'll tell you something. I like snow. All of a sudden, I like snow. I used to hate it. Remember, Lillian, how I used to hate the winter? Always I took my vacation in the winter. My wife and I, every winter. Florida, California. But now I go for walks. If I told you how much I walked in the snow tonight, and that's a blizzard out there. I'll bet you at least six, seven inches. I walked from the office to the garage. Forty-two blocks. It was so clear out. Like a lunatic, I started walking up Broadway. I got to a Hundred and Eighteenth Street, I suddenly stopped, I said, "What am I, crazy?" It was so bracing outside. I want you to know, Evelyn, I did not wear rubbers, I did not wear galoshes. I came home, I was soaking wet, and I feel wonderful. So you're going to Florida? Your first time, right? You'll have a wonderful time. It's the height of the season, Jack, did you make reservations? Evelyn, give me a knife. So when are you going, Monday? Are you going by plane, train, what? *(He suddenly pauses while paring the apple and slaps the back of an upholstered chair)* I'm going to tell you something. I just feel wonderful. Listen, as long as you're here. I've got something to tell you. I figured I'd drive up tomorrow night and see you, but as long as you're here. I'll go see Paul tomorrow. How is he, by the way, and Elizabeth? I haven't seen them in a couple of weeks. Well, anyway, did Evelyn tell you anything?

THE SISTER

I didn't say nothing. You told me to say nothing, and that's what I said.

THE MANUFACTURER

Well, I've decided to get married again.

(THE DAUGHTER goes for her cigarettes again.)

THE DAUGHTER

You're going to get married, Pa?

THE MANUFACTURER

Well, I'll tell you the whole story.

THE DAUGHTER

(Fishing in her purse for cigarettes)

Do we know the woman, Pa?

THE MANUFACTURER

Well, you might. I don't know. She's a girl works up in my office. You probably saw her there. A blond girl. The receptionist, sits in front of Caroline.

(THE SON-IN-LAW again proffers his pack of cigarettes to his wife, who shakes her head and gets out one of her own.)

THE SON-IN-LAW

Congratulations, Jerry.

THE MANUFACTURER

Thank you. I think you should know, she's quite a young girl. Twenty-four years old. She's younger than you are, Lillian. I've been seeing her for a couple of months, and it just seems that this is it.

(*The brief enthusiasm of the previous moment seems to have filtered out. A short silence fills the room.* THE SISTER, *who had turned abruptly away at* THE MANUFACTURER's *announcement, rubs her brow nervously with the tips of her fingers.* THE SON-IN-LAW *sends a cautious look to his wife and then looks back to the floor.* THE DAUGHTER *sits down again, takes a long puff on her cigarette.* THE MANUFACTURER *purses his lips.*)

THE DAUGHTER
(*Smiling briefly*)
Well, that's wonderful, Pa. I'm very happy for you.

THE MANUFACTURER
Thank you, sweetheart, thank you. Nothing definite has been set. The girl has to get a divorce, she's in the process now. I'd like you to meet the girl. I'm sure you'll like her. We'll have to set up some kind of dinner. (*He considers the carpeting at his feet, takes a deep sigh*) So that's it, that's my announcement.

THE SISTER
(*Suddenly moves to her brother, bursting out*)
Jerry, what are you doing? Do you know what you're doing? What's the matter with you?

THE MANUFACTURER
Evelyn, let me stop you before you even start.

THE SISTER
Honest to God, for God's sakes. All right, you come in, you tell me, a twenty-four-year-old girl. All right. What's the matter with you? You're a sensible man, for the love of God, honest to God. Our brother Herman, who is a fool—all right, this I could expect from him. But you're the sensible one. For God's sakes, what's the matter with you?

(THE MANUFACTURER *has moved a few steps toward his daughter.*)

THE MANUFACTURER
(*To his daughter, with a vague smile*)
I have to admit, Lillian, I expected a little more enthusiasm from you.

(THE DAUGHTER *looks up, smiles briefly.*)

THE DAUGHTER
I'm just a little shocked, Pa, to tell you the truth.

THE MANUFACTURER
It's really not such a shocking thing. I'm going to get married, that's all. Of course, she's a young girl, and this presents a number of problems, but…

THE SISTER
(*To* THE SON-IN-LAW)

It never works out. I could tell you ten cases. When I had my apartment in Brooklyn, there was a man in the building, fifty-nine years old, he ran away with a sixteen-year-old girl. It was in the papers and everything. What a scandal. His wife had a nervous breakdown. (*Turns to her brother*) Jerry, don't do something you'll regret the rest of your life. You're fifty-three years old. You're a man settled in habit. You like to come home, you watch television. You want to get married, marry somebody your own age. Who is this girl? I want to know. Who is this girl? She sees a nice rich fellow, has a good business, makes a good living. She sees herself living in a fancy apartment, fancy clothes....

THE MANUFACTURER

Evelyn, don't get so excited. You're beginning to say a lot of foolish things.

THE SISTER

Is she going to move in here?

THE MANUFACTURER

A married couple usually live together.

THE SISTER
(*Throwing up her hands and moving away*)

All right! You want to marry her, marry her. You want me to move out of the house? All right, I'll pack my clothes, I'll move out.

THE MANUFACTURER

Is that what's bothering you?

THE SISTER

What's bothering me is you're making a fool of yourself.

THE MANUFACTURER

All right, Evelyn...

THE SISTER

You're making a fool of yourself, Jerry. I'm telling you right to your face. All right, you want to have an affair with a girl, all right. But marriage? Don't be a fool. It never works out. Max Coleman—you remember Max Coleman? I could tell you a hundred cases. Max Coleman married a girl of thirty-four, already a young woman, not a kid any more, and you saw what happened. One year, and they were divorced. (THE MANUFACTURER *turns from his sister and moves slowly to his daughter.* THE SISTER *suddenly calls out*) Is she Jewish?

THE MANUFACTURER
(Sitting down beside his daughter)
Does that matter in this day and age?

THE SISTER
(Paces nervously to another corner of the room, mutters)
All right, you want me to move out, I'll pack my clothes, I'll move out.
(THE MANUFACTURER looks at his daughter.)

THE MANUFACTURER
Lillian, I sense you're not entirely happy about the whole idea.

THE DAUGHTER
Pa, for heaven's sakes, you come in the room, you tell me you're going
to get married to some girl. Give me a chance to digest it.

THE SISTER
(Calling out from her corner)
Do you remember Harry Wolfson? Used to live on Eastern Parkway
when we used to live in Brooklyn. He also had a big romance with a young
girl. A man gets to middle age, and he begins to worry about...

THE MANUFACTURER
What's so terrible about middle age? I'm physically in tip-top shape. Nat
Phillips has been trying to get me interested in golf. Son of a gun, I'm
going to take him up on it.

THE SISTER
Max Coleman married a girl of thirty-four, already a young woman, not
a kid any more, and in one year...

THE MANUFACTURER
Max Coleman is an idiot, was an idiot, and always will be.

THE SISTER
Jerry, we went to Paul's New Year's Eve party last year. A bunch of young
people, dancing and drinking. Didn't you tell me you felt out of place? For
heaven's sakes, your own daughter Lillian is older than this girl. A young
girl, twenty years old, what does she want? She wants night clubs, dancing. She's not going to sit with you, watch television every night. And
don't say you're in such tiptop shape. You're not such an athlete any more.
You've been complaining about your back for a good couple of years.

THE MANUFACTURER
Don't you think I considered all this? I'm a businessman, you know. I
don't jump into propositions.

THE SISTER
Are you kidding yourself this girl's in love with you or something?

THE MANUFACTURER

Evelyn, this is really none of your goddam business.

THE SISTER

You said you wanted to discuss it.

THE MANUFACTURER

(With sudden sharpness)

I made an announcement! I didn't open the floor for discussions! I'm not a kid we're deciding to send to summer camp or not. I'm not a family problem.

THE SISTER

(Throwing up her hands and turning away)

All right! All right!

THE DAUGHTER

All right, Pa...

THE SISTER

You want me to pack my clothes, I'll move out, that's all.

THE DAUGHTER

(Taking the older woman's arm)

All right, Evelyn, don't get so upset.

(THE SISTER'S *eyes have become red.*)

THE SISTER

(Shielding her eyes with a hand)

My whole life I gave up for my brothers and sisters. My whole life. Mama died, who brought up the family? My whole life I gave up.

(She turns away from the others, moves quickly across the room.)

THE MANUFACTURER

Nobody said you have to move out. Maybe we'll get a bigger apartment. I don't know. I haven't thought about it.

THE SISTER

(Shrilly)

I wouldn't live in the same house with that tramp!

THE MANUFACTURER

(Angrily)

All right! Shut up!

THE DAUGHTER

All right, Pa, all right.

THE MANUFACTURER

For God's sakes, the world isn't coming to an end. I'm just going to get married.

THE DAUGHTER
(*Escorting him to a chair*)
All right, Pa, don't get so angry.
(*A sudden, swift, inexplicable silence sweeps over the room, thick with the edges of unresolved angers.* THE MANUFACTURER *plucks at his trouser leg with nervous fingers.* THE DAUGHTER *sits down on the couch. Then, suddenly,* THE SISTER *whirls abruptly and goes sullenly up into the anteroom, disappearing into the apartment.* THE MANUFACTURER *looks up briefly, scowling at her departing back. He mutters to no one in particular, but really to his daughter.*)

THE MANUFACTURER
All she's worried about is she's going to have to move out of the house. She's the older sister, you know, so she feels everybody has to get her okay. That's why Herman never got married, do you know that? She wouldn't approve of any girl.

THE DAUGHTER
Pa, her position in your house is threatened, and she's fighting, that's all.

THE MANUFACTURER
(*The anger flowing out of him*)
This was not an easy decision for me. To get married, you know, at my age, and to a girl young enough to be my daughter...Don't you think I have doubts about what I'm doing? You know Walter Lockman tried to commit suicide yesterday?

THE DAUGHTER
No, I didn't know, Pa.

THE MANUFACTURER
Everybody gets to a certain age there, when suddenly old age with white hair, sitting in the park playing checkers...who wants to be an old fool? I'll tell you something. It's important to me that a young girl finds me attractive. I didn't know it was so important, but it's important. (*He leans to his daughter, a vague note of pleading slipping into his voice*) She needs me, you understand, Lillian? It's been a long time since somebody needed me. My kids are all grown up, with children of their own. I'm a man who has to give of himself, I...(*He turns his face away and scowls. For a moment, nobody says anything. Then he stands, ostensibly looks for his jacket, which is draped over the back of the chair. He goes to it*) I don't have to justify myself. I decided to get married, that's all.

THE DAUGHTER
Nobody said no, Pa.

THE MANUFACTURER
(Finding a cigar and taking it out)

She's a very sweet girl. Very bright, very clever. But emotionally, she's really immature. A neglected girl. She's so hungry for love. Like an orphan. She has to know twenty-four hours a day that you love her. *(Coming back to his daughter)* All right, so who's perfect? Apparently, I'm attracted to childish women. Your mother, she should rest in peace, till the day she died she was fifteen years old. *(Sits down again, leans across to his daughter, the pleading naked on his face)* But this girl is sweet, Lillian, I can't tell you. She has such delight in her. Like a baby. *(He looks at her, his eyes wide and beseeching)* Do you think I'm making a fool of myself, Lillian?

THE DAUGHTER
(Drops her eyes, frowns)

Well, Pa, it's really not my business to interfere in your life.

THE MANUFACTURER

At least, a few years of happiness I'll have. Even a few years of happiness, you don't throw away.

THE DAUGHTER

I never met the girl, of course...
(THE DAUGHTER scowls, looks away, then stands.)

THE MANUFACTURER

Your opinion is very important to me, Lillian. I'll be honest with you. I'm not sure of myself in this thing. *(THE DAUGHTER is looking around for her cigarettes again)* Don't go home yet, Lillian.

THE DAUGHTER

I'm just looking for my cigarettes, Pa.
(Her husband offers his pack; she takes one.)

THE MANUFACTURER
(Rising and following her)

What I'm afraid, you see, is like Walter Lockman needs prostitutes maybe I need a young bride.

THE SON-IN-LAW
(Standing suddenly)

Jerry, you love her?

THE MANUFACTURER
(Turns to his son-in-law)

Like a schoolboy.

THE SON-IN-LAW

And she loves you? So that's the whole thing. Get married.

THE DAUGHTER
(Snapping at her husband with rather sudden intensity)

Sit down and stay out of this. It's none of your business. (THE SON-IN-LAW, *stung a little, shuffles back to his chair.* THE DAUGHTER *turns to her father)* Pa, I'm going to be frank with you. The relationship, to say the least, seems to be a neurotic one. The girl is obviously infantile in many ways. Otherwise, she wouldn't have to look to older men. I don't know the girl, but obviously she is very dependent, very infantile. And the whole relationship doesn't sound to me like the basis for a sound marriage. It sounds to me more like a father-daughter relationship than a husband-wife. It sounds like you want to adopt her, rather than marry her.

THE SON-IN-LAW
(Sitting in his chair, without looking up)

Your father's nobody's fool, Lilly.

THE DAUGHTER

Jack, please...

THE SON-IN-LAW

The man wants to get married. All he wants to know is that you're happy for him.

THE DAUGHTER

I don't want him to do something he'll regret the rest of his life. *(There is something familiar about the sentence she has just said that is unpleasant to* THE DAUGHTER *and makes her frown)* I'm just saying, weigh the circumstances.

THE MANUFACTURER
(Stands but avoids the eyes of the others)

All right, all right. We discussed it enough. I don't want to talk about it any more. *(He puts the cigar down on an ash tray, crosses slowly to a window, looks out at the heavy snow.* THE SISTER *appears in the anteroom)* I'd go out for a walk, except it's snowing so much. I can't stand snow. I wish I was going to Florida with you. I'd like to go to bed. I'm tired. I'm usually asleep by this hour. When you get to my age...
(He breaks off, once more aware of his age.)

THE DAUGHTER

Pa, all I'm trying to say is...

THE MANUFACTURER
(Crying out)

All right! I don't want to talk any more about it, do you hear me!
(He starts up to the anteroom, but his sister's presence makes him turn,

and instead he goes to the chair over which his jacket is draped, and takes it.)

THE DAUGHTER

Pa, why don't you come home with Jack and me, don't go in to work tomorrow, spend a long week end at our house?

THE SISTER

(As her brother moves into the anteroom to go to the closet)

Jerry, where are you going? Go to bed, for God's sakes. What are you going down for, a paper, what?

THE MANUFACTURER

(Getting his coat out of the closet, mutters)

Look, leave me alone for a couple of minutes.

THE DAUGHTER

(Coming to him in the anteroom)

What did you say, Pa? I didn't hear what you said.

THE MANUFACTURER

(Turns to his daughter and cries out more in pain than in anger)

I said, "Leave me alone!"

(Carrying his coat, he wrenches the door open and exits from the apartment. The door closes heavily behind him. THE SISTER *lets out a deep sigh and comes down into the living room.)*

THE SISTER

All right, all right, it's not so bad, it's not so bad. He's all upset now. Tomorrow he'll be sulking. In a couple of days he'll be all right, same old Jerry. One thing I know, a man gets to middle age, God alone knows.

THE DAUGHTER

(Coming down into the living room to her husband, who is standing and glowering at the floor)

I knew something like this was going to happen. He lives here lonely. His friends have all died or moved to California. Naturally, he's going to...

THE SON-IN-LAW

Come on, let's go home.

THE DAUGHTER

(To her husband, who has walked to the anteroom)

Listen, Jack, I really don't think I can get away Monday for Florida. My father is going through a very crucial period now, and...

THE SON-IN-LAW

(Slowly bursting out with all the repressed submissiveness of years. He stares at his wife, the words stumbling out)

Boy, you're great! Boy, you're great! Sure, the trouble with Evelyn, she got a neurotic attachment! Holy Jesus Christ! He came to you, he says he's going to get married, and you whack him across the face with some two-bit psychology! Can't go to Florida now! I knew it! I knew it! Your father needs you! Oh, sure, boy! Your father needs you like a hole in the head! How many times I heard that? My father needs me! You need your father, that's what! I knew we weren't going to Florida! I knew it!

THE DAUGHTER
Jack...

THE SON-IN-LAW
You're the one! You! You! Who's all tied up with your father! Took me two years to get you to move to New Rochelle! Couldn't live half an hour away from your father!

THE DAUGHTER
Now, listen, Jack...

THE SON-IN-LAW
Shut up! I'm talking now! I'm going to Florida, you hear me?! I don't care whether you come! Everything is for your father! Three times a week you got to call him on the phone! I'm your husband, goddammit, you know that? Jesus Christ! How about me?! I want to go away for a vacation! How about thinking about me sometimes instead of your goddam father?! *(The shrill, fierce, tortured fury is so new to him that he feels physically sick. He stands, hunched a little, his face forward, his mouth open as if he were retching, his breath coming in the deep, exhausted way of a truly ill man. Then he says quietly, his eyes closed)* I'm sorry, Lillian, I'm sorry. Come on, let's go home.

> *(He turns and shuffles to the front door, where he waits. His wife, who is standing, pained and shocked at the outburst, guilty, confused, shamed, now moves slowly to the steps of the living room.)*

THE DAUGHTER
(Looking at the floor as she goes)
I didn't know you felt so strongly about my father, Jack. *(She goes up into the anteroom)* Would you like to have a cup of coffee before we start driving? *(Turning to her aunt)* Evelyn, is there any coffee? *(She turns back to her husband)* Jack...

THE SON-IN-LAW
(At the door, looking down)
Come on, let's go. It's late, and I got to drive the sitter home yet.
> *(THE SON-IN-LAW disappears out into the landing. THE DAUGHTER frowns, pauses, turns to her aunt.)*

THE DAUGHTER
So, Evelyn, would you call me and let me know what happens?

THE SISTER

Listen, don't worry. You go home with Jack. He's tired and nervous.

THE DAUGHTER

(Nods nervously)

So good-bye. Call me if something happens.

THE SISTER

Nothing's going to happen.

THE DAUGHTER

All right, so call me.

(She goes out, closing the door behind her. THE SISTER *stands a moment, then turns to pick up the fruit bowl.)*

Curtain

ACT III

SCENE 1

No sooner is the stage dark than the lights come up brightly in THE GIRL's *apartment. It is the same night.* THE MOTHER *and* THE KID SISTER *are seated in the living room, listening to* THE HUSBAND, *a young man in his late twenties, slim, dark, attractive in the diffident fashion of Montgomery Clift. He seems to be a pleasant, controlled young man, and is dressed neatly except for a somewhat flashy collar and necktie. He sits, his cigarette dangling from between two long fingers.*

THE HUSBAND

...I look in to see if there's any mail. The clerk says, "There's a special delivery letter for you." So I see it's from Betty, so I open it up. The first sentence is the greatest. "Dear George. I want a divorce."

THE MOTHER

Oh, my God.

THE HUSBAND

"I'm interested in another man. I want a divorce."

THE MOTHER

Oh, my God, I never knew about this, George.

THE HUSBAND

That's the night I called you three o'clock in the morning, New York time.

THE MOTHER
(To THE KID SISTER*)*

Did you know she wrote a letter to George?

THE KID SISTER

No, I didn't know anything, Ma.

THE HUSBAND
(Suddenly singing effortlessly, improvising tonelessly)

"Man, I want that woman..." (I wrote this one day. I felt so torchy one day, I just noodled with the piano, and it just came out). "Man, I want that woman...wahde-oodle-la-da-doo-dee...Wherever she may be. My arms,

71

my lips, my body says, 'Baby, come to me.'" Simple little lyric. Mel Torme
was out there. I played it for him. He was very excited about it.

*(He stands, moves around gracefully but a little nervously as he looks for
an ash tray.)*

THE KID SISTER

There's one right there on the table, George.

THE HUSBAND

(Finds the ash tray)

I don't know. I'm beginning to think there's something wrong with
women as a class. Don't get me wrong—I like women. I'm okay that way,
don't worry about that. I can hand you a long list of references, believe me.
But women, you know, don't seem to have the capacity to just yak it up.
The only time Betty was happy was when she was crying. In my limited
experience, it seems women like to be hurt. They always seem to love you
more after they cry. *(Smiling with great sweetness now)* Betty, you know,
sometimes I'd tease her, and she would cry. I don't know. I was just kidding around. But after she cried, she was always so beautiful. I never raised
a hand to her, though, I'll tell you that. You're a woman, Mrs. Mueller. Do
you agree with me?

THE MOTHER

(Not sure what he is talking about)

About what, George?

THE HUSBAND

I like women. Don't get me wrong. But for laughs, men are more fun to
be with, don't you think? My mother always used to say that. "You have to
break a woman's heart before she's happy." My mother is a tough old lady,
I'll tell you that. She tamed my old man pretty fast. Poor bastard.

THE MOTHER

Don't use that kind of language, George.

THE HUSBAND

Oh, I'm sorry, Mrs. Mueller. *(Looking at his watch)* Hey, it's twelve
o'clock, you know that?

THE MOTHER

I don't know what time she gets in any more.

THE HUSBAND

How long she been going out with this man?

THE MOTHER

She used to stay out till two, three o'clock in the morning, even when
she was in high school. I never knew where she was.

THE HUSBAND

She was a virgin, Mrs. Mueller, when we got married.

THE MOTHER

Oh, thank God for that.

THE HUSBAND

I still don't know what happened that last night. I happened to wake up four o'clock in the morning, she was gone. I look in the bathroom, she ain't there. But who figured a divorce? I figured I forgot her birthday, something like that. Suddenly, I get a letter from out of the blue, she wants a divorce. That hurt, you know? Your wife wants a divorce, the inference is that you failed as her husband. That's a reflection on me as a man. I took quite a kidding around about that. All the guys in the band, you know? "What's the matter, couldn't you keep her happy." I took quite a kidding around.

(THE GIRL *appears on the landing, cannot find her keys, rings the bell.*)

THE MOTHER

She must have forgot her keys.

THE HUSBAND

(*To* THE KID SISTER, *as he puts on his jacket*)

So I was telling you about Marlene Dietrich. Man, I tell you, that woman is architectured.

THE KID SISTER

You know who I think is beautiful? Janet Leigh.

THE HUSBAND

Oh, yeah, sure, she's a nice one, that one.

(THE MOTHER *opens the front door.*)

THE GIRL

I forgot my keys, Mother. It's really snowing outside. Did I wake you up?

THE MOTHER

George is here.

THE GIRL

(*Frowns*)

George? Where, here? (*She lets the door close and moves quickly through the foyer to the living-room doorway.* THE HUSBAND *rises from his chair*) Well, for Pete's sakes. Hello, George, you look just fine...

THE HUSBAND

You look great yourself.

THE MOTHER
(Coming in through the living-room doorway)
He called about ten minutes after you left the house. So I told him you
were on a date, so we were just sitting around talking, that's all.

THE GIRL
Well, you look just wonderful, all brown. Why don't you sit down while
I hang up my coat. My mother says your mother says you got a staff job at
NBC.
*(She goes back into the foyer, down to the hall closet, and hangs her wet
coat on the outside of the door. THE HUSBAND follows her to the doorway.)*

THE HUSBAND
(Calls down the foyer to her)
Well, not exactly. I got a buddy of mine, staff piano man at NBC, and
he says he can get me in, probably one of the smaller networks. Tony was
trying to round up a four-piece combination for a night club spot in San
Francisco. But it didn't look good to me, and you know me and Lou
Waters never got along.

THE GIRL
(Coming back up the foyer)
That was the horn man.

THE HUSBAND
Yeah, some horn man! He couldn't blow his nose, what a horn man. So
Eddie Johnson, he used to play in the pit in the Roxy before they put in
Cinemascope—I think you met him once—he wrote me, he said there's
going to be a spot open on WPAT, that's out in New Jersey, for a good staff
piano man with a classical background. So I figured that's steady work, a
couple of hundred bucks a week, so I wired Eddie: "See what you can do
for me." So I took the plane in. I mean, after I got your letter, you know.
*(THE GIRL has come into the living room and has been listening, leaning
against the couch.)*

THE GIRL
How's your mother?

THE HUSBAND
Oh, she's fine. You look great, Betty.
*(THE GIRL sits down on the couch. Her mother and sister are already seat-
ed. A silence hangs over the four of them.)*

THE KID SISTER
So what other stars did you see out there, George?

THE HUSBAND
I caught Sinatra one show. He was at the Sands. Lou Rocco dropped in

one night, he sat in for me, so I went over to the Sands, catch Sinatra. Man, he was the greatest. He had laryngitis. He couldn't hit anything over middle F. He had to whisper all his songs. But he was up there for an hour and a half. They wouldn't let him off the stage. The greatest, that man, the greatest. *(Again the uneasy silence. He turns to* THE MOTHER*)* Would you mind very much, Mrs. Mueller, if Betty and I went for a walk?

THE GIRL
I don't want to go for a walk.

THE MOTHER
Go on out for a walk. He isn't going to kill you.

THE GIRL
I got to get up early tomorrow.

THE HUSBAND
I think you owe me a few minutes in private, Betty. After all, you write me a letter, tell me you want a divorce...

THE MOTHER
Listen, Alice and I can go in our rooms, and you could talk right here.

THE GIRL
Ma...

THE MOTHER
For heaven's sakes...

THE GIRL
(Suddenly)
There's nothing to talk about because I just want a divorce because I'm getting married.
(This statement causes a moment's silence.)

THE MOTHER
(Coldly)
Who? To him?

THE GIRL
Yes.
(She stands.)

THE MOTHER
I'm not going to let you marry a man old enough to be your father. A Jewish man like that. *(*THE GIRL *moves away, somewhat like an animal at bay, moves out of the room into the foyer.* THE MOTHER *follows her, herself deeply stirred)* You're always telling me I never took an interest in you! In your school, and things like that! Well, all right! All right! I'm taking an interest in you now! I'm not going to let you throw away the rest of your life!

I'm your mother! You listen to what I tell you!
> (*They are coming down the foyer now, to the front door.*)

THE GIRL
> (*Crying out*)

Ma! Leave me alone!

THE MOTHER

I'm only thinking what's good for you! For you!

THE GIRL
> (*Screaming*)

Just leave me alone, please! Will you leave me alone!

THE MOTHER
> (*In a fury of desperation*)

For God's sakes! (*She turns, not far from tears, and hurries back to the living room, where* THE HUSBAND *and* THE KID SISTER *stand, embarrassed by the short outburst of screaming*) Oh, for God's sakes, everybody in this building must have heard everything going on in this house! Everything. (*She sits down and begins to cry a little.* THE GIRL *remains in the foyer, by the front door, leaning against the wall, trying to control herself.* THE MOTHER, *talks out loud, to no one in particular*) I don't believe in divorce. You make your bed, you lie in it. My husband wrote me sixteen years ago from Canton, Ohio, he said he wanted a divorce. I said, "You made your bed, you lie in it." The whole neighborhood knows about her and her sugar daddy. I'm ashamed to show my face in the street.
> (*She cries again, biting her lip, making no effort to shield her face.*)

THE HUSBAND
> (*Nervously, after a moment, to* THE KID SISTER)

What did she do, go out?
> (THE KID SISTER *shrugs. At this moment,* THE GIRL *opens the door and does go out onto the landing. The sound of the door closing is heard by the others.*)

THE HUSBAND

She looks good, you know? Listen, I think I'll go out and see if I can calm her down.
> (*He ambles out into the foyer and down to the front door.*)

THE MOTHER
> (*To* THE KID SISTER)

How's your school coming? Are you having any trouble in school?
> (THE HUSBAND *opens the door and looks out.* THE GIRL, *standing on the landing, looks briefly up at him.*)

THE HUSBAND

What are you doing out here, come on in the house.

THE GIRL

I don't want to come in the house.

THE HUSBAND

It's cold out here, you want me to get your coat?

THE GIRL

Would you, please? It's hanging right on the closet there.
(THE HUSBAND *reaches over and pulls the wet coat down from the closet door and goes out onto the landing. The door closes behind him. He helps his wife into her coat.*)

THE HUSBAND

You remember Lou Angosino? You met him once. He was the guy from the union came up the house one time. I think he sat at a table once at Birdland once with us. He made a pass at you. He was out in Vegas. He sends his regards.

THE GIRL

George, I'd like to know why you came back. I mean it, really.

THE HUSBAND

What do you mean, why did I come back? I suddenly get a letter from my wife out of the blue, saying she wants a divorce.

THE GIRL

You said on the phone that you wouldn't contest my divorce. I told you I was sending you a letter from my lawyer which you had to sign.

THE HUSBAND

What are we talking about this out here for? Let's go somewheres where we can talk.

THE GIRL

I don't want to go anywheres.

THE HUSBAND

I'll get my coat, we'll go down, we'll have a beer somewheres.

THE GIRL

George, I'm tired. I'm getting divorced, and I'm getting married, and now you turn up, and it's just a little too much for me.
(THE HUSBAND *looks at the dirty tiles of the landing.*)

THE HUSBAND

Listen, the landlord, what's his name, wrote me, wanted to know if we were moving out. What did you do, give him my address?

THE GIRL

What? Yes, I gave him your address.

THE HUSBAND

I sent him a check for two months.

THE GIRL

What is it that's so terrible about marrying an older man? Lots of girls marry older men.

THE HUSBAND

Well, you know.

THE GIRL

You know what?

THE HUSBAND

Well, you figure a girl who's running around with an old man, he's usually got a lot of dough, and he buys her fur coats. I'm not saying that's you, because I know you're not a bimbo. But that's the picture you have when you see some beautiful girl on some old man's arm.

THE GIRL

It was nothing like that.

THE HUSBAND

It's understandable, you know, you've been here alone for a couple of months, and you know, it's like when guys get separated from their wives when they're in the army. I used to know a girl whose husband was in the army. This was before we got married, I mean. But she was lonely, you know. It didn't mean she didn't love her husband. But every now and then, she'd give me a call. It was just a physical thing. I mean, that's understandable. But I just can't see you with this old man.

THE GIRL

I'm going in.
    (She rises, starts for the door.)

THE HUSBAND

I'm only going to be in tonight and tomorrow. I got to fly back tomorrow night. I got two more weeks to fill out in Vegas. Give me twenty minutes, will you?

THE GIRL
    (Looks at him for a moment)

George, you're just going to make a pass at me. If you want to talk, I'll be glad to. *(Turns to him)* I've thought so much about us. You need a girl who doesn't need you, and I need too much from everybody. We' re so wrong for each other, I wonder why we ever got married. (THE HUSBAND *has begun to make a tentative pass at her. She pushes his arm away with annoyance)* Cut it out. That's just what I mean.

THE HUSBAND

Let's go have a beer somewheres.

THE GIRL
(With slowly graduated anger)
What do you think, I'm going to go to bed with you? What do you think I am?

THE HUSBAND

Take it easy, will you? I flew all the way back here, I had a two-hour layover in Los Angeles, just to see you. I suddenly get a letter out of the blue, my wife wants a divorce. Maybe I'm a little hurt. Maybe you ought to hear my side.

THE GIRL

It took me four days to write that letter so you wouldn't think I was blaming you.

THE HUSBAND

I won't stand in the way of a divorce, if you want it. What the hell, I don't want any wife that don't want me. I didn't know you were so miserable with me. What did I do? I don't know what I did that you say you were so miserable with me. I thought I was a pretty good husband. What did I do? I thought I kept you pretty happy.

THE GIRL

George, what would you do with a woman if you couldn't make a pass at her?

THE HUSBAND

The trouble with you is I've always got to make you cry.

THE GIRL

I'm going in.

THE HUSBAND
(Now he is trying to embrace her)
Don't tell me you didn't miss me.

THE GIRL
(Trying to avoid the embrace)
I'm going in. I don't feel well.

THE HUSBAND

Betty…

THE GIRL

I don't feel well.

THE HUSBAND

I missed you so much I used to go crazy.

THE GIRL

I don't feel well.

THE HUSBAND

What did I do wrong, Betty? Whatever I did wrong, I won't do it again.

THE GIRL

I don't feel well.

THE HUSBAND

I swear I won't do it again.

(*He finally manages to kiss her. She responds for a moment, then throws him off violently. She sinks to the floor, sobbing. As he watches her,*

The lights fade slowly

Scene 2

THE MANUFACTURER's *apartment, an hour and a half later. It is now a little after 1:00* A.M. *The only light is from a reading lamp in the living room.* THE SISTER *is seated on the soft chair beneath it, reading a newspaper. She wears a knitted wool sweater.*

For a moment, she presents a solitary tableau. Then the door to the apartment is heard being opened, and THE MANUFACTURER *enters.* THE SISTER *rises but doesn't move to him.* THE MANUFACTURER *takes off his coat and hat, places them in the foyer closet. He seems in control of himself.*

THE MANUFACTURER
(Mumbling)
It's stopped snowing.

THE SISTER
What did you say, Jerry?

THE MANUFACTURER
(He closes the closet door and comes down into the living room)
I'm so tired I don't even feel like washing myself. I feel like falling down on the bed with my clothes on and going to sleep. Lillian and Jack went home?

THE SISTER
Yeah, they went about ten minutes after you went out. Listen, the girl called. She called twice actually. She called about twenty minutes after you went out, and she called again about a half an hour ago.

*(*THE MANUFACTURER *sinks down onto the seat, not visibly affected by this information.)*

THE MANUFACTURER
What did she say? She want me to call her back?

THE SISTER
She just wanted to know if you was in.

*(*THE MANUFACTURER *glances at his watch.)*

THE MANUFACTURER
It's twenty after one. Do you think I should call her? *(The phone suddenly rings.* THE MANUFACTURER *frowns. He rises and goes to the phone as it rings again. He picks it up. On phone)* Hello?...Hello, Betty, how are you? I just came in the house...No, no, I just came in the house. I went out for a walk

and I just...Yes, I told them. Did you tell your family?...Well, where are you?...It's half-past one, dear.... Well, what exactly is the trouble?...Oh. When did he come in? *(He listens for a long moment, his eyes closed)* Betty, I think we should both go to sleep and...All right, would you like me to come pick you up?...Well, where could we meet? I'd ask you up here except my sister...

THE SISTER

Ask her, ask her, I'm going to sleep anyway.

THE MANUFACTURER
(Frowns on phone)

Do you want to come up here?...I'll come and pick you up...I don't want you walking in the streets this hour of the night...All right, grab a cab...All right, sweetheart.
(He hangs up.)

THE SISTER

What did she want?

THE MANUFACTURER

Her husband is in town.
(He stands with great weariness.)

THE SISTER

Do you want me to put up a pot of coffee?

THE MANUFACTURER

Would you, Evelyn? I'd appreciate it a great deal.

THE SISTER

Sure.
(She starts for the anteroom but pauses when her brother speaks.)

THE MANUFACTURER

If it'll make you feel any better, Evelyn, I think she wants to call the whole business off. The first thing she says to me on the phone is, "Did you tell your family yet?" Her husband's in town. The whole thing has become so messy. A divorce, a whole messy business. Really, something you could find on page four of the *Daily News*.
(He moves around the room, hands in pockets, enclosed once again in his quiet, introspective cage of amiability.)

THE SISTER

Jerry, take off those wet shoes, you're going to catch a good cold. I'll get a towel, you'll wipe your feet. I'll bring you the shawl to put around your legs. It's freezing in here. We haven't had steam since twelve o'clock. I want you to complain tomorrow about that.

(She starts for the anteroom again.)

THE MANUFACTURER
(A little irritated)

Don't bring me no shawl. I'm not an old man to sit here with a shawl around my legs.

(But THE SISTER *has disappeared off into the apartment.* THE MANU-FACTURER *continues to move around the room, his brows thick and knitted. Aware he is alone now, he suddenly permits himself the luxury of an animal-like grunt of pain. Then he quickly shakes his head to clear it of its confusion.* THE SISTER *returns with a towel, a heavy, long foot shawl and a fresh pair of socks.* THE MANUFACTURER *regards her balefully.)*

THE SISTER

All right. Just dry your feet and put on a new pair of socks, that's all.

*(*THE MANUFACTURER *sits down and, with some wheezing, bends to take off his shoes.)*

THE MANUFACTURER

I'll tell you something funny. I knew she was going to call tonight. I had a feeling, when I came in the house, you were going to tell me she called. *(His sister hands him the towel and he begins to dry his feet)* The truth of the matter is, this marriage is not a good idea. I was going to take her to dinner tomorrow and tell her. *(He stands, frowns, assembles his thoughts)* It would be like living in a foreign country and not speaking the language. Expatriates. It won't work. I tell you, I'm amazed how swept away I was by impulse. I was drunk. The whole last couple of months, I was pie-eyed. Drunk with vanity. Drunk with middle age. Well, listen, it was a wonderful experience.

THE SISTER

Jerry, put on these socks.

(He moves around in his bare feet, scowling.)

THE MANUFACTURER

I'll remember this girl as one of the sweetest things in my life. But it was candy. I'm too old to eat candy. You can't build a permanent life on candy.

THE SISTER

I told Lillian, "Your father, don't worry about him, he'll come home, he'll be the same sensible Jerry."

*(*THE MANUFACTURER *walks around, his face drawn now, the pain visible beneath his self-control.)*

THE MANUFACTURER
(Muttering)

You know, I love her, Evelyn. What should I tell you, I don't love her? I love her. I'm trying very hard to be sensible about this business, but my head feels like it's going to explode like a bomb. She tells me her husband is at her house. You don't think I'm not jealous? You know what just flashed through my mind right now? Maybe she went to bed with him. You know that makes me feel sick? I feel sick. Why should she call me one-thirty in the morning? Something must have happened there. I said to her, "It's half-past one, for God's sakes." No, she wants to see me right away. *(He throws up his hands)* Have you ever seen me in a state like this? Is there anything more pathetic than a middle-aged man who falls in love? I'll never be sure if she really loves me. I held her in my arms, and she told me she loved me, and even as she was saying the words, I was thinking, "She's caught up in the moment." She called me on the phone five minutes ago. I was very calm. *(Thoroughly agitated)* Calm. My whole stomach fell out. What can she see in me, a man with a paunch, for God's sakes?! A hundred good-looking young fellows will chase her around the block, what can she want from me?! I mean, let's face the facts, for God's sakes! She doesn't love me! All right, she loves me! I'm a nice man, I got a kind heart. But she doesn't love me like...I don't know what. It's sweet what we have, but it isn't in the fingers, in the muscles. It isn't love, you know what I mean? It isn't a man and a woman. *(He turns away, almost shaking from his lack of articulateness)* I don't know what! All I know is I'm trembling and I'm nervous. Go make the coffee, will you, Evelyn? I don't like you to see me like this.

THE SISTER
(Moving a step toward him, with genuine compassion)

Jerry...

THE MANUFACTURER

All right! All right! It's over! I'm going to tell her it's over. *(He looks away, quite upset now, trying to regain his usual control)* It dies hard. Do you know what I mean, Evelyn? *(He turns back to her)* It dies hard. I feel that something inside me is dying right now. You know what it is? *(He stares at her, his face illumined by a stumbling and almost ineffable insight)* I want to be loved by a woman. And that want dies hard. When you give up that want, it's a very painful thing to go through.

(He furrows his brow and rubs his closed eyes.)

THE SISTER

Jerry, for heaven's sakes, you're a successful man, you got a fine business, you got...

THE MANUFACTURER

I would appreciate being alone right now.

THE SISTER

Listen, Jerry...

THE MANUFACTURER

(Profoundly tired, he is shading his eyes with his hand now)

Evelyn, I feel lousy, and I would like to just be alone for a couple of minutes.

THE SISTER

I'll go put on the electric coffee maker.

THE MANUFACTURER

Please.

(THE SISTER moves off into the apartment, carrying the shoes and socks. THE MANUFACTURER paces around the room, frowning, grimacing. He finds himself by the window, looking out into the dark, lightless street. He stands there a moment, and then he begins to cry, quietly, unostentatiously. He suddenly feels cold and rubs his hands. He goes to his chair and sits down again, hunched within its confines, so that he seems smaller. His shoulders are drawn together and his arms are between his knees to protect him against his shivering. He seems older, almost like a little old man. His eye is caught by the shawl lying on the arm of the chair, and, frowning, he takes it, unfolds it over his legs, tucks it in around his feet, and just sits, huddled and tired and cold. The doorbell chimes. THE MANUFACTURER rises quickly, extricating himself from his shawl. For a moment, he doesn't know whether or not to put on the clean socks, then decides to answer the door in his bare feet. THE GIRL enters.)

THE GIRL

Jerry, I just realized it's half-past one and...

THE MANUFACTURER

It's all right, it's all right.

THE GIRL

I couldn't sleep. I wanted to see you because I need to be near you. I couldn't just stay home alone.

THE MANUFACTURER

It's all right, sweetheart, come in.

THE GIRL

I felt so foolish when I was coming over here. I was going to tell the cab driver to take me back, but I had already told you I was coming and you were waiting for me and...

THE MANUFACTURER

Give me your coat, sweetheart.

THE GIRL
(As he helps her out of her coat)

How do you feel, Jerry?

THE MANUFACTURER

I'm fine. How do you feel?
(THE GIRL, freed of her coat, moves nervously down into the living room. THE MANUFACTURER hangs her coat in the closet)

THE MANUFACTURER

I have some coffee going in the kitchen.

THE GIRL

I'm confused, very confused, and yet I feel very sure. There are so many things I wanted to tell you before…and I never said.
(At this moment, THE SISTER appears, cautiously curious. She darts a quick glance at THE GIRL.)

THE SISTER
(In a low voice, to her brother)

Listen, the coffee is on. It'll be ready in a couple of minutes. You'll hear the bell ring.
(THE GIRL turns at her voice.)

THE MANUFACTURER

Evelyn, this is Mrs. Betty Preiss.

THE SISTER

How do you do, pleased to meet you.

THE GIRL

How do you do?

THE SISTER

So I'll say good night. I'm going to sleep.
(She turns away..)

THE MANUFACTURER

Good night, Evelyn.
(THE GIRL nods good night. THE SISTER exits. THE MANUFACTURER closes the closet door and comes down into the living room.)

THE GIRL

Listen to me, Jerry. This much I know. I love you. I told my husband, maybe there's something wrong with loving an older man, but any love is better than none. What would I do if I didn't have you, Jerry? I'd go running around like I always did all my life, running to the movies, watching television, jumping into bed with someone I don't even like—I might even marry somebody just so I won't be alone. That's what I've been doing all my life, just filling in the hours, killing time, and then go to sleep, and say, "Well I managed to get through another day." Keeping myself busy so I won't be alone. Well, life has meaning for me when I'm with you. That's more than most people have. I wanted you to know that's how I feel, and I want you more than anything in the world.

THE MANUFACTURER

Even a few years of happiness you don't throw away. We'll get married. *(He looks at her as she sits gazing up at him)* I'll go turn off the percolator before my sister gets up.

(He moves out into the anteroom, and then disappears quickly into the apartment. For a moment, THE GIRL remains seated. Then she stands and takes a few aimless steps. The off-stage buzzing noise of the percolator stops, and THE MANUFACTURER reappears in the anteroom.)

THE MANUFACTURER

Do you want to go outside? I feel like walking forty blocks in the snow. *(He goes to the chair and starts to put on his socks. THE GIRL moves around the room, comfortably, amiably. He sees the shawl, throws it aside in a rather extravagant gesture. They both laugh.)*

Curtain

The Tenth Man

To Tyrone Guthrie

THE TENTH MAN *was first presented by Saint Subber and Arthur Cantor at The Booth Theatre, New York City, November 5, 1959, with the following cast:*

(In Order of Appearance)

THE CABALIST	Arnold Marlé
THE SEXTON	David Vardi
SCHLISSEL	Lou Jacobi
ZITORSKY	Jack Gilford
ALPER	George Voskovec
FOREMAN	Jacob Ben-Ami
THE GIRL (EVELYN FOREMAN)	Risa Schwartz
ARTHUR LANDAU	Donald Harron
HARRIS	Martin Garner
THE RABBI	Gene Saks
KESSLER BOYS	{ Alan Manson Paul Marin
THE POLICEMAN	Tim Callaghan

Directed by Tyrone Guthrie
Settings and lighting by David Hays
Costumes by Frank Thompson
Associate: Caroline Swann

An Orthodox Synagogue

ACT I

Before the Morning Prayers.

ACT II

Scene 1: The Morning Prayers.

Scene 2: Before the Afternoon Prayers.

ACT III

The Exorcism.

ACT I

Interior of the synagogue of the Congregation Atereth-Tifereth Yisroel.
It is a poor congregation, and the synagogue is actually a converted shop. A
raised platform surrounded by a railing contains the lectern and the Holy Ark.
This altar is surrounded by rows of plain wooden folding chairs which constitute
the seating accommodations for the congregation. On the far side of the altar is
an old desk at which THE RABBI *presides when teaching Hebrew school.*
A partitioned area downstage right is THE RABBI's *study, a crowded little cubi-*
cle containing a battered mahogany desk and chair, an old leather armchair, a
worn leather couch, and piles of black prayer books. On the walls are old framed
pictures of bearded patriarchs in desolate obsession over their Talmuds and perhaps
a few familiar scenes from the Old Testament.
Downstage is a metal heating unit. There is a second heating unit upstage, and
a door leading apparently to a bathroom. The front door is stage left.
It is 6:30 A.M. on a cold winter day.
At rise, THE CABALIST *stands in the middle of the synagogue, entirely wrapped*
in a thick white linen prayer shawl with broad black stripes, praying silently from
a heavy prayer book that rests on the railing of the altar. Suddenly he pauses in
his intense devotions, clutches at the railing as if to keep himself from falling. We
have the impression that he is faint, near to swooning. He is a small, bearded
man, in his seventies; his face is lean and lined, his eyes sunken and hollow. He
wears a small black skullcap from beneath which stick out gray forelocks and side-
curls—a testament to his orthodoxy. After a moment, he regains his strength and
returns to his prayers.
Three men hurry into the synagogue out of the oppressive cold of the street.
They are THE SEXTON, SCHLISSEL *and* ZITORSKY. *They all wear heavy over-*
coats and gray fedoras. SCHLISSEL *and* ZITORSKY *are in their early seventies.*
THE SEXTON *is a small, nervous, bespectacled man of forty-eight. We know he is*
a sexton because he carries a huge ring of keys. The men rub their hands for
warmth and huff and puff and dart quick looks at THE CABALIST, *who is obliv-*
ious to their entrance.

SCHLISSEL

Close the door.
  (Light pours down on the synagogue as THE SEXTON *flicks on the wall*

switch. THE SEXTON *scurries upstage to fuss with the heater in the rear of the synagogue.* SCHLISSEL *and* ZITORSKY *shuffle downstage to a small uncovered heater and stand silently—indeed a little wearily—for a moment.* SCHLISSEL *sighs)*

SCHLISSEL

So how goes it with a Jew today?

ZITORSKY

How should it go?

SCHLISSEL

Have a pinch of snuff.

ZITORSKY

No, thank you.

SCHLISSEL

Davis won't be here this morning. I stopped by his house. He has a cold. His daughter-in-law told me he's still in bed.

ZITORSKY

My daughter-in-law, may she grow rich and buy a hotel with a thousand rooms and be found dead in every one of them.

SCHLISSEL

My daughter-in-law, may she invest heavily in General Motors, and the whole thing should go bankrupt.

ZITORSKY

Sure, go have children.

SCHLISSEL

The devil take them all.

THE SEXTON

(Scurrying downstage; to THE CABALIST *as he passes)*
Hirschman, are you all right?
(He flutters, a small round ball of a man, to the door of THE RABBI'S *office, which he now opens with one of the many keys on his chain.)*

SCHLISSEL

Foreman won't be here today.

ZITORSKY

What's the matter with Foreman?

SCHLISSEL

His granddaughter today. This is the morning.

ZITORSKY

Oh, that's right. Today is the morning.

SCHLISSEL

Listen, it's better for everybody.

ZITORSKY

Sure.

SCHLISSEL

I told Foreman, I said: "Foreman, it's better for everybody." The girl is becoming violent. I spoke to her father. He said to me they live in terror what she'll do to the other children. They came home one night, they found her punching one of the little children.

ZITORSKY

Well, what can you do?

SCHLISSEL

What can you do? You do what they're doing. They're putting her back in the institution.

ZITORSKY

Of course. There she will have the benefit of trained psychiatric personnel.

SCHLISSEL

The girl is incurable. She's been in and out of mental institutions since she was eleven years old. I met the psychiatrist there, you know, when I was up there to visit Foreman last week. I discussed the whole business with him. A fine young fellow. The girl is a schizophrenic with violent tendencies.

(ZITORSKY *considers this diagnosis for a moment, then sighs.*)

ZITORSKY

Ah, may my daughter-in-law eat acorns and may branches sprout from her ears.

SCHLISSEL

May my daughter-in-law live to be a hundred and twenty, and may she have to live all her years in *her* daughter-in-law's house.

(THE SEXTON *has been tugging a large opened brown cardboard carton out of* THE RABBI's *office, from which he now extracts two velvet bags which he hands to* SCHLISSEL *and* ZITORSKY. *A fifth old Jew now enters from the street, a patrician little man with a Vandyke beard and a black homburg. His name is* ALPER. *He bursts into shrill prayer as he enters.*)

ALPER

(Chanting)

"As for me in the abundance of thy loving kindness will I come into thy house; I will worship toward thy holy temple in the fear of thee. How goodly are thy tents, O Jacob..."

> *(As precipitously as the prayer had begun, it now drops into nothing more than a rapid movement of lips.* THE SEXTON *acknowledges* ALPER'S *arrival with a nod and darts back into* THE RABBI'S *office, where he plunks himself behind the desk and begins hurriedly to dial the phone.* ALPER'S *voice zooms abruptly up into a shrill incantation again)*

ALPER

"...in the truth of thy salvation. Amen!"

SCHLISSEL

Amen.

ZITORSKY

Amen.

> *(*ALPER *joins the other two old men, and they stand in silent, rueful speculation.)*

THE SEXTON
(On phone)

Hello, Harris? This is Bleyer the Sexton. Come on down today, we need you. Foreman won't be here. Davis is sick. We won't have ten men for the morning prayers if you don't come down...Services start in twenty minutes. Hurry up...Wear a sweater under your coat...All right...

> *(He hangs up, takes a large ledger from the desk, and begins nervously to examine its pages.)*

SCHLISSEL

Hirschman slept over in the synagogue again last night. Have you ever seen such pietistic humbug?

ALPER

Well, he is a very devout man. A student of the cabala. The Rabbi speaks of him with the greatest reverence.

SCHLISSEL

Devout indeed. I assure you this lavish display of orthodoxy is a very profitable business. I was told confidentially just yesterday that his board and food are paid for by two foolish old women who consider him a saint.

ALPER

It can't cost them very much. He's been fasting the last three days.

SCHLISSEL

And the reason he sleeps in the synagogue so frequently is because his landlady does not give him heat for his own room in the mornings.

ZITORSKY

Ah, go be an old man in the winter.

ALPER

I must say, I really don't know what to do with myself on these cold days.

SCHLISSEL

I'm an atheist. If I had something better to do, would I be here?

ZITORSKY

You know what would be a nice way to kill a day? I think it would be nice to take a trip up to Mount Hope Cemetery and have a look at my burial plot. A lovely cemetery. Like a golf course, actually. By the time one gets there and comes back, the whole day has been used up. Would you like to come? I'll pay both your fares.

ALPER

Why not? I have never been to Mount Hope. I have my burial plot on Mount Zion Cemetery.

ZITORSKY

Oh, that's a beautiful cemetery.

ALPER

Yes, it is. My wife wanted to buy plots in Cedar Lawn because her whole family is buried there, but I wouldn't hear of it.

ZITORSKY

Oh, Cedar Lawn. I wouldn't be buried in Cedar Lawn.

ALPER

It's in such a bad state. The headstones tumble one on top of the other, and everybody walks on the graves.

ZITORSKY

They don't take care in Cedar Lawn. My wife once said, she should rest in peace, that Cedar Lawn was the tenement of cemeteries.

ALPER

A well-turned phrase.

ZITORSKY

She had a way with words, God grant her eternal rest.

ALPER

I'd like you to come to Mount Zion sometime, see my plot.

ZITORSKY

Maybe we could make the trip tomorrow.

SCHLISSEL

Listen to these two idiots, discussing their graves as if they were country estates.

ZITORSKY

Where are you buried, Schlissel?

SCHLISSEL

Cedar Lawn.

ALPER

Well, listen, there are many lovely areas in Cedar Lawn. All my wife's
family are buried there.

ZITORSKY

Come with us, Schlissel, and have a look at my grave.

SCHLISSEL

Why not? What else have I got to do?

(ALPER *now slowly goes about the business of donning his prayer shawl and
phylacteries, which he takes out of a velvet prayer bag. Among Jews,
prayer is a highly individual matter, and peripatetic to the bargain. The
actual ritual of laying on the phylacteries is a colorful one.* ALPER *extracts
his left arm from his jacket and rebuttons his jacket so that his shirt-sleeved
left arm hangs loose. Then, the shirt sleeve is rolled up almost to the shoulder, and the arm phylactery, a long thin black leather thong, is put on by
wrapping it around the left arm seven times, three times around the palm,
and three times around the middle finger. All this is accompanied by rapidly recited prayers, as is the laying on of the head phylactery. All the while*
ALPER *walks, bending and twisting at the knees, raising his voice occasionally in the truly lovely words of incantation. In a far upstage corner,* THE
CABALIST *huddles under his enveloping white tallith—prayer shawl—his
back to everyone else, deeply involved in his personal meditations. The synagogue itself is a shabby little place, the walls yellowed and cracked, illumined by a fitful overhead bulb. There is indeed at this moment a sense of
agelessness, even of primitive barbarism. During this,* THE SEXTON *has
dialed a second number.*)

THE SEXTON

Hello? Mr. Arnold Kessler, please…How do you do? This is Mr. Bleyer
the Sexton at the synagogue. Perhaps you recall me…Did I wake you up?
I'm terribly sorry. As long as you're up, according to my books, your father
died one year ago yesterday, on the eleventh day in the month of Shvat,
may his soul fly straight to the heavenly gates, and how about coming
down with your brother and saying a memorial prayer in your father's
name?…Let me put it this way, Mr. Kessler. You know we can't have
morning prayers without a quorum of ten men. If you and your brother
don't come down we won't have a quorum…As a favor to me…Kessler,
may your children be such devoted sons, and bring your brother. You are
doing a good deed. Peace be with you. Hurry up.

(*He hangs up, sits frowning, totaling up on his fingers the number of men he has, scowls. In the synagogue,* ALPER's *voice rises for a brief moment.)*

ALPER

"...And it shall be to thee for a sign upon thy hand, and for a memorial between thy eyes..."

(THE SEXTON rises abruptly from his chair and bustles out of the office to the front door of the synagogue.)

THE SEXTON

(To nobody in particular)

Listen, I'm going to have to get a tenth Jew off the street somewheres. I'll be right back. Schlissel, will you please fix that bench already, you promised me.

(He exits. SCHLISSEL *nods and picks up a hammer. For a moment, only the singsong murmur of the rapid prayers and the upstage tapping of* SCHLISSEL's *hammer fill the stage. The front door to the synagogue now opens, and a sixth old Jew peers in. He is a frightened little wisp of a man, named* FOREMAN. *He is obviously in a state. He darts terrified looks all about the synagogue, and then abruptly disappears back into the street, leaving the synagogue door open. Nobody noticed his brief appearance. A moment later, he is back, this time leading a slim young girl of eighteen wearing a topcoat, who is also distracted. The old man herds her quickly across the synagogue to* THE RABBI's *office, pushes her in, and closes the door behind her. She stands in* THE RABBI's *office, almost rigid with terror.* FOREMAN *scuttles back to close the front door.* SCHLISSEL *looks up and notices* FOREMAN *and nods to him; he nods back. Like his friends,* FOREMAN *wears a heavy winter coat and a worn fedora some sizes too small for him. He stands and watches the others apprehensively. At last* ALPER *reaches the end of his laying on of the phylacteries, his voice climbing to a shrill incantation.)*

ALPER

(To FOREMAN, *moving slowly as he prays)*

"...And it shall be for a sign upon thy hand, and for frontlets between thy eyes; for by strength of hand the Lord brought us out from Egypt. Amen!"

FOREMAN

(Muttering, his head bobbing nervously)

Amen!

ALPER

I thought you weren't coming down today, Foreman.

FOREMAN
(His mouth working without saying anything. Finally, he says)
Alper...

ALPER
You seem agitated. Is something wrong?

FOREMAN
(Staring at his friend)
Alper, I have her here.

ALPER
You have who here?

FOREMAN
I have my granddaughter Evelyn here. I have her here in the Rabbi's office.

ALPER
What are you talking about?

FOREMAN
I took her out of the house while nobody was looking, and I brought her here. I am faint. Let me sit down.
(He sinks onto a chair. His friend regards him with concern.)

ALPER
Here, David, let me take your coat.

FOREMAN
Alper, I have seen such a thing and heard words as will place me in my grave before the singing of the evening service. "Blessed art Thou, O Lord, King of the Universe, who hath wrought the wonders of the world." *(Suddenly half-starting from his seat)* I must speak to Hirschman! This is an affair for Hirschman who has delved into the cabala and the forbidden mysteries of numbers.

ALPER
Sit down, Foreman, and compose yourself. *(FORMAN sinks slowly back onto his chair)* Why did you bring her here? Foreman, you are my oldest friend from our days in the seminary together in Rumni in the Province of Poltava, and I speak to you harshly as only a friend may speak. You are making too much out of this whole matter of the girl. I know how dear she is to you, but the girl is insane, for heaven's sakes! What sort of foolishness is this then to smuggle her out of your son's home? To what purpose? Really, Foreman, a gentle and pious man like you! Your son must be running through the streets at this moment shouting his daughter's name. Call him on the phone and tell him you are bringing her back to him.

(FOREMAN *stares at his friend, his pale eyes filled with tears.*)

FOREMAN

Alper...

ALPER

David, my dear friend, make peace with this situation.

FOREMAN
(*Whispering*)

She is possessed, Alper. She has a dybbuk in her. A demon! It spoke to me. (*He stares down at the floor at his feet, a numb terror settling over his face*) It spoke to me. I went into my granddaughter this morning to comfort her, and I said: "How are you?" And she seemed quite normal. She has these moments of absolute lucidity. (*He looks desperately at his friend again*) She seemed to know she was being taken to the institution again. Then suddenly she fell to the floor in a swoon. I said: "Evelyn, what's the matter?" And she looked up at me, and it was no longer her face, but a face so twisted with rage that my blood froze in my body. And a voice came out of her that was not her own. "Do you know my voice?" And I knew it. I knew the voice. God have mercy on my soul. I stood there like a statue, and my granddaughter lay on the floor with her eyes closed, and the voice came out of her, but her lips never moved. "David Foreman, son of Abram, this is the soul of Hannah Luchinsky, whom you dishonored and weakened in your youth, and the Gates of Heaven are closed to me." And my granddaughter began to writhe on the floor as if in the most horrible agony, and she began to laugh so loudly that I was sure my son and daughter-in-law in the living room could hear. I flung the door open in panic, and my son and daughter-in-law were sitting there talking, and they heard nothing. And I tell you shrieks of laughter were coming from this girl on the floor. And I closed the door and besought God, and finally the dybbuk was silent. May God strike me down on this spot, Alper, if every word I tell you is not true.

(ALPER *has slowly sat down on an adjacent chair, absolutely enthralled by the story. He stares at* FOREMAN.)

ALPER

A dybbuk?

FOREMAN
(*Nodding*)

A dybbuk. Could you believe such a thing?

ALPER

Who did the dybbuk say she was?

FOREMAN

You should remember her. Hannah Luchinsky.

ALPER

The name is vaguely familiar.

FOREMAN

You remember Luchinsky, the sexton of the Rumni seminary, with his three daughters? Hannah was the handsome one who became pregnant, and they threw stones at her, called her harlot, and drove her out of the city.

ALPER
(Recognition slowly coming over him)

Ooohhh.

FOREMAN

I was the one who debased her.

ALPER

You? You were such a nose-in-the-books, a gentle and modest fellow. Dear me. A dybbuk. Really! What an extraordinary thing. Schlissel, do you want to hear a story?

SCHLISSEL
(Coming over)

What?

ALPER
(To ZITORSKY, *who ambles over)*

Listen to this. Foreman is telling a story here that will turn your blood into water.

SCHLISSEL

What happened?

FOREMAN

What happened, Schlissel, was that I went in to see my granddaughter this morning and discovered that she was possessed by a dybbuk. Now, please, Schlissel, before you go into one of your interminable disputations on the role of superstition in the capitalist economy, let me remind you that I am a follower of Maimonides and...

SCHLISSEL

What are you talking about?

FOREMAN

A dybbuk! A dybbuk! I tell you my granddaughter is possessed by a dybbuk! Oh, my head is just pounding! I do not know which way to turn.

SCHLISSEL

What are you prattling about dybbuks?

ALPER

(To SCHLISSEL*)*

The voice of Hannah Luchinsky spoke to him through the lips of his granddaughter.

ZITORSKY

Oh, a dybbuk.

SCHLISSEL

What nonsense is this?

ALPER

(To FOREMAN*)*

Are you sure?

FOREMAN

(Angrily)

Am I sure? Am I a peasant who leaps at every black cat? Have I ever shown a susceptibility to mysticism? Have you not seen me engaging Hirschman over there in violent disputation over the fanatic numerology of the cabala? Have I not mocked to his very face the murky fantasy of the Gilgul with wispy souls floating in space? Really! Am I sure! Do you take me for a fool, a prattler of old wives' tales? Really! I tell you I heard that woman's voice as I hear the cold wind outside our doors now, and saw my granddaughter writhing in the toils of possession as I see the phylactery on your brow this moment. I was a teacher of biology for thirty-nine years at the Yeshiva High School. A dedicated follower of the great Rambam who scoffed at augurs and sorcerers! For heaven's sakes! Really! I report to you only what I see! *(He strides angrily away, and then his brief flurry of temper subsides as abruptly as it flared)* My dear Alper, please forgive this burst of temper. I am so distressed by this whole business that I cannot control my wits. I assure you that it is as hard for me to believe my own senses as it is for you.

ZITORSKY

When I was a boy in Lithuania, there was a young boy who worked for the butcher who was possessed by the dybbuk.

SCHLISSEL

(Scornfully)

A dybbuk. Sure. Sure. When I was a boy in Poland, I also heard stories about a man who lived in the next town who was possessed by a dybbuk. I was eight years old, and, one day after school, my friends and I walked barefoot the six miles to the next town, and we asked everybody, "Where is the man with the dybbuk?" And nobody knew what we were talking about. So I came home and told my mother: "Mama, there is no man with a dybbuk in the next town." And she gave me such a slap across the face that I turned around three times. And she said to me: "Aha! Only eight years old and already an atheist." Foreman, my friend, you talk like my mother, who was an ignorant fishwife. I am shocked at you.

FOREMAN

Oh, leave me be, Schlissel. I have no patience with your pontificating this morning.

ALPER

Don't let him upset you, Foreman. The man is a Communist.

FOREMAN

He is not a Communist. He is just disagreeable.

SCHLISSEL

My dear fellow, I have never believed in God. Should I now believe in demons? A dybbuk. This I would like to see.

FOREMAN
(Furiously)

Then see!
(He strides to the door of THE RABBI's office and wrenches the door open. The others gingerly follow him to the opened doorway and peer in. THE GIRL—EVELYN—stares at them, terrified. In a thunderous voice, FORE-MAN cries out—)

FOREMAN

Dybbuk! I direct you to reveal yourself!
(THE GIRL stares at the four patently startled old men, and then suddenly bursts into a bloodcurdling shriek of laughter. The four old men involuntarily take one step back and regard this exhibition wide-eyed.)

FOREMAN

What is your name?

THE GIRL

I am Hannah Luchinsky.

FOREMAN

Who are you?

THE GIRL

I am the whore of Kiev, the companion of sailors.

FOREMAN

How come you to be in my granddaughter's body?

THE GIRL

I was on a yacht in the sea of Odessa, the pleasure of five wealthy merchants. And a storm arose, and all were lost. And my soul rose from the water and flew to the city of Belgorod where my soul appealed to the sages of that city. But since I was debauched they turned their backs on me.

FOREMAN

And then?

THE GIRL

Then my soul entered the body of a cow who became insane and was brought to slaughter and I flew into the body of this girl as if divinely directed.

FOREMAN

What do you want?

THE GIRL

I want the strength of a pure soul so that I may acquire that experience to ascend to heaven.

FOREMAN

I plead with you to leave the body of this girl.

THE GIRL

I have wandered through Gilgul many years, and I want peace. Why do you plague me? There are those among you who have done the same as I and will suffer a similar fate. There is one among you who has lain with whores many times, and his wife died of the knowledge.

ZITORSKY
(Aghast)

Oh, my God!

THE GIRL
(Laughing)

Am I to answer questions of old men who have nothing to do but visit each other's cemeteries?

ZITORSKY
(Terrified)

A dybbuk...a dybbuk...

FOREMAN

Evelyn...Evelyn...She is again in a catatonic state.

(THE GIRL *now sits in* THE RABBI's *chair, sprawling wantonly, apparently finished with the interview. The four old men regard her a little numbly. They are all quite pale as a result of the experience. After a moment,* FOREMAN *closes the door of* THE RABBI's *office, and the four old men shuffle in a silent group downstage, where they stand, each reviewing in his own mind the bizarre implications of what they have seen.* FORE- MAN *sinks into a chair and covers his face with his hands. After a long, long moment,* ZITORSKY *speaks.)*

ZITORSKY

Well, that's some dybbuk, all right.

SCHLISSEL

The girl is as mad as a hatter and fancies herself a Ukrainian trollop. This is a dybbuk?

ALPER

I found it quite an unnerving experience.

ZITORSKY

She caught me dead to rights. I'll tell you that. I was the one she was talking about there, who trumpeted around with women. Listen, when I was in the garment business, if you didn't have women for the out-of-town buyers, you couldn't sell a dozen dresses. Oh, I was quite a gamy fellow when I was in business, a madcap really. One day, my wife caught me in the shop with a model—who knew she would be downtown that day?— and from that moment on, my wife was a sick woman and died three years later, cursing my name with her last breath. That was some dybbuk, all right. How she picked me out! It gave me the shivers.

ALPER

Did you notice her use of archaic language and her Russian accent? The whole business had an authentic ring to me.

SCHLISSEL

What nonsense! The last time I was up to Foreman's, the girl confided to me in a whisper that she was Susan Hayward. A dybbuk! Ever since she was a child Foreman has been pumping her head full of the wretched superstitions of the Russian Pale, so she thinks she is a dybbuk. The girl is a lunatic and should be packed off to an asylum immediately.

(ALPER *regards* SCHLISSEL *with a disapproving eye; he then takes* SCHLISSEL's *arm and leads him a few steps away for a private chat.)*

ALPER

Really, Schlissel, must you always be so argumentative? We are all here agreed that we have a dybbuk in our company, but you always seem intent on being at odds with everyone around you. Really, look at poor Foreman, how distraught he is. Out of simple courtesy, really, for an old friend, can you not affect at least a silence on the matter? And, after all, what else have you got to do today? Ride two and a half hours to look at Zitorsky's tomb- stone? When you stop and think of it, this dybbuk is quite an exciting affair. Really, nothing like this has happened since Kornblum and Milsky had that fist fight over who would have the seat by the East Wall during the High Holidays.

ZITORSKY
(Ambling over)
That's some dybbuk, all right.

SCHLISSEL
(Frowning)
All right, so what'll we do with this dybbuk now that we got it?

ALPER
It seems to me, there is some kind of ritual, an exorcism of sorts.

ZITORSKY
Maybe we should tell the Rabbi.

SCHLISSEL
A young fellow like that. What does he know of dybbuks? A dybbuk must be exorcised from the body by a rabbi of some standing. You can't just call in some smooth-shaven young fellow fresh from the seminary for such a formidable matter as a dybbuk. This Rabbi has only been here two months. He hardly knows our names.

ALPER
He's right. You have to get a big rabbi for such a business.

SCHLISSEL
What has to be done is we must get in touch with the Korpotchniker Rabbi of Williamsburg, who has inherited the mantle of the great Korpotchniker of Lwów, whose fame extends to all the corners of the world.

ZITORSKY
Oh, a sage among sages.

ALPER
I was about to suggest the Bobolovitcher Rabbi of Crown Heights.

SCHLISSEL
Where do you come to compare the Bobolovitcher Rabbi with the Korpotchniker?

ALPER
I once attended an afternoon service conducted by the Bobolovitcher, and it was an exalting experience. A man truly in the great tradition of Chassidic rabbis.

ZITORSKY
A sage among sages, may his name be blessed for ever and ever.

SCHLISSEL

It shows how much you know. The Bobolovitcher Rabbi is a disciple of
the Korpotchniker and sat at the Korpotchniker's feet until a matter of
only a few years ago.

ALPER

Listen, I'm not going to argue with you. Either one is fine for me.

SCHLISSEL

The Korpotchniker is the number one Chassidic rabbi in the world. If
you're going to involve yourself at all, why not go straight to the top?

ALPER

All right, so let it be the Korpotchniker.

ZITORSKY

For that matter, the Lubanower Rabbi of Brownsville is a man of great
repute.

SCHLISSEL

The Lubanower! Really! He's a young man, for heaven's sakes!

ALPER

Zitorsky, let it be decided then that it will be the Korpotchniker.

ZITORSKY

I only made a suggestion.

SCHLISSEL

The question is how does one get to the Korpotchniker? One does not
drop into his home as if it were a public library. One has to solicit his secretary and petition for an audience. It may take weeks.

ALPER

I do think, Schlissel, we shall have to get a more accessible rabbi than
that. Ah, here is Hirschman, who I am sure can give us excellent counsel
in this matter.

(THE CABALIST *has indeed finished his prayers and is shuffling downstage,
a small, frightened man.* FOREMAN *leaps from his chair.*)

FOREMAN

Hirschman!

(*Everyone crowds around* THE CABALIST.)

ZITORSKY

Oh, boy, Hirschman, have we got something to tell you!

ALPER

Zitorsky, please. Hirschman, you are a man versed in the cabala, a man
who prays with all the seventy-two names of the Most Ancient of the
Ancient Ones.

> **FOREMAN**
> *(Blurting out)*

Hirschman, my granddaughter is possessed by a dybbuk!

> **THE CABALIST**
> *(Starting back in terror)*

A dybbuk!

> **ALPER**

Foreman, please, one does not announce such a thing as baldly as that.

> **THE CABALIST**

Are you sure?

> **FOREMAN**

Hirschman, as a rule, I am not given to whimsy.

> **THE CABALIST**

Was it the soul of a woman wronged in her youth?

> **FOREMAN**

Yes.

> **THE CABALIST**

I heard her cry out last night. I awoke for my midnight devotions, and as I prayed I heard the whimpering of a woman's soul. *(A strange expression of wonder settles over his face)* I have fasted three days and three nights, and I dismissed the sound of this dybbuk as a fantasy of my weakened state. For only those to whom the Ancient One has raised his veil can hear the traffic of dybbuks. Is this a sign from God that my penitence is over? I have prayed for such a sign. I have felt strange things these past days. Sudden, bursting illuminations have bleached mine eyes, and I have heard the sounds of dead and supernatural things.

> *(He lifts his worn little face, his eyes wide with wonder. The others are put a little ill-at-ease by this effusive outburst.* FOREMAN, *indeed, is quite overwhelmed.)*

> **ALPER**

Actually, Hirschman, all we want to know is if you knew the telephone number of the Korpotchniker Rabbi.

> (THE CABALIST *with some effort brings himself back to the moment at hand.)*

> **THE CABALIST**

He is my cousin. I will call him for you.

> *(He moves slowly off, still obsessed with some private wonder of his own, to the phone on the outside wall of* THE RABBI's *office.)*

ALPER
(Quite awed)
Your cousin? You are the Korpotchniker's cousin, Hirschman?

ZITORSKY
(Hurrying after THE CABALIST*)*
You'll need a dime, Hirschman.
(He gives THE CABALIST *the ten-cent piece.)*

ALPER
Schlissel, the Korpotchniker's cousin, did you hear? Apparently, he's not such a humbug.

SCHLISSEL
I tell you, he gives me the creeps, that Hirschman.
*(*THE CABALIST *has dialed a number on the wall phone.* FOREMAN *stands at his elbow, hunched with anxiety.)*

THE CABALIST
(To FOREMAN, *gently)*
Where is she, the dybbuk?

FOREMAN
In the Rabbi's office.

THE CABALIST
You are wise to go to the Korpotchniker. He is a Righteous One among the Righteous Ones. We were quite close as children until I abandoned the rabbinate. *(On the phone, in soft, gentle tones)* Hello? Is this Chaim son of Yosif…This is Israel son of Isaac…And peace be unto you…There is a man here of my congregation who feels his granddaughter is possessed by a dybbuk and would seek counsel from my cousin…He will bless you for your courtesy. Peace be unto you, Chaim son of Yosif. *(He hangs the receiver back in its cradle and turns to* FOREMAN*)* Give me a paper and pencil. *(The others, who have crowded around to hear the phone call, all seek in their pockets for a paper and pencil and manage to produce an old envelope and a stub of a pencil between them)* That was the Korpotchniker's secretary, and you are to go to his home as quickly as you can. I will write the address down for you. It is in Williamsburg in Brooklyn. And you will be received directly after the morning services.
(He gives FOREMAN *the address, sweeps his prayer shawl on and retires upstage again for continued devotions.)*

FOREMAN
Thank you, Hirschman. The eye of the Lord will be open to you in the time of your need.

ZITORSKY

Oh, Williamsburg. That's quite a ride from here.

SCHLISSEL

What are you talking about? Foreman, you take the Long Island Railroad to Atlantic Avenue Station, where you go downstairs, and you catch the Brooklyn subway.

ALPER

Maybe, I should go along with you, David, because a simple fellow like you will certainly get lost in the Atlantic Avenue Station, which is an immense conflux of subways.

SCHLISSEL

What you do, Foreman, is you take the Long Island Railroad to the Atlantic Avenue Station, where you take the Double G train on the lower level...

ALPER

Not the Double G train.

SCHLISSEL

What's wrong with the Double G?

ALPER

One takes the Brighton train. The Double G train will take him to Smith Street, which is a good eight blocks' walk.

SCHLISSEL

The Brighton train will take him to Coney Island.

ALPER

Foreman, listen to what I tell you. I will write down the instructions for you because an innocent fellow like you, if they didn't point you in the right direction, you couldn't even find the synagogue in the morning. Where's my pencil?

(He has taken the paper and pencil from FOREMAN's *numb fingers and is writing down the traveling instructions.)*

FOREMAN

(Staring off at the wall of THE RABBI's *office)*
What shall I do with the girl? I can't leave her here.

ALPER

Don't worry about the girl. She knows me. I'm like a second grandfather to her.

FOREMAN

I don't like to leave her. Did I do right, Alper? Did I do right, kidnaping her this morning and bringing her here? Because the psychiatrist said we must prepare ourselves that she would probably spend the rest of her life in mental institutions. The irrevocability of it! The rest of her life! I was in tears almost the whole night thinking about it. Perhaps this produced a desperate susceptibility in me so that I clutch even at dybbuks rather than believe she is irretrievably insane. Now, in the sober chill of afterthought, it all seems so unreal and impetuous. And here I am bucketing off to some forbidding rabbi to listen to mystical incantations.

ALPER

The Korpotchniker is not a rogue, Foreman. He is not going to sell you patent medicine. He will advise you quite sensibly, I am sure.

FOREMAN
(Buttoning his coat)
Yes, yes, I shall go to see him. You shall have to hide her till I come back. My son has probably called the police by now, and sooner or later they will come here looking for her.

ALPER

Don't worry about it. I won't leave her side for a moment.

FOREMAN

I better tell her I'm going. She'll be frightened if she looks for me, and I'm not here.
(He hurries quickly to THE RABBI's office, where he stands a moment, regarding THE GIRL with mingled fear and tenderness. THE GIRL has sunk into the blank detachment of schizophrenia and stares unseeingly at the floor.)

SCHLISSEL

So the girl is a fugitive from the police. The situation is beginning to take on charm.

ALPER

Look at Schlissel. The retired revolutionary. As long as it's against the law, he believes in dybbuks.

SCHLISSEL

I believe in anything that involves a conspiracy.
(At this point, the front door bursts open, and THE SEXTON returns with the announcement—)

THE SEXTON

I've got a tenth Jew!

ZITORSKY

Sexton, have we got something to tell you!

SCHLISSEL
(Shushing him abruptly)
Sha! Idiot! Must you tell everyone?

THE SEXTON
(He leans back through the open door to the street and says to someone out there)
Come in, come in…
(A fine-looking, if troubled, young fellow in his middle thirties enters; he is dressed in expensive clothes, albeit a little shabby at the moment, as if he had been on a bender for the last couple of days. His name is ARTHUR LANDAU. *He stands ill-at-ease and scowling, disturbed in aspect. His burberry topcoat hangs limply on him.* THE SEXTON *has scooted to an open carton, from which he takes out a black paper skullcap, nervously talking as he does.)*

THE SEXTON
Harris didn't come in yet?

SCHLISSEL
No.

THE SEXTON
The two Kessler boys, I called them on the phone, they didn't show up yet? *(He thrusts the skullcap into* ARTHUR's *hand)* Here's a skullcap, put it on.
*(*ARTHUR *takes the skullcap absently, but makes no move to put it on. He is preoccupied with deep and dark thoughts.* THE SEXTON *heads for the front door.)*

THE SEXTON
The Rabbi's not here yet?

SCHLISSEL
He'll be here in a couple of minutes.

THE SEXTON
It's only seven minutes to the services. Listen, I'm going to the Kesslers'. I'll have to pull them out of their beds, I can see that. I'll be right back. *(To* ARTHUR*)* You'll find some phylacteries in the carton there. Alper, give the man a prayer book. Sure, go find ten Jews on a winter morning.
(He exits, closing the front door.)

FOREMAN
(As he comes out of the office)
All right, I'm going. She didn't eat anything this morning, so see she gets some coffee at least. Let's see. I take the Long Island Railroad to Atlantic Avenue Station. Listen, it has been a number of years since I have

been on the subways. Well, wish me luck. Have I got money for carfare? Yes, yes. Well...well...my dear friends, peace be with you.

ALPER

And with you, Foreman.

ZITORSKY

Amen.

FOREMAN
(Opening the door)

Oh, it's cold out there.
(He exits, closing the door.)

ALPER

He'll get lost. I'm sure of it.

ZITORSKY

Oh, have you ever seen such excitement? My heart is fairly pounding.

ALPER

Oh, it's just starting. Now comes the exorcism. That should be something to see.

ZITORSKY

Oh, boy.

SCHLISSEL

Oh, I don't know. You've seen one exorcism, you've seen them all.

ZITORSKY

You saw one, Schlissel?

SCHLISSEL

Sure. When I was a boy in Poland, we had more dybbuks than we had pennies. We had a fellow there in my village, a mule driver, a burly chap who reeked from dung and was drunk from morning till night. One day, he lost his wits completely, and it was immediately attributed to a dybbuk. I was a boy of ten, perhaps eleven, and I watched the whole proceedings through a hole in the roof of the synagogue. A miracle-working rabbi who was passing through our district was invited to exorcise the dybbuk. He drew several circles on the ground and stood in the center surrounded by four elders of the community, all dressed in white linen and trembling with terror. The miracle-worker bellowed out a series of incantations, and the poor mule driver, who was beside himself with fear, screamed and...hello, Harris...

(This last is addressed to a very, very old man named HARRIS, who is making his halting way into the synagogue at this moment. He barely nods to the others, having all he can do to get into the synagogue and close the door.

SCHLISSEL *continues his blithe story.)*

SCHLISSEL

...and fell to the floor. It was a marvelous vaudeville, really. I was so petrified that I fell off the roof and almost broke a leg. The miracle-worker
wandered off to work other miracles and the mule driver sold his mule and
went to America where I assume, because he was a habitual drunkard and
an insensitive boor, he achieved considerable success. Our little village had
a brief month of notoriety, and we were all quite proud of ourselves.

ALPER

Oh, it sounds like a marvelous ceremony.

SCHLISSEL

Of course, they don't exorcise dybbuks like they used to. Nowadays, the
rabbi hangs a small amulet around your neck, intones, "Blessed art Thou,
O Lord," and that's an exorcism.

ALPER

Oh, I hope not.

SCHLISSEL

Really, religion has become so pallid recently, it is hardly worth while
being an atheist.

ZITORSKY

I don't even know if I'll come to see this exorcism. I'm already shivering
just hearing about it.

ALPER

Well, you know, we are dealing with the occult here, and it is quite
frightening. Hello there, Harris, how are you?
*(By now, the octogenarian has removed his overcoat, under which he wears
several layers of sweaters, one of which turns out to be one of his grandson's
football jerseys, a striped red garment with the number 63 on it. For the
rest of the act, he goes about the business of putting on his phylacteries.*
ALPER *claps his hands.)*

ALPER

Well, let me find out if we can help this young Jew here. *(He moves
toward* ARTHUR LANDAU, *smiling)* Can I give you a set of phylacteries?

ARTHUR

(Scowling—a man who has had a very bad night the night before)
I'm afraid I wouldn't have the first idea what to do with them.

ALPER

You'll find a prayer shawl in one of these velvet bags here.

ARTHUR

No, thank you.

ALPER

(Offering a small black prayer book)

Well, here's a prayer book anyway.

ARTHUR

Look, the only reason I'm here is a little man stopped me on the street, asked me if I was Jewish, and gave me the impression he would kill himself if I didn't come in and complete your quorum. I was told all I had to do was stand around for a few minutes wearing a hat. I can't read Hebrew and I have nothing I want to pray about, so there's no sense giving me that book. All I want to know is how long is this going to take, because I don't feel very well, and I have a number of things to do.

ALPER

My dear young fellow, you'll be out of here in fifteen or twenty minutes.

ARTHUR

Thank you.

(He absently puts the black paper skullcap on his head and sits down, scowling, on one of the wooden chairs. ALPER regards him for a moment; then turns and goes back to his two colleagues.)

ALPER

(To SCHLISSEL and ZITORSKY)

To such a state has modern Jewry fallen. He doesn't know what phylacteries are. He doesn't want a shawl. He can't read Hebrew.

ZITORSKY

I wonder if he's still circumcised.

(ARTHUR abruptly stands.)

ARTHUR

I'd like to make a telephone call. *(Nobody hears him. He repeats louder)* I said, I'd like to make a telephone call.

ALPER

(Indicating the wall phone)

Right on the wall there.

ARTHUR

This is a rather personal call.

ALPER

There's a phone in the Rabbi's office there.

(ARTHUR crosses to THE RABBI's office.)

SCHLISSEL

Well, look about you, really. Here you have the decline of Orthodox Judaism graphically before your eyes. This is a synagogue? A converted grocery store, flanked on one side by a dry cleaner and on the other by a shoemaker. Really, if it wasn't for the Holy Ark there, this place would look like the local headquarters of the American Labor Party. In Poland, where we were all one step from starvation, we had a synagogue whose shadow had more dignity than this place.

ALPER

It's a shame and a disgrace.

ZITORSKY

A shame and a disgrace.

(*In* THE RABBI's *office* ARTHUR *is regarding* THE GIRL *with a sour eye.*)

ARTHUR

Excuse me. I'd like to make a rather personal call.

(THE GIRL *stares down at the floor, unhearing, unmoving, off in a phantasmic world of her own distorted creation.* ARTHUR *sits down at* THE RABBI's *desk, turns his shoulder to* THE GIRL, *and begins to dial a number.*)

SCHLISSEL

Where are all the Orthodox Jews? They have apostated to the Reform Jewish temples, where they sit around like Episcopalians, listening to organ music.

ALPER

Your use of the word "apostasy" in referring to Reform Jews interests me, Schlissel. Is it not written in Sifre on Deuteronomy, "Even if they are foolish, even if they transgress, even if they are full of blemishes, they are still called sons?" So, after all, is it so terrible to be a Reform Jew? Is this not an interesting issue for disputation? Oh, my God!

(*He wheels and starts back for* THE RABBI's *office. The same thought has been entering the other two old fellows' minds, as has been indicated by a growing frown of consternation on each of their faces. They follow* ALPER *to* THE RABBI's *office, where he opens the door quickly and stares in at* ARTHUR LANDAU. *The latter is still seated at* THE RABBI's *desk, waiting for an answer to his phone call; and* THE GIRL *is still in her immobilized state.* ARTHUR *casts such a baleful eye at this interruption that the three old men back out of the office and close the door. They remain nervously outside the door of the office. At last, someone responds to* ARTHUR's *phone call.*)

ARTHUR
(On the phone, shading his face, and keeping his voice down)
Hello, Doctor, did I wake you up? This is Arthur Landau…Yes, I know.
Do you think you can find an hour for me this morning?…Oh, I could be
in your office in about an hour or so. I'm out in Mineola. My ex-wife lives
out here with her parents, you know. And I've been blind drunk for—I just
figured it out—three days now. And I just found myself out here at two
o'clock in the morning banging on their front door, screaming…(THE
GIRL's *presence bothers him. He leans across the desk to her and says—)* Look,
this is a very personal call, and I would really appreciate your letting me
have the use of this office for just a few minutes.
   (THE GIRL looks up at him blankly.)

THE GIRL
(Hollowly)
I am the Whore of Kiev, the companion of sailors.
   *(The bizarreness of this stops ARTHUR. He considers it for a moment, and
   then goes back to the phone.)*

ARTHUR
(On the phone)
No, I'm still here. I'm all right. At least, I'm still alive. *(He hides his face
in the palm of one hand and rubs his brow nervously)* I've got to see you, Doc.
Don't hang up on me, please. If my analyst hangs up on me, that'll be the
end. Just let me talk a couple of minutes…I'm in some damned synagogue.
I was on my way to the subway. Oh, my God, I've got to call my office. I
was supposed to be in court twice yesterday. I hope somebody had the
brains to apply for an adjournment. So it's funny, you know. I'm in this
damned synagogue. I'll be down in about an hour, Doctor…Okay. Okay…
I'm all right…No, I'm all right…I'll see you in about an hour. *(He hangs
up, hides his face in the palms of both hands and slowly pulls himself together.
After a moment, he looks up at THE GIRL, who is back to staring at the floor. He
frowns, stands, goes to the door of the office, opens it, gives one last look at THE
GIRL, and closes the door behind him. He finds himself staring at the inquiring
faces of the three old men)* Listen, I hope you know there's a pretty strange
girl in there.
   *(The old men bob their heads nervously. ARTHUR crosses the synagogue to
   a chair and sits down, his face dark with his emotions. The three old men
   regard him anxiously. After a moment, SCHLISSEL approaches ARTHUR.)*

SCHLISSEL
A strange girl, you say?

> ARTHUR

Yes.

> SCHLISSEL

Did she say anything?

> ARTHUR

She said: "I am the Whore of Kiev, the companion of sailors."

> SCHLISSEL

That was a very piquant statement, wouldn't you say?

> ARTHUR

Yes, I think I would call it piquant.

> SCHLISSEL

What do you make of it?

> ARTHUR
> *(Irritably)*

Look, I'm going. I have a hundred things to do. I...

> SCHLISSEL

No, no, no. Sit down. For heaven's sakes, sit down.

> ALPER
> *(Hurrying over)*

Don't go. Oh, my, don't go. We need you for a tenth man. We haven't had ten men in the morning in more than a week, I think.

> ZITORSKY
> *(On* ALPER's *tail)*

Two weeks, at least.

> *(At this point,* HARRIS, *who has finally divested himself of his muffler and the heavy, ribbed sweaters which were over his jacket, is now wrapped in a prayer shawl and bursts into a high, quavering prayer.)*

> HARRIS

"Blessed art thou, O Lord, our God, King of the Universe, who hath sanctified us by his commandments and..."

> *(The words dribble off into inaudibility.* ARTHUR LANDAU *darts a startled look at the old man, not being prepared for this method of prayer, and moves a few nervous steps away from the other old men, then stands rubbing his brow, quite agitated.)*

> ALPER
> *(Whispering to* SCHLISSEL*)*

So what happened in there? Did she say anything?

> SCHLISSEL

Yes, she said she was the Whore of Kiev, and the companion of sailors.

ALPER

Oh dear me.

SCHLISSEL

I'm afraid we shall have to get her out of the Rabbi's office because if she keeps telling everybody who walks in there that she is the Whore of Kiev, they will pack us all off to the insane asylum. And let us be quite sensible about this situation. If Foreman has kidnaped the girl, he has kidnaped her, however kindly his motives—not that I expect the police to regard a dybbuk as any kind of sensible explanation. Whatever the case, it would be a good idea to keep the girl a little less accessible. *(The wall phone rings)* Ah! I'll tell you who that is. That's Foreman's son calling to find out if Foreman and the girl are here. *(The phone rings again)* Well, if you won't answer it, I'll answer it.

(He crosses to the wall phone.)

ALPER

We could take her to my house. Everybody is still sleeping. We'll put her in the cellar.

(The phone rings again. SCHLISSEL *picks up the phone.)*

SCHLISSEL
(On the phone)

Hello. *(He turns to the others and nods, indicating he was right in guessing the caller. The other two old men move closer to the phone)* Mr. Foreman, your father isn't here...Listen, I tell you, he isn't here...I wouldn't have the slightest idea. I haven't seen her since I was up to your house last Tuesday. Isn't she home?...If he comes in, I'll tell him...Okay...*(He hangs up and turns to the other two)* Well, we are in it up to our necks now.

ALPER
(Stripping off his phylacteries)

So shall we take her to my house?

SCHLISSEL

All right. Zitorsky, go in and tell her we are going to take her some place else.

ZITORSKY
(Not exactly inspired by the idea)

Yeah, sure.

SCHLISSEL
(To ZITORSKY*)*

For heaven's sakes, Zitorsky, you don't really believe that's a dybbuk in there.

ZITORSKY

If that's no dybbuk, then you go in and take her.
(SCHLISSEL *shuffles slowly to the door of* THE RABBI's *office.*)

SCHLISSEL
(Pausing at the closed office door)

It's getting kind of complicated. Maybe we ought to call Foreman's son and tell him she's here and not get involved.

ZITORSKY

Oh, no!

SCHLISSEL

Ah, well, come on. What can they do to us? They'll call us foolish old men, but then foolishness is the only privilege of old age. So, Alper, you'll deal with her. You know how to talk to her, and we'll hide her in your cellar. So we'll have a little excitement. (*He opens the door, and the three old men regard* THE GIRL *as she sits in sodden, detached immobility*) Listen. Alper, let's get along, you know. Before the Sexton comes back and starts asking us where we're all going.

(ALPER *nods apprehensively and takes a few steps into the office.*)

ALPER
(To THE GIRL, *who doesn't actually hear him or know of his presence)*

How do you do, my dear Evelyn. This is Alper here. (*She makes no answer.* ALPER *turns to the other two*) She's in one of her apathetic states.

ZITORSKY
(Darting back into the synagogue proper)

I'll get your coat, Alper.

SCHLISSEL
(Looking around to see if ARTHUR *is paying any attention to what's going on;*
he is not)

Well, take her by the arm.

ALPER

Evelyn, your grandfather suggested we take you to my house. You always liked to play with the children's toys in my cellar there, you remember? Come along, and we'll have a good time.

ZITORSKY
(Giving SCHLISSEL *an overcoat)*

Here. Give this to Alper.
(*He hurries off to the front door of the synagogue.*)

HARRIS
(In the process of laying on his phylacteries)
"And from thy wisdom, O Most High God, Thou shalt reserve for me..."
(He dribbles off into inaudibility.)

ALPER
(Placing a tentative hand on THE GIRL's *shoulder)*
Evelyn, dear...
(She looks up, startled.)

ZITORSKY
(Leaning out the front door, searching up and down the street)
Oh, it's cold out here.

ALPER
(To SCHLISSEL, *who is hurriedly putting on his own overcoat)*
I have a feeling we're going to have trouble here.

SCHLISSEL
I've got your coat here.

ALPER
Evelyn...*(A strange animal-like grunt escapes* THE GIRL, *and she begins to moan softly)* Evelyn dear, please don't be alarmed. This is Mr. Alper here who has known you since you were born.
(He is getting a little panicky at the strange sounds coming out of THE GIRL, *and he tries to grab her arm to help her to her feet. She bursts into a shrill scream, electrifying everybody in the synagogue with the exception of* THE CABALIST, *who is oblivious to everything.* ZITORSKY, *who has just closed the front door, stands frozen with horror.* ARTHUR, *sunk in despondency, looks up, startled. The old man,* HARRIS, *pauses briefly, as if the sound has been some distant buzzing, and then goes back to his mumbled prayers.)*

ALPER
Evelyn, my dear girl, for heaven's sakes...

THE GIRL
(Screaming out)
Leave me alone! Leave me alone!

ARTHUR
(Coming to SCHLISSEL, *who shuts the office door quickly)*
What's going on in there?

SCHLISSEL
It's nothing, it's nothing.

THE GIRL
(Screaming)
They are my seven sons! My seven sons!

ALPER
(Who is trying earnestly to get out of the office)
Who closed this door?

ZITORSKY
(Reaching for the front door)
I'm getting out of here.

SCHLISSEL
Where are you going?
(But ZITORSKY has already fled into the street.)

ARTHUR
(To SCHLISSEL)
What's all this screaming?
(ALPER, at last out of the office, comes scurrying to SCHLISSEL.)

ALPER
I put my hand on her arm to help her up, and she burst into this fit of screaming.
(ARTHUR strides to the open doorway of the office. THE GIRL stares at him, hunched now in terror, frightened and at bay.)

ARTHUR
(To SCHLISSEL)
What have you been doing to this girl?

SCHLISSEL
The girl is possessed by a dybbuk.

ARTHUR
What?

SCHLISSEL
(To ALPER)
Zitorsky ran out in the street like a kangaroo.

ALPER
Listen, maybe we should call somebody.

ARTHUR
Listen, what is this?

ALPER
My dear young man, there is no reason to alarm yourself. There is an insane girl in the Rabbi's office, but she appears to have quieted down.

ARTHUR

What do you mean, there's an insane girl in the Rabbi's office?

ALPER

Yes, she is a catatonic schizophrenic, occasionally violent, but really, go back to your seat. There is no cause for alarm.

ARTHUR

Am I to understand, sir, that it is a practice of yours to keep insane girls in your Rabbi's office?

ALPER

No, no. Oh, dear, I suppose we shall have to tell him. But you must promise, my dear fellow, to keep this whole matter between us. (*To* SCHLISSEL) Zitorsky, you say, took to his heels?

SCHLISSEL

Absolutely flew out of the door.

ALPER

Well, I really can't blame him. It was quite an apprehensive moment. I was a little shaken myself. (*He peeks into the office*) Yes, she seems to be quite apathetic again. I think we just better leave her alone for the time being.

ARTHUR

Look, what is going on here?

ALPER

My dear fellow, you are, of course, understandably confused. The girl, you see, is possessed by a dybbuk.

ARTHUR

Yes, of course. Well, that explains everything.

ALPER

Well, of course, how would he know what a dybbuk is? A dybbuk is a migratory soul that possesses the body of another human being in order to return to heaven. It is a Lurian doctrine, actually tracing back to the Essenes, I suppose, but popularized during the thirteenth century by the Spanish cabalists. I wrote several articles on the matter for Yiddish periodicals. My name is Moyshe Alper, and at one time I was a journalist of some repute. (ZITORSKY *appears in the doorway again, peering nervously in*) Come in, Zitorsky, come in. The girl is quiet again.

(ZITORSKY *approaches them warily.*)

ARTHUR

Look, are you trying to tell me you have a girl in there you think is possessed by some demon? Where is her mother or father or somebody who should be responsible for her?

ALPER

If there were someone responsible for her, would she be insane in the first place?

ARTHUR

Of course, this is none of my business...

ALPER

You are a good fellow and let me put you at ease. The girl is in good hands. Nobody is going to hurt her. Her grandfather, who adores her more than his own life, has gone off for a short while.

ZITORSKY

To Williamsburg on the Brighton train.

SCHLISSEL

The Brighton train takes you to Coney Island.

ZITORSKY

You said the Double G.

ALPER

All right, all right.

ARTHUR

Of course, this is none of my business.

ALPER

(To ARTHUR*)*

I can understand your concern; it shows you are a good fellow, but really the matter is well in hand.

(The front door opens and there now enter THE SEXTON *and two young men in their thirties, apparently the* KESSLER *boys, who are none too happy about being roused on this cold winter morning. They stand disconsolately around in the back of the synagogue.)*

THE SEXTON

Here are two more, the Kessler boys.

ALPER

Now we'll have ten for a quorum.

ZITORSKY

Kessler? Kessler? Oh, yes, the stationery store. I knew your father.

(There is a general flurry of movement. THE SEXTON *hurries about the ritual of baring his left arm, donning the prayer shawl and phylacteries, walking nervously about, mumbling his prayers rapidly.* ARTHUR, *quite disturbed again, looks into* THE RABBI'S *office at* THE GIRL, *then moves slowly into the office.* THE GIRL *is again in a world of her own. He closes*

the door and studies THE GIRL. SCHLISSEL, ALPER *and* ZITORSKY *watch him warily, taking off their overcoats again and preparing to stay for the impending services.* HARRIS' *shrill quavering voice suddenly leaps up into audibility again.)*

HARRIS

"Thou shalt set apart all that openeth the womb of the Lord, and the firstling that cometh of a beast which thou shalt have, it shall belong to the Lord..."

SCHLISSEL
(To ALPER)

What are we going to do when the Rabbi tries to get into his office? He'll see the girl, and that will be the end of our exorcism. What shall we tell the Rabbi?

(The front door of the synagogue opens, and THE RABBI *comes striding efficiently in, right on cue. He is a young man in his early thirties, neatly dressed if a little threadbare, and carrying a briefcase.)*

ZITORSKY

Peace be with you, Rabbi.

THE RABBI

Peace be with you.

ALPER
(Intercepting THE RABBI *as he heads for his office)*

How do you do, Rabbi.

*(*THE RABBI *nods as he strides to the door of his office, where* SCHLISSEL *blocks the way.)*

SCHLISSEL

We have ten men today, Rabbi.

THE RABBI

Good. *(He reaches for the door to his office)* I'll just get my phylacteries.

ALPER
(Seizing ZITORSKY's *phylacteries)*

Oh, here, use these. It's late, Rabbi.

THE RABBI
(Taking the phylacteries)

Fine. Well, let's start the services.

(He turns back to the synagogue proper. From all around, each man's voice rises into prayer.)

The Curtain Falls

ACT II

SCENE 1

Fifteen minutes later.
ZITORSKY *is reading the prayers. He stands before the lectern on the raised platform, singing the primitive chants.*

ZITORSKY
"And we beseech thee according to thine abundant mercies, O Lord..."

THE SEXTON
Young Kessler, come here and open the Ark.
(The younger KESSLER *ascends the platform and opens the Ark by drawing the curtains and sliding the doors apart.)*

ZITORSKY
"And it came to pass, when the ark set forward, that Moses said, Rise up, O Lord, and Thine enemies shall be scattered, and they that hate Thee shall flee before Thee. For out of Zion shall go forth the Law, and the word of the Lord from Jerusalem."
(Immediately, the rest of the quorum plunges into a mumbled response: "Blessed be Thy name, O Sovereign of the World! Blessed be Thy crown, and Thy abiding place!" Jewish prayers are conducted in a reader-congregation pattern, although frequently the reader's vocalized statement and the congregation's mumbled responses merge and run along simultaneously. In this specific moment of prayer, when the Ark has been opened and the Torah is about to be taken out, the demarcation between reader and congregation is clear-cut. The sliding brown wooden doors of the Ark are now open. THE SEXTON *is reaching in to take out the exquisitely ornamented Torah, which, when its lovely brocaded velvet cover is taken off, will show itself to be a large parchment scroll divided on two carved rollers. When* THE SEXTON *gets the Torah out, he hands it carefully to* ZITORSKY, *who has been chosen this day for the honor of holding the Torah until it is to be read from.* ZITORSKY, *who, as today's reader, has been reading along with the congregation although more audibly, now allows his voice to ring out clearly, marking the end of this paragraph of prayers.)*

127

ZITORSKY

"...May it be Thy gracious will to open my heart in Thy Law, and to grant my heart's desires, and those of all Thy people Israel, for our benefit, throughout a peaceful life." *(Pause)* "Magnify the Lord with me, and let us exalt His name together."

(Again, the congregation leaps into mumbled response. "Thine, O Lord, is the greatness, and the power, and the glory, and the victory, and the majesty..." ZITORSKY marches solemnly to the front of the lectern, carrying the Torah before him. Each man kisses the Torah as it passes him. There is now the ritual of removing the velvet cover, and the Torah is laid upon the lectern. ZITORSKY, HARRIS, and THE SEXTON form a hovering group of three old betallithed Jews over it. THE RABBI stands rocking slightly back and forth to the left of the lectern. Off the raised platform, but immediately by the railing, stands THE CABALIST, rocking back and forth and praying. ALPER and SCHLISSEL stand at various places, mumbling their responses. The two KESSLER boys have removed their coats and wear prayer shawls, but still stand as close to the front door as they can. ARTHUR LANDAU stands, leaning against the wall of THE RABBI's office, quite intrigued by the solemn prayers and rituals. THE GIRL is still in THE RABBI's office, but she is standing now, listening as well as she can to the prayers. Her face is peaceful now and quite lovely. Again ZITORSKY's voice rises to indicate the end of a paragraph of prayer.)

ZITORSKY

"Ascribe all of your greatness unto our God, and render honor to the Law."

(There is now a quick mumbled conference among the three old Jews at the lectern, then THE SEXTON suddenly leans out and calls to the two KESSLER boys in the rear.)

THE SEXTON

Kessler, you want to read from the Torah?

THE ELDER KESSLER

No, no, no. Get somebody else.

THE SEXTON

Alper?

(ALPER nods and makes his way to the lectern. THE SEXTON's voice, a high, whining incantation, rises piercingly into the air, announcing the fact that Moyshe son of Abram will read from the Torah.)

THE SEXTON

Rise up, Reb Moses Ha'Kohan, son of Abram, and speak the blessing on the Torah. "Blessed be He, who in His Holiness gave the Law unto his people Israel, the Law of the Lord is perfect."

                            CONGREGATION
                          (Scattered response)
"And ye that cleave unto the Lord your God are alive every one of you
this day."

                                ALPER
          (Now at the lectern, raises his head and recites quickly)
"Blessed is the Lord who is to be blessed for ever and ever."

                            CONGREGATION
"Blessed is the Lord who is to be blessed for ever and ever."

                                ALPER
"Blessed art Thou, O Lord our God, King of the Universe, who hast
chosen us from all peoples and hast given us Thy Law. Blessed art Thou,
O Lord, who givest the Law."

                            CONGREGATION
Amen!

                             THE SEXTON
"And Moses said…"
          *(There are now four mumbling old Jews huddled over the lectern. It all
          becomes very indistinguishable;* THE SEXTON's *piercing tenor rises audibly
          now and then to indicate he is reading.* ALPER *moves into the reader's posi-
          tion and begins to read from the Torah, bending his knees and twisting his
          body and hunching over the Torah, peering at the meticulous Hebrew let-
          tering inscribed therein.* SCHLISSEL *and the* KESSLER *boys find seats where
          they were standing, as does* THE CABALIST. THE RABBI *and* HARRIS *are
          seated on the raised platform. In* THE RABBI's *office,* THE GIRL *decides to
          go out into the synagogue proper. She opens the door and moves a few steps
          out.* ARTHUR *hears her and turns to her warily.)*

                              THE GIRL
                       (Quite lucid and amiable)
Excuse me, sir, are they reading from the Torah now?
          (She peers over ARTHUR's *shoulder toward the old men at the lectern.)*

                               ARTHUR
Yes, I think so.
          *(He watches her carefully. She seems all right now. Still, there is some-
          thing excessively ingenuous about her, a tentative, wide-eyed, gently smil-
          ing innocence.)*

                              THE GIRL
Is my grandfather here?

(*She peers nervously around the synagogue.*)

ARTHUR

Which one would be your grandfather?

THE GIRL
(*Growing panic*)

No, he's not here. I see Mr. Alper, but I don't see my grandfather.

ARTHUR

I'm sure he will he back soon.
(*His calmness reassures her.*)

THE GIRL
(*She studies this strange young man*)

I think all synagogues should be shabby because I think of God as being very poor as a child. What do you think of God as?

ARTHUR

I'm afraid I think of God as the Director of Internal Revenue.
(THE GIRL *laughs brightly and then immediately smothers her laughter, aware she is in a solemn synagogue.*)

THE GIRL

You're irreverent. (*Frowning, she goes into* THE RABBI's *office, plops down on his swivel chair, and swivels back and forth, very much like a child.* ARTHUR *follows her tentatively, studying her cautiously, yet taken by her ingenuousness. She darts a quick frightened look at him*) Were you in here just before?

ARTHUR

Well, yes.

THE GIRL

Did I—did I say anything?

ARTHUR
(*Amiably*)

Well, yes.

THE GIRL
(*Sighing*)

I see. Well, I might as well tell you. I've been to several mental institutions. (*She looks quickly at him. He smiles at her*) You don't seem very disconcerted by that.

ARTHUR

Oh, I expect it might be hard to find somebody who couldn't do with occasional confinement in a mental institution.
(*In the synagogue,* THE SEXTON *now calls* HARRIS *to read from the Torah.*)

THE GIRL
(She frowns)

Did my grandfather say when he would be back or where he was going?
(She starts from her seat frightened again.)

ARTHUR

I understand he'll be back soon.

THE GIRL

Are you the doctor?

ARTHUR

No. You don't have to be the least bit afraid of me.

THE GIRL
(She brightens)

My grandfather and I are very close. I'm much closer to him than I am to my own father. I'd rather not talk about my father, if you don't mind. It's a danger spot for me. You know, when I was nine years old, I shaved all the hair off my head became that is the practice of really Orthodox Jewish women. I mean, if you want to be a rabbi's wife, you must shear your hair and wear a wig. That's one of my compulsive dreams. I keep dreaming of myself as the wife of a handsome young rabbi with a fine beard down to his waist and a very stern face and prematurely gray forelocks on his brow. I have discovered through many unsuccessful years of psychiatric treatment that religion has a profound sexual connotation for me. Oh, dear, I'm afraid I'm being tiresome again about my psychiatric history. Really, being insane is like being fat. You can talk about nothing else. Please forgive me. I am sure I am boring you to death.

ARTHUR

No, not at all. It's nice to hear somebody talk with passion about anything, even their insanity.

THE GIRL
(Staring at him)

The word doesn't bother you?

ARTHUR

What word?

THE GIRL

Insanity.

ARTHUR

Good heavens, no. I'm a lawyer. Insanity in one form or another is what fills my anteroom. Besides, I'm being psychoanalyzed myself, and I'm something of a bore about that too. You are a bright young thing. How old are you?

THE GIRL

Eighteen.

ARTHUR

(*Staring at her*)

My God, you're a pretty kid! I can hardly believe you are psychopathic. Are you very advanced?

THE GIRL

Pretty bad. I'm being institutionalized again. Dr. Molineaux's Sanitarium in Long Island. I'm a little paranoid and hallucinate a great deal and have very little sense of reality, except for brief interludes like this, and I might slip off any minute in the middle of a sentence into some incoherency. If that should happen, you must be very realistic with me. Harsh reality is the most efficacious way to deal with schizophrenics.

ARTHUR

You seem well read on the matter.

THE GIRL

I'm a voracious reader. I have so little else to do with myself. Will you come and visit me at Dr. Molineaux's hospital? I am awfully fond of you.

ARTHUR

Yes, of course, I will.

THE GIRL

It won't be as depressing an experience as you might think. If I am not in the violent ward, I will probably be allowed to go to the commissary and have an ice-cream soda with you. The worst of an insane asylum is really how poorly dressed the inmates are. They all wear old cable-stitched sweaters. I do like to look pretty. (*A vacuous look is beginning to come across her face*) They ask me to be in a lot of movies, you know, when I have time. Did you see *David and Bathsheba* with Susan Hayward? That was really me. I don't tell anybody that. They don't want me to make movies. My mother, I mean. She doesn't even go to synagogue on Saturday. You're the new Rabbi, you know. Sometimes, I'm the Rabbi, but they're all afraid of me. The temple is sixty cubits long and made of cypress and overlaid with gold. The burnished Roman legions clank outside the gates, you know. Did you see *The Ten Commandments*? I saw that Tuesday, Wednesday. I was in that. I was the girl who danced. I was in that. Mr. Hirschman is here, too, you know, and my grandfather. Everybody's here. Do you see that boy over there? Go away. Leave us alone. He's insane. He's really Mr. Hirschman the Cabalist. He's making a golem. You ought to come here, Rabbi.

ARTHUR
(Who has been listening fascinated, now says firmly)
I am not the Rabbi, Evelyn.
(She regards him briefly.)

THE GIRL
Well, we're making a golem and...

ARTHUR
You are not making a golem, Evelyn.
(She pauses, staring down at the floor. A grimace of pain moves quickly across her face and then leaves it. After a moment, she mumbles—)

THE GIRL
Thank you. *(Suddenly she begins to cry and she throws herself on* ARTHUR'S *breast, clinging to him, and he holds her gently, caressing her as he would a child)* Oh, I can't bear being insane.

ARTHUR
(Gently)
I always thought that since the insane made their own world it was more pleasurable than this one that is made for us.

THE GIRL
(Moving away)
Oh, no, it is unbearably painful. It is the most indescribable desolation. You are all alone in deserted streets. You cannot possibly imagine it.

ARTHUR
I'm afraid I can. I have tried to commit suicide so many times now it has become something of a family joke. Once, before I was divorced, my wife stopped in to tell a neighbor before she went out to shop: "Oh, by the way, if you smell gas, don't worry about it. It's only Arthur killing himself again." Suicides, you know, kill themselves a thousand times, but one day I'll slash my wrists and I will forget to make a last-minute telephone call, and there will be no stomach-pumping Samaritans to run up the stairs and smash my bedroom door down and rush me off to Bellevue. I'll make it some day—I assure you of that.

THE GIRL
(Regarding him with sweet interest)
You don't look as sad as all that.

ARTHUR
Oh, I have made a profession of ironic detachment. It depresses me to hear that insanity is as forlorn as anything else. I had always hoped to go crazy myself some day since I have apparently no talent for suicide.

THE GIRL

I always thought life would be wonderful if I were only sane.

ARTHUR

Life is merely dreary if you're sane, and unbearable if you are sensitive. I cannot think of a more meaningless sham than my own life. My parents were very poor so I spent the first twenty years of my life condemning the rich for my childhood nightmares. Oh, I was quite a Bernard Barricade when I was in college. I left the Communist Party when I discovered there were easier ways to seduce girls. I turned from reproaching society for my loneliness to reproaching my mother, and stormed out of her house to take a room for myself on the East Side. Then I fell in love—that is to say, I found living alone so unbearable I was willing to marry. She married me because all her friends were marrying somebody. Needless to say, we told each other how deeply in love we were. We wanted very much to be happy. Americans, you know, are frantic about being happy. The American nirvana is a man and his wife watching television amiably and then turning off the lights and effortlessly making the most ardent love to each other. Television unfortunately is a bore and ardent love is an immense drain on one's energy. I began to work day and night at my law office, and besides becoming very successful, I managed to avoid my wife entirely. For this deceit, I was called ambitious and was respected by everyone including my wife, who was quite as bored with me as I was with her. We decided to have children, because we couldn't possibly believe we were that miserable together. All this while I drove myself mercilessly for fear that if I paused for just one moment, the whole slim, trembling sanity of my life would come crashing down about my feet without the slightest sound. I went to a psychoanalyst who wanted to know about my childhood, when I could barely remember whether I took a taxi or a bus to his office that day. I began to drink myself into stupors, pursuing other men's wives, and generally behaving badly. One morning, I stared into the mirror and could barely make out my features. Life is utterly meaningless. I have had everything a man can get out of life—prestige, power, money, women, children, and a handsome home only three blocks from the Scarsdale Country Club, and all I can think of is I want to get out of this as fast as I can. (*He has become quite upset by now, and has to avert his face to hide a sudden welling of tears. He takes a moment to get a good grip on himself, readopts his sardonic air and says—*) As you see, I have quite a theatrical way when I want to.

THE GIRL
(*Brightly*)

Oh, I think you are wonderfully wise.

ARTHUR

Oh, it was said best by your very own King Solomon, the wisest man who ever lived, when he wrote Ecclesiastes.

THE GIRL

Oh, King Solomon didn't write Ecclesiastes. That was written by an anonymous Jewish scholar in Alexandria. I wouldn't put too much stock in it. Weariness was all the rage among the Hellenized Jews.

ARTHUR
(Staring at her)

You are an amazing kid.

(She smiles back at him exuberantly, unabashedly showing her fondness for him. It embarrasses him, and he turns away. He opens the door and looks out into the synagogue, where the reading of the Torah has come to an end.)

THE RABBI
(Singing out)

"Blessed art thou, O Lord our God, King of the Universe, who hast given us the Law of truth, and hast planted everywhere life in our midst. Blessed art Thou, O Lord, who givest the Law."

(There is a scattered mumbled response from the old men in the synagogue. ZITORSKY now takes the Torah and holds it up above his head and chants.)

ZITORSKY

"And this is the Law which Moses set before the children of Israel, according to the commandment of the Lord by the hand of Moses." *(The four men on the platform form a small group as ZITORSKY marches slowly back to the Ark carrying the Torah. A mumble of prayers rustles through the synagogue. ZITORSKY's voice rises out)* "Let them praise the name of the Lord; for His name alone is exalted."

(He carefully places the Torah back into the Ark. A rumble of prayer runs through the synagogue. All the men in the synagogue are standing now.)

ARTHUR
(Turning to THE GIRL)

They're putting the Torah back. Is the service over?

THE GIRL

No. I have a wonderful book I want to give to you. Mr. Hirschman, our Community Cabalist, gave it to me. It is called the Book of Splendor, a terribly mystical book. And you are a mystic, you know.

ARTHUR

Oh, am I?

THE GIRL

Yes. I never met anyone who wanted to know the meaning of life as desperately as you do. I have to get the book for you.

> (SCHLISSEL *pokes his head into the office and indicates to* ARTHUR *that he is needed outside.*)

ARTHUR

I think they need me outside.

> (*He moves to the door.*)

THE GIRL

Yes, we really shouldn't have been talking during the service.

> (ARTHUR *goes out of the office, closing the door behind him. He joins* SCHLISSEL, *who is a few steps away, muttering the prayers.*)

ARTHUR
> (*Shaking his head*)

What a pity, really. A lovely girl. What a pity. Now, you look like a sensible sort of man. What is all this nonsense about demons? You really should call her father or mother or whoever it is who is responsible for her.

SCHLISSEL

Young man, if we called her father he would come down and take her away.

ARTHUR

Yes. That would be the point, wouldn't it?

SCHLISSEL

Then what happens to our exorcism?

ARTHUR

What exorcism?

SCHLISSEL

Listen, we've got to exorcise the dybbuk.

ARTHUR
> (*Aghast*)

Exorcism!

> (THE SEXTON *leans over the railing of the platform and admonishes them in a heavy whisper.*)

THE SEXTON

Sssshhhh!

> (SCHLISSEL *promptly turns back to muttering his prayers.* ARTHUR *stares at him with vague disbelief.*)

ARTHUR

Are you serious?

> (ZITORSKY's *voice rises up loud and clear.*)

ZITORSKY

"...And it is said, and the Lord shall be king over all the earth; on that day shall the Lord be One, and his Name One."

(THE CONGREGATION, which had been sitting, now stands again. THE SEXTON leans over the railing and calls to the KESSLER boys.)

THE SEXTON

Kessler, stand up. Now is the time for your memorial prayers.

(The two KESSLER boys nod, stand, and look unhappily down at their prayer books. HARRIS pokes a palsied finger onto a page to show them where to read, and the two young men now begin to read painstakingly and with no idea of what they are reading.)

KESSLER BOYS

"Magnified and sanctified be His great Name in the world which He hath created according to His will. May He establish His kingdom in your lifetime and in your days, and in the lifetime of all the house of Israel, speedily and at a near time; and say ye, Amen."

CONGREGATION

Amen. "Let His great Name be blessed for ever and ever."

KESSLER BOYS

"Blessed, praised, and glorified, exalted, extolled and honored, adored, and lauded, be the Name of the Holy One, blessed be He, beyond, yea, beyond all blessings and hymns, praises and songs, which are uttered in the world, and say ye, Amen."

CONGREGATION

Amen.

(The front door to the synagogue bursts open and FOREMAN thrusts himself in, obviously much distraught; not so distraught, however, that he doesn't automatically join in the "Amen.")

KESSLER BOYS

"May there be abundant peace from heaven, and life for us and for all Israel; and say ye, Amen."

CONGREGATION

Amen.

KESSLER BOYS

"May he who maketh peace in his high places, make peace for us and for all Israel, and say ye, Amen."

CONGREGATION

Amen.

(The synagogue bursts into a quick mumble of prayers, except for SCHLIS-

SEL, *who scurries over to* FOREMAN. FOREMAN *stares at him, white with panic.*)

SCHLISSEL

What happened? You got lost? You took the Long Island Railroad to Atlantic Avenue Station, and you got lost in the Atlantic Avenue Station?

FOREMAN

What Atlantic Avenue Station? I couldn't even find the Long Island Railroad!

SCHLISSEL

Idiot! You are an innocent child! Really! Services are over in a minute, and I'll take you myself.

(ALPER *is leaning over the railing of the platform, making obvious gestures, as if to ask what had happened. Even* ZITORSKY *looks up from his hunched position at the lectern.* SCHLISSEL *announces in a heavy whisper, as he starts to put on his coat—*)

SCHLISSEL

He couldn't even find the Long Island Railway Station.

(ALPER *clasps his brow.* THE SEXTON *turns around to* SCHLISSEL *and admonishes him with a heavy "Ssshhh!!!"* FOREMAN *has begun walking about, mumbling the prayers by heart, automatically a part of the service again. As he passes* SCHLISSEL, *he indicates with a jerk of his head that he would like to know of the well-being of his granddaughter*)

SCHLISSEL

She's all right. Don't worry about her.

(FOREMAN *nods and continues mumbling his prayers. In* THE RABBI'S *office,* THE GIRL, *who has been sitting pensively, now stands, puts her coat on, goes out of the office, calmly crosses to the rear of the synagogue, and exits through the front door. Absolutely no one is aware she has gone.* THE CONGREGATION *now bursts into a loud prayer, obviously the last one of the service, since the men on the platform begin to meander off, and all those who are still wearing their phylacteries begin to strip them off, even as they say the words of the prayer.*)

CONGREGATION

"He is the Lord of the Universe, who reigned ere any creature yet was formed.

At the time when all things were made by His desire, then was His name proclaimed King.

And after all things shall have had an end, He alone, the dreadest one shall reign;

Who was, who is, and who will be in glory."

(SCHLISSEL, ALPER, ZITORSKY, *and* FOREMAN *have all rattled quickly through this fine paean, impatient to close off the service, while the others continue the terminal recital. The four old men form a huddled group by the front door.*)

ALL FOUR
(Rattling it off)
"And with my spirit, my body, also; the Lord is with me, and I will not fear. Amen."

ALPER
Amen, what happened?

SCHLISSEL
I'm taking him myself right away.

ZITORSKY
What happened, you got lost?

FOREMAN
I asked this fellow in the street, I said: "Could you..."

SCHLISSEL
(To ALPER, *pointing to* ARTHUR*)*
Listen, keep an eye on that fellow there. He wants to tell the Rabbi about the girl. All right, listen. I shall have to lead Foreman by the hand to Korpotchniker. All right, listen, we're going. Good-bye. Peace be unto you.

ALPER
Take the Long Island Railroad to the Atlantic Avenue Station. Then take the Brighton train.

SCHLISSEL
Oh, for heaven's sakes. Are you presuming to tell me how to get to Williamsburg?

ALPER
All right, go already.

SCHLISSEL
(Muttering as he leads FOREMAN *out the door)*
The Brighton train. If we took the Brighton train, we would spend the day in Coney Island.
(He exits with FOREMAN, *closing the door. The rest of* THE CONGREGA-TION *has finally come to the end of the service.*)

CONGREGATION
(Their scattered voices rising to a coda)
"And with my spirit, my body also; the Lord is with me, and I will not
fear. Amen!"

ZITORSKY and ALPER

Amen!
*(There is a flurry of dispersion. The two KESSLER boys mumble good-byes
and disappear quickly out into the street, buttoning their coats against the
cold. HARRIS, who is slowly and tremblingly removing his phylacteries, continues slowly to dress himself again throughout the rest of the scene. THE
SEXTON now scurries about, gathering the various phylacteries and prayer
shawls and putting them back into the velvet prayer bags and then putting
all the velvet bags and prayer books back into the cardboard carton they
were all taken from, an activity he pursues with his usual frenetic desperation. Only THE RABBI and THE CABALIST continue to say a few extra
prayers: "The Thirteen Principles of Faith," etc. THE CABALIST reads
them sitting down, hunched over his prayer book. ALPER and ZITORSKY
have genuine cause for alarm concerning ARTHUR LANDAU, for he has
ambled down to the platform, where he stands waiting for THE RABBI to
finish his prayers. They watch ARTHUR guardedly. HARRIS suddenly
decides to be communicative. He lifts his old face to ALPER and ZITORSKY.)*

HARRIS

Ah, am I thirsty!

ALPER
(Watching ARTHUR carefully)

Good.
*(THE RABBI, having finished his last prayer, now turns and starts down
from the platform. ARTHUR steps forward to meet him.)*

ARTHUR

Rabbi...

THE RABBI
(Walking by him)

I'll be with you in just a moment.
(He strides directly to his office. ALPER leaps to intercept him.)

ALPER

Rabbi...

THE RABBI
(Continuing into his office)

I'll be with you in a minute, Alper.
(He goes into his office and closes the door. ALPER clasps his brow and

shrugs. ZITORSKY *mutters an involuntary "Oy." They both nod their heads and wait with the sufferance that is the badge of all their tribe.* ARTHUR *moves a few steps to* THE RABBI's *door and also waits. In the office,* THE RABBI *sits down—all business—and dials a number. Then he speaks into the phone.)*

THE RABBI

I'd like to make a person-to-person call to Rabbi Harry Gersh in Wilmington, Delaware. The number in Wilmington is Kingswood 3-1973…Thank you…

(He hums a snatch of the service. ALPER *knocks lightly on the door, and, receiving no answer, opens the door and comes into the office. He stares—open-mouthed—noting the absence of* THE GIRL. *He tugs at his Vandyke beard in contemplation)*

THE RABBI

Yes, Alper?

ALPER

Well, I'll tell you, Rabbi…*(He scowls, a little flustered, then turns and goes out of the office)* Excuse me.

THE RABBI
(On the phone)

Locust 6-0932.

ALPER
(To ZITORSKY*)*

She's not there.

ZITORSKY

She's not there?

ALPER

I'll have to go out and look for her.

(Frowning in contemplation, ALPER *puts his coat on slowly and exits from the synagogue.* THE RABBI *is still on the phone. His voice rises to the pitch usually used for long-distance calls.)*

THE RABBI

Harry, how are you, this is Bernard here, I'm sorry I wasn't in last night, my wife Sylvia said it was wonderful to hear your voice after all these years, how are you, Shirley, and the kids, oh, that's wonderful, I'm glad to hear it. Harry, my wife tells me you have just gotten your first congregation and you wanted some advice since I have already been fired several times…Good, how much are you getting?…Well, five thousand isn't bad for a first congregation although I always thought out-of-town paid better. And what is it, a one-year contract?...Well, what kind of advice can I give you? Especially you, Harry. You are a saintly, scholarly, and truly pious man, and you have no business being a rabbi. You've got to be a go-getter, Harry, unfortunately. The synagogue I am in now is in an unbelievable state of neglect and I expect to see us in prouder premises within a year. But I've got things moving now. I've started a Youth Group, a Young Married People's Club, a Theatre Club which is putting on its first production next month, *The Man Who Came to Dinner*, I'd like you to come, Harry, bring the wife, I'm sure you'll have an entertaining evening. And let me recommend that you organize a little-league baseball team. It's a marvelous gimmick. I have sixteen boys in my Sunday School now... Harry, listen, what do I know about baseball?...Harry, let me interrupt you. How in heaven's name are you going to convey an awe of God to boys who will race out of your Hebrew classes to fly model rocket ships five hundred feet in the air exploding in three stages? To my boys, God is a retired mechanic...Well, I'm organizing a bazaar right now. When I hang up on you, I have to rush to the printer's to get some raffles printed, and from there I go to the Town Hall for a permit to conduct bingo games. In fact, I was so busy this morning, I almost forgot to come to the syna-gogue...(*He says gently*) Harry, with my first congregation, I also thought I was bringing the word of God. I stood up in my pulpit every Sabbath and carped at them for violating the rituals of their own religion. My congre-gations dwindled, and one synagogue given to my charge disappeared into a morass of mortgages. Harry, I'm afraid there are times when I don't care if they believe in God as long as they come to the synagogue...Of course, it's sad...Harry, it's been my pleasure. Have I depressed you?...Come and see us, Harry...Good luck...Of course. Good-bye.

(*He hangs up, stands, starts looking around for his briefcase, and strides out into the synagogue still searching for it. He is interrupted by* ARTHUR.)

ARTHUR

Rabbi, I have to hurry off, but before I go I would like to talk to you about that girl in your office. These old men tell me she is possessed by a demon, and I think they are intending to perform some kind of an exor-cism. I must caution you that that girl should be treated only by compe-tent psychiatrists and the most frightful harm might come to her if she is subjected to anything like— Look, do you know about this exorcism, because I cannot believe you would tolerate any...

THE RABBI

(*Who has been trying very hard to follow all this*)

I'm afraid you have me at a disadvantage.

ARTHUR

I'm talking about the girl in your office.

THE RABBI

I'm somewhat new here and don't know everybody yet by name. Please be patient with me. Now, I take it you want to get married.

(*For a moment* ARTHUR *briefly considers the possibility he's not really awake.*)

ARTHUR
(*Pensively*)

This whole morning is beginning to seem absolutely...Rabbi, there is a girl in your office who is insane.

THE RABBI

In my office? (THE RABBI *is suddenly distracted by* ZITORSKY, *who has been wandering around the synagogue, looking up and down between the rows of chairs, and is now looking into the bathroom at the upstage end of the synagogue*) Mr. Zitorsky, what are you doing?

ZITORSKY
(*To* ARTHUR, *who is moving quickly to* THE RABBI's *office*)

Well, have you ever seen such a thing? The girl has vanished into thin air.

(*He shuffles to* THE RABBI, *absolutely awe-struck by it all.*)

ARTHUR
(*Now examining the interior of* THE RABBI's *office*)

I suspect something more mundane, like simply walking out the door.

(*He moves quickly to the front door, which now opens, and* ALPER *returns, frowning with thought.*)

ALPER
(*To* ARTHUR)

Well, is that something or isn't it? I looked up and down, I couldn't see her.

(ARTHUR *scowls and goes out into the street, where he stands looking up and down.*)

THE RABBI

Mr. Zitorsky, if you will just tell me what this is all about.

ZITORSKY
(*His eyes wide with awe*)

Rabbi, Mr. Foreman brought his granddaughter down this morning, and he said: "She is possessed by a dybbuk!" Well, what can you say when someone tells you something like that?

THE RABBI

Oh, Mr. Foreman's granddaughter. Yes, of course, I see.

ZITORSKY

So he took us into your office where she was standing, and it spoke to us! What an experience! You cannot imagine! The voice of the dybbuk spoke to us. It was like a hollow echo of eternity, and the girl's whole body was illuminated by a frame of light! Fire flashed from her mouth. All of us were there, ask Alper here, he'll tell you. I swear this on my soul the girl began to rise into the air!

ALPER

Actually, Zitorsky is coloring the story a little.

ZITORSKY

(Riveted by the marvelousness of the fantasy)

What are you talking about? You saw it with your own eyes!

ALPER

Well, it was an experience, I must say.

THE RABBI

And the girl has gone now.

ZITORSKY

Into the air about us.

THE RABBI

And where is Mr. Foreman?

ALPER

He went to Brooklyn.

THE RABBI

What in heaven's name for?

ALPER

To see the Korpotchniker Rabbi.

THE RABBI

(Quite impressed)

The Korpotchniker?

ZITORSKY

Certainly! Maybe you don't know this, but Hirschman is his cousin.

THE RABBI

Mr. Hirschman? I have to admit I didn't know that.

ZITORSKY

Oh, sure. Listen, Hirschman is the first-born son of the original Korpotchniker.

ALPER

I am afraid we are drifting from the point.

THE RABBI
(Frowning)
The girl probably went home. Why don't you call the girl's home, Mr.
Alper, and find out if she's there? I think you are a very close friend of the
family.

ARTHUR
(Who has come back into the synagogue)
Well, thank God for the first rational voice I've heard today.

ALPER
(Nodding his head sadly)
Yes, I suppose I had better call her father.

ARTHUR
(Buttoning his coat)
Fine. (Glancing at his watch) Gentlemen, if you don't need me for any-
thing anymore, I would like to get to my analyst. Good morning.
(He strides to the door.)

THE RABBI

Peace be unto you.
(ARTHUR pauses at the front door, a little amused at the archaic greeting.)

ARTHUR

Peace be unto you, Rabbi.
(He opens the door and goes out.)

THE RABBI

Who was that fellow?

ZITORSKY

Who knows? The Sexton found him on the street.

THE RABBI
(Buttoning his own coat)
Well, I have to be down at the printer's. A dybbuk. Really. What an
unusual thing. Is Mr. Foreman a mystical man? By the way, Mr. Alper—
Mr. Zitorsky—you weren't at the meeting of the Brotherhood last night.
I think you should take a more active interest in the synagogue. Did you
receive an announcement of the meeting? Please come next time. (He finds
his briefcase) Ah, there it is, good. (He heads for the door) I would like to
know what the Korpotchniker said about this. Will you be here later
today? I'll drop in. Let me know what happens. You better call the girl's
family right away, Alper. Good morning. Peace be with.

ALPER *and* ZITORSKY

Peace be with you, Rabbi.

(THE RABBI *exits. The two old men regard each other a little balefully and then shuffle to* THE RABBI's *office, where* ALPER *sits down and puts his hand on the phone, resting it on the receiver, quite depressed by the turn of events. In the synagogue,* THE CABALIST *is huddled in prayer, and* THE SEXTON *has gotten a broom out and is sweeping an upstage area. A long moment of hushed silence fills the stage.*)

ALPER
(His hand still on the phone)

Zitorsky, let us reason this out.

ZITORSKY

Absolutely.

ALPER
(The Talmudic scholar)

If I call the girl's home, there are two possibilities. Either she is home or she is not home. If she is home, why call? If she is not home, then these are two possibilities. Either her father has already called the police, or he has not called the police. If he has already called the police, then we are wasting a telephone call. If he has not called the police, he will call them. If he calls the police, then there are two possibilities. Either they will take the matter seriously or they will not. If they don't take the matter seriously, why bother calling them? If they take the matter seriously, they will rush down here to find out what we already know, so what gain will have been made? Nothing. Have I reasoned well, Zitorsky?

ZITORSKY

You have reasoned well.

ALPER

Between you and me, Zitorsky, how many people are there on the streets at this hour that we couldn't spot the girl in a minute? Why should we trouble the immense machinery of the law? We'll go out and find the girl ourselves.

(They are both up in a minute, buttoning their coats and hurrying to the front door, where they pause.)

ZITORSKY
(Regarding ALPER with awe)

Alper, what a rogue you are!

(ALPER accepts the compliment graciously, and they both dart out into the street. Then, out of the hollow hush of the stage, THE CABALIST's *voice rises*

into a lovely chant as he rocks back and forth, his eyes closed in religious ecstasy.)

THE CABALIST
(Singing slowly and with profound conviction)
"I believe with perfect faith in the coming of the Messiah, and though he
   tarry, I will wait daily for his coming.
I believe with perfect faith that there will be a resurrection of the dead
   at the time when it shall please the Creator,
   blessed be His name,
   and exalted the remembrance of him for ever and ever."
   (The front door opens, and THE GIRL *comes rushing in, holding a beautifully bound leather book. She looks quickly around the synagogue, now
   empty except for* THE SEXTON *and* THE CABALIST, *and then hurries to*
   THE RABBI's *office, which is of course also empty. A kind of panic sweeps
   over her, and she rushes out into the synagogue again, to* THE SEXTON.)

THE GIRL
Mr. Bleyer, the young man that was here, do you know…*(She whirls as
the front door opens behind her and* ARTHUR *comes in. We have the feeling he
also has been, if not running, at least walking very quickly. He and* THE GIRL
stare at each other for a moment. Then she says to him—) I went home to get
this book for you. I wanted you to have this book I told you about.

ARTHUR
(Quietly)
I just simply couldn't go till I knew you were all right.
   *(For a moment they stand poised, staring at each other. Then she sweeps
   across the stage and flings herself into his arms.)*

THE GIRL
(Crying out)
Oh, I love you. I love you. I love you…
   (They stand, locked in embrace. THE CABALIST's *voice rises again in a
   deeply primitive chant, exquisite in its atavistic ardor.)*

THE CABALIST
"For Thy salvation I hope, O Lord! I hope, O Lord, for thy salvation. O
   Lord, for Thy salvation I hope!
For Thy salvation I hope, O Lord! I hope, O Lord, for Thy salvation! O
   Lord, for Thy salvation I hope!"

The Curtain Falls

Scene 2

*It is now several hours later. A silent, dozing quiet has settled over the syna-
gogue. Indeed,* THE CABALIST *has dozed off over a thick tome at the upstage desk
on the far side of the altar, his shawl-enshrouded head lying on his book.* THE
GIRL, *too, is napping, curled up in the worn leather armchair in* THE RABBI's
office. THE SEXTON *is sitting like a cobbler on a chair stage left.* ALPER *and
ZITORSKY sit drowsily on two wooden chairs, center stage. Only* ARTHUR *moves
restlessly around the synagogue. He looks into* THE RABBI's *office, checking on
THE GIRL, studies her sleeping sweetness, somehow deeply troubled. All is still, all
is quiet.*

In the synagogue, THE CABALIST *awakens suddenly and sits bolt upright, as if
he has just had the most bizarre dream. He stares wide-eyed at the wall in front
of him. He rises, and moves slowly downstage, his face a study in quiet awe.
Apparently, he has had a profoundly moving dream, and he puts his hand to his
brow as if to keep his thoughts from tumbling out. An expression of exaltation
spreads across his wan, lined, bearded old face. His eyes are wide with terror.*

THE CABALIST
(Whispering in awe)
"Blessed be the Lord. Blessed be the Lord. Blessed be the Lord." *(He
stands now almost at the footlights, staring out over the audience, his face illuminated with ecstasy. He cries out)* Praise ye the Lord! Hallelujah! Praise ye the
Lord! Hallelujah! It is good to sing praises unto our God; for it is pleasant
and praise is seemly. Praise ye the Lord! Hallelujah!
*(ALPER has watched THE CABALIST with drowsy interest. THE CABALIST
turns and stares at him.)*

THE CABALIST
My dear friends, my dear, dear friends...
*(Tears fill his old eyes, and his mouth works without saying anything for a
moment.)*

ALPER
Are you all right, Hirschman?

THE CABALIST
(Awed by an inner wonder)
I was studying the codification of the Law, especially those paragraphs
beginning with the letters of my father's name—because today is my
father's day of memorial. I have brought some honey cake here, in my

father's memory. I have it somewhere in a paper bag. Where did I put it? I brought it here last night. It is somewhere around—and as I studied, I dozed off and my head fell upon the Book of Mishna. Oh, my dear friends, I have prayed to the Lord to send me a dream, and He has sent me a dream. I dreamt that I was bathing in a pool of the clearest mountain water. And a man of great posture appeared on the bank, and he said to me: "Rabbi, give me your blessing, for I go to make a journey." And I looked closely on the man, and it was the face of my father. And I said unto him: "My father, why do you call me Rabbi? For did I not lustfully throw away the white fringed shawl of the rabbinate and did I not mock the Lord to thy face? And have I not spent my life in prayer and penitence so that I might cleanse my soul?" And my father smiled upon me, and his bearded face glowed with gentleness, and he said unto me: "Rise from your bath, my son, and put upon you these robes of white linen which I have arrayed for you. For thy soul is cleansed and thou hast found a seat among the righteous. And the countenance of the Lord doth smile upon thee this day. So rise and rejoice and dance in the Holy Place. For thine is eternal peace and thou art among the righteous." Thus was the dream that I dreamt as my head lay on the Book of Mishna. *(He lifts his head and stares upward)* The Lord shall reign for ever. Thy God, O Zion, unto all generations. Praise ye the Lord. Hallelujah! *(He stares distractedly around him)* Where is the wine, Sexton? The wine! There was a fine new bottle on Friday! I have been given a seat among the righteous! For this day have I lived and fasted! I have been absolved! Hallelujah! Hallelujah!— Ah, the cakes! Here! Good!—*(He is beginning to laugh)* I shall dance before the Holy Ark! Sexton! Sexton! Distribute the macaroons that all may share this exalted day! The Lord hath sent me a sign, and the face of my father smiled upon me!

> *(As abruptly as he had begun to laugh he begins to sob in the effusion of his joy. He sinks onto a chair and cries unashamedly.)*

ALPER

My dear Hirschman, how delighted we are for you.

THE SEXTON

> *(Offering some honey cake to ZITORSKY)*

You want some cake there, Zitorsky?

ZITORSKY

I'll have a little wine too as long as we're having a party.

> *(THE SEXTON scurries off to the lectern, the bottom of which is a cabinet containing various sacramental things and wine.)*

ARTHUR
(Who has been watching all this, rather taken by it)
What happened?

ALPER
Mr. Hirschman has received a sign from God. His father has forgiven him, and his soul has been cleansed.

ARTHUR
That's wonderful.

ZITORSKY
(To THE SEXTON, *now pouring wine from a decanter)*
I'll tell you, Bleyer, if you have a little whiskey, I prefer that. Wine makes me dizzy.

THE SEXTON
Where would I get whiskey? This is a synagogue, not a saloon.

ZITORSKY
(Taking his glass of wine)
Happiness, Hirschman.

ALPER
Some wine for our young friend here. *(To* ARTHUR*)* Will you join Mr. Hirschman in his moment of exaltation?

ARTHUR
Yes, of course.
*(*THE SEXTON, *who is pouring the wine and sipping a glass of his own as he pours, has begun to hum a gay Chassidic tune. He hands* ARTHUR *his glass.)*

ZITORSKY
(Handing his glass back for a refill)
Oh, will Schlissel eat his heart out when he finds out he is missing a party.

ALPER
(Making a toast)
Rabbi Israel, son of Isaac, I think it is fitting we use your rabbinical title—we bow in reverence to you.

THE CABALIST
(Deeply touched)
My dear, dear friends, I cannot describe to you my happiness.

ZITORSKY
There hasn't been a party here since that boy's confirmation last month. Wasn't that a skimpy feast for a confirmation? Another glass, please,

Sexton. Oh, I'm beginning to sweat. Some confirmation party that was! The boy's father does a nice business in real estate and all he brings down is a few pieces of sponge cake and one bottle of whiskey. One bottle of whiskey for fifty people! As much whiskey as I had couldn't even cure a toothache. Oh, boy, am I getting dizzy. When I was a boy, I could drink a whole jar of potato cider. You remember that potato cider we used to have in Europe? It could kill a horse. Oh, boy, what kind of wine is that? My legs are like rubber already.

(ZITORSKY *suddenly stamps his foot and executes a few brief Chassidic dance steps.*)

ALPER

This is not bad wine, you know. A pleasant bouquet.

ZITORSKY
(*Wavering over to* ARTHUR)

Have a piece of cake, young man. What does it say in the Bible? "Go eat your food with gladness and drink your wine with a happy mind?" Give the boy another glass.

ARTHUR
(*Smiling*)

Thank you. I'm still working on this one.

(THE CABALIST *suddenly raises his head and bursts into a gay Chassidic chant.*)

THE CABALIST
(*Bursting into song*)

"Light is sown,
  sown for the righteous,
  and joy for the upright,
  the upright in heart.
Oh,
  light is sown,
  sown for the righteous…"

ZITORSKY
(*Gaily joining in*)

"and joy for the upright,
  the upright in heart.
Oh!"

(THE CABALIST *and* ZITORSKY *take each other's shoulders and begin to dance in the formless Chassidic pattern. They are in wonderful spirits.*)

"light is sown,
  sown for the righteous…"

(THE SEXTON and ALPER join in, clapping their hands and eventually joining the dance so that the four old Jews form a small ring, their arms around each other's shoulders, their old feet kicking exuberantly as they stamp about in a sort of a circular pattern.)

ALL

"...and joy for the upright,
the upright in heart."
Oh!
Light is sown,
sown for the righteous,
and joy for the upright,
the upright in heart.

(Round and round they stomp and shuffle, singing out lustily, sweat form-ing in beads on their brows. The words are repeated over and over again until they degenerate, from the shortness of breath of the singers, into a "bi-bu-bu-bi-bi-bi-bi-bi-bi-bibibi." ARTHUR watches, delighted. Finally, ALPER, gasping for breath, breaks out of the ring and staggers to a chair.)

THE CABALIST

A good sixty years I haven't danced! Oh, enough! Enough! My heart feels as if it will explode!

(He staggers, laughing, from the small ring of dancers and sits down, gasping for air.)

ALPER

Some more wine, Hirschman?

THE CABALIST
(Gasping happily)

Oh!

(ZITORSKY looks up, noticing THE GIRL, who, awakened by the romping, has sidled out into the synagogue and has been watching the gaiety with delight. ZITORSKY eyes her wickedly for a moment; then advances on her, his arm outstretched, quite the old cock-of-the-walk.)

ZITORSKY

Bi-bi-bi-bi-bi-bi-bi...

(He seizes her in his arms and begins to twirl around, much to her delight. She dances with him, her skirts whirling and her feet twinkling, laughing at the sheer physical excitement of it all. ZITORSKY supplies the music, a gay chant, the lyrics of which consist of: "Bi-bi-bi-bi-bi-bi-bi-bi...")

THE CABALIST

The last time I danced was on the occasion of the last Day of the Holiday of Tabernacles in 1896. I was seventeen years old. *(A sudden frightened frown sweeps across his face. He mutters)* Take heed for the girl, for the dybbuk will be upon her soon.

ALPER
(Leaning to him)
What did you say, Israel son of Isaac?
(THE CABALIST *turns to* THE GIRL *dancing with* ZITORSKY, *and stares at her.)*

THE CABALIST
Let the girl rest, Zitorsky, for she struggles with the dybbuk. Behold.
(THE GIRL *has indeed broken away from* ZITORSKY *and has begun an improvised dance of her own. The gaiety is gone from her face and is replaced by a sullen lasciviousness. The dance she does is a patently provocative one. She dances slowly at first, and then with increasing abandon and wantonness.* ZITORSKY *recoils in horror.* THE GIRL *begins to stamp her feet and to whirl more and more wildly. Her eyes grow bold and flashing and she begins to shout old Gypsy words, a mongrel Russian, Oriental in intonation.* THE CABALIST *now slowly moves to* THE GIRL, *who, when she becomes aware of his coming close, abruptly stops her dance and stands stock-still, her face a mask of extravagant pain.* THE CABALIST *regards her gently.)*

THE CABALIST
Lie down, my child, and rest.
(At this quiet suggestion, THE GIRL *begins to sway as if she is about to faint.)*

THE GIRL
I feel so faint, so faint.
(She sinks slowly to the floor, not quite in a swoon, but on the verge. ARTHUR *races to her side.)*

ARTHUR
Do we have any water here?

ALPER
Wine would be better. Sexton, give her some wine.
(THE SEXTON *hurries with some one's glass.)*

ARTHUR
(Holding THE GIRL's *head)*
Is she a sickly girl?

ALPER
(Bending over them)
She was never sick a day in her life.

THE SEXTON

Here's the wine.

ZITORSKY

(*To* THE SEXTON)

Did I tell you? Did I tell you?

THE GIRL

I feel so faint. I feel so faint.

ARTHUR

(*Bringing the glass of wine to her lips*)

Sip some of this.

THE GIRL

(*Murmuring*)

Save me...save me...

THE CABALIST

The dybbuk weakens her. I have seen this once before.

THE SEXTON

(*To* ZITORSKY)

When you told me about this dybbuk, I didn't believe you.

ZITORSKY

So did I tell you right?

THE SEXTON

Oh, boy.

ARTHUR

Help me get her onto the chair in there.

ALPER

Yes, of course.

THE SEXTON

Here, let me help a little.

(*Between them, they manage to get* THE GIRL *up and walk her slowly to* THE RABBI's *office, where they gently help her lie down on the leather sofa.*)

THE CABALIST

(*To* ZITORSKY)

They haven't heard from Mr. Foreman yet?

ZITORSKY

No, we're waiting.

THE CABALIST

(*Frowning*)

It is not that far to Williamsburg. Well, the girl will sleep now.

(He walks slowly to the door of THE RABBI's *office, followed by a wary* ZITORSKY. ALPER *returns to the synagogue proper to join the other old men, and, for the briefest of moments,* ARTHUR *finds himself alone with* THE GIRL, *holding her head gently in his arms. Suddenly he kisses her brow and lightly strokes her hair. He rises quickly as the others return.)*

ARTHUR

I think she's fallen asleep.

ALPER

Thank heavens for that.

ARTHUR

Look, I'm going to call her family. She may be quite ill. I think we'd all feel a lot better if she were in the hands of a doctor. If one of you will please give me her home phone number…*(Just a little annoyed, for nobody answers him)* Please, gentleman, I really don't think it's wise to pursue this nonsense any longer.

THE CABALIST

It is not nonsense. I do not speak of dybbuks casually. As a young man, I saw hundreds of people come to my father claiming to be possessed, but, of all these, only two were true dybbuks. Of these two, one was a girl very much like this poor girl, and, even before the black candles and the ram's horn could be brought for the exorcism, she sank down onto the earth and died. I tell you this girl is possessed, and she will die, clutching at her throat and screaming for redemption unless the dybbuk is exorcised. *(He stares at the others and nods his head)* She will die. Wake the girl. I will take her to the Korpotchniker myself.

ALPER

Zitorsky, wake the girl. I will get her coat. Sexton, call a taxicab for Rabbi Israel. (ALPER, *who had been reaching for* THE GIRL's *coat, is stayed by* ARTHUR. *He looks up at the young man)* Young man, what are you doing?

ARTHUR

Mr. Alper, the girl is sick. There may be something seriously wrong with her.

ALPER

Young man, Rabbi Israel says she is dying.

ARTHUR

Well, in that case certainly, let me have her home telephone number.

ALPER

(Striding into THE RABBI's *office)*

You are presuming in matters that are no concern of yours.

ARTHUR
(Following)
They are as much my concern as they are yours. I have grown quite fond
of this girl. I want her returned to the proper authorities, right now. If
necessary, I shall call a policeman. Now, let's have no more nonsense.
*(ALPER sinks down behind the desk, glowering. A moment of silence fills
the room. Then* THE CABALIST, *who has been standing in the rear of the
office and watching with quiet interest, says—)*

THE CABALIST
The young man doesn't believe in dybbuks?

ARTHUR
I'm afraid not. I think you are all behaving like madmen.
(THE CABALIST considers this answer for a moment.)

THE CABALIST
I will tell you an old Chassidic parable. A deaf man passed by a house in
which a wedding party was going on. He looked in the window and saw all
the people there dancing and cavorting, leaping about and laughing.
However, since the man was deaf and could not hear the music of the fid-
dlers, he said to himself: "Ah, this must be a madhouse." Young man,
because you are deaf, must it follow that we are lunatics?

ARTHUR
You are quite right. I did not mean to mock your beliefs, and I apologize
for it. However, I am going to call the girl's father, and, if he wants to have
the girl exorcised, that's his business. *(He sits down behind the desk, puts his
hand on the receiver, and looks up at* ALPER*)* Well?

THE CABALIST
Give him the number, Mr. Alper. *(*ALPER *fishes an old address book out of
his vest pocket, thumbs through the pages, and hands the open book to* ARTHUR,
who begins to dial) There is no one home in the girl's house. Her father,
who wishes only to forget about the girl, has gone to his shop in the city,
and, at this moment, is overeating at his lunch in a dairy restaurant. The
stepmother has taken the younger children to her sister's. The girl's doctor has called the police and has gone about his rounds, and the police are
diffidently riding up and down the streets of the community, looking for
an old Jew and his granddaughter. *(*ARTHUR *says nothing, but simply waits
for an answer to his ring.* THE CABALIST *sits down on the arm of the couch to
contemplate. At last he says—)* I cannot understand why this young man does
not believe in dybbuks.

ALPER
It is symptomatic of the current generation, Rabbi Israel, to be utterly

disillusioned. Historically speaking, an era of prosperity following an era of hard times usually produces a number of despairing and quietistic philosophies, for the now prosperous people have found out they are just as unhappy as when they were poor. Thus when an intelligent man of such a generation discovers that two television sets have no more meaning than one or that he gets along no better with his wife in a suburban house than he did in their small city flat, he arrives at the natural assumption that life is utterly meaningless.

> THE CABALIST
>
> What an unhappy state of affairs.
>
> (ARTHUR *returns the receiver to its cradle.*)
>
> ARTHUR
> *(Muttering)*
>
> Nobody home.
>
> THE CABALIST
> *(To* ARTHUR*)*
>
> Is that true, young man that you believe in absolutely nothing?
>
> ARTHUR
>
> Not a damn thing.
>
> THE CABALIST
>
> There is no truth, no beauty, no infinity, no known, no unknown.
>
> ARTHUR
>
> Precisely.
>
> THE CABALIST
>
> Young man, you are a fool.
>
> ARTHUR
>
> Really. I have been reading your book—the Book of Zohar. I am sure it has lost much in the translation, but, sir, any disciple of this abracadabra is presuming when he calls anyone else a fool.
>
> (ARTHUR *produces from his jacket the book* THE GIRL *gave him, and extends it to* THE CABALIST, *who accepts it, frowning.*)
>
> THE CABALIST
>
> You have been reading the Book of Zohar. Dear young man, one does not read the Book of Zohar, leaf through its pages, and make marginal notes. I have entombed myself in this slim volume for sixty years, raw with vulnerability to its hidden mysteries, and have sensed only a glimpse of its passion. Behind every letter of every word lies a locked image, and behind every image a sparkle of light of the ineffable brilliance of Infinity. But the concept of the Inexpressible Unknown is inconceivable to you. For you are a man possessed by the Tangible. If you cannot touch it with your fin-

gers, it simply does not exist. Indeed, that will be the epithet of your generation—that you took everything for granted and believed in nothing. It is a very little piece of life that we know. How shall I say it? I suggest it is wiser to believe in dybbuks than in nothing at all.

ARTHUR

Mr. Hirschman, a good psychiatrist—even a poor one—could strip your beliefs in ten minutes. You may think of yourself as a man with a God, but I see you as a man obsessed with guilt who has invented a God so he can be forgiven. You have invented it all—the guilt, God, forgiveness, the whole world, dybbuks, love, passion, fulfillment—the whole fantastic mess of pottage—because it is unbearable for you to bear the pain of insignificance. None of these things exist. You've made them all up. The fact is, I have half a mind to let you go through with this exorcism, for, after all the trumpetings of rams' horns and the bellowing of incantations and after the girl falls in a swoon on the floor—I assure you, she will rise up again as demented as she ever was, and I wonder what bizarre rationale and mystique you will expound to explain all that. Now, if the disputation is at an end, I am going to call the police.
(He picks up the receiver again and dials the operator.)

ALPER

Well, what can one say to such bitterness?

THE CABALIST
(Shrugs)
One can only say that the young man has very little regard for psychiatrists.
(The front door to the synagogue bursts open, and FOREMAN *and* SCHLISSEL, *come hurtling in, breathing heavily and in a state of absolute confusion.* ALPER *darts out into the synagogue proper and stares at them.)*

SCHLISSEL

Oh, thank God, the synagogue is still here!

ALPER

Well?

SCHLISSEL
(He can hardly talk, he is so out of breath)
Well, what?

ALPER

What did the Korpotchniker say?

SCHLISSEL

Who knows?! Who saw the Korpotchniker?! We've been riding in subways for four hours! Back and forth, in this train, in that train! I am convinced there is no such place as Williamsburg and there is no such person as the Korpotchniker Rabbi! I tell you, twice we got off at two different stations, just to see daylight, and, as God is my witness, both times we were in New Jersey!

FOREMAN

Oh, I tell you, I am sick from driving so much.

ALPER

Idiot! You didn't take the Brighton train!

SCHLISSEL

We took the Brighton train! (*He waves both arms in a gesture of final frustration*) We took all the trains! I haven't had a bite to eat all morning. Don't tell me about Brighton trains! Don't tell me about anything! Leave me alone, and the devil take your whole capitalist economy!

(ZITORSKY, THE SEXTON *and* THE CABALIST *have all come out to see what the noise is all about. Even* ARTHUR *is standing in the office doorway, listening to all this.*)

SCHLISSEL

We asked this person, we asked that person. This person said that train. That person said this train. We went to a policeman. He puts us on a train. The conductor comes in, says: "Last stop." We get out. As God is my witness, New Jersey. We get back on that train. The conductor says: "Get off next station and take the other train." We get off the next station and take the other train. A man says: "Last stop." We get out. New Jersey!

(*In* THE RABBI's *office,* THE GIRL *suddenly sits bolt upright, her eyes clenched tight in pain, screaming terribly, her voice shrill with anguish.*)

FOREMAN

(*Racing to her side*)

Oh, my God! Evelyn! Evelyn! What is it?!

(THE GIRL *clutches at her throat and screams.*)

THE GIRL

Save me! Save me! Save me!

(ZITORSKY *and* THE SEXTON *begin to mutter rapid prayers under their breath.*)

ALPER

(*Putting his arm around* FOREMAN)

David, she's very ill. We think she may be dying.

(ARTHUR *has raced to* THE GIRL. *He sits on the couch beside her and takes her in his arms.*)

ARTHUR

Call a doctor.

FOREMAN
(In a panic, to ALPER*)*
He says I should call a doctor.
*(*ARTHUR *puts his hand to his brow and shakes his head as if to clear it of shock and confusion.)*

ALPER
(Crossing to THE CABALIST*)*
Save her, Rabbi Israel. You have had your sign from God. You are among the righteous.
*(*ARTHUR *turns slowly and regards the silent betallithed form of the little* CABALIST.*)*

ARTHUR
(To THE CABALIST, *his voice cracking under emotions he was unaware he still had)*
For God's sakes, perform your exorcism or whatever has to be done. I think she's dying.
*(*THE CABALIST *regards* ARTHUR *for a moment with the profoundest gentleness. Then he turns and, with an authoritative voice, instructs* THE SEXTON.*)*

THE CABALIST
Sexton, we shall need black candles, the ram's horn, prayer shawls of white wool, and there shall be ten Jews for a quorum to witness before God this awesome ceremony.

THE SEXTON
Just plain black candles?

THE CABALIST
Just plain black candles.
*(*THE SEXTON *is already hurrying into his coat.* ALPER *moves quietly up to* FOREMAN, *standing in the office doorway, and touches his old friend's shoulder in a gesture of awe and compassion.* FOREMAN, *at the touch, begins to cry and buries his shaking old head on his friend's shoulder.* ALPER *embraces him.)*

ZITORSKY
(In the synagogue, to SCHLISSEL*)*
I am absolutely shaking—shaking.
*(*ARTHUR, *having somewhat recovered his self-control, sinks down behind the desk, frowning, confused by all that is going on, and moved by a complex of feeling he cannot understand at all.)*

The Curtain Falls

ACT III

Half an hour later.

At rise, THE GIRL *is sitting in* THE RABBI's *office, perched on the couch, nervous, frightened, staring down at her restlessly twisting fingers.* FOREMAN *sits behind* THE RABBI's *desk, wrapped in his own troubled thoughts. He wears over his suit a long white prayer shawl with thick black stripes, like that worn by* THE CABALIST *throughout the play.*

Indeed, all the men now wear these ankle-length white prayer shawls, except ARTHUR, *who, at rise, is also in* THE RABBI's *office, deep in thought.*

THE CABALIST *stands downstage left, his prayer shawl hooded over his head; he is leafing through a volume, preparing the prayers for the exorcism.*

THE SEXTON *is standing by the wall phone, the receiver cradled to his ear, waiting for an answer to a call he has just put in. He is more or less surrounded by* ALPER, SCHLISSEL, *and* ZITORSKY.

ZITORSKY
How about Milsky the butcher?

ALPER
Milsky wouldn't come. Ever since they gave the seat by the East Wall to Kornblum, Milsky said he wouldn't set foot in this synagogue again. Every synagogue I have belonged to, there have always been two kosher butchers who get into a fight over who gets the favored seat by the East Wall during the High Holy Days, and the one who doesn't abandons the congregation in a fury, and the one who does always seems to die before the next High Holy Days.

SCHLISSEL
Kornblum the butcher died? I didn't know Kornblum died.

ALPER
Sure. Kornblum died four years ago.

SCHLISSEL
Well, he had lousy meat, believe me, may his soul rest in peace.
(THE SEXTON *has hung up, recouped his dime, reinserted it, and is dialing again.*)

ZITORSKY
(*To* THE SEXTON)
No answer?

161

(THE SEXTON *shakes his head.*)

THE SEXTON

I'm calling Harris.

SCHLISSEL

Harris? You tell an eighty-two-year old man to come down and make a tenth for an exorcism, and he'll have a heart attack talking on the phone with you.

THE SEXTON
(Dialing)

Well, what else am I to do? It is hard enough to assemble ten Jews under the best of circumstances, but in the middle of the afternoon on a Thursday it is an absolute nightmare. Aronowitz is in Miami. Klein the furrier is at his job in Manhattan. It is a workday today. Who shall I call? *(He waits for someone to answer)* There are many things that I have to do. The tapestries on the Ark, as you see, are faded and need needlework, and the candelabras and silver goblet for the saying of the Sabbath benediction are tarnished and dull. But every second of my day seems to be taken up with an incessant search for ten Jews...*(On the phone)* Hello, Harris. Harris, this is Bleyer the Sexton. We need you badly down here in the synagogue for a quorum...If I told you why, you wouldn't come...All right, I'll tell you, but, in God's name, don't tell another soul, not even your daughter-in-law...

SCHLISSEL

My daughter-in-law, may she grow like an onion with her head in the ground.

THE SEXTON
(On the phone)

Hirschman is going to exorcise a dybbuk from Foreman's granddaughter...I said, Hirschman is...A dybbuk. That's right, a dybbuk...Right here in Mineola...That's right. Why should Mineola be exempt from dybbuks?

ALPER
(Thinking of names)

There used to be a boy came down here every morning, about eight, nine years ago—a devout boy with forelocks and side-curls—a pale boy, who was studying to be rabbi at the seminary.

THE SEXTON
(On the phone)

Harris, this is not a joke.

SCHLISSEL

Chwatkin.

ALPER

That's right, Chwatkin. That was the boy's name. Chwatkin. Maybe we could call him. Does he still live in the community?

SCHLISSEL

He's a big television actor. He's on television all the time. Pinky Sims. He's an actor.

ZITORSKY

Pinky Sims? That's a name for a rabbinical student?

THE SEXTON

Put on your sweater and come down.

ALPER

(*To* THE SEXTON, *who has just hung up*)

So Harris is coming?

THE SEXTON

Yes, he's coming. So with Harris, that makes eight, and I am frankly at the end of my resources. I don't know who else to call.

ALPER

This is terrible. Really. God manifests Himself in our little synagogue, and we can't even find ten Jews to say hello.

THE SEXTON

I shall have to go out in the street and get two strangers. (*Putting on his coat*) Well, I don't look forward to this at all. I will have to stop people on the street, ask them if they are Jewish—which is bad enough—and then explain to them I wish them to attend the exorcism of a dybbuk—I mean, surely you can see the futility of it.

ALPER

(*To* THE CABALIST, *who is crossing now en route to the office*)

We can only get eight. A disgrace. Really. We shall not have the exorcism for lack of two Jews.

THE SEXTON

(*On his way out*)

All right, I'm going.

(*He exits.*)

ZITORSKY

(*To* SCHLISSEL)

In those days when I was deceiving my wife, I used to tell her I was entertaining out-of-town buyers. I once told her I was entertaining out-of-town buyers every night for almost three weeks. It was a foolhardy thing to do because even my wife could tell business was not that good. So one night she came down to my loft on Thirty-Sixth Street and walked in and caught me with—well, I'm sure I've told you this story before.

SCHLISSEL

Many times.

(THE CABALIST *enters the office. Upon his entrance,* THE GIRL *stands abruptly, obviously deeply disturbed and barely in control of herself. She turns from* THE CABALIST *and shades her eyes with her hand to hide her terror.* FOREMAN *looks up briefly. He seems to be in a state of shock.* THE CABALIST *sits down on the couch, letting his heavy prayer shawl fall back on his shoulders, and studies his hands folded patiently between his knees. After a moment, he speaks.*)

THE CABALIST
(*Quietly*)

Dybbuk, I am Israel son of Isaac. My father was Isaac son of Asher, and I wear his fringed shawl on my shoulders as I talk to you.

(*Upon these words,* THE GIRL *suddenly contorts her form, as if seized by a violent cramp. She clutches her stomach and bends low, and soft sobs begin to come out of her*)

THE CABALIST

Reveal yourself to me.

THE GIRL
(*In the voice of the dybbuk*)

I am Hannah Luchinsky.

(*In the synagogue,* ALPER, SCHLISSEL, *and* ZITORSKY *begin to edge— quite frightened—to the open office door.* ARTHUR *watches from his seat behind* THE RABBI's *desk.*)

THE CABALIST

Why do you possess this girl's body?

THE GIRL
(*Twisting and contorting; in the voice of the dybbuk*)

My soul was lost at sea, and these is no one to say the prayers for the dead over me.

THE CABALIST

I will strike a bargain with you. Leave this girl's body through her smallest finger, doing her no damage, not even a scratch, and I shall sit on wood for you for the First Seven Days of Mourning and shall plead for your soul for the First Thirty Days and shall say the prayers for the dead over you three times a day for the Eleven Months and light the Memorial Lamp each year upon the occasion of your death. I ask you to leave this girl's body.

(THE GIRL *laughs quietly.*)

THE GIRL
(In the voice of the dybbuk)

You give me short weight, for you will yourself be dead before the prayers for the new moon.

(In the office doorway, the three old men shudder. FOREMAN *looks up slowly.* THE CABALIST *closes his eyes.)*

THE CABALIST
(Quietly)

How do you know this?

THE GIRL
(In the voice of the dybbuk)

Your soul will fly straight to the Heavenly Gates, and you will be embraced by the Archangel Mihoel.

THE CABALIST

Then I enjoin the Angel of Death to speed his way. Dybbuk, I order you to leave the body of this girl.

*(THE GIRL's *face suddenly flashes with malevolence.*)*

THE GIRL
(In the voice of the dybbuk, shouting)

No! I seek vengeance for these forty years of limbo! I was betrayed in my youth and driven to the Evil Impulse against my will! I have suffered beyond belief, and my spirit has lived in dunghills and in piles of ashes, and I demand the soul of David son of Abram be cast through Gilgul for the space of forty years times ten to gasp for air in the sea in which I drowned...

FOREMAN
(Standing in terror)

No! No!

THE GIRL
(In the voice of the dybbuk)

...so that my soul may have peace! A soul for a soul! That is my bargain.

FOREMAN
(Shouting)

Let it be then! Leave my granddaughter in peace and I will give my soul in exchange.

THE CABALIST
(With ringing authority)

The disposition of David son of Abram's soul will not be decided here.

It's fall and ascent has been ordained by the second universe of angels. The bargain cannot be struck! Dybbuk, hear me. I order you to leave the body of this girl through her smallest finger, causing her no pain nor damage, and I give you my word, prayers will be said over you in full measure. But if you abjure these words, then must I proceed against you with malediction and anathema.

THE GIRL
(Laughs)

Raise not thy mighty arm against me, for it has no fear for me. A soul for a soul. That is my bargain.

(THE GIRL *suddenly begins to sob.*)

THE CABALIST
(To ALPER*)*

We shall have to prepare for the exorcism.

ALPER

I thought that would be the case.

THE GIRL
(Sitting down on the couch, frightened, in her own voice)

I am so afraid.

FOREMAN

There is nothing to fear. It will all be over in a minute, like having a tooth pulled, and you will walk out of here a cheerful child.

SCHLISSEL
(Ambling back into the synagogue proper with ZITORSKY *and* ALPER*)*

I tell you, I'd feel a lot better if the Korpotchniker was doing this. If you are going to have a tooth pulled, at least let it be by a qualified dentist.

ZITORSKY

I thought Hirschman handled himself very well with that dybbuk.

SCHLISSEL
(To ALPER *and* ZITORSKY*)*

If I tell you all something, promise you will never throw it back in my face.

ZITORSKY

What?

SCHLISSEL

I am beginning to believe she is really possessed by a dybbuk.

ZITORSKY

I'm beginning to get used to the whole thing.

(THE CABALIST *has stood and moved upstage to the rear wall of the syna-*

gogue, where he stands in meditation. FOREMAN *is sitting again, somewhat numb, beside his granddaughter. After a moment,* THE GIRL *speaks.)*

THE GIRL
I am very frightened, Arthur.

ARTHUR
(Rises)
Well, I spoke to my analyst, as you know, and he said he didn't think this exorcism was a bad idea at all. The point is, if you really do believe you are possessed by a dybbuk...

THE GIRL
Oh, I do.

ARTHUR
Well, then, he feels exorcism might be a good form of shock treatment that will make you more responsive to psychiatric therapy and open the door to an eventual cure. Mr. Hirschman assures me it is a painless ceremony. So you really have nothing to be frightened of.

THE GIRL
Will you be here?

ARTHUR
Of course. Did you think I wouldn't?
(FOREMAN moves slowly out into the synagogue, as if to ask something of THE CABALIST.*)*

THE GIRL
I always sense flight in you.

ARTHUR
Really.

THE GIRL
You are always taking to your heels, Arthur. Especially in moments like now when you want to be tender. I know that you love me, or I couldn't be so happy with you, but the whole idea of love seems to terrify you, and you keep racing off to distant detachments. I feel that if I reached out for your cheek now, you would turn your head or, in some silent way, clang the iron gates shut on me. You have some strange dybbuk all of your own, some sad little turnkey, who drifts about inside of you, locking up all the little doors, and saying, "You are dead. You are dead." You do love me, Arthur. I know that.

ARTHUR
(Gently)
I wish you well, Evelyn. We can at least say that.

THE GIRL

I love you. I want so very much to be your wife. *(She stares at him, her face glowing with love. She says quietly)* I will make you a good home, Arthur. You will be very happy with me.

(He regards her for a moment, caught by her wonder. He reaches forward and lightly touches her cheek. She cannot take her eyes from him)

THE GIRL

I adore you, Arthur.

ARTHUR
(With deep gentleness)

You are quite mad.

(They look at each other. ARTHUR stands.)

THE GIRL

You think our getting married is impractical.

ARTHUR

Yes, I would say it was at the least impractical.

THE GIRL

Because I am insane and you are suicidal.

ARTHUR

I do think those are two reasons to give one pause.

THE GIRL

Well, at least we begin with futility. Most marriages take years to arrive there.

ARTHUR

Don't be saucy, Evelyn.

THE GIRL
(Earnestly)

Oh, Arthur, I wouldn't suggest marriage if I thought it was utterly unfeasible. I think we can make a go of it. I really do. I know you have no faith in my exorcism...

ARTHUR

As I say, it may be an effective shock therapy.

THE GIRL

But we could get married this minute, and I still think we could make a go of it. I'm not a dangerous schizophrenic; I just hallucinate. I could keep your house for you. I did for my father very competently before he remarried. I'm a good cook, and you do find me attractive, don't you? I love you, Arthur. You are really very good for me. I retain reality remarkably well with you. I know I could be a good wife. Many schizophrenics function quite well if one has faith in them.

ARTHUR
(*Touched by her earnestness*)
My dear Evelyn...

THE GIRL
I don't ask you to have faith in dybbuks or Gods or exorcisms—just in me.
(*He gently touches her cheek.*)

ARTHUR
How in heaven's name did we reach this point of talking marriage?

THE GIRL
It is a common point of discussion between people in love.
(*He kneels before her, takes her hand between his.*)

ARTHUR
(*Tenderly*)
I do not love you. Nor do you love me. We met five hours ago and exchanged the elementary courtesy of conversation—the rest is your own ingenuousness.

THE GIRL
I do not remember ever being as happy as I am this moment. I feel enchanted.
(*They are terribly close now. He leans to her, his arms moving to embrace her. And then he stops, and the moment is broken. He turns away, scowls, stands.*)

THE GIRL
You are in full flight again, aren't you?

ARTHUR
I reserve a certain low level of morality which includes not taking advantage of incompetent minors.

THE GIRL
Why can't you believe that I love you?

ARTHUR
I simply do not believe anybody loves anyone. Let's have an end to this.
(*He is abruptly aware that their entire love scene has been observed by the old men, who are clustered together in the open doorway of* THE RABBI's *office, beaming at them. With a furious sigh,* ARTHUR *strides to the door and shuts it in the old men's faces. He turns back to* THE GIRL, *scowling*) Really, this is all much too fanciful. Really, it is. In an hour, you will be back to your institution, where I may or may not visit you.

(THE GIRL *sits down slowly.*)

THE GIRL

If I were not already insane, the thought that I might not see you again would make me so.

ARTHUR

I don't know what you want of me.

THE GIRL
(One step from tears)
I want you to find the meaning of your life in me.

ARTHUR

But that's insane. How can you ask such an impossible thing?

THE GIRL

Because you love me.

ARTHUR
(Cries out)
I don't know what you mean by love! All it means to me is I shall buy you a dinner, take you to the theatre, and then straight to our tryst, where I shall reach under your blouse for the sake of tradition while you breathe hotly in my ear in a pretense of passion. We will mutter automatic endearments, nibbling at the sweat on each other's earlobes, all the while gracelessly fumbling with buttons and zippers, cursing under our breath the knots in our shoelaces, and telling ourselves that this whole comical business of zipping off our trousers is an act of nature like the pollination of weeds. Even in that one brief moment when our senses finally obliterate our individual alonenesses, we will hear ringing in our ears the reluctant creaking of mattress springs.

(THE GIRL *stares at him, awed by this bitter expostulation.*)

THE GIRL

You are possessed.

ARTHUR

At your age, I suppose, one still finds theatrical charm in this ultimate of fantasies, but when you have been backstage as often as I have, you will discover love to be an altogether shabby business of cold creams and costumes.

THE GIRL
(Staring at him)
You are possessed by a dybbuk that does not allow you to love.

ARTHUR
(Crying out again in sudden anguish)
Oh, leave me alone! Let's get on with this wretched exorcism!
(He strides to the door, suddenly turns, confused, disturbed, and would say something, but he doesn't know what. He opens the door to find the old men patiently waiting for him with beaming smiles. This disconcerts him and he turns to THE GIRL *again and is again at a loss for words. She stares at the floor.)*

THE GIRL
We could be very happy if you would have faith in me.
(He turns and shuffles out of THE RABBI's *office.)*

ARTHUR
(To the old men)
It was tasteless of you to gawk at us.
(He continues into the synagogue, trailed by the old men. He sits and is immediately surrounded by the old men.)

FOREMAN
Are you interested in this girl, young man, because my son is not a rich man, by any means, but he will give you a fine wedding, catered by good people, with a cantor...

ZITORSKY
And a choir.

FOREMAN
...Possibly, and a dowry perhaps in the amount of five hundred dollars which, believe me, is more than he can afford. However, I am told you are a professional man, a lawyer, and the father of the bride must lay out good money for such a catch.

ALPER *and* ZITORSKY
Sure...Absolutely.

FOREMAN
Of course, the girl is an incompetent and you will have to apply to the court to be appointed the committee of her person...

ALPER
...A formality, I assure you, once you have married her.

FOREMAN
As for the girl, I can tell you first hand, she is a fine Jewish girl...

ZITORSKY
Modest...

ALPER

Devout...

FOREMAN

...And she bakes first-rate pastries.

ARTHUR
(Staring at the gay old men with disbelief)
You are all mad, madder than the girl, and if I don't get out of here soon,
I shall be as mad as the rest.

ZITORSKY

A beauty, young man. Listen, it is said—better a full-bosomed wife than
to marry a Rothschild.

SCHLISSEL

Leave the man alone. We have all been miserably married for half a century ourselves. How can you in good faith recommend the institution?

ALPER

The girl is so obviously taken with him. It would be a good match.

FOREMAN
(Anxiously)
Perhaps, he is married already.

ALPER
(To ARTHUR*)*
My dear fellow, how wonderful to be in love.

ARTHUR

I love nothing!

THE CABALIST

Yes. The girl's quite right. He is possessed. He loves nothing. Love is an
act of faith, and yours is a faithless generation. That is your dybbuk.
(The front door of the synagogue opens, and THE SEXTON *slips quickly in,
quietly closing the door.)*

ARTHUR
(To THE CABALIST*)*
Don't you think it's time to get on with this exorcism?

THE CABALIST

Yes.
(He moves to the door of THE RABBI's *office, where he regards the supine
form of* THE GIRL *on the couch.)*

ALPER
(To THE SEXTON*)*
Did you get anybody?

(THE SEXTON *moves in his nervous way down into the synagogue. He has obviously been on the go since he left; sweat beads his brow, and he is breathing heavily.*)

THE SEXTON
(*Unbuttoning his coat and wiping his brow*)
Gentlemen, we are in the soup.

SCHLISSEL
You couldn't find anybody?

THE SEXTON
Actually, we have nine now, but the issue of a quorum has become an academic one. Oh, let me catch my breath. The Rabbi will be here in a few minutes.

ALPER
The Rabbi?

THE SEXTON
I saw him on Woodhaven Boulevard, and he said he would join us. Harris is on his way already. I saw him coming down the hill from his house. But the whole matter is academic.

ALPER
You told the Rabbi we need him to exorcise the girl's dybbuk?

THE SEXTON
Well, what else was I to say? He asked me what I needed a quorum for at one o'clock in the afternoon, and I told him, and he thought for a moment, and he said: "All right, I'll be there in a few minutes." He is quite a nice fellow, something of a press agent perhaps, but with good intentions. Oh, I am perspiring like an animal. I shall surely have the ague tomorrow. I have been running all over looking for Jews. I even went to Friedman the tailor. He wasn't even in town. So let me tell you. I was running back here. I turned the corner on Thirty-Third Road there, and I see parked right in front of the synagogue a police patrol car.
(*The others start.*)

ALPER
(*Looking up*)
Oh?

THE SEXTON
That's what I mean when I say we are in the soup.

SCHLISSEL
Did they say something to you?

THE SEXTON

Sure they said something. I tell you, my heart gave such a turn when I saw that police car there. They were sitting there, those two policemen, big strapping cossacks with dark faces like avenging angels, smoking cigarettes, and with their revolvers bulging through their blue overcoats. As I walked across the street to the synagogue, my knees were knocking.

ALPER

When was this? It was just now?

THE SEXTON

Just this second. Just before I came in the door...Hello, Harris, how are you?

(This last to the octogenarian, who, bundled in his heavy overcoat, muffler, and with his hat pulled down on his head, has just entered the synagogue.)

ZITORSKY

(To THE SEXTON*)*

So what happened?

HARRIS

(In his high shrill voice, as he unbuttons his overcoat)

Gentlemen! Have you heard about this dybbuk?

SCHLISSEL

Harris, we were all here at the time he called you.

THE SEXTON

Harris, did you see the police car outside?

SCHLISSEL

So what did the policeman say?

THE SEXTON

(Unbuttoning his collar and wiping his neck with a handkerchief)

This big strapping fellow with his uniform full of buttons looks up, he says: "You know a man named David Foreman? We're looking for him and his granddaughter, a girl, eighteen years old." Well?! Eh! Well, are we in the soup or not?

(SCHLISSEL goes to the front door, opens it a conspiratorial crack, and looks out.)

ARTHUR

I don't think the police will bother you if you get your exorcism started right away. They won't interrupt a religious ceremony, especially if they don't know what it is.

THE CABALIST
(Who has made up his own mind)
Sexton, fetch the black candles, one for each man.
(THE SEXTON scurries to THE RABBI's office, where the black candles are lying on the desk, wrapped in brown grocery paper.)

ARTHUR
(Moving to the front door)
I'll stand by the door and talk to the police if they come in.

SCHLISSEL
(Closing the front door)
They're out there all right.

THE CABALIST
(He looks about the little synagogue, immensely dignified now, almost beatified in his authority. The others wait on his words)
I shall want to perform the ablutions of the Cohanim. Is there a Levite among you?

SCHLISSEL
I am a Levite.

THE CABALIST
You shall pour the water on my hands.
(THE SEXTON scoots across the synagogue, carrying black candles to everyone.)

HARRIS
(Looking distractedly about)
What are we doing now? Where is the dybbuk?

ALPER
Harris, put on a prayer shawl.

HARRIS
(Moving nervously to the office door)
Is this actually a serious business then? Where is the dybbuk? Tell me because Bleyer the Sexton told me nothing...
(His words drift off into a mumble. He enters the office, sees THE GIRL sitting rigidly on the chair. He starts at the sight of her, snatches a prayer shawl from the carton, and, quite in terror, darts back into the synagogue.)

THE CABALIST
There is nothing in the Book of Codes which gives the procedure for exorcism, so I have selected those passages to read that I thought most apt. For the purpose of cleansing our souls, we shall recite the Al-chait, and we shall recite that prayer of atonement which begins: "Sons of man such as

sit in darkness." As you pray these prayers, let the image of God in any of His seventy-two faces rise before you.

ALPER
(Crossing into THE RABBI's *office)*
I'll get the books.

THE SEXTON
(Giving SCHLISSEL *a metal bowl and a pitcher)*
Fill it with water.

SCHLISSEL
I'm an atheist. Why am I mixed up in all this?

ALPER
We do not have a quorum. Will this be valid?

THE CABALIST
We will let God decide.

THE SEXTON
When shall I blow the ram's horn?

THE CABALIST
I shall instruct you when.

HARRIS
(Putting on his shawl)
What shall I do? Where shall I stand?

ZITORSKY
(To HARRIS*)*
Stand here, and do not be afraid.
*(*FOREMAN *comes out of* THE RABBI's *office carrying a long white woolen prayer shawl, which he gives to* ARTHUR.*)*

FOREMAN
(To ARTHUR*)*
I will show you how to put it on.
(He helps ARTHUR *enshroud himself in the prayer shawl.* SCHLISSEL *comes out of the washroom carefully carrying his brass bowl and the pitcher filled with water. He goes to* THE CABALIST, *who holds his white hands over the basin.* SCHLISSEL *carefully pours the water over them.* THE CABALIST *speaks with great distinctness.)*

THE CABALIST
"Blessed art Thou, O Lord our God, King of the Universe, who hath sanctified us by his commandments, and has commanded us to cleanse our hands."

ALL

Amen.

(The others watch until the last of the water has been poured over his hands. A sudden silence settles over the synagogue. They are all standing about now, eight men, cloaked in white, holding their prayer books. THE CABALIST *dries his hands on a towel handed to him by* SCHLISSEL. *He puts the towel down, rolls his sleeves down, takes his long shawl and, with a sweep of his arms, raises it over his head, lifts his face, and cries out—)*

THE CABALIST

"Thou knowest the secrets of eternity and the most hidden mysteries of all living. Thou searchest the innermost recesses, and tryest the reins and the heart. Nought is concealed from thee, or hidden from thine eyes. May it then be thy will, O Lord our God and God of our fathers, to forgive us for all our sins, to pardon us for all our iniquities, and to grant us remission for all our transgressions."

(As one, the other old men sweep their shawls over their heads and begin the ancient recital of their sins. They all face the Ark, standing in their places, bending and twisting at the knees and beating upon their breasts with the clenched fists of their right hands. They all pray individually, lifting their voices in a wailing of the spirit. ARTHUR *remains silent.)*

ALL

"For the sin which we have committed before thee under compulsion, or of our own will;

and for the sin which we have committed before thee in hardening of the heart!

For the sin which we have committed before thee unknowingly:"

ZITORSKY

And for the sin which we have committed before thee with utterance of the lips."

FOREMAN

"For the sin which we have committed before thee by unchastity;"

SCHLISSEL

"For the sin which we have committed before thee by scoffing;"

HARRIS

"For the sin which we have committed before thee by slander;

And for the sin which we have committed before thee by the stretched-forth neck of pride:"

(It is a deadly serious business, this gaunt confessional. The spectacle of the eight men, cloaked in white, crying out into the air the long series of their sins and their pleas for remission, has a suggestion of the fearsome bar-

barism of the early Hebrews. They stand, eyes closed, and in the fervor of communication with God, their faces pained with penitence. The last of the old men, HARRIS, *finally cries out the last lines of supplication, his thin voice all alone in the hush of the synagogue)*

"And also for the sins for which we are liable to any of the four death penalties inflicted by the court—stoning, burning, beheading, and strangling; for thou art the forgiver of Israel and the pardoner of the tribes of Jeshurun in every generation and beside thee we have no king, who pardoneth and forgiveth."

(Again, the silence falls over the stage.)

THE CABALIST

"Children of men, such as sit in darkness and in the shadow of death, being bound in affliction and iron, He brought them out of darkness, and the shadow of death."

THE OTHERS

"Children of men, such as sit in darkness and in the shadow of death, being bound in affliction and iron, He brought them out of darkness, and the shadow of death."

THE CABALIST

"Fools because of their transgressions and because of their iniquities are afflicted."

THE OTHERS

"Fools because of their transgressions and because of their iniquities are afflicted."

THE CABALIST

"They cry unto the Lord in their trouble, and He saveth them out of their distress."

(The repetition of the lines has its cumulative effect on ARTHUR. *His lips begin to move involuntarily, and soon he has joined the others, quietly muttering the words.)*

ARTHUR *and* THE OTHERS

"They cry unto the Lord in their trouble, and He saveth them out of their distress."

THE CABALIST

"Then He is gracious unto him and saith:"

ARTHUR *and* THE OTHERS

"Then He is gracious unto him and saith:"

THE CABALIST

"Deliver him from going down to the pit; I have found a ransom."

                                ARTHUR *and* THE OTHERS
"Deliver him from going down to the pit; I have found a ransom."
                                    THE CABALIST
Amen.

                                ARTHUR *and* THE OTHERS
Amen.

                                    THE CABALIST
Bring the girl in, Mr. Foreman.
                (FOREMAN *nods and goes into* THE RABBI'S *office.*)
                                        ALPER
                                  (*To* SCHLISSEL)
I don't like it. Even if the Rabbi comes, there will only be nine of us. I
am a traditionalist. Without a quorum of ten, it won't work.
                                      SCHLISSEL
                                    (*Muttering*)
So what do you want me to do?
                (*In* THE RABBI'S *office,* FOREMAN *touches* THE GIRL'S *shoulder, and she
                starts from her coma-like state and looks at him.*)
                                      FOREMAN
Come. It is time.
                (*She nods nervously and sits up. There is a vacuous look about her, the
                vague, distracted look of the insane.*)
                                      THE GIRL
                                  (*Quite numbly*)
Where are you taking me? My mother is in Rome. They put the torch
to her seven sons, and they hold her hostage. (*She rises in obedience to her
grandfather's arm as he gently escorts her out of the office into the synagogue
proper. All the while she maintains a steady drone of rattling gibberish*) Where
were you yesterday? I asked everybody about you. You should have been
here. We had a lot of fun. We had a party, and there were thousands of
people, Calebites and Bedouins, dancing like gypsies.
                (*She suddenly lapses into a sullen silence, staring at the ground, her shoul-
                ders jerking involuntarily. The others regard her uneasily.*)
                                      THE SEXTON
Shall I take the ram's horn out?
                                    THE CABALIST
Yes.
                (THE SEXTON *produces the horn-shaped trumpet from the base of the pul-
                pit. The front door of the synagogue now opens, and a tall, strapping young*

POLICEMAN, *heavy with the authority of his thick blue overcoat, steps one step into the synagogue. He stands in the open doorway, one hand on the latch of the door, his attitude quite brusque—as if he could not possibly get his work done if he had to be polite.*)

THE POLICEMAN

Is Rabbi Marks here?

(ALPER *throws up his arms in despair. The others alternately stare woodenly at* THE POLICEMAN *or down at the floor.* ARTHUR, *still deeply disturbed, rubs his brow.* THE CABALIST *begins to pray silently, only his lips moving in rapid supplication.*)

THE SEXTON

No, he's not.

THE POLICEMAN

I'm looking for a girl named Evelyn Foreman. Is that the girl?

(*He indicates* THE GIRL.)

ALPER

(*Moving away, muttering*)

Is there any need, Officer, to be so brusque or to stand in an open doorway so that we all chill to our bones?

THE POLICEMAN

(*Closing the door behind him*)

Sorry.

SCHLISSEL

(*To* ZITORSKY)

A real cossack, eh? What a brute. He will take us all to the station house and beat us with night sticks.

THE POLICEMAN

(*A little more courteously*)

A girl named Evelyn Foreman. Her father has put out a call for her. She's missing from her home. He said she might be here with her grandfather. Is there a Mr. David Foreman here?

(*Nobody says anything.*)

ALPER

You are interrupting a service, Officer.

THE POLICEMAN

I'm sorry. Just tell me, is that the girl? I'll call in and tell them we found her.

(SCHLISSEL *suddenly advances on* THE POLICEMAN.)

SCHLISSEL

First of all, where do you come to walk in here like you were raiding a poolroom? This is a synagogue, you animal. Have a little respect.

THE POLICEMAN

All right, all right, I'm sorry. I happen to be Jewish myself.
(ALPER *looks up quickly.*)

ALPER

You're Jewish? (ALPER *turns slowly to* THE SEXTON) Sexton, our tenth man.

THE SEXTON

Alper, are you crazy?

ALPER

A fine, strapping Jewish boy. (*To* THE POLICEMAN) Listen, we need a tenth. You'll help us out, won't you?

SCHLISSEL
(*Strolling nervously past* ALPER)
Alper, what are you doing, for God's sakes?

ALPER

We have to have ten men.

SCHLISSEL

What kind of prank is this? You are an impossible rogue, do you know that?

ALPER
(*Taking* SCHLISSEL *aside*)
What are you getting so excited about? He doesn't have to know what it is. We'll tell him it's a wedding. I think it's funny.

SCHLISSEL

Well, we will see how funny it is when they take us to the basement of the police station and beat us with their night sticks.

ALPER

Night sticks. Really, Schlissel, you are a romantic. (*Advancing on* THE POLICEMAN) I tell you, Officer, it would really help us out if you would stay ten or fifteen minutes. This girl—if you really want to know—is about to be married, and what is going on here is the Ritual of Shriving.

ZITORSKY

Shriving?

ALPER

A sort of ceremony of purification. It is a ritual not too commonly practiced any more, and I suggest you will find it quite interesting.

HARRIS
(To SCHLISSEL*)*

What is he talking about?

SCHLISSEL

Who knows?
*(*THE POLICEMAN *opens the door and calls to his colleague outside.)*

THE POLICEMAN

I'll be out in about ten minutes, Tommy, all right? *(He opens the door wider for* THE RABBI, *who now comes hurrying into the synagogue, still carrying his briefcase)* Hello, Rabbi, how are you?
*(*THE RABBI *frowns, a little confused at* THE POLICEMAN's *presence.)*

THE RABBI

Hello, Officer, what are you doing here?
(He moves quickly to his office, taking stock of everything as he goes: the seven old men and ARTHUR *in their white shawls, and* THE GIRL *standing woodenly in the center of the synagogue.* ALPER *and* ZITORSKY *greet him with hellos, at which he nods back.)*

THE POLICEMAN

They've asked me to make a tenth for the shriving.

THE RABBI
(Frowning as he darts into his office)

Shriving? *(He opens his desk to get out his own large white shawl, unbuttoning his coat as he does. He notes* ALPER, *who has followed him to the doorway)* What is the policeman doing here?

ALPER

We needed a tenth.
(In the synagogue, THE POLICEMAN *speaks amiably to* ZITORSKY.*)*

THE POLICEMAN

This is the girl, isn't it? *(*ZITORSKY *nods his head bleakly)* What's really going on here?
(In THE RABBI's *office,* THE RABBI *sweeps his large shawl over his shoulders.)*

ALPER

We have said Al-chait and a prayer of atonement and we are waiting now just for you.
*(*THE RABBI *frowns in troubled thought, slips his skullcap on as he slips his fedora off. In the synagogue,* ZITORSKY *shuffles to* SCHLISSEL.*)*

ZITORSKY
(Indicating THE POLICEMAN *with his head, he mutters)*

He knows, he knows.

SCHLISSEL

Of course. Did Alper expect to get away with such a collegiate prank? (*In* THE RABBI's *office,* THE RABBI *finishes a rapid, silent prayer, standing with his eyes closed. He looks up at* ALPER *now.*)

THE RABBI

I would rather not take any active role in this exorcism. I am not quite sure of my rabbinical position. But it would please me a great deal to believe once again in a God of dybbuks. (*He walks quickly past* ALPER *out into the synagogue.* ALPER *follows*) Well, we are ten. (*A silence falls upon the gathered men.*)

FOREMAN

May God look upon us with the eye of mercy and understanding, and may He forgive us if we sin in our earnestness.

THE OTHERS

Amen.

THE CABALIST

Sexton, light the candles. (THE SEXTON *lights each man's candle.* THE CABALIST *advances slowly to* THE GIRL, *who stands slackly, her body making small occasional jerking movements, apparently in a schizophrenic state.* THE CABALIST *slowly draws a line before* THE GIRL *with the flat of his toe. He speaks quietly.*)

THE CABALIST

Dybbuk, I draw this line beyond which you may not come. You may not do harm to anyone in this room. (*The old men shift nervously in their various positions around the synagogue.* THE CABALIST *turns to* THE SEXTON.)

THE CABALIST

Open the Ark. (THE SEXTON *moves quickly up to the altar and opens the brown sliding doors of the Ark, exposing the several scrolls within, standing in their handsome velvet coverings.* THE CABALIST *moves slowly back to his original position; he says quietly—*)

THE CABALIST

Dybbuk, you are in the presence of God and His Holy Scrolls. (THE GIRL *gasps*) I plead with you one last time to leave the body of this girl. (*There is no answer*) Then I will invoke the curse of excommunication upon your pitiable soul. Sexton, blow Tekiah. (THE SEXTON *raises the ram's horn to his lips, and the eerie, frightening tones shrill out into the hushed air.*)

THE CABALIST

Sexton, blow Shevurim.

(Again, THE SEXTON *raises the ram's horn and blows a variation of the first hollow tones.)*

THE CABALIST

Sexton, blow Teruah.

(A third time, THE SEXTON *blows a variation of the original tones.)*

THE CABALIST

Sexton, blow the Great Tekiah, and, upon the sound of these tones, dybbuk, you will be wrenched from the girl's body and there will be cast upon you the final anathema of excommunication from all the world of the living and from all the world of the dead. Sexton, blow the Great Tekiah.

(For the fourth time, THE SEXTON *raises the ram's horn to his lips and blows a quick succession of loud blasts. A silence falls heavily on the gathered men, the notes fading into the air. Nothing happens.* THE GIRL *remains as she was, standing slackly, her hands making involuntary little movements.* FOREMAN's *head sinks slowly on his chest, and an expression of deep pain covers his face.* THE CABALIST *stares steadily at* THE GIRL. *Suddenly,* ARTHUR *begins to moan softly, and then with swift violence a horrible scream tears out of his throat. He staggers one brief step forward. At the peak of his scream, he falls heavily down on the floor of the synagogue in a complete faint. The echoes of his scream tingle momentarily in the high corners of the air in the synagogue. The others stand petrified for a moment, staring at his slack body on the floor.)*

ALPER

My god. I think what has happened is that we have exorcised the wrong dybbuk.

*(*THE POLICEMAN *starts toward* ARTHUR's *limp body.)*

THE POLICEMAN

All right, don't crowd around. Let him breathe.

THE CABALIST

He will be all right in a moment.

ZITORSKY

If I didn't see this with my own eyes, I wouldn't believe it.

THE RABBI

Hirschman, will he be all right?

THE CABALIST

Yes.

SCHLISSEL
(With simple devoutness)
Praise be to the Lord, for His compassion is everywhere.
(HARRIS sinks down onto a chair, exhausted and terrified by the whole experience. THE RABBI moves slowly down and stares at ARTHUR as SCHLISSEL, ZITORSKY and ALPER help him to a chair.)

ALPER
How are you, my dear fellow?

ARTHUR
(Still in a state of shock)
I don't know.

THE SEXTON
(Coming forward with some wine)
Would you like a sip of wine?

ARTHUR
(Taking the goblet)
Yes, thank you very much. *(Turning to look at THE GIRL)* How is she?
(Her schizophrenic state is quite obvious. ARTHUR turns back, his face furrowed and his eyes closed now in a mask of pain.)

SCHLISSEL
Was it a painful experience, my friend?

ARTHUR
I don't know. I feel beyond pain. *(Indeed, his hands are visibly trembling as if from cold; his face is rigid and masklike. Words become more difficult to say)* I feel as if I have been reduced to the moment of birth, as if the universe has become one hunger.
(He seems to be almost on the verge of collapse.)

ALPER
A hunger for what?

ARTHUR
(Whispering)
I don't know.

THE CABALIST
For life.
(At these words, ARTHUR sinks back into his chair, exhausted.)

ARTHUR
Yes, for life. I want to live. *(He opens his eyes and begins to pray quietly)* God of my fathers, you have exorcised all truth as I knew it out of me. You have taken away my reason and definition. Give me then a desire to wake in the

morning, a passion for the things of life, a pleasure in work, a purpose to sorrow...*(He slowly stands, for a reason unknown even to himself, and turns to regard the slouched figure of* THE GIRL*)* Give me all of these things in one— give me the ability to love. *(In a hush of the scene, he moves slowly to* THE GIRL *and stands before her crouched slack figure)* Dybbuk, hear me. I will cherish this girl, and give her a home. I will tend to her needs and hold her in my arms when she screams out with your voice. Her soul is mine now—her soul, her charm, her beauty—even you, her insanity, are mine. If God will not exorcise you, dybbuk, I will. *(To* THE GIRL*)* Evelyn, I will get your coat. We have a lot of things to do this afternoon. *(He turns to the others)* It is not a simple matter to get somebody released from an institution in New York. *(He starts briskly across to* THE RABBI's *office and pauses at the door)* Officer, why don't you just call in and say you have located the girl and she is being brought to her father. *(To* MR. FOREMAN*)* You'd better come along with us. Would somebody get my coat? We will need her father's approval. We shall have to stop off at my office and have my secretary draw some papers.
    *(*MR. FOREMAN *has hurriedly gotten* THE GIRL's *coat,* ARTHUR's *coat, and his own. In this rather enchanted state, these three drift to the exit door.)*

THE POLICEMAN
Rabbi, is this all right?

THE RABBI
Yes, quite all right.

ARTHUR
(Pausing at the door, bemused, enchanted)
Oh—thank you all. Good-bye.

ALL
Good-bye.

ZITORSKY
Go in good health.

ALPER
Come back and make a tenth for us sometime.
    *(*ARTHUR *smiles and herds* THE GIRL *and* FOREMAN *out of the synagogue. The door closes behind them.)*

SCHLISSEL
(Sitting with a deep sigh)
Well, what is one to say? An hour ago, he didn't believe in God; now he's exorcising dybbuks.

ALPER

(Pulling up a chair)

He still doesn't believe in God. He simply wants to love. (ZITORSKY *joins the other two)* And when you stop and think about it, gentlemen, is there any difference? Let us make a supposition...

(As the curtain falls, life as it was slowly returns to the synagogue. The three old men engage in disputation, THE CABALIST *returns to his isolated studies,* THE RABBI *moves off into his office,* THE SEXTON *finds a chore for himself, and* THE POLICEMAN *begins to button his coat.)*

The Curtain Falls

Gideon

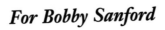

For Bobby Sanford

GIDEON *was first presented by Fred Coe and Arthur Cantor at The Plymouth Theatre, New York City, N.Y., on November 9, 1961, with the following cast:*

(In Order of Appearance)

THE ANGEL	Fredric March
JOASH	Mitchell Jason
ABIMELECH	Victor Kilian
HELEK	Martin Garner
JETHER	Robert Weiss
GIDEON	Douglas Campbell
TIRZAH	Florence Anglin
HAGLAH	Anna Berger
WOMEN OF MANASSEH	{ Bathsheba Garnett Gubi Mann Ilene Tema
SHILLEM	Eric Berry
JAHLEEL	David Hooks
HEZEKIAH	Alan Manson
MALCHIEL	Mark Lenard
PURAH	George Segal
ZEBAH	Alan Bergmann
ZALMUNNA	Paul Marin
SOLDIERS	{ Bernard Chessler Tom Klunis Amnon Meskin Meir Ovadia
OZNI	David Hooks
SECOND ELDER	Martin Garner
THIRD ELDER	Victor Kilian
WOMEN OF SUCCOTH	{ Florence Anglin Anna Berger Bathsheba Garnett Gubi Mann Ilene Tema
ORPAH	Lorraine Egypt
MAHLAH	Bathsheba Garnett
MILCAH	Ilene Tema
ADINOAB	Gubi Mann

Directed by Tyrone Guthrie
Sets and lighting by David Hays
Costumes by Domingo A. Rodriguez
Produced in association with Carnegie Productions, Inc.

TIME: 1100 B.C.

ACT I

ACT II

ACT I

"Now the angel of the Lord came and sat under the oak at Ophrah, which belonged to Joash, the Abiezrite, as his son Gideon was beating out wheat in the wine press to hide it from the Midianites."

SCENE 1

The time is June, 1100 B.C.

The scene is the hill country of Manasseh, west of the Jordan River in Biblical Palestine.

Stage right is a wine press. Upstage of the wine press is a terebinth tree. Upstage center is a crude, stone sacrificial altar. Stage left is a black Bedouin-like tent.

At rise, a man with a black beard, almost entirely enshrouded in long black Mosiac robes, is leaning against the terebinth tree. He is an ANGEL.

Enter the elders, JOASH, ABIMELECH, and HELEK, followed by a frightened boy of twelve, whose name is JETHER. The elders are all in their sixties. They wear variously colored robes. They hurry to the stone altar upstage center, lift their faces and begin to wail softly. They beat their breasts, pour ashes from the altar's hearth over their heads.

JOASH
(Crying out)
O Mighty Ba-al! Progenitor of Oxen! Rider of the Clouds and the Bringer of Rain! Hear the entreaty of your servant Joash...

ABIMELECH
...and of Abimelech his kinsman.

JOASH
Hear the entreaty of Joash of the house of Abiezer of the tribe of Manasseh.

HELEK
O Puissant Ba-al!

JOASH

O Mighty Ba-al! Hear the voice of your servant Joash!

ABIMELECH

Do not ignore Abimelech his kinsman.

HELEK

Nor Helek son of Zoar.

JOASH

All-potent Father! O Mighty Ba-al! The Midianites are upon us again!
*(The four men burst into fresh wailing. They beat their breasts. They pour
ashes on their heads. They rend their garments.)*

JOASH

We have seen their tents in Gilead on the other side of the Jordan River.
Every year, for eight years, they have thundered up from the desert of
Havilah, one hundred thousand swarming nomads, their camels and their
flocks. Like locusts, they devour everything before them, the harvests of
Reuben, the barley of Gad. And now they are here again, this vast savage
multitude. From our hills, we have seen the glint of their earrings and the
golden crescents that hang from their camels. As far as the eye can see,
their black tents darken the land of Gilead. Soon they will cross the Jordan
and devour us here.

HELEK

Woe is Manasseh! Woe unto us here in Manasseh!

JOASH

They will take our daughters to be their servants.

ABIMELECH

O Divine Ba-al! Save us! Redeem us!
Smite them with plagues, smite them with lightning.
Strike with your cudgels.

JOASH

Give us a hero,
A redeemer, a savior.
Raise up a prince who will lead us in battle!
Raise up a hero!
You donkey! What have you brought here?
*(This last, needless to say, was hardly addressed to Ba-al, but rather to a
strapping, good-natured, bearded fellow in his late thirties named
GIDEON, who has just entered carrying the carcass of a newly slaughtered
young goat. He pauses at this greeting.)*

GIDEON

Father, I am bringing the sacrifice, as you asked me.

JOASH

A bullock! A bullock! I said to slaughter a bullock, Gideon, not a kid!

GIDEON

Oh, I heard you to say a kid.

ABIMELECH

Oh, let's get on with this sacrifice.

JOASH

My son Gideon has brought in a kid instead of a bullock.

ABIMELECH

Well, offer the kid then. We all want to get back to our tents and hide whatever we can before the Midianites come.

JOASH

(*Taking the kid from* GIDEON *and putting it on the altar, muttering*)

Five sons I had; four were killed by the Midianites, and this is the one who was spared. (*Pulling his knife from its scabbard*) Now, does anyone remember the ritual we followed last year?

HELEK

It didn't help much last year so I shouldn't worry too much about repeating it exactly.

ABIMELECH

You dip your hand in the blood of the sacrifice and sprinkle it on the horns of the altar and...

JOASH

Yes, yes, I remember all that. It's the portion I'm asking about. How much of the animal do we actually offer? Does the right shoulder and upper right joint sound familiar to anyone?

HELEK

No, no, the proper portion for a sacrifice to My Lord Ba-al is the two cheeks, the stomach, the shoulders and all the fat thereof.

JOASH

Oh, I know that's not right.

ABIMELECH

(*Reaching impatiently for the knife in* JOASH's *hand*)

Oh, let me do it.

JOASH

No, I'm chief of the clan.

ABIMELECH

Well, finish up with it then.

JOASH

(Dipping his hand into the blood of the sacrificial kid and sprinkling some on the ground)

It's a mangy little animal. Why don't we just offer up the whole kid and be done with it?

ABIMELECH

Good.

JOASH

(Now rubbing the blood on the tips of the horns of the altar)

Gideon, while I'm doing this—there are some sheaves of wheat that I brought into the tent. Beat them out and put the threshed wheat in a sack, and hide the sack in that cave we used last year.

GIDEON

Yes, Father.

JOASH

(Now applying some blood to his forehead, the thumb of his right hand, and to the toe of his right foot. He nudges ABIMELECH)

You see the point? We shall have to thresh the wheat harvest by hand and in secret. If the Midianites see us threshing the wheat on the hilltop, they will know we have had a good harvest, and it shall go all the worse with us.

ABIMELECH

Oh, that is true. And I have just sent our cousin Lamech up to the threshing floor on the hill. Gideon, you had better send someone up to the threshing floor straightaway to tell Lamech to come down before the Midianites see him.

GIDEON

Yes, Uncle. *(He turns to the boy JETHER)* Jether, my son, go to the threshing floor and tell Lamech to come down straightaway.

(JETHER, far more interested in the ritual at the altar, pays his father no attention.)

HELEK

(To JOASH)

You forgot to sprinkle the blood seven times around the altar.

JOASH

No, no, I've already done that.

GIDEON

(Annoyed at his son's indifference, he appeals to his father)

Father, he never does what I ask him.

JOASH
(Peremptorily to the boy)
Go to Lamech and bring him down from the threshing floor.
(The boy leaps to his charge, exiting upstage and around the tent.)

ABIMELECH
What shall we do with the herds this year?

HELEK
Well, let us finish with the prayers, and then we can decide what to do
with the women and the cattle.

ABIMELECH
I hear wailing. The women have heard the news.
(Indeed, far offstage left, we can hear the keening of women. JOASH *turns
back to the altar.)*

JOASH
O My Lord Ba-al, you are god over all other gods. And let the people
say...

THE OTHER ELDERS
Amen.
*(*GIDEON *goes into the tent, and hoists several large sheaves of wheat
effortlessly onto his shoulders.)*

JOASH
You have banished Yam to the waters.
You seize the womb of Anath and you are sire to eagles,
And you are father to the grape.
And let the...
(He pauses to watch his son GIDEON *carrying the sheaves of wheat upstage and
around the tent)* Where are you going now?

GIDEON
(Turning)
Do you speak to me, Father?

JOASH
I said where are you going?

GIDEON
I am taking these sheaves of wheat, as you asked me to, up to the threshing floor on the hill and...

ABIMELECH
Up to the threshing floor! You witless ass! You have just sent your son
to tell Lamech to come down from the threshing floor!

GIDEON

But, Uncle, my father has asked me to thresh these sheaves of wheat...

JOASH

I said to beat them out! Beat them out in the wine press!

GIDEON
(Utterly confused)

Beat the wheat out in the wine press?

HELEK

What a donkey!

JOASH

Gideon, if you go up to the threshing floor, the Midianites will see you. They are only across the river. Do you want them to know we are reaping a good harvest? Go to the wine press, you goat, and beat out the sheaves with a stick.

(Enter two women, TIRZAH and HAGLAH, in a state of panic. They wear blue and purple robes.)

THE WOMEN

Oh, my lord Joash, the Midianites are upon us!

JOASH

Yes, yes, we know about that. We are offering prayers to Ba-al now. *(ABIMELECH suddenly bolts for the wings)* Where are you going?

ABIMELECH

I have my own fields to reap!

(He exits.)

JOASH
(To THE WOMEN)

Foolish ladies, you must get back to your gleaning. *(To HELEK, who is also bolting away)* We haven't finished the prayers!

HELEK
(Exiting)

Bother the prayers!

THE WOMEN

See how Israel is brought low, how the elders scurry. As lions shall they devour the daughters of Israel.

JOASH
(Weakly)

Oh, it is all too much for me.

(He enters the tent and squats gloomily down on his haunches.)

GIDEON
(Calling from the wine press)
Shall I continue beating out the wheat, Father?

JOASH
Yes! *(Mutters)* Donkey.

(HAGLAH, GIDEON's mother, goes off. TIRZAH, GIDEON's wife, remains, moving in and out of view in the tent as she gathers the stores of the household and puts them in baskets. There is a moment of silence, interrupted only by the pounding of GIDEON's stick as he beats at the kernels of wheat in the wine press. The black-bearded ANGEL, who has been watching it all from the shade of the terebinth tree, now steps forward to GIDEON and regards the big fellow, whacking away at the wheat.)

THE ANGEL
The Lord is with you, O mighty man of valor. *(GIDEON, who had not noticed the ANGEL till now, looks up, a little startled)* I said, the Lord is with you, O mighty man of valor.

(This greeting, needless to say, disconcerts GIDEON. He darts a quick look back to the tent to see if anyone is around to take the fellow off his hands. He pounds a few more whacks, then smiles sheepishly at the stranger, raises his hand in a gesture of "Be right back," and shuffles quickly into the tent. His father is squatting unhappily on his haunches in the middle of the tent.)

GIDEON
Father, there is a very strange fellow by our terebinth tree.

JOASH
Well, give him what cakes we have on the hearth and show him the road to Schechem.

GIDEON
(Hurriedly gathering cakes)
I was beating the wheat, you see, and this fellow suddenly came up, saying…*(He hurries out of the tent, across to the stranger now perched on the edge of the wine press. He offers the cakes and a skin of water)* We have only these. We are very oppressed here. But you must hurry south before the Midianites come. I will show you the road. One makes for Schechem and then into Ephraim, and then others will show you the roads to Judah. I must get to my work. I have this wheat to beat here. It is a slow business. *(GIDEON picks up his beating stick and gets back to his work. But the calm stranger unnerves him. THE ANGEL sits perched on the edge of the wine press amiably munching the flat cakes he has been given)* Sir, it is hard for me to do my work if you sit there like that.

THE ANGEL
(Affably)

I am the Lord your God, Gideon, who brought you out of the iron furnace of Egypt and delivered you from bondage.

(GIDEON considers this announcement for a moment.)

GIDEON

Well, as you say, sir. Now, let me be about my work.

THE ANGEL

I am the Lord your God, Gideon. I have heard your groans under the Midianite yoke. You have cried out to Ba-al, but it is my ears that heard. My wrath was hot against you, for you have bowed down and served the Amorite gods and the Ba-als of the Canaanites. My name is Jealous, Gideon, for I am a Jealous God; and I have delivered you into the hands of the Midianites. But I have remembered the covenant I made with Jacob and the bargain I struck with Moses, and I will redeem you from the Midianite oppression. For My Name is the Loving God, the Gracious God, the Merciful God, and I have hearkened to your groans.

(This is all a little too much for poor GIDEON. He makes a few half-hearted whacks at the wheat in the wine press, nods his head nervously a few times.)

GIDEON
(Mutters)

Excuse me. *(He turns and shuffles back across the stage to his father's tent and goes in again)* It is a very strange stranger, indeed, Father. He seems a Hebrew from the cut of his beard, but I—it would be better if you came forth and dealt with him.

JOASH
(In despair)

Leave me be, Gideon.

(GIDEON nods nervously and takes a few tentative steps out of the tent, and would perhaps have made his way back to the wine press, but he is petrified into a halt by the sudden booming of the stranger's voice. THE ANGEL is now standing in all his black majestic height, and he roars out in volcanic tones.)

THE ANGEL

I am the Lord your God who brought you out of the house of Egypt! With signs and wonders I delivered you from bondage! Ten plagues I hurled at Pharaoh to awe you with my might. I drove back the sea with a strong east wind, and Israel walked through the waters! The horse and the rider I cast into the sea, but you walked through water! Would that not be a sign enough? Would that not be wonder enough? But you are a stubborn people! From that day to this have you rebelled against the Lord! Did I not rain bread from the heavens? Did I not strike water from the rock at Horeb? How long will you murmur against me? I shattered the walls of Jericho with trumpets. Thirty-one kings with their cities and walls did I give into your hand! But this mighty God was not enough for you! A cult of whores did you require! Mincing priests with crushed testicles! You have made cuttings in your skin and tattoos upon your brows! You have reveled before eyeless gods! You have debauched before stumps of trees! You are a stiff-necked people! You have done evil in mine eyes!

(GIDEON, *now thoroughly unnerved by what seems a raging lunatic, looks back to the tent to see why his father and wife haven't come running out at this outburst. But the two people in the tent do not seem to have heard.*)

GIDEON
(*Nervously*)
Sir, I do not know why you are so enraged.

THE ANGEL
Gideon, do you not know me? It is hardly four generations since Moses. Do not the young men know my name any more? I am your Lord Yahweh, the Kinsman of Jacob, who was the father of all the houses in Israel.

GIDEON
I have heard the old men talk of My Lord Yahweh.

THE ANGEL
Well, I am he.

GIDEON
I shall not say you are not.

THE ANGEL
I tell you I, even I, am he!

GIDEON
Pray, sir, do not shout.

THE ANGEL
What a stiff-necked fellow you are!

GIDEON
(*Thoroughly distressed*)
What would you have me say? I am a poor farmer, beating out wheat in his wine press. Suddenly, a black-bearded stranger appears at my elbow and shouts at me: "I am your God!" Well, I find this all an unusual business. I do not hold everyday traffic with gods. I said: "Very well." What else should I have said? And you have abused me roundly and hold me

back from my pressing work.

THE ANGEL

I did not mean to discomfort you.

GIDEON

And now that I am put to it, I will tell you plainly—I do not believe in gods. I am not all as witless as my fellows sometimes think me. I have thought about these matters lately, and I do not believe in gods. You say that you are the god, Yahweh. The fact is, sir, in these parts, you are but a minor divinity. When I was a boy, you were more highly thought of, I think. But we Abiezrites are poor men, hill farmers. Our soil is hard, and we must pray for fertility, so we adopted a goddess with breasts and a womb, Ishtar—a sportive lady, I must say; her festivals are lively times. A farmer, you see, needs a romping god. And Yahweh, as I recall, was grim. Oh, sir, we have had all manner of gods here—the Bull-El, Yam, Mot, pin-breasted Ashtartes, Anu, Anath, the Mother Goddess of the wonderful womb, and now we have added the rain Ba-al of Beth-shean! And to all these gods I gave my full and primitive awe. I truly, truly served them. For I am a child in many ways and truly thought the wind did love me, and that the thunder was angry at something I did, and that I sliced our poor Lord Ba-al in half as I sickled my wheat, for such is the story, you know, that Ba-al dies each year at harvest. How I wailed as I reaped! I truly, truly thought the air was cluttered with fierce powers. But lately I have come to wondering.

THE ANGEL

Gideon...

GIDEON

(Indicating the sacrificial kid)

What god will eat this sacrifice? Only that black bird. You say god to me, but I am a farmer, sir; I know a crow for a crow. A carrion crow is not much of a god really; I can chase him away with a stick.

THE ANGEL

Dear Gideon...

GIDEON

I have never asked of any god more than my own, that my trees bear olives, that my ewes bear lambs, the natural increase of things, no special favor. I did ask for seven sons; I have but one.

THE ANGEL

You shall have seventy sons, I promise you. And I shall redeem you from the Midianites.

GIDEON

Perhaps so. But lately, as I say, I have come to wondering.

THE ANGEL

Let us be friends, Gideon. For I am, in truth, the Lord your God, and I would have you believe in me. *(There is something so gentle about the black-bearded stranger that* GIDEON *must look at him)* The Lord is with you, O mighty man of valor.

(GIDEON *looks quickly away, then squats on his haunches in the manner of the East.)*

GIDEON

If the Lord is with us, sir, then why are we as we are? In my time, it has always been hard for a Hebrew.

(THE ANGEL *now squats beside* GIDEON, *as two Oriental farmers might sit for a chat.)*

THE ANGEL

Come, we will talk as kinsmen, for I am the first of your tribe. I like you, Gideon; you are a straightforward man.

GIDEON

Well, you are quick to temper, I see, but there is a sweetness in you.

THE ANGEL

Then, we are friends.

GIDEON

Brothers, since you say so.

THE ANGEL

My brother then, you are a farmer. You know the ways of covenants. When you sell your cow to the caravan and the merchant gives you nothing in exchange, you will rise in anger, I should think.

GIDEON

Aye.

THE ANGEL

It is a breach, is it not?

GIDEON

It is a breach.

THE ANGEL

Well, so it is with me. I have made covenant with the people of Israel, and they have defaulted. I have filled my part of the contract. I promised Jacob I would make of him a great people, and indeed I did. Jacob was but a wandering Aramaean with a household of seventy people when I sent him down into Egypt. And when I led them out of the land of Egypt, the house of Jacob had become six hundred families, rich with flocks and servants. And I gathered the whole full twelve tribes of them at Mount Nebo by the Jordan River. And I put the matter to them plainly there. "Look here," spoke I, "let us renew this covenant of ours, so that things are clear between us. I shall give this land across the Jordan to you, and you shall prosper there. Your part of the bargain is simple enough. You shall not bow down to any other god. I am the Lord your God, and there is no other god. You shall not serve any other god." Could it have been more plainly stated?

GIDEON

No, it was plainly said.

THE ANGEL

Well, after Moses came Joshua, and after Joshua, there rose a new generation in Israel who knew not the Lord, and they played the harlot after the Amorite gods. And such gods, really! A stone lady with a bulbous belly! As you say, with more colorful rites than mine perhaps, but I really did think you Hebrews were a cleverer breed than that. Do you really think if you lay with a priestess, your seed will fecundate barley? Come, Gideon, this is merely magic and not fitting for a noble house. It is beyond my understanding—really it is!—what you see in these other gods. The men of Sumer pray to the moon, but your god made the moon and many moons like it. The Philistines bow down to a flea, and the Egyptians—oh, well, the Egyptians will pray to anything. Cats, fish, vermin, frogs, rams, bulls, asps and adders, anything really. But your god is no cat. Nor can his likeness be chipped from stone. Not by gold nor red carbuncle can your god be wrought. Your god is beyond dimension. Your god, Hebrew, is beyond all other gods. Your god is all. Your god is everything. I am what is. I am the Lord! What was it we were talking of?

GIDEON

You were saying our fathers bowed down to other gods.

THE ANGEL

Your fathers indeed! Have *you* not bowed down to Marduk? And now it is Ishtar and the rain Ba-al of Beth-shean. And so I have given you into the hands of the Midianites. (*He has risen now to his full godlike majesty. His voice booms out*) This one last time shall I redeem you! This one last time, ye Hebrews! (GIDEON *looks nervously around, surprised that nobody seems to hear* THE ANGEL) But if you break faith with me one more time, then cursed shall you be in the city and cursed shall you be in the field! You shall serve your enemies in nakedness! I shall make brutes of you! Your women shall eat their own afterbirth! Your men shall eat their sons in hunger. Among

all nations, you shall find no rest! For I am the Lord! I am the Lord! I am
the Lord! *(He is abruptly affable again)* I shall raise up from among you a
redeemer, and he shall deliver you from the Midianites.

GIDEON
(Terrified now)
How shall we know this redeemer?

THE ANGEL
I shall come to him in the guise of a stranger, and I shall say unto him:
"The Lord is with you, O mighty man of valor."
(GIDEON *nods his head slowly. Then he scowls as he begins to understand.)*

GIDEON
I?

THE ANGEL
You shall be the redeemer. Gideon the son of Joash, the son of Abiezer,
the son of Gilead, the son of Machir, the son of Manasseh.

GIDEON
You cannot be serious.

THE ANGEL
You shall be the redeemer.

GIDEON
Sir, I am Gideon, the donkey of the clan. Ask anyone in Ophrah or on
the hills. They shall tell you Gideon is a good enough fellow but an ass.
Will you gird a donkey and make him your general? Of course, it is a
prank. I am often the butt of such pranks. It is a prank, is it not? Of course.
Ho! Gideon the general! What an idea! *(He looks anxiously at* THE ANGEL
who seems quite serious about the whole matter) Sir, I am not a soldier. I
wouldn't know which end of the sword is haft.

THE ANGEL
You are a mighty man of valor.

GIDEON
I will not hear any more of this. Really, I...the very idea of it has put me
at my wit's end. Who will join Gideon's army?

THE ANGEL
The spirit of the Lord shall come upon you, and all Israel shall heed
your words.

GIDEON
No, no, sir, I will have no part of this.
(Enter HELEK, *running from stage right. He is aghast with panic and
quite out of breath.)*

HELEK
(Shouting)

They come! They come! The Midianites come!

ABIMELECH'S VOICE
(Offstage left)

They come! They come! Midian comes!

HELEK
(Hurrying across to the tent)

Joash! They come! The shepherds have seen them. They are crossing the river.

JOASH
(At his tent flap)

Oh, dear me!

(ABIMELECH comes hurtling in from stage left.)

ABIMELECH

They have entered the river! Lamech has seen them from the threshing floor! *(He flings himself down before the altar)* O Mighty Ba-al! Let it be quick and done with this year!

JOASH
(Walking about at a loss)

Is there time to gather the elders and hold council?

(Far offstage, THE WOMEN begin a long, ululating wail.)

THE ANGEL
(To GIDEON)

Sound the trumpet, man of valor, and gather your army.

(GIDEON, who has quite forgotten the stranger in this flurry of panic, turns and regards him blankly.)

JOASH
(Shaking with fear and indecision)

Each man must do what is right in his own eyes. Take what you can and run for the caves.

GIDEON
(Crosses to JOASH)

Father, I pray you, talk with this stranger, for he frightens me.

JOASH

What stranger?

GIDEON

The man by the terebinth tree.

JOASH

The terebinth tree?

GIDEON

The black-bearded man in the heavy black robes. His hand is outstretched towards us.

JOASH

There is no man by the terebinth tree. Have you lost your wits entirely?

(GIDEON turns slowly and stares at THE ANGEL as THE WOMEN OF MANASSEH enter, lamenting. JETHER, the boy, is with them, terrified and clutching at his mother's robe.)

THE WOMEN

The Kings of Midian ford the Jordan.
The blood of Gilead drips from their swords.

THE ELDERS

O! We are oppressed!

THE WOMEN

The quiet Jordan heaves with waves.
Thousand on thousand push into the water.
They come! They come! Midian comes!

THE ELDERS

O! We are wounded and suffer!

THE ANGEL
(To GIDEON, who is staring with wide-eyed interest at him)

The spirit of the Lord is upon you, Gideon, and the people shall do as you tell them.

(GIDEON turns slowly to the elders.)

GIDEON
(In a state of possession)

Rise up, ye elders!
Hear the oracle of Gideon, the son of Joash,
The oracle of the man whose eye is opened!
The Lord of Jacob will redeem you.
The God of Moses is here,
And the Midianites will flee before you seven ways!

(The elders look up from their postures of prostration.)

HELEK

On my head, is this Gideon who prophesies?

(He stands slowly.)

GIDEON

Sound the trumpet, Father! Gather the Abiezrites upon this hill. We shall make war with Midian. *(He seizes his fathers' sacrificial knife from the altar and, with a quick, violent stroke slashes off a section of* HELEK's *robe)* Send messengers throughout Manasseh. This is what they shall say to the chiefs of Manasseh: "Whosoever does not come out after Gideon, thus shall my sword be brought down upon him." Let them come to me at Harod. There shall we gather an army. The battle shall be met in three days' time. It is the word of the Lord! The trumpet, Father! Go fetch the horn and sound it! *(*JOASH *shuffles dumbly into his tent)* It is the word of the lord, Helek. *(*HELEK *turns blankly and exits slowly off stage right. To* ABIMELECH*)* Send men servants to Asher, to Naphtali and to Zebulun. Take a yoke of oxen and chop them into pieces, and let your men servants say this to the chiefs: "Whoever does not come out after Gideon, thus shall it be done to his herds." The Lord is with you.

A WOMAN

We have raised up a savior!
*(*ABIMELECH *nods his head numbly and moves slowly off stage left.)*

GIDEON

Rise, ye women, and take the aged and children to the stronghold at Schechem. If you come into your monthly weakness in these three days, hide ye from the others, for it is an unclean thing and a bad omen for the battle.

THE WOMEN
(Rising and intoning)

We have raised up a savior.
As a lion does he rise up.
As the wild ox who gores the foe.
*(*THE WOMEN *exeunt stage left. The boy,* JETHER, *pauses a moment to regard his father with new interest.* GIDEON *beams at him and the boy exits.* JOASH *comes out of the tent, carrying a large silver trumpet.* GIDEON *stares at him blankly. Now,* JOASH *lets loose a mighty blast.* GIDEON *winces against the loud clarion.)*

JOASH

Shall we sound the horn again, my lord Gideon?
*(*GIDEON *turns, startled at this appellation. It pleases him. He looks at* THE ANGEL *who nods approval. He smiles.)*

GIDEON

Yes, I suppose we had better.
(The fact is that GIDEON *is very pleased by his new prominence; he is not*

quite sure of what has happened but is quite pleased nevertheless. JOASH
sounds the trumpet again, its blast reverberates throughout the theatre.
GIDEON *tugs at his beard as he considers the whole remarkable incident
favorably.)*

The curtain comes down quickly.

"Then Jerubaal (that is, Gideon) and all the people who were with him, rose early and encamped beside the spring of Harod; and the camp of Midian was north of them by the hill of Moreh in the valley."

SCENE 2

The hill at Harod. It is late afternoon, three days later.
Upstage is a small spur of a hill. On the spur is GIDEON's *tent. Downstage of this spur is a second smaller spur. Both spurs drop away to stage level some feet from the right wing. They are separated by a small defile.*
At rise, GIDEON *is seated downstage against the lower spur. His chin rests gloomily on the palm of his right hand. He is accoutered for war: he wears a leather corselet which chafes him and a leather baldric studded with iron pieces.*
In the tent are SHILLEM *the Naphtalite and* JAHLEEL *the Zebulunite.* SHILLEM *is a grizzled old warrior in his late sixties. He wears a brass cuirass, a woolen helmet with lappets, a leather belt and greaves. He holds a mighty warbow over which he fusses throughout the scene.* JAHLEEL *is a man in his fifties, robed and turbaned. He squats on the carpets.* PURAH, *the manservant of* GIDEON, *stands guard stage left of the tent. He is armed with a mattock. One or two* SOLDIERS *are occasionally visible upstage of the tent.*
Enter two warriors in their late forties. They are HEZEKIAH *and* MALCHIEL. HEZEKIAH *is stripped to the waist and wears a short skirtlike garment that comes to the knees. A pouch of stones, slung over his shoulder, dangles at his hip. He carries a sling.* MALCHIEL *wears a knee-length tunic, girdled by a leather belt, and holds a spear. They poke their heads into the tent.*

HEZEKIAH
Peace be with you, is this the tent of Gideon?

SHILLEM
Aye.

HEZEKIAH
We are the captains from Asher. I am Hezekiah of the house of Immah.

MALCHIEL
I am his brother Malchiel of the house of Immah.

SHILLEM

Peace be unto you. I am Shillem, captain of Naphtali, and there sits Jahleel the Zebulunite.

(PURAH, *at last aware that someone is going into the tent, wheels and brandishes his mattock.*)

PURAH

Who enters the tent of Gideon?

SHILLEM

Rest, rest, sentry, it is only the captains from Asher.

(*At* PURAH's *challenge,* GIDEON *stood and peeked over his spur to see the new arrivals. Now he squats again.*)

SHILLEM

The sentry is an imbecile. I can't step out of this tent to yawn that he doesn't challenge me with his plowshare. Well, how many have you brought with you?

HEZEKIAH

Eight thousand. We are pitched at the southern foot of the hill.

SHILLEM

Eight thousand fishermen from Asher. Well, that brings us now to thirty-two thousand. Well, we are fully met, the hosts of Israel. Thirty-two thousand fishers and husbandmen, armed with mattocks and trammels, a few dirks and darts, harpoons, and some old battle-axes, and flint axes at that. Ha! Not ten archers in the lot. I captained fifty men for Barak when we drove Sisera down the slopes of Tabor into the Kishon River. I mention it, not to bore you with an old warrior's tales, but to say merely that I know the shape of an army, and in truth, captains of Zebulun and Asher, this is an undistinguished garrison we have gathered here. We had expected the men of Asher yesterday.

HEZEKIAH

Yes, well, it wasn't easy to gather eight thousand men to make war simply because a zealot named Gideon suggested it. I mean, a messenger from Manasseh, brandishing a chopped-up cow, came racing up to the gates of my city, shouting: "Whosoever does not come out after Gideon," and so forth and so forth—well, it's hard to take that sort of thing seriously. I didn't want to come at all, but my brother Malchiel here is a more enthusiastic follower of prophets.

MALCHIEL

(*A fanatic sort*)

We have been told this Gideon is a charismatic man and that he walks in a blinding circle of light.

SHILLEM

Well, not too blinding. I wouldn't put him down as completely reckless, but he does seem to lack a forceful grip on things.

JAHLEEL

Aye.

SHILLEM

I took our general, Gideon, up to the crest of this hill this morning. We lay on our bellies and looked down on the Midianite camp in the valley. Their tents stretch ten miles from Shunem to the foothills of Gilboa. If I had to hazard a number, I would count them at a hundred thousand.

JAHLEEL

And there are another twenty thousand Amalekites who ride with them.

SHILLEM

And Gideon prophesied we should smite the Midianites on the third day, and this is the third day.

JAHLEEL

And late in the afternoon of the third day.

SHILLEM

Well, as I say, we looked down upon this awesome multitude, and I said to Gideon: "My General, what plan of battle have you for this?" "I haven't the beginnings of an idea," he said, "have you?" And that was this morning.

HEZEKIAH

You mean we have no plan of battle?

SHILLEM

Absolutely none at all. So I have been conceiving a clever shift or two. Still, we are badly favored in this battle, badly favored. (*He takes a small branch and begins marking the ground at their feet*) Well, attend. Here we sit on the hill of Harod. Here lay the Midianites in the Valley of Jezreel below.

(*The others gather around him. Downstage,* THE ANGEL, *in excellent spirits, enters.* GIDEON *offers him a quick, sulky look.*)

GIDEON

Where have you been?

THE ANGEL

(*A little surprised at this sulkiness*)

Why are you suddenly so cross? When I left you this morning, you flung yourself at my feet, kissed the hem of my robe and vowed eternal love to me. Now, what occasions this new petulance? Oh, come, Gideon, I have grown so fond of you these past three days. And it is lovely here at Harod at this hour. See all this arbutus; it is a sweet night.

GIDEON

This corselet my uncle gave me chafes.

THE ANGEL

(*Squatting down beside* GIDEON)

Oh, take it off. I told you yesterday to take it off. It is much too hot for leather. But you will posture as a general and swagger among the troops. You have your baldric on backwards, I might add.

GIDEON

My manservant Purah said this was the way.

THE ANGEL

And put away that poniard. You will not need it. A handsome one though. Here, let me look at it. Made of an antelope's horn. Is it also your uncle's?

GIDEON

Yes.

THE ANGEL

Very handsome.

GIDEON

The old man Shillem of Naphtali is driving me out of my wits.

THE ANGEL

A vain old man, why do you listen to him?

GIDEON

He keeps clutching my arm and saying: "What have you in the way of a battle plan?" Well, what am I to say? The men of Asher have finally come. Their captains sit in my tent now. "What is the plan of battle?" they shall say. And what am I to answer? The people shout at me as I walk among the tents: "We've left half a harvest in the field. The first grapes will be ripening in a week! We want to be home!" "The Lord of Moses is with you," I answer, "and you shall not fear." Well, I shall have to have something cleverer to say than that, for they grumble a great deal. I said we would engage the Midianites in three days' time, and it is the third day now. And you went off this morning, and here it is dusk. I've been looking for you all through the hills. And you say wherefore do I sulk?

THE ANGEL

You shall have your battle plan. Have no fear.

GIDEON

Why have you kept it secret?

THE ANGEL

You never asked me for it. You have been sporting among the people, playing the prince. I watched you shout orders from your tent and gravely scratch maps on the ground. This rodomontade was your diversion; I would not spoil it for you. And I meant you also to know your own incompetence. It shall not be said, when this victory over Midian is won, that it was won by Gideon or any other general. This victory shall be mine. It shall be a miracle. It shall be clear to all Israel that only the hand of God delivered them.

GIDEON

Pray, sir, what is the plan?

THE ANGEL

You shall require three hundred lamps, each filled with an hour's oil.

GIDEON

Three hundred lamps?

THE ANGEL

And three hundred horns.

GIDEON

What manner of horns?

THE ANGEL

Any manner so long as each can blow a loud blast. Go see to these requisitions quickly. It is dusk now, and night falls abruptly in June.

GIDEON

Pray, sir, these three hundred lamps—what is the reason for these three hundred lamps and three hundred horns?

THE ANGEL

Yes, another thing. The Midianites will flee seven ways before you this night.

GIDEON

This night? It is tonight then, the battle?

THE ANGEL

In panic shall they flee down the Jordan valley. They will try to escape across the Jordan at Beth-barah which is in Ephraim. Therefore, send messengers into Ephraim, and let them say to the chiefs of Ephraim: "Set men at Beth-barah and smite the Midianites as they flee to the fords." Quickly, Gideon, for these are matters of the moment.

GIDEON

Sir, these lamps—I cannot flatly march into that tent, saying "Get three hundred lamps and three hundred horns," turn on my heel and flatly walk out again. My captains shall, with some justification, think it a strange instruction.

THE ANGEL
(Ending all argument)

I am the Lord.

*(*GIDEON *scowls, darts a probing look or two at* THE ANGEL, *then turns and starts climbing up the defile between the spurs.)*

JAHLEEL
(At the tent flap)

Attend! He comes!

SHILLEM
(Coming to the tent flap)

Ho, Gideon! The captains of Asher are here with eight thousand men!

PURAH
(Whirling and challenging GIDEON*)*

Who approaches the tent of Gideon?

GIDEON
(Wearily)

It is only I, Purah, it is only I.

SHILLEM
(As GIDEON *clambers up to the upper spur)*

We have contrived a plan of assault, O General, suggested by Joshua's tactics when he captured the City of Ai. It is our plan to entice the Amalekites off the slopes of Gilboa by sending...

HEZEKIAH

Peace be with you, Gideon.

GIDEON

Peace be with you, men of Asher.

SHILLEM

...by sending a small band of decoys to the east to—

GIDEON

Captains of Asher, gather from your men three hundred lamps, each filled with an hour of oil, and three hundred horns for blowing.

(This gives everybody something to think about for a moment.)

SHILLEM

Three hundred lamps and three hundred horns. What is the purpose of three hundred lamps and three hundred horns?

GIDEON

You know as much as I. So spoke the Lord to me, and so I speak it to you. *(To* JAHLEEL*)* Captain of Zebulun, send three messengers to the proud prince of Ephraim at Shiloh. Let them say this: "Guard the fords at Beth-barah. This very night, the Midianites, fleeing in panic, will try to cross the Jordan there. Let them smite the Midianites, preserve not one that breathes." Straightaway now, all of you.

MALCHIEL

It is tonight then, that the battle is met?

GIDEON

So spoke the Lord to me.

SHILLEM

Three hundred lamps, each with an hour's oil in it. What are we to do with three hundred lamps?

JAHLEEL

Pray, Gideon, a sensible forethought this guarding the fords at Beth-barah where the Midianites shall flee in panic. What still bears consideration—to me at least—is how does one get the Midianites to flee there in panic?

GIDEON

I am as curious as you.
(He turns on his heel and starts down the defile again.)

SHILLEM

As gods go, this Lord Yahweh has a whimsical turn of mind, don't you think? Three hundred trumpets. Ha!

MALCHIEL

It is said that with the blowing of trumpets, Joshua took Jericho.

SHILLEM

Well, there was more to it than that, I'm sure. Joshua had a sizable command of a thousand families.

HEZEKIAH
(Dubiously)

I shall go gather the requisitions.
(He exits.)

SHILLEM

My plan, I thought, had considerable merit. You see, having drawn off the Amalekites...

PURAH
(Whirling to challenge GIDEON *en route back)*

Who passes there?

GIDEON

Oh, in the name of heaven, you donkey, it is only I!

SHILLEM

Having drawn off the Amalekites, we retire quickly to the east of the Jordan in Gad, where we would reassemble the hosts...

JAHLEEL

I had better go send messengers to the proud prince of Ephraim.
(*He exits.*)

MALCHIEL

He did not seem especially compelling, this Gideon. We have diviners in Dor whose eyes flash with actual flame. How is this Gideon when prophecy comes upon him? The priests of Cybele leap into the air, slash themselves with knives, spinning and shrieking in Corybantic frenzy till they sink to the ground, self-bloodied eunuchs. The signs have not been good for this battle, Captain of Naphtali. Our men of Acco say a shark washed ashore the day before with a fish in his teeth still wriggling. It is a bad foreboding.

(GIDEON *has rejoined* THE ANGEL *downstage. He is waiting a little anxiously for* THE ANGEL, *who is deep in thought, to speak.*)

THE ANGEL

How many men have you in your camp?
(GIDEON *calculates for a moment.*)

GIDEON

Thirty-two thousand with the eight thousand from Asher.

THE ANGEL

Too many. We shall have to cut your forces down.

GIDEON
(*Unashamedly alarmed*)

Cut them down?

THE ANGEL

If Midian is defeated by thirty-two thousand, then will Israel vaunt itself, saying: "It was by our own hand that we were delivered." And, yea, they shall know it was by the hand of God alone. Now, therefore, go to your chiefs and say: "Proclaim in the ears of the people, saying: 'Whoever is fearful and trembling, let him return home.'"

GIDEON

Oh, dear me!

THE ANGEL

Quickly, Gideon.

GIDEON

Pray, sir, you have charged me to go to my chiefs and say: "Proclaim in the ears of the people, saying: 'All those who are fearful and trembling, they may return to their farms.'"

THE ANGEL

Aye.

GIDEON

Pray, sir, if we were to proclaim in the ears of the people, saying: "All those who are fearful and trembling, you may return to your farms," then, sir, would you see such a sweeping exodus as would make you pale. These hills would be desolate in an hour. And I, in all probability, will be leading the pack.

THE ANGEL

Quickly, Gideon, for we mean to make battle tonight.

GIDEON

This cuirass is unendurable! Why didn't you tell me one wears an undergarment with these things? I had to learn it from Shillem this morning. "Do you not have a sagum underneath?" he said. I didn't even know what a sagum was. He studied me for a moment, unfavorably, to say the least. Oh, sir, surely you must see the consequences—even I who do not know what a sagum is can see that if we tell the fearful of heart to go home we shall be left with a shocking small army, a few reluctant husbands and some larking boys who think this whole matter a frolic. Oh, no, sir, I pray you! Shall I say to my chiefs: "We are outnumbered four to one. Therefore we are too many"? They think me a howling jackal as it is. And they shall think you the same. If you had only seen their faces when I passed on that matter of the oil lamps. They looked, to put the kindest word on it, they looked askance at me. Oh, this cuirass!

THE ANGEL
(Rising into his lordly fury and roaring out)

I am the Lord! I have said I shall redeem the house of Israel! With one man, if I choose it so, shall I redeem you! *(GIDEON looks nervously back to see if they are being overheard)* Gideon, take heed! My anger waxes hot against you! I shall consume you with my wrath! I shall open the earth, and I shall swallow you up into the earth!

GIDEON
(Rather cowed)

All right, pray, do not shout, sir. All right, it shall be done. *(He turns and with a show of petulance, starts back up the defile. PURAH, ever-alert fellow, wheels again to challenge him, but GIDEON wearily waves him back. GIDEON calls as he clambers up to the upper spur)* Chiefs of Zebulun, Asher, and Naphtali...*(*JAHLEEL, *who is back by now,* MALCHIEL, *and* SHILLEM *rise as* GIDEON *enters the tent)* Well, harken to this. It is the word of the Lord, spoken in a voice of thunder. You are each to go to your separate camps and proclaim in the ears of your people, saying: "Whoever is fearful and trembling, let him return home."

SHILLEM

Are you insane?

GIDEON
(His own temper exploding)
Well, what am I to do? It is the word of the Lord! He spoke it to me; I speak it to you! I too am ill-disposed to this idea! If we are to talk of those who tremble and fear, well, sir, I am surely captain of *that* army! This dreadful cuirass, may it be cursed, and all who put it on them! *(He wrenches at the bindings of the cuirass as he storms about)* If you think you can manage matters better, Naphtalite, well, then, you are general now; I am done with being general! I have been hearing nothing these past two days but what a wily warrior you are. *You* can parley with the Lord. I don't know why he picked on me in the first place!

SHILLEM

Peace, peace, Gideon.

GIDEON
Go and parley with him yourself if you think you can reap a better crop from him than I! He stands at the foot of that second spur, a large man with a black beard, robed in black linen of such richness as you have never seen. Murmur to him, if you will! Show the stiffness of your neck to him; not to me.

JAHLEEL
But the Lord keeps himself invisible to all but you.

GIDEON
Well, perhaps, I am insane. Have you ever considered that? Not every man who sees a vision is a prophet! You may all be gathered here at the fancy of a maniac! At any moment, I may drop down to all fours and howl like a laboring heifer! *(He wrenches the cuirass off and throws it down angrily)* Ah! That's better! Look at me, welted and raw. And my baldric was on backwards. My manservant shall feel my stick soon enough for that. Well, I shall say once more what was enjoined me by this angel whom only I can see. The Lord Yahweh feels that an army of thirty-two thousand Israelites will detract from the miraculous nature of his deliverance. He wants a smaller army. So go forth to your separate peoples and proclaim in their

ears, saying: "Whoever is fearful and trembling, let him return home."
(The chiefs look questioningly at one another, shrug, and troop out of the tent.
GIDEON *stands wearily for a moment; then goes out of the tent and calls to*
PURAH) Purah, go and charge my captains of Manasseh: "Go among the
tents of Manasseh and proclaim in the ears of the men, saying: 'All those
who fear the battle tonight may go home.'" *(A delighted smile breaks across*
PURAH's *face and he leaps to his charge)* And return here to me. I shall need
you.

> *(Some of his joy abated,* PURAH *exits. It is noticeably dark on stage now.*
> *Evening is come. After a moment,* THE ANGEL *strolls up the defile and*
> *goes into the tent.)*

THE ANGEL

Well, they have gone to do as you bid them. You were truly lordly in
your wrath.

GIDEON

Thank you.

THE ANGEL

Now then—by sending the fearful home, you will be left with an army
of ten thousand men. And this will still be too many.

GIDEON

I had expected as much.

THE ANGEL

Of these ten thousand who shall be left, three hundred are such great
cowards they are even too frightened to escape. You shall know them by
the following test: you shall take the ten thousand down to the springs of
Harod and let them drink of the water. And those that kneel down to
drink, cupping their hands, these shall you send home to their farms. And
those that lap the water, as a dog laps, these shall number three hundred.
These three hundred, Gideon, shall be your band of deliverers.

GIDEON

For my curiosity alone, why those who lap the water as a dog laps?

THE ANGEL

These three hundred are such frightened men they shall lie upon their
bellies and lap furtively for fear the Midianites might hear even their
drinking.

GIDEON

Well, then, an army of three hundred uncompromising cowards, armed,
I assume, with the three hundred oil lamps and the three hundred horns.

THE ANGEL

Ah! You see the battle plan then!

GIDEON

What battle plan?

THE ANGEL

It is an artful ruse. Place one hundred men at Shunem, one hundred more to the north at Endor, and a third company you shall keep right here with you. Then, upon a signal, all three companies shall light their lanterns, wave them in the air, all the while blowing loud blasts on their trumpets. The Midianites will then flee in panic down the valley to Beth-barah where you have already planned a savage greeting for them.

(GIDEON regards THE ANGEL for a long moment in a manner that can only be called quizzical.)

GIDEON

This is the plan for which you had me assemble four tribes of Israel to make war?

THE ANGEL

Aye.

GIDEON

One company of cowards in Shunem, another in Endor, and the third here, waving lanterns and blowing trumpets—that is the substance of it?

THE ANGEL

Aye.

GIDEON

Sir, I have heard at least five plans from that old fraud Shillem that I would deem more probable.

THE ANGEL

Well, it is intended to be a miracle, Gideon.

GIDEON

Oh, that is clear enough. *(He strides out of the tent, throwing up his arms in a gesture of deep annoyance)* It is a silly plan, sir! A blithe and silly plan! Three hundred tooting cowards will not send a hundred thousand and more men of Midian ranting down the Jordan Valley. The Midianites will simply look up and say: "What is that tooting?" Then they will unsheathe their scimitars, root us out and slash us up. It is a preposterous plan! And see how clear this night! A full moon, not a cloud! No night for hidden warfare, this! That olive bush one mile hence is visible. See! See! The chiefs have told the fearful they can go home. See how they race for their tents. Whisk! That one was folded quickly. And there!, that man is already scuttling down the slope to the caravan road to Bezek. How they scramble! Come and see! *(The ANGEL ambles out of the tent to join GIDEON on the spur)* How many did you compute would be left? Ten thousand? A rash estimate, my Lord. There will not even be three hundred from which to cull your cowards.

THE ANGEL

Whatever has come over you?

GIDEON

I'm finished with being a soldier.

THE ANGEL

You believed in me this morning.

GIDEON

Yes, then I did, but now I don't.

THE ANGEL

I have given you proofs of my godhood. I have performed wonders at your whim. Yesterday, at this very hour, you tested me. "See," you said, "I place this fleece of wool upon this hill. Now, prove to me you are truly the Lord. In the morning, let me see a heavy dew upon this fleece; but let there be no dew at all on the hill. The hill shall be dry, the fleece alone wet." And I performed this prodigy for you.

GIDEON

Yes, you did.

THE ANGEL

In the morning, it was as you asked. The hill was dry; the fleece was conclusively wet. You seemed convinced. You were effusive in your faith this morning.

GIDEON

Yes, I know. I fell to the ground, didn't I? And shouted: "Turn away from me! Show me not your face! For I have seen the face of the Lord, and I will surely die!" I hope nobody saw us. But then you went off. The sun rose fully up, and the tents around me came awake with the shouts of mortal men. I looked down at the sopping piece of wool in my hand; it seemed a soggy thing to have served a miracle. The fact is, all this dew on the fleece is really not much more than any conjurer's artifice. The diviners of Phrygia are said to change sticks into snakes—I should like to see that. And then I thought: Well, it's one thing to do sleight of hand with pieces of wool but quite another to smite one hundred and twenty thousand Midianites. Oh, well, you know how doubts will gallop. Within an hour, I had arrived at full despair.

THE ANGEL
(Snorts)

I too can make sticks into snakes. What manner of snake will you have?

An asp? A python? A horned viper? Oh, Gideon, would you have your God a wandering magician, slapping a timbrel and kicking his heels?

GIDEON
Do not rise in wrath against me, sir.

THE ANGEL
I am not in wrath. I am plainly confused. And sore at heart. I have loved you, and you have turned your back.

GIDEON
I do find you personable, sir.

THE ANGEL
Personable! Gideon, one does not merely fancy God. I demand a splendid love from you, abandoned adoration, a torrent, a storm of love.

GIDEON
I'm afraid I'm not the splendid sort, my Lord.

THE ANGEL
I shall make you love me. I'll do another miracle for you, if that will bolster you. The moon is too manifest for you, is it? Shall I eclipse it? Come, tell me what manner of miracle would please you.

GIDEON
No miracles at all. I have no faith in miracles; they are too easily denied. (*He scowls unhappily down at his feet. Then, his face slowly brightens, and he turns to* THE ANGEL, *bursting with an idea*) If you could send me a dream, my Lord...

THE ANGEL
A dream?

GIDEON
Yes, a dream. I put great stock in dreams.

THE ANGEL
A dream? You will not honor my miracles performed open-handedly before your eyes, but you put great stock in dreams.

GIDEON
Oh, sir, it is a well-known fact that dreams portend the future. If I could but have a dream, or, better yet, some other man's. The dreams of other men are frequently more significant.

THE ANGEL
What a devious mind man has developed. Well, then, what would you say to a royal dream? The dream, let us say, dreamed last night by Zalmunna or Zebah, the kings of Midian?

GIDEON

Oh, well, sir, such a dream, of course, would be most portentous. But surely I would not...

THE ANGEL

See then, there in that defile, two men, crowned by rubied aigrettes. I really think this must be Zebah and Zalmunna, kings of Midian. Yes, one sees the vivid colors of their tunics now. Royally caparisoned. Oh, that *is* good linen.

(At this point, enter ZEBAH *and* ZALMUNNA. *They are indeed richly caparisoned. Their jeweled crowns, girdles, sheaths, earrings and pendants glisten and gleam in the moonlight. They are both deeply involved with troubled thoughts.)*

ZEBAH

And that is not all. Let us pause here in this quiet spot, for I must tell you of this dream.

(They pause at the foot of the spur.)

THE ANGEL
(Sotto voice to GIDEON*)*

What luck! We are going to hear his dream.

*(*GIDEON *doesn't answer. He has been staring at the kings of Midian in utter amazement, mouth agape and eyes bulging, ever since they were first pointed out to him.)*

ZEBAH
(To ZALMUNNA*)*

Hear, then, this dream of Zebah, king of Midian. Behold, I dreamed a dream; and lo, a cake of barley bread tumbled into the camp of Midian and came to my tent, and struck it so that it fell, and turned it upside down, so that the tent lay flat. What meaning do you put on this, Zalmunna?

ZALMUNNA

It is an evil dream, Zebah. This is no other than the sword of Gideon the son of Joash, a man of Israel; into his hand God has given Midian and all the host. (ZEBAH *clutches his head with both hands and moans softly.* ZAL-MUNNA *looks nervously around)* Come, let us hurry from this spot. It is frightening here. I hear flappings and flutterings. What are you staring at?

ZEBAH
(So frightened he can hardly talk. He points upward)

The moon! The moon!

*(*ZALMUNNA *looks up, and terror sweeps across his face.)*

ZALMUNNA

Eclipsed! It is eclipsed!

ZEBAH

Ay!

ZALMUNNA
(Tugging at his fellow king)

Oh! Come! Come!

(He finally tugs ZEBAH *from his petrified fright, and they rush off. On the upper spur,* GIDEON, *now spotted by the only light on the black stage, stares after the fleeing kings. The expression of astonishment he wore all through this last sudden incident now slowly changes to aghast awe. He stares up at the darkened moon, and then slowly turns to* THE ANGEL.*)*

GIDEON
(Backing slowly away in awe; whispering)

Holy! Holy! Holy! Thou art the Lord! Thou art truly the Lord! *(He suddenly cringes, hides his face in his hands)* O! Turn away from me. I have seen the face of the Lord, and I will die!

THE ANGEL
(Moves slowly to GIDEON; *gently)*

Do not fear, you will not die. I am but a personation of the Lord.

*(*GIDEON *sinks to his knees and embraces the knees of* THE ANGEL. *He slowly lifts his face. His countenance gleams; his lips are parted in a smile of inspirited exaltation. He begins to chant in the fashion of Oriental psalmody.)*

GIDEON

Give ear, O Heavens! God our Lord is One!
Hear, O Kings; give ear, O princes! Glory!
Proclaim the Name of God, to Him I sing!
A psalm of love to God, the Lord of Israel!
I love Thee, Lord.
Holy! Holy! Holy!

(The lights dim out slowly.)

Curtain

"So Gideon and the three companies blew the trumpets and broke
the jars, holding in their left hands the torches, and in their right
hands the trumpets to blow and they cried: 'For the Lord and for
Gideon!'"

Scene 3

*A ridge overlooking the fords at Beth-barah, some hours later that night.
At rise,* THE ANGEL *is standing patiently stage right, regarding the battlefield
about him. Two Hebrew* SOLDIERS *hurtle in from downstage right.*

FIRST SOLDIER

For the Lord and for Gideon!
> *(He sounds a blast on his trumpet and disappears over the ridge. The* SEC-
> OND SOLDIER *pauses briefly to loot one of the bodies on the ground.)*

SECOND SOLDIER

For the Lord and for Gideon!
> *(He exits over the ridge. Enter* GIDEON, *running in from downstage left,
> panoplied for war again, sweaty and exultant, and waving his flambeau.)*

GIDEON
(Shouting)

For the Lord and for Gideon!
> *(He rushes to the crest of the ridge where he stands and blows a triumphant
> blast on his trumpet.)*

THE ANGEL

Gideon...

GIDEON
(Shouting down into the valley)

You men of Ephraim, there by the river! Can you hear me? What is the
outcome here? Have you the kings of Midian, Zebah and Zalmunna, in
your hand?

THE ANGEL

Gideon...
> *(A* THIRD SOLDIER *dashes in from the wings.)*

THIRD SOLDIER
(Shouting)

For the Lord and for Gideon!

(He exits over the ridge.)

GIDEON
(Shouting after him)
Naphtalite! Go to the river bank! Send me a captain of Ephraim to report the events that have happened here at Beth-barah!

THE ANGEL
Gideon...
(GIDEON, at last aware of THE ANGEL, turns and regards him with shocked and unbelieving eyes, then bursts into exultant laughter.)

GIDEON
My Lord, we have won the battle! Were you there at the beginning? Did you see the slaughter that took place in Jezreel? At least thirty thousand Midianites dead in Jezreel alone. Carpeted! I say Jezreel is carpeted with Midian's dead! You cannot put your foot down but there is a body underneath it. I say thirty thousand—perhaps more—countless! countless!—and another forty or fifty thousand, trampled, slashed, drowned in their flight down the Jordan Valley to here. It was hideous! Oh, look on this, a child! And that absurd camel there, it makes me cry. *(Indeed he has suddenly begun to cry.* THE ANGEL *proffers him a leather skin of water)* Thank you. Oh, I am weary. Picture, if you can, the sleeping camp of Midian at ten o'clock last night. Their tents lay darkly east and west across the Jezreel valley. Some oxen lowed, a clink here and there as the Midianite sentries took up the middle watch. I lit my lamp and shouted: "For the Lord and for Gideon!" On this signal, my three hundred men, now widely spaced in three troops, as you directed, shouted: "For the Lord and for Gideon!", blew trumpets, smashed pottery, stamped their feet and made as much noise as they could. Down below us, the men of Midian came yawning from their tents to see what all the clamor was. Then, suddenly, the cattle in the western camp were in stampede. They came crashing eastward through the tents, raising up a storm of dust so that no man knew his brother. The Midianites in the east, thinking themselves besieged, leaped into the dust with their swords, and the Midianites of the west, fleeing before their cattle, found themselves engaged in war with their own brothers until, my Lord, the whole vast multitude, one hundred thousand men and women, their young and old and all their animals, fled in shrieking frenzy to the Jordan River. I stood upon the hill at Harod, transfixed by the sight of it!
(A FOURTH SOLDIER *enters, shouting.)*

FOURTH SOLDIER
For the Lord and for Gideon!
(He exits.)

GIDEON

Then, at the Jordan, down from the hills came the men of Naphtali and Asher and the houses of Manasseh with their sickles and plowshares, and reaped the Midianites as so much wheat. At last, the shreds and tatters of this mighty host came splashing into the shoals here at Beth-barah, where the men of Ephraim sprang from their ambush and smote the survivors until surely there is not one left that breathes. The vultures will be flapping thick tomorrow. I see the soldiers have begun to gather the stray cows and sheep. There is much looting going on. Indeed, I stripped a corpse myself just before. *(He indicates a jeweled sheath on his baldric, and tries to pull out the falcate sword from the sheath; he can't get it out)* They have a strange curved sword, these Midianites, with the honed edge outward. One slashes away. It seems awkward. Oh, my Lord, it came to pass, as you said. One hundred and twenty thousand Midianites lie slain this night. How great you are, my Lord, and how impermanent is man. *(He begins to snicker and giggle)* Forgive me, my Lord, forgive me...*(In a moment, he has yielded to a spasm of uncontrollable laughter. He stands, clutching his sides, shouting and wheezing, lurching about, stumbling over bodies. He manages to squeeze out bursts of sentences)* Oh, my Lord! You will not believe this! Oh! It is so comical, let me gather my wits! Oh, I am a foolish ass indeed! Oh! Oh! Oh! My Lord, one hundred twenty thousand Midianites were slain this night, the entire host of them, or so it seems! Oh! Oh! One hundred twenty thousand of them slain, and I, the captain of the hosts of Israel...Oh! Oh! Oh!...and I, my Lord, I, the captain of the hosts, did not so much as unsheathe my dagger! I took no part at all in the whole bloody battle! Do you understand, my Lord? Oh! I never got within a mile of a Midianite! I watched the whole night from the hills! *(It is too much for him. GIDEON has to lie down flat on his back. Tears of laughter stream from his eyes. After a moment, he sits up, spent and sighing)* Forgive me, my Lord. I have been shaken badly this night. I am not my own master.

THE ANGEL

It is not yet finished, Gideon. The kings of Midian with fifteen thousand of their men have escaped across the river.

GIDEON

Oh? I shall have to gather my three hundred men.
(Wearily he starts to rise.)

THE ANGEL

No, no, rest, Gideon. There are some moments yet till dawn. You shall pursue after Zebah and Zalmunna then.

GIDEON
(Lying back exhausted on the ground)
The kings of Midian...

THE ANGEL
The kings of Midian are halfway to the walled city of Karkor. You will have them in your hand tomorrow night. Now rest and spend this interlude with me.

GIDEON
(Closing his eyes)
Have I found favor in your eyes tonight, my Lord?

THE ANGEL
(Gently)
Indeed you have.
(THE ANGEL *now sits cross-legged besides* GIDEON's *resting body. A silence falls between the two.*)

GIDEON
(After a moment)
Have you loved many men, my Lord?

THE ANGEL
I love all men. It is my essence.

GIDEON
I mean, men with whom you have truly commerced face-to-face as you have with me.

THE ANGEL
Five or six, perhaps.

GIDEON
Were they as pleasing to you as I am, my Lord?

THE ANGEL
(Smiling)
What a vain fellow you are.

GIDEON
Understand, my Lord, I do not hold these other loves to your discredit.

THE ANGEL
Are you being kind to me, Gideon? Now you must own that is vain of you. And you are something of a prig too, taking this high moral tone, even if I were no more than the dissolute lady you seem to think me.

GIDEON
Oh, my Lord, you are God, and your name is One!

THE ANGEL

I am just teasing you, Gideon.

GIDEON

I love you more than I have ever loved anyone.

THE ANGEL

I know you do.

GIDEON

I thought of nothing but you the whole night. I am possessed by all the lunacy of love. If I could, I would cover you with veils, God, and keep you hidden behind the curtains in my tent. Oh! Just say again you love me, God.

THE ANGEL

I do, Gideon.

GIDEON

I do not know why. I must say, I do not know why.

THE ANGEL

I hardly know why myself, but then passion is an unreasonable thing. *(He leans back against a rock, rather pensive)* Let me consider. I have loved five men, or six if I add in Phinehas, but I could not say I truly loved Phinehas. Phinehas was high priest in the years that followed Joshua, and we spoke ten times or so of sacerdotal things, the setting of the year's calendar, such matters as that. A nice man, Phinehas, good family, son of Eleazar the son of Aaron—you cannot be better bred than that; but, still, not my sort. Too pinch-penny with his passions. The costive soul makes priests; it does not make lovers. Abraham, Isaac, Jacob of course...Joshua. But the man I most loved was Moses.

GIDEON

Yes?

THE ANGEL

I loved him very much. I do not think I shall love any man so much again. And he was scarcely Hebrew. He was bred as an Egyptian and married a gentile woman. Yes, I think the man was still uncircumcised the day I first beheld him herding sheep at Horeb, a hulking, harelipped, solitary man, quite unattractive really, stammered, dour—nay, say sullen—lacking wit, one of those ever-earnest fellows. Yet I fancied Moses from the very first. Gaunt he stood against the crags of Horeb, a monumentally impassioned man. It is passion, Gideon, that carries man to God. And passion is a balky beast. Few men ever let it out the stable. It brooks no bridle; indeed, it bridles you; it rides the rider. Yet, it inspirits man's sessile soul above his own inadequate world and makes real such things as beauty, fancy, love, and God and all those other things that are not quite molecular but are. Passion is the very fact of God in man that makes him other than a brute. I must own, Gideon, yours was an old and cold and settled soul, and I huffed and puffed quite a bit before I found the least flame of passion in you.

GIDEON

What is it that you love in me, my Lord? These other men were saints or prophets, but I am an ordinary sort. I am as all men are.

THE ANGEL.

Well, perhaps *that* is your special attraction, your ordinariness. I would have plain men love me, not just saints.

GIDEON

Well, that isn't very nice.

THE ANGEL

Oh, Gideon, you are difficult.

GIDEON

Well, I do not think it gratifying to be loved for one's lack of distinction. *(He stands, ruffled)* I thought I managed my duties well tonight.

THE ANGEL

Indeed, you did.

GIDEON

To speak plainly, I think I make a good show of being a general. I have a commanding voice and am not unhandsome in my armor.

THE ANGEL

You make a splendid figure.

GIDEON

You find me amusing.

THE ANGEL

Well, you are a pompous ass.

GIDEON

Yes, so I am. *(His natural good humor returns, and he laughs agreeably at himself)* Oh, it is indeed the truth, God. Like all modest men, I am impossibly vain. I amuse even myself, strutting about, shouting—well, not really shouting; I'm cleverer than that at the charade. I put myself forth more as the calm but resolute general, imperative but not forbidding. What a peacock I am! It is amusing, isn't it?

THE ANGEL

It is.

(GIDEON *sits down beside* THE ANGEL, *a little sad now.*)

GIDEON

I have had very little esteem in my life, my Lord, and I do not think there is much harm in my relishing this one moment of honor. I have this one son, Jether, who is twelve years old, the son of my first wife, and even he uses me lightly. I am not esteemed, my Lord, even in my own tent, and this has given me great pain.

(THE ANGEL *regards* GIDEON *compassionately.*)

THE ANGEL

I shall give you seventy sons, Gideon; they shall praise your name. You shall know the ardor of many wives.

GIDEON

I should like that.

THE ANGEL

Oh, Gideon, I shall bless you. I shall make your fields to prosper. I shall make your cattle fat. Your father shall kneel before you and embrace your knees. All Israel shall say: "Regard Gideon; he is the most blessed of men, for he is beloved of God." You seem displeased by all this good fortune.

(*This last in reference to a scowl deepening on* GIDEON's *brow.*)

GIDEON

Yes, well, all this greatness, all this good fortune which you will make mine, will not really be mine. It is all but a gift from God. There is no honor that reflects to me in it at all, merely that I am beloved of God.

THE ANGEL

Well, that is a somewhat less than gracious thing to say. The love of God will not suffice for you indeed.

GIDEON
(*Ashamed*)

I spoke coarsely, Lord. Forgive me.

THE ANGEL

I wonder if this vanity of yours is as ingenuous as it seemed, and if it is not a sinister thing rather. What is vanity in man really, but the illusion that he has a purpose? Do not presume to matter, Gideon, for in the house of God you matter not. My universe is large beyond your knowing; there is no beginning, there is no end to it. You are a meaningless thing and live only in my eye. I shall make you great, Gideon, because I love you; but it is merely my caprice. If you displease me, I shall destroy you in a whim of temper. To love me, Gideon, you must abandon all your vanities. They are presumptuous and will come between us.

GIDEON
(Truly penitent)

Oh, my Lord, that could never be.

THE ANGEL

Consider how you have already reduced me to some kind of clever if wanton lady who finds you handsome and sends you into battle with her handkerchief.

GIDEON

My Lord, I...

THE ANGEL

Surely, I shall see you tomorrow vaunting yourself before the armies, saying it was by your hand, and not mine, that Israel was redeemed from the Midianites.

GIDEON

Oh, my Lord, I would sooner cut my throat with this—*(He wrenches at his Midianite sword again, and again it sticks to its scabbard)*—with this—Oh! How do they manage with these things? At any rate, if I could get it out of its scabbard, I would slit my throat with it before I derogated you, my Lord.

THE ANGEL
(Laughing)

Oh, Gideon. I love you, and I will exalt you over all men. But I fear you will betray me.

> *(GIDEON gives up on the sword, turns to THE ANGEL and regards him with manifest devotion. He kneels before THE ANGEL, takes the latter's hand and presses it to his lips.)*

GIDEON
(Fervently)

The Lord is my God, the Lord is One. He is vast, ineffable, the maker and the mover of all things, and He has paused to love me; shall I ask for other blessings? God, do not fear my vanity. I will never betray you.

> *(THE ANGEL, touched, gently strokes the bowed head before him. Enter tired SOLDIERS, straggling slowly across the stage.)*

SOLDIER
(Wearily)

For the Lord and for Gideon.

> *(They disappear over the ridge. The first streaks of dawn are now lightening the sky. THE ANGEL marks the coming of day.)*

THE ANGEL

It's morning now, Gideon.

(He is interrupted by the entrance of SHILLEM. *That is, two soldiers enter, bracing a rubber-legged and wheezing* SHILLEM *between them. Despite his dreadful condition, the old man holds fast to his warbow.* THE ANGEL *notes* SHILLEM's *entrance with a smile)*

THE ANGEL

The troops of Shillem have come.

SHILLEM
(Gasping; to the two SOLDIERS*)*

Here—set me here.
(The two SOLDIERS *sit him gently down, propped up against a large rock, where he slumps, all but dead of exhaustion.)*

GIDEON

Oh, Shillem! I told you to stay behind. You will exhaust yourself with all this racing up and down these hills. *(To* THE ANGEL*)* The old popinjay fell in a faint five minutes after the slaughter in Jezreel began. It seems the sight of blood sickens him.

THE ANGEL
(Laughing)

Go then, Gideon, and find Shethulah, the prince of Ephraim. He's very arrogant and will not like a man from Manasseh such as you ordering him about.

GIDEON

Oh, dear. *(To the two* SOLDIERS*)* Go and join your fellows on the river bank. I will be shortly there.
(The two SOLDIERS *exit.)*

THE ANGEL
(To GIDEON*)*

The spirit of the Lord shall be with you.
(He exits with a casual wave of his hand.)

GIDEON
(Giving SHILLEM *his skin of water)*

Here, drink this and rest.
(It is more than SHILLEM *can manage to even raise the skin of water to his lips. It dangles slackly from his fingers.)*

SHILLEM

Oh, Gideon, tell no one, I beg you, that I swooned at the sight of battle.

GIDEON

Shillem, my old captain, we are all wretched cowards, the full three hundred of us.

SHILLEM

I spent the night, hiding in a cave, clutching my warbow.

GIDEON

Yes, I know. Now, rest here. I must go find the proud prince of Ephraim and learn the state of things here at Beth-barah.

(He exits over the ridge. SHILLEM, *alone now, allows himself a sob or two.)*

SHILLEM

Oh, how despicable I am. Let all men know that Shillem is a coward, a rabbit, a...

(He breaks off as HEZEKIAH *and* MALCHIEL *and two* SOLDIERS *enter from stage right, waving their lamps and shouting:)*

HEZEKIAH, MALCHIEL, SOLDIERS

For the Lord and for Gideon!

(They are about to clamber across the ridge when HEZEKIAH *sees* SHILLEM *sprawled downstage.* HEZEKIAH *comes puffing down to the old man, sits beside him, crosses his legs.)*

HEZEKIAH
(Sighing)

Well, we seem to have won the war and decimated the entire host of Midian—how did we ever manage to do that? Well, I daresay we shall find sensible explanations for everything. You were with Gideon, were you not? That put you in the thick of it. Did you kill many of the enemy?

(A brief struggle for virtue ensues in SHILLEM.*)*

SHILLEM
(Mumbling)

Two or three.

HEZEKIAH

Two or three, did you say?

SHILLEM

Dozen.

HEZEKIAH

Two or three dozen!

SHILLEM

Yes, I was with Gideon, as you say, when the Midianite herds broke into stampede. Seeing the Midianites disconcerted, I led a charge down from my hill, panicking the foe into headlong flight to the Jordan valley. This, I would have to say, was the pivotal point of the battle.

*(*MALCHIEL, *who has been walking slowly about the stage examining the battlefield, now looks up, his bold, fanatic eyes blazing in his dark, sweated face.)*

MALCHIEL

We have heard fantastic stories of Gideon's deeds. A woman of Manasseh told us she saw Gideon leap from a tree into a pack of ten Midianites and smite them all with ten strokes of his spear.

SHILLEM

She told you all wrong. His weapon was an ox-goad, and there were twenty of the foe, not ten.

HEZEKIAH

Twenty?

MALCHIEL

Twenty men did Gideon smite with an ox-goad! Here, look on this! A serpent has coiled itself upon this fallen Midianite. This augurs significantly.

HEZEKIAH
(Nudging SHILLEM)

My brother is adroit at divination.

MALCHIEL
(With fanatic fervor)

What manner of god is this Yahweh of Gideon's? His incarnation is the bull; his ideogram is the coiled serpent.
(He scoops up a handful of dirt and lets it fall back to the ground. He kneels and studies the patterns it makes.)

HEZEKIAH
(Winking at SHILLEM)

My brother divines from the configurations of the ground and sees great significance in pebbles.

MALCHIEL
(Studying the geomantic pattern)

Regard. A crescent moon and, here again, a coiled viper upon a cloven heart. Oh, dazzling among gods is this Yahweh; he is both sun and moon; and Gideon is his only son. Behold! The morning star! Gideon is single among men as the morning star is single in the heavens! Sing praise! Cry out for Gideon! The son of Yahweh, the bull-god! Ay!
(He stands stiffly upright and promptly falls into a dead faint. SHILLEM, rather taken aback by this, sits up with a start.)

HEZEKIAH

He'll be all right. He is given to these ecstatic moments.

SHILLEM

Is he really?

HEZEKIAH

He spends much time with Phoenician priests who are emotional. But I prefer to find more reasonable explanations for things than gods. I am not a little known in my own city of Kanah as a scholar and have predicted several eclipses. I read and write a competent Egyptian hand and have some knowledge of medicinal herbs. Actually, I attracted some attention in learned circles a few years ago with my theory of the ecliptic of the sun; you may have heard something of that.

SHILLEM

Look here, are we to leave your brother lying around like that?

HEZEKIAH

I think that when all the facts are known, this improbable battle will seem more probable. It was a clever stratagem of Gideon's, stampeding the cattle; and, of course, your opportune assault on the Midianite flank explains much of the enemy's panic. Piece by piece, the events of the night become less mystical.

SHILLEM

On my soul!

(This last refers to the entrance of SHETHULAH, *a prince of Ephraim, followed by several* SOLDIERS, *who loom up from the upstage side of the ridge.* SHETHULAH *is holding aloft two grisly decapitated heads.)*

SHETHULAH

Behold the heads of Oreb and Zeeb, princes of Midian, the sons of the kings of Midian. *(*MALCHIEL *remains in his trance.* HEZEKIAH *rises)* Which of you three is Gideon the son of Joash the Abiezrite?

SHILLEM

He has gone to the river to find the prince of Ephraim.

SHETHULAH

I am the prince of princes of Ephraim. I am Shethulah the son of Elishama, the son of Ammihud, the son of Ephraim, the son of Joseph. Bring forth this Gideon, send men after him so that he may account to me for what he did, that he has made war on Midian but he did not ask my counsel? Is not Ephraim the prince among all the tribes of Israel, the most populous in number, the richest in wealth? Who shall lead the tribes of Israel in war? Shall it not be Ephraim?

*(*HEZEKIAH *considers this statement with scholarly detachment.)*

HEZEKIAH

(To SHILLEM*)*

These Ephraimites are so superior really, There's no historical basis for it at all, you know.

SHETHULAH

Captain of Asher, go with your men down to the valley and chop off the hands of all the dead that we may make a count of how many slain.

HEZEKIAH

Sir, it's all very well to play the proud prince with the chief of Naphtali here and me, but I suggest you be more humble when Gideon comes. Know the manner of man this Gideon is. Know that Gideon leaped from a tree and smote—*(Turns to* SHILLEM*)* How many did you say, twenty?

SHILLEM

Did I say twenty? Oh, well, in that case, it was nearer forty.
(For a long moment, HEZEKIAH studies SHILLEM with the scientist's skeptical eye. Then, he turns back to SHETHULAH.)

HEZEKIAH

Eighty men did Gideon smite with an ox-goad.

SHETHULAH
(Very impressed)

Eighty men!
(At this moment, MALCHIEL springs up to his feet with a shrill cry.)

MALCHIEL

Ay! The vision of Malchiel! The oracle of a man whose eye is opened! Hear the history of Gideon.

SHILLEM
(Crying out)

Tell us your vision, oh, holy man!

HEZEKIAH
(Seizing the elbow of the startled SHETHULAH)

My brother, sir, is adroit at divination and not to be taken lightly.
(GIDEON appears, coming up from the far side of the ridge. He pauses on the crest to hear MALCHIEL's testimony. At the same time, THE ANGEL enters and stands downstage right, watching.)

MALCHIEL
(In a trance)

The great god, Yahweh, the god of Moses, who is the bull, who is the lion; in his left hand is a crescent sword, in his right hand is a ball of fire; he saw a woman of Manasseh. He leaned over her lips. He raised his voice and said: "Behold her lips are as sweet as a bunch of grapes." In the perfume of the cedars did they lay. When dawn broke, a cloud black as night rose from heaven's foundations. The great god Yahweh rose into the sky in a chariot of lapis lazuli and gold. In the arms of the Manassehite woman he placed an infant. On its brow was coiled the sacred asp. Behold! It was Gideon, the man-god, the son of Yahweh, the redeemer of Israel, the man of valor, the god Gideon!

(A silence follows this enthusiastic statement.)

GIDEON
(From the crest of the ridge)

Oh, Malchiel, you cannot be serious.

(All whirl at the sound of GIDEON's *voice.* MALCHIEL *falls to his knees and prostrates himself.)*

SHILLEM

There, ye Ephraimites, stands Gideon, who with an ox-goad smote one hundred men!

*(*GIDEON *bursts into laughter.)*

GIDEON

A hundred men! Oh, Shillem, what a fearful fiction! What have you been telling this noble man? For you, sir, must surely be Shethulah, the prince of princes in Ephraim.

(He descends in obsequious haste from the ridge. For a moment he and SHETHULAH, *who is now in abject awe of* GIDEON, *vie with each other in the gestures of deference.)*

SHETHULAH
(Humbly proffering the decapitated heads of the Midianite princes to GIDEON)

Behold the heads of Oreb and Zeeb, the princes of Midian.

GIDEON

Don't give them to me. I wouldn't know what to do with them. Hang them on the walls of your city. I think that is the practice. *(Winking at* THE ANGEL*)* How many did he have me killing with an ox-goad, one hundred? *(He bursts into laughter; to* SHETHULAH*)* The truth is, great lord, I killed no Midianites at all.

*(*SHETHULAH *looks up startled.)*

SHETHULAH

You killed no Midianites at all?

GIDEON
(Beaming)

Not a one.

(Rage sweeps across the Ephraimite prince's face. He is furious at being gulled and regards SHILLEM *and* HEZEKIAH *with a fierce eye.)*

SHETHULAH

Then, Gideon, you shall account to me for what you have done, that you made war against Midian and did not seek my counsel. Shall Manasseh lead the hosts and Ephraim be the scavengers? Did not Jacob bless Ephraim before his brother, saying: "Ephraim shall be greater than his brother Manasseh"? I shall take command of the hosts of Israel now, Gideon!

(He seizes a whip from one of the soldiers and would lash GIDEON *but is intercepted by* GIDEON.*)*

GIDEON

Hear, O Ephraimite! Do not contend with me for glory, for it is neither yours nor is it mine! This glory is the Lord's! Give praise to the Lord for he has triumphed gloriously. Bow down!

(All sink to their knees and bow their heads down to the ground. GIDEON *surveys the supplicating backs for a moment, then turns and slowly walks to where* THE ANGEL *stands stage right, regarding* GIDEON *with effulgent love.* GIDEON *prostrates himself before* THE ANGEL.*)*

GIDEON

Did you truly fear my vanity? Oh, timeless and immane God, I yearn after you and seek only to be pleasing in your eye.

THE ANGEL

Rise up, good Gideon, and pursue after the kings of the enemy.

*(*GIDEON *stands.)*

GIDEON

Rise up! We have more war to make! These are my charges to you all. Let the Ephraimites count the dead and bury them that the land may be clean of carrion and that the jackals may not overrun us. Captains of Asher and Naphtali, come with me. We shall pursue after the kings of Midian.

(The others all stand. Again, GIDEON *tries to wrench his Midianite sword from its scabbard to flourish it, but again it sticks. Flourishing his empty hand instead, he shouts.)*

GIDEON

For Gideon and for the Lord!

(He leaps out of view over the ridge. SHILLEM, HEZEKIAH, MALCHIEL, *and* SOLDIERS, *brandishing their weapons, exit quickly after him.)*

SHILLEM, HEZEKIAH, MALCHIEL *and* SOLDIERS

For Gideon and for the Lord!

*(*SHETHULAH *and his Ephraimite* SOLDIERS *follow after them, shouting.)*

EPHRAIMITES

For Gideon and for the Lord!

(They exit over the ridge. THE ANGEL *is now left alone onstage, frowning thoughtfully. He detaches himself from the arch and shuffles to center stage*

where he tugs at his beard pensively.)

THE ANGEL
(Muttering)

"For Gideon and for the Lord," indeed. It used to be: "For the Lord and for Gideon."

(He shrugs in the ageless Hebrew fashion and strides offstage left.)

The curtain comes down quickly.

ACT II

"And the elders of Succoth said, Are Zebah and Zalmunna in your hand, that we should give bread to your army? And Gideon said, Therefore when the Lord has delivered Zebah and Zalmunna into my hand, then I will tear your flesh."

SCENE 1

A threshing floor on a hill by the city of Succoth.
The time is two days later in the afternoon.
At rise, there are three senior gentlemen, obviously prisoners, standing disconsolately at stage left. A rope joins their necks, and their hands are tied in front of them. These are the elders of Succoth. There are supposed to be seventy-four more of them offstage. We can perhaps see one or two. A guard stands in attendance on them. A second soldier stares off upstage over a parapet. He is apparently a LOOKOUT.
THE ANGEL now appears, climbing up to the top of the threshing floor. He stands a moment, amiably looking around. Suddenly the LOOKOUT straightens to attention and shouts:

THE LOOKOUT
Gideon is here! He is at the gates!

VOICE
(Off)
He comes! Gideon comes!
(Shouts and alarum are heard offstage; SHILLEM suddenly looms up out of the pit, clambering up to the threshing floor.)

SHILLEM
Prepare the feast! Soldiers, clear the space before the gates! Maidens, bring fruit here, bring wine! Bring skewers of meat for Gideon!
(More shouts and alarum off down in the pit. WOMEN OF SUCCOTH come scurrying up bearing bowls of pomegranates, grapes, figs, slabs of steaming mutton, and skins of wine. SHETHULAH, the Ephraimite prince, also

enters, champing away on a leg of lamb as he does. Both he and SHILLEM
are nicely drunk. SHILLEM *regards the elders standing stage right.)*

SHILLEM

The elders of Succoth, are they all here? Seven and seventy of them?
Oh, you wretched chiefs of Succoth! You will surely die today. This is what
Gideon charged me this morning: "Go in advance, Shillem," said he, "my
mighty captain, and capture the seven and seventy elders of Succoth, for
they are Hebrews; yet, they jeered at the word of the Lord. The wrath of
God is hot against them and they shall die." *(A ram's horn is heard far offstage. Shouting down into the pit)* Bugler, sound your trumpet!

*(The ram's horn sounds offstage, closer than before, and a bugler onstage
responds. The stage crowds up with people.)*

ALL
(Singing)

Hosanna! Hosanna!
Make melody to Gideon!
Barak has slain his thousands!
But Gideon tens of thousands!
He is as the wild ox who gores the foe!
Barak has slain his thousands!
But Gideon tens of thousands!
O Israel! O Israel!
Israel! Israel!

VOICES

They are here! They are here! Gideon is here!
(Indeed, MALCHIEL *comes bouncing up to the top of the threshing floor,
where he stands addressing the multitude in the pit.)*

MALCHIEL

We have won the battle of Karkor! With twenty thousand men of
Reuben and Gad, we smote the last of Midian! There is not one left that
breathes! Great was the glory of Barak, of Ehud and Othniel, but sovereign is the glory of Gideon. Bow down!

*(Everyone on the threshing floor and presumably everyone in the pit bends
low in homage. A hush falls on the stage. In the midst of it,* GIDEON *enters
climbing up from the pit, followed by* HEZEKIAH *and two* WOMEN *who
thrust baskets of grapes and pomegranates at the conquering hero.)*

FIRST WOMAN

The first grapes of the year, my lord Gideon.

SECOND WOMAN

The first of the summer fruits, my lord Gideon.

(GIDEON *seems pleased by all this homage. He surveys the pit below him rather grandly.* THE ANGEL *now crosses to* GIDEON *and claps him heartily on the back.* GIDEON *turns startled. A quick look of apprehension sweeps over his face. He wheels on the obeisant people around him and below him and thunders out.*)

GIDEON

Be still, you foolish people! Am I the Lord that you bring me first fruits? Make no god of me! It was the Lord that redeemed you from Midian! Rise up, then, rise up! *(He looks for approval from* THE ANGEL, *and almost stumbles over a maiden at his feet. She is a darkly savage and sinuous thing of fourteen, a marriageable age in those days)* Rise up, you silly woman. Whose maiden is this?

SHILLEM

She is Orpah the daughter of the elder Ozni, standing there.

GIDEON

The daughter of Ozni? He was most guilty of all the elders. Poor maiden, her father shall die first. *(Turns to the elders, raising a foreboding finger at them)* Regard the elders of Succoth!

OZNI

(An elder, flinging himself at GIDEON's *feet)*
O, Puissant Gideon, hear our suffrage.

A SECOND ELDER

Pity us, my lord.

A THIRD ELDER

O, pity us, sire.

GIDEON

One day ago, you elders, my three hundred men and I, hot in pursuit of Zebah and Zalmunna, came to these gates. And you seven and seventy elders of Succoth with Ozni the son of Deuel at your head came forth to meet us. "Pray," I said, "give loaves of bread to the people who follow me; for they are faint, and I am pursuing after Zebah and Zalmunna, the kings of Midian." And you all did taunt me. "Are Zebah and Zalmunna already in your hand," you said to me, "that we should give bread to your army?" "These are the soldiers of the Lord!" I said. "Give them food, or will you mock the Lord?" And you, Ozni, son of Deuel, then said: "Show us Zebah and Zalmunna in your hand, and we shall give you loaves of bread." Well, then, bring forth Zebah and Zalmunna!

(*Enter* ZEBAH *and* ZALMUNNA, *their hands tied in front of them, their necks joined by a rope. They are guarded by two* SOLDIERS.)

GIDEON

Behold! Zebah and Zalmunna, the kings of Midian, are in my hand!
(The two kings drop to their knees, place their faces at GIDEON's *feet.* GIDEON *puts a foot on the neck of* ZEBAH.)

GIDEON

We do not practice mutilation in Israel. I shall kill you plainly, Zebah and Zalmunna.
(With a quick, strong, downward thrust, GIDEON *plunges his spear into* ZEBAH's *ribs. The Midianite king emits a short, strangled gasp and topples over dead. The spear remains in* GIDEON's *hand, now dripping red with blood. With a second quick thrust, he dispatches* ZALMUNNA, *who screams out shrilly and falls, the spear protruding slantwise from under his arm. A frightened silence fills the stage.)*

GIDEON

This was Midian, a violent tribe. They lived ten generations. They are no more. As it was with the kings of Midian, O elders, so shall it be with you. (GIDEON *wrenches the spear loose from* ZALMUNNA's *body, turns, strides to the elders on the tower, raising his spear above his head)* The Voice of the Lord came to me, thundering: "Smite the elders of Succoth, preserve not one, so that all Israel may know the fear of God!"
(But the sheer piteousness of the three old men before him stays his hand. Mutely, they stare up at him, tears streaming down their cheeks. One of the WOMEN *breaks into a high-pitched wail.* GIDEON *lowers his spear, darts a nervous look at* THE ANGEL.)

GIDEON

Well, I'm faint; I marched all day. Set food and wine before me that I may eat and drink. I shall kill these old men after that. *(The* WOMEN *scurry off.* GIDEON *addresses the host of people onstage)* Give praise to the Lord, for he is the kinsman, he is the rock, he is a man of war. Bow down!
(The people all go down upon their knees and bow their heads forward so that their brows touch the floor between their hands—the full salaam. GIDEON *regards the stage of bowed backs, then turns and looks for* THE ANGEL, *now downstage right again.* GIDEON, *ambles over, rubbing his neck and sighing wearily.)*

GIDEON

I slept two hours last night, if that much, and ache in every bone. We left Karkor at break of day. It is almost thirty miles and a mountainous route. I had not thought to see you here, my Lord.

THE ANGEL

Will you not embrace me?

GIDEON

Oh, indeed, yes, of course.

(He kneels quickly, kisses the hem of THE ANGEL's *robe, and stands.)*

THE ANGEL

That was perfunctory, Gideon.

GIDEON

Well, I made battle all last night, God, and marched all day and ate nothing but some figs and cake. I do not feel affectionate at the moment.

THE ANGEL

You are not pleased that I am here.

GIDEON

Well, I have many things to do, my Lord. It would be better if you waited for me at my tent at Ophrah.

THE ANGEL

Like your other wives.

GIDEON

You are being quarrelsome. You know you are more than wife to me. I am on edge and close to temper, and I pray you, leave me to myself for the moment.

THE ANGEL

As you say. I shall wait beside your tent at Ophrah for you.

GIDEON

I should be home within a day or two.

THE ANGEL

Will you not embrace me before I go?

(GIDEON sighs a brief sigh of exasperation, goes to his knees again, and brushes the hem of THE ANGEL's *robe with his lips.* THE ANGEL *starts off, but* GIDEON, *still on his knees, calls him.)*

GIDEON

Oh, my Lord.

THE ANGEL
(Turning)

Yes?

GIDEON
(Standing)

My Lord, about these elders of Succoth here. You came to me in a dream last night and said: "Smite them all, preserve not one that breathes." Yet, I wonder, is that not perhaps too harsh a penalty? They seem so piteous a lot of senior gentlemen. And they are Hebrews, my

Lord. They are our people.

THE ANGEL

They made light of the Lord. Will you pass by while men make light of me?

GIDEON

I thought perhaps to scourge them with whips, forty lashes less one for each. That would surely instruct them in the fear of God.

THE ANGEL

These men are utter wretches, Gideon. Of all the clans of Gad, these men of Succoth have done most evilly in mine eyes. I have had it in mind several times to strike them down.

GIDEON

I pity them, my Lord.

THE ANGEL

It is not just this matter of their taunting you. The men of Succoth have married their sons to the daughters of Moab and practice the ways of Moab. They lie with men as with a woman and uncover the nakedness of their own daughters. They eat unslaughtered meat with its carrion blood still in it, oppress the stranger and revile the widow and the orphan. They are a miscreant folk. Smite these elders, every one, Gideon, preserve not one, so that all Israel may hear and fear, so that the name of the Lord shall be a name of terror in their hearts, and they shall walk in my ways again.

GIDEON

Well, I shall kill them then since you wish it.

THE ANGEL

Oh, Gideon, you make so much of death. You must not be so temporal. It is all right for the bulk of men to fear death, for in death they fear me. But, in truth, there isn't anything to it at all. Nothing happens, nothing changes; the essence of things goes on. You see, you measure things in time, but there is no time in truth. You live now ten million years ago and are at this moment ten million years hence, or more; for there are no years. The slaying of seventy-seven elders happens but it does not happen, for they live even so and have died before, and all is now, which was and is forever. Oh, dear, I see this is heavy going for you.

GIDEON

Well, I follow you here and there a bit; not everything of course.

THE ANGEL

Well, you shouldn't bother your head with all these speculations anyway. I am the final truth of all things, Gideon, so you need only love me and live your life as I will it for you, and it shall be a seemly thing.

GIDEON

My point, you see, is that I pity these old men.

THE ANGEL

Of course you do. But you are being vain again, for to pity a man's death is to say his life was significant, which it isn't. Now, let us have an end to this. Go and smite the elders, I am the Lord.

GIDEON

As you say.

THE ANGEL

(*Turning to go*)

Then, peace be with you, Gideon. I shall wait for you beside your tent.

GIDEON

(*Nervously shuffling his feet*)

My Lord—

THE ANGEL

Yes?

GIDEON

My Lord—oh, how shall I say it? My Lord, the people have made much of me these past few days. Well, as you see, even here in Succoth. But what an ovation was accorded to me at Mahanaim! Great crowds gathered along the highway and shouted my name. Maidens came forth with dancing and with timbrels. I fancy that sort of thing, as, of course, you know. And twice today, Malchiel there, who is an enthusiastic man, stood up before thousands—at Mahanaim and at Jogbehah too—and called me king, and the people shouted as with one voice: "Amen!" I would like to be king, my Lord.

THE ANGEL

But Gideon—

GIDEON

I could hardly sleep last night for thinking of myself as king. That demon vanity crept into my tent like a succubus and had me trying on different crowns, diadems from Babylon and pschents from Egypt. I finally dropped off, having decided I looked best with no crown at all, a modest king, receiving the ambassadors from Armenia while plowing his own fields, distinguishable from his servants only by his noble bearing. Well, you know what a vain ass I am. Oh, Lord, could I not be king of Israel?

THE ANGEL

Gideon, I am king of Israel. To say Israel needs another king suggests I am inadequate.

GIDEON
(In a burst of temper)

I do not think I ask so very much! I do not say I will usurp your throne. I only ask for a nominal crown and a few trappings. Some purfled robes, perhaps a modest palace. You are ever accusing me of wishing to cheat you! Indeed, I meant to make your name greater. I would build altars for you and enforce your laws. All I ask was a bit of pomp because I am a vain fellow and like to preen before the people. Well, then I am vain! That is my manner! You could indulge me in this minor frailty. Just this one time!

THE ANGEL
(Furiously)

Do you shout at the Lord?

GIDEON
(Striding angrily about)

I have served you well, have I not? You vowed you would exalt me above my fellows. And do not say you did not, because you did. You said you would bless me and that you would do such and such, and, in particular, you said you would exalt me above my fellows.

THE ANGEL

Gideon, beware!

GIDEON
(Turning sulkily away)

I warned you I was in a temper.

THE ANGEL

You are a presumptuous man!

GIDEON

Nor is it an easy thing to love you, God.

THE ANGEL

I struck Korah down, and all his household, for less cause than this. I opened the ground and swallowed them, he and his household, and Dathan and Abiram, and all their households. I made Miriam a leper white as snow for less insubordinate ways, and she was a prophetess of the Lord and a sister to Moses. I burnt to death the sons of Aaron, who were priests, enveloped them in flame for a mere breach of hieratic conduct. Then what shall I do with you, Gideon, who shout at the Lord?

(GIDEON, squatting down on his haunches at the opposite end of the stage, is still sullen.)

GIDEON

I did not mean to shout.

THE ANGEL

I will not make you king over these people, for they shall see a king and forget about the Lord. They shall bow down to the king, and they shall not bow down to me. They will seek blessings from this king who cannot bless and fear this king who cannot frighten. Therefore I am the king over Israel, and the people shall bow down to me and fear me and seek my blessings. Surely, this is dear to you.

GIDEON
(Mutters, sulking)

Yes, yes, yes.

THE ANGEL

Oh, Gideon, let us not quarrel, for I love you.

GIDEON

I am in this sullen temper. I cannot seem to master it.

THE ANGEL
(Crossing to GIDEON *and squatting beside him)*

You are worn with battle and marching. Then rest and let me see your true and amiable self next time we meet.

GIDEON

Do not be kind to me, my Lord. I shall only cry.

THE ANGEL

I said I shall exalt you above your fellows, and I shall. I vowed seventy sons to you; well, then, know that both your wives at home are now with child. Indeed, from this moment, all women shall plead to be your wives. Now that should please you. (GIDEON *works up a shallow smile)* Come, give me your hand. If I have given you some hurt, then take my hand and show me it is over with. (GIDEON, *keeping his eyes petulantly down, lets* THE ANGEL *take his hand and clasp it)* No, eat and rest; then go and smite the elders of this city as I have instructed you, preserve not one.
*(*GIDEON *nods bleakly.)*

GIDEON

I would be left to myself now, my Lord.

THE ANGEL

Of course. *(He stands)* I shall wait for you beside your tent at Ophrah. Before I go, will you not say you love me?

GIDEON
(Mutters)

I love you, God.

THE ANGEL
(Sighs)

Peace be with you, Gideon.

GIDEON

Peace be with you, my Lord.

(THE ANGEL *turns and exits down the ladder.* GIDEON *bows his head and murmurs*)

GIDEON

Hallowed, sanctified, glorious, magnified, holy is the Lord. The Lord is perfect, he shall reign for ever and ever. (*He looks up, notes* THE ANGEL *is gone. He stands, regards the stage of bowed backs. He is still in a black temper*) Rise up! Rise up! I asked for food. Bring me water to bathe my feet. (*He indicates the bodies of* ZEBAH *and* ZALMUNNA) And get rid of that carrion there.

(*The people rise quickly. The* WOMEN *scurry up from the pit, bringing steaming meat, bowls of fruit and skins of wine to where the various captains are gathered.* GIDEON *crosses to them.*)

GIDEON

Here, give me that skin of wine before you've drunk it all.

SHILLEM
(*Giving a skin of wine to* GIDEON)

I was telling these Ephraimites, O Gideon, how last night at Karkor four Midianites descended on me in a bunch...

(*He sees* GIDEON *is in no mood for campfire stories and breaks off.* ORPAH *has made herself* GIDEON's *handmaiden. As he stands, scowling and swilling the wine, she unwraps his girdle and unwinds his ankle-length outer garment.*)

GIDEON

It is not easy to be loved by God, I tell you that.

SHILLEM

What did you say, my lord Gideon?

GIDEON

Perhaps you chiefs and princes think it is a splendid state to be loved by God; well, it is not. Do this, do that, such-and-such, so-and-so, constant demands, and what does one get for a thank you? Ah, well, let us not speak of it any more. It only puts me in a fury.

(GIDEON *wrenches a chunk of meat from the bowl beside him and champs angrily at it. His ugly mood has cast rather a pall over all the others onstage. During the above speech, the maiden* ORPAH *is called to one side*

by her father, OZNI, *the elder. By dumb show, they make clear a plot is
hatching. She suddenly whirls away from her father, her eyes flashing. She
gives her tabret a good whack and stamps her foot. Then she turns her full
voluptuous attention on* GIDEON, *who has looked briefly up at her.* ORPAH
*lifts her face high and chants out in the high-pitched manner of Oriental
song.)*

ORPAH

Wherefore do they lament, the virgins of Succoth?
Let them weep for their fathers tomorrow.
Rejoice, ye maidens of Israel!
Rejoice and dance at the gates!
See the blood of Midian!
See how it gels in the dust!
Rejoice, ye virgins of Israel!
It is not thy blood in the dust!
Recall how they ripped thee, Virgins.
They defiled thee on the highways.
Then rejoice, O Virgin of Israel!
Thy blood remains clean for thy marriage.
On the night of thy wedding, O Virgin,
Shall thy blood for the first time be seen.
Thy husband shall flourish thy nightdress
And shout: "See the stains of innocence!"
Sing praise, O maidens, to Gideon!
Let thy husbands cry out: "Amen!"
Hosanna!

(She smashes her tabret and leaps into savage dance. The SOLDIERS *and
captains, needless to say, find her dance diverting.)*

SHILLEM

The hot sun and the wine and the dancing rouse the blood, do they not?

SHETHULAH

Aye.

GIDEON

Aye.

*(*GIDEON *watches the voluptuous dance with evident interest. Suddenly,
with a swoop,* ORPAH *sinks to the ground at* GIDEON's *feet and remains
huddled, trembling, prostrate. The elder,* OZNI, *cannily noting the appreciation* GIDEON *entertains for his daughter, scrambles closer to* GIDEON,
*pulling along with him the other two elders whose necks are joined to his
by a rope.)*

OZNI

Oh, my lord Gideon, I see my maiden daughter Orpah here is pleasing in your eye. Could you think of her—well, in a manner of speaking—as a sacrifice of atonement that we wretched men of Succoth offer up to you? Take my daughter here as wife, great Gideon, and be merciful with us and spare our lives.

SECOND ELDER

Spare us, my lord.

(GIDEON *sullenly regards the piteous old faces staring at him, takes a good look at the girl again, considers the suggestion for a moment.*)

GIDEON

Well, it is an interesting idea. But it can't be done. It was the word of the Lord that you must die; I cannot gainsay God. *(Fairly drunk now, he turns, glowering, to his captains)* I spoke to the Lord about this, you know. I said: "They are such piteous old wretches, and they are our own brothers. Must I kill them?" "Oh," spoke the Lord, "indeed you must!" And he told me some wild farrago of things concerning the temporal inadequacies of man, now, was and is and all manner of things like that. Oh, let me say again, it is not an easy thing to love God. One must transcend all the frailties of man. Do you not think I would like this juicy doxy here for a wife? But even that is denied me. *(He seizes another skin of wine, takes a long swallow, and squats down on his haunches, belligerently drunk)* I would ask of you, have I done well by the Lord?

SHETHULAH

Indeed you have.

GIDEON

Is there anyone here—I protest, is there anyone here who has ever heard me reprehend the Lord in any way?

SHILLEM

You have praised his name with every breath.

GIDEON

Well, then, what comes of this? I spoke with the Lord and said: "The people think of me as their king, and I think it sensible that I should be king over these people. All other peoples have kings. There are kings in Tyre, Byblos, Boetia, in every Phoenician city, and the Egyptians indeed have had a full pedigree of pharaohs. They are well into their twenty-third dynasty by now."

HEZEKIAH

Twentieth.

GIDEON

Twentieth? Well, twentieth then. It does not belittle the argument. The point is, great empires are in the making in Asshur and in Babylon. Shall we always be the subject people?

MALCHIEL

(Showing interest for the first time)

And let the people say:

THE CAPTAINS

Amen.

GIDEON

In these words did I speak to the Lord: "Shall we not be a mighty nation too? May I not sit upon a throne as well as Tiglath-Pileser? Let Syria raise bowls of silver tribute above their heads to me! We are the crossroads of Asia here! Let the caravans from Aram pay duty on Gideon's highways!"

MALCHIEL

And let the people say:

THE CAPTAINS

Amen!

GIDEON

I would make a good king, I think.

SHILLEM

Oh, and I might be your vizier.

GIDEON

Well, you shall have to do without your vizierate and I without my crown. For these ambitions are vanity and show a lack of faith in God. The Lord brushed the whole idea aside and terrified me with horrible deaths for just the mentioning of it.

(MALCHIEL *drops suddenly to one knee before* GIDEON, *his zealot's eyes glowing.*)

MALCHIEL

Be our king, Gideon, and rule over us. This is the moment now to take the crown. The victory over Midian does make the other kings of Canaan tremble at your name. You have but to show your might of twenty thousand men before the gates of Megiddo or of Dor, and the Girgashite kings will fall in the dust before you and pay you tribute.

SHETHULAH

The Jebusites rule Jerusalem and the Amorites Beth-Shean. But stretch forth your palm, and these kings will put their cities in it.

GIDEON

Nay, nay, my captains, do not press me.

MALCHIEL

Does not all Israel cry out for a king? We shall be as a nation among nations. What say you, captain of Ephraim?

SHETHULAH

Let him be our king and rule over us.

MALCHIEL

What say you, chief of Naphtali?

SHILLEM

Let him be our king.

MALCHIEL
(Standing)

And my brother here and I are Asher. Reuben and Gad sit twenty thousand strong at the foot of the hill. Will Judah say nay to his redeemer? Will not Benjamin cry out: "Amen." You will give the Sea back to Zebulun and return Dan's inheritance wrenched from him by the Philistines. There will be peace again in Israel, and travelers will not fear the highways. For you will be "the Good King Gideon," and the land shall prosper. And let the people say:

ALL

Amen!

(GIDEON sits cross-legged on the skins, his head bowed, the cynosure of all eyes. He looks up, deeply moved.)

GIDEON
(Gently)

Nay, I will not rule over you, and my son will not rule over you; the Lord will rule over you. *(He rises and regards the assembled host around and below him)* You shall love the Lord your God with all your soul and with all your heart and with all your might, for he is in truth our king, and we need no other. *(To his captains)* I have been insolent and have made the Lord unattractive in your eyes with my grumbling. *(He turns back to all the people, raises his hands high)* Come, let us give offering up to God. We have taken much spoil; this is the portion I ask for myself: give me all the golden rings Midian wore in his ears and all the golden crescents Midian hung about the necks of his camels. I shall melt these golden things and make a sacred golden garment as a gift to the Lord. I shall set it on a high place by my tent, and in the sun it shall be seen for many miles. All who see it shall think of the Lord and remember his great victory. And let the people say:

ALL

Amen!

GIDEON

Give me my spear! The spirit of the Lord is upon me, and I shall kill these elders!

(MALCHIEL puts GIDEON's spear into his hand. GIDEON turns sharply, face set, and strides to where OZNI and the two other prostrate ELDERS are still hunched over on their knees, backs bowed in abject fear. GIDEON raises the spear above his head and cries out in a mighty voice.)

GIDEON

The Lord our God is a wrathful God! His name is the Great and the Mighty and the Terrible God, the Devouring God! Let not his wrath be raised against you as with these taunting men! *(He stands a moment, spear upraised, and then a look of horror crosses his face. Slowly he brings the spear down and lets it dangle from his hand. He stands a moment, trembling with a kind of dread)* I cannot do it. Let them live, Shillem, scourge them, if you will, with whips, with briars of the wilderness and thorns. For surely man must have more meaning than this.

(He shuffles disconsolately, even guiltily, a few steps away, casting a nervous look up to heaven.)

SHILLEM

Well then, soldiers, go gather me briars from the wilderness and thorns and make a scourge for me. *(He nudges OZNI gently)* Well, it is better than being killed isn't it?

OZNI

(Delight slowly spreading across his face)

Yes. I suppose it is.

SHILLEM

(To GIDEON)

The girl, Gideon, is yours, you know.

(GIDEON, who had quite forgotten about ORPAH, is delighted at being reminded. He sweeps her over his shoulder and carries her off. The people of Succoth, needless to say, spring up into great rejoicing. The WOMEN smash tabrets and cymbals and dance enthusiastically. The ELDERS gaily sing out.)

ELDERS

Hosanna! Hosanna!
Sing glory to Gideon!
His name is Merciful.
He has redeemed us from Midian!

The land is free, O Israel!
Thy sons stand up, O Israel!
Thy daughters dance, O Israel!
Hosanna! Hosanna!
> (*The* ELDERS, *escorted by* SOLDIERS, *start offstage; the* WOMEN *dance; the stage is a scene of tumultuous revelry.*)

The curtain comes quickly down.

"And Gideon made an ephod of it and put it in his city, in Ophrah; and all Israel played the harlot after it there, and it became a snare to Gideon and to his family."

Scene 2

The same as Act I, Scene 1; by the tents of JOASH.
It is two days later.
At rise, THE ANGEL *is striding about the stage, glowering and furious. He looks down the road to Schechem.*

THE ANGEL
Ah, here he comes, hugging to his chest the sacred golden garment he has made for me. Oh, he shall know my wrath, indeed he shall.
(*Enter* GIDEON, *huffing and puffing, holding the golden ephod to his chest with both hands. It is crudely made but recognizable as a simple waist-length garment with shoulder-straps, and it glitters and glistens hand-somely.* ORPAH *follows a few wifely paces behind, robed and veiled, and carrying a large bundle of her belongings on her head.* THE ANGEL *regards* GIDEON'S *entrance with a cold eye and speaks in an icy tone.*)

THE ANGEL
The Lord is with you, O mighty man of valor.

GIDEON
(*Startled*)
Oh! Peace be with you, my Lord. (*He sets the golden ephod down atop the altar upstage*) This is for you, my Lord. I fashioned it myself. My Lord, I must have some few words with you, but first let me make my presence known to my father and my wives. Oh, here stands my new wife, Orpah the daughter of Ozni. Uncover your face, my wife, so that the Lord may look upon you. Here, here, he stands by the tree here.
(ORPAH *lowers her veil and turns blankly to the tree.*)

THE ANGEL
(*Coldly*)
Very handsome.

GIDEON
Yes. Well, let me go embrace my father and make my presence known.

I hope my gift finds favor in your eye.

THE ANGEL

Go and seek your father.

GIDEON

Yes, well, in a moment then. *(He takes* ORPAH's *arm and starts for the tent)* He is invisible to you then, too. (ORPAH *nods, looks nervously back to the tere-binth tree)* He is in a black temper.

*(*JOASH *comes bursting out of the tent.)*

JOASH

He is here! He is here among us! Come forth to greet him! Oh, my son, come let me embrace you.

(From out of the tent now pour TIRZAH, MAHLAH, HAGLAH, MILCAH, ADINOAB, *and* JETHER, GIDEON's *son. They all stand at the tent flap star-ing in mute adoration at the returning hero.* JOASH *embraces* GIDEON.)

JOASH

Oh, my son, what honor you have brought to this house! The people of Abiezer are waiting for us now up on the threshing hill. Now, that you have come, we shall start the festival of summer fruits. Oh, Gideon, I am most blessed of fathers. Let water be brought that he may bathe his feet.

GIDEON

My father, this is a Gadite woman who is my wife. Her name is Orpah daughter of Ozni of the house of Eliasaph, a princely house. Give her your blessing and make her welcome in your tent.

JOASH

(To ORPAH, *bowing low at his feet)*

Rise up, my daughter, take off your veil. You are in your own home.

GIDEON

(Embracing HAGLAH*)*

My mother, let me embrace you. *(To* TIRZAH *and* MAHLAH*)* My wives, this is the Gadite Orpah. Bring water that she may bathe her feet and drink. She is dear to me; honor her.

JOASH

Sit, my son, and let us attend you.

(Skins have been spread on the ground. GIDEON *and* ORPAH *sit on them and have their feet bathed and are served cakes and water.* GIDEON *looks anxiously back to* THE ANGEL, *then tries to give his attention to his fam-ily.)*

GIDEON

These other ladies here are the widows of my brothers. This is my son,

Jether, a pensive boy. His uncles call him donkey as they once called me. Well, you shall have sweeter names now. You are the only son of Gideon.

MAHLAH

Nay, nay, my lord. Oh, let my lord be told.

JOASH

Your wife Mahlah is with child again.

TIRZAH

And I do think the same, my lord. I too have passed my time.

GIDEON
(Scowls, darts a nervous look at THE ANGEL*)*

Yea, God did promise me seventy sons. *(Turns back to* JETHER *with a gentle smile and takes the boy's hand)* But this is Jether, my first-born, who shall be a prince in Manasseh after me and whose opinion I hold dear.
(The boy stares up at him in open-mouthed adulation.)

JOASH

Oh, my son, we have heard such stories of your gallantry in war. Every passing soldier adds fifty to the host of Midianites you have slain.

GIDEON

Oh, I slew a few perhaps.
*(*THE ANGEL *snorts and throws up his hands.)*

THE ANGEL

Oh!
*(*GIDEON *turns to* THE ANGEL, *his face appealing for indulgence, but he receives only a baleful glare.)*

GIDEON
(Turning sadly back to his son)

In truth, I killed no Midianites at all. These stories you have heard are but the usual legends of the battlefield.

JOASH

Your father was the general, boy. He stands behind and regards the course of things so that he may direct the overall tactic and maneuver.

GIDEON

Yes, yes, that is true, of course.

JOASH

It was your father who conceived the plan to stampede the Midianite cattle with lamps and trumpets.

GIDEON

Ah, there, of course, I must take the credit, and—*(He looks back to* THE ANGEL, *who glowers at him again)* Well, even this was not my doing. The

Lord our God instructed me what to do; I merely did it.

(*The boy,* JETHER, *is obviously disappointed by this, and* GIDEON *is pained by his disappointment.*)

JOASH

But there passed through here just yesterday a prince of Asher whose name was Hezekiah the son of Immah, who expounded to us for many hours on the war and said that Gideon was among the great generals.

GIDEON

Did he say that indeed?

JOASH

Aye, and this Hezekiah is well known as a scholar and knows many things.

GIDEON

Oh, indeed, he predicts the eclipses of the moon and has measured the ecliptic of the sun as it revolves around the earth.

JOASH

And this Hezekiah described the history of the war, and indeed God did not enter into it at all. "We are all men of reason here," he said, "and need not explain all things in supernatural ways. The savage will say God gave us into the hand of the Midianites," said Hezekiah, "but was it not in fact the economic conditions of drought in the desert that drove the Midianites upon us." And then he said: "Was it the spirit of God that aroused the tribes of Israel to rebel, or was it not rather the need to protect our growing cities, our increase in caravan trade, and the beginnings of our mercantile interests? Is the panic of the one hundred and twenty thousand Midianites so hard to understand when one realizes the superstitious spirit of the men of Midian? For these were a primitive people with a crumbling social fabric. All that was needed was a bold and ingenious general who could exploit these weaknesses of Midian." And, indeed, Gideon, that was you.

(GIDEON *considers this explanation a moment.*)

GIDEON

Well, it is not altogether illogical, is it?

JOASH

"Indeed," said this Hezekiah, "who is this Yahweh of Gideon's? Has anyone seen him or heard his words? Only Gideon." It was Hezekiah's contention, Gideon, that Yahweh was a masterful fiction you created to inspirit the troops.

GIDEON
(Eagerly)

Now, how did his reasoning go again? It was the economic conditions prevailing in the desert of Havilah that...

THE ANGEL
(Roaring)

Gideon! Will you countenance this pomander of utter nonsense?
(The smile disappears from GIDEON's *face, and he sighs unhappily.)*

GIDEON

Ah. *(He regards his son anxiously)* It is none of it true, my son. It was the Lord our God who gave us into the hand of Midian, for we had bowed down to false gods, and it was the Lord our God who redeemed us by the strength of his hand alone. Yea, though none of you may see nor hear him, he is here among us now, and I see and hear him. There is no honor due me at all, but that I am the device of God.

*(*JETHER, *embarrassed by his father's humility, lowers his eyes and shuffles away upstage.* GIDEON *watches him go anxiously.)*

JOASH
(Now suddenly terrified)

He is here among us, did you say, the Lord our God?

GIDEON
(Watching his son)

Aye.

*(*JOASH *immediately prostrates himself to the ground as do all the others onstage, excepting* JETHER—*who has suddenly noticed the glistening ephod on the upstage altar—and* GIDEON, *who is watching him. The boy approaches the ephod to examine it.)*

THE ANGEL

Do not let him touch it, Gideon. It is a thing of God, and he will die.
(The boy reaches out to touch the ephod.)

GIDEON
(Crying out)

Do not touch it! It is holy! You will die!

JOASH
(Looking up)

My son, you have carried it in your hands for twenty miles.

GIDEON

I have given it to God, and it is holy now. Not you nor I nor the Levite priests of God may touch it, for it is a holy thing.

JOASH

Behold the sacred golden garment Gideon has made for God!

GIDEON

(Stands and faces THE ANGEL*)*

There is no putting it off, my Lord, but I must have a word with you.

THE ANGEL

And I with you, Gideon.

GIDEON

(To his father)

My father, go and make ready for the festival on the hill. Let my new wife be taken to my tent. Leave me here alone. I must speak with the Lord.

(The others rise quickly and exit off into the tent. For a moment, the stage is silent, GIDEON *downstage in frowning concentration and* THE ANGEL *upstage waiting in cold anger. Then* GIDEON *turns to* THE ANGEL.*)*

GIDEON

My Lord, we have always spoken plainly with each other.

THE ANGEL

I am not pleased with this golden ephod you have made. It is a pagan thought to think your God wears golden undercoats.

GIDEON

I fashioned it for love of you, my Lord.

THE ANGEL

Indeed, you did not, but as a wily gift to turn aside my wrath. You betrayed me at Succoth, Gideon. I charged you to slay the elders, and you did not. Shall you say who shall die and who shall live? I am the Lord. I kill, and I make alive. Shall you gainsay me? Have you seen the end of time? Do you know the beginning and what came before that? Do you know whence you rose? Do you know where you go? Are you God now that you give life where I have taken it away?

GIDEON

I pitied the old men, my Lord.

THE ANGEL

And I watched you sit there now, greedily believing all of Hezekiah's chimera and claptrap about the socio-economic conditions in the desert of Havilah—you, who have seen the Lord face-to-face and beheld his wonders.

GIDEON

Well, Hezekiah is well spoken of as a scholar. He knows all about the ecliptic of the sun as it revolves around the earth.

THE ANGEL

The sun does not revolve around the earth, you imbecile; the earth revolves about the sun.

GIDEON

Oh, that is patent nonsense, my Lord. The sun obviously revolves around the earth.

THE ANGEL

Oh! I do not know how I bear with you!

GIDEON
(*Crying out*)

Oh, my Lord, let me go!

THE ANGEL

Let you go?

GIDEON

We have made a covenant of love between us, you and I. Release me from that covenant.

THE ANGEL

Are you suggesting some sort of divorce between your God and you?

GIDEON

We make an ill-matched pair, my Lord. You surely see we never meet but tempers rise between us. It is too much for me, this loving God. I cannot manage it. I am a plain man and subject to imperfect feelings. I shall betray you many times, and you shall rise in wrath against me and shall punish me with mighty penalties, and I cannot continue in this way, my Lord. Oh, let me say it plainly. I do not love you, Lord, and it is unreasonable to persist with each other when there is no love.

THE ANGEL
(*Startled*)

You do not love me?

GIDEON

I tried to love you, but it is too much for me. You are too vast a concept for me. To love you, God, one must be a god himself. I did not kill the elders of Succoth, and I shall tell you why. I raised my spear above their heads, but in that moment I felt a shaft of terror that chills me even now. It was as if the nakedness of all things was exposed to me, and I saw myself and all men for what we truly are, suspensions of matter, flailing about for footholds in the void, all the while slipping back screaming into endless suffocations. That is the truth of things, I know, but I cannot call it truth. It is too hideous, an intolerable state of affairs. I cannot love you, God, for it makes me a meaningless thing.

THE ANGEL
(Thoroughly exasperated)

Oh!

GIDEON

My Lord, it is elemental in me to aspire to be greater than myself. This is your own doing, for you gave me passion that I might raise myself to you. You have uncovered your nakedness before me. How shall I think myself an aimless brute now?

THE ANGEL

I meant you to love me, but you are merely curious. You have no feeling for me then at all?

GIDEON

I fear you, God. I am in mortal dread of you. Perhaps, that is the only love a man can give his god.

THE ANGEL
(Deeply hurt)

What shall we do then, Gideon?

GIDEON

Let me go, God.

THE ANGEL

Let you go—whatever does that mean? Gideon, there is no divorce from God. I am truth and exist. You cannot deny that I am. I stand palpably here before you, as real as rock, a very actual thing with whom you have commerced face-to-face.

GIDEON

Aye, my Lord. I see you and hear you. So I beg of you, my Lord—go from my sight. Make not your presence known to me again that I might say: "God is a dream, a name, a thought, but not a real thing."

THE ANGEL

But I am a real thing.

GIDEON

I would pretend that you were not.
   (THE ANGEL *is a little startled at this.*)

THE ANGEL

Let me review this. You would pretend God is not, although you know that he is, so that you might be a significant creature which you know you are not. Oh! This is beyond even God's understanding! And you do not love me! I found you a mournful farmer, and I have loved you and raised you up and uncovered your soul, and gave you many satisfactions. And now you turn on me like a disgruntled husband and would send me packing back to my father's tent. This was not the case when you needed me, was it? Oh! What protestations of ardor you made then! And I was susceptible enough to think the man did love me. I have been too kind with you, indeed I have! If fear is all the love you have for me, then you shall fear me, Gideon. You betrayed me at Succoth. You have given the life of men greater value than the word of God. Behold then, Gideon! Know that there is a God, and that his will is all there is. As I blessed you for your love, so shall I punish you for your infidelity. You did not slay the seven and seventy elders of Succoth. Then, the seventy sons I promised you shall die in their stead.

GIDEON
(Sinks to the ground, stricken)

Oh!

THE ANGEL

They shall die in bitterness by each other's hands. As you contend with me, so shall they contend among themselves.

GIDEON

Oh, God, this is most cruel!

THE ANGEL

It seems just weight to me. Behold then, Gideon. I give life and I take it away. I bless, and I punish. I am pleased, and I rise in wrath. This is the law of the universe; there is no other.

GIDEON
(Shriveled now into a terrified ball on the ground)

Oh, my Lord, I cannot continue in this way! (GIDEON *frozen in terror, huddles hunched against further lashes of punishment. After a moment, he looks slowly up, his face drawn into an expression of intense anguish. His eye is caught by the appearance of* JETHER, *who has shuffled out of the tent and would come to his father but sees that the latter is on his knees in profound prayer)* Spare me at least my one only son, my Lord. I have never known his love. His mother taught him her contempt, but now, I think, he might love me, and I would like that, God.

> (JOASH, ORPAH *and the other* WOMEN *now come out of the tent, stop at the sight of* GIDEON, *on his knees in prayer, and stand silent and a little frightened.)*

GIDEON

Behold mine own small world of people there. Could I not pretend there is some reason for their being here? Pretend, my Lord, no more than that. Let me have at least some bogus value.

THE ANGEL
(Gently)

I am truth, Gideon. I cannot vary.

(GIDEON *bows his head, utterly crushed. Then he slowly looks up again, but apparently does not see* THE ANGEL *immediately.*)

GIDEON

My Lord?

THE ANGEL

Yes?

(GIDEON *looks around the stage.*)

GIDEON

God?

THE ANGEL

I am by the wine press now.

GIDEON

God?

THE ANGEL

Here, Gideon, by the press.

GIDEON

Are you still here?

THE ANGEL

Here, over here.

GIDEON
(Standing)

Ah, yes, you do seem blurred. My Lord, I asked you one small thing, that I might delude myself with some spurious grandeur.

THE ANGEL

And I answered: "No, it will not do." You want the universe to please your eye, Gideon, and not mine. You would be God yourself. Hear me well, O Hebrew. I am a jealous God and brook no other gods, not even you. Why have I come here at all but to put an end to false idols? You have done well in pulling down the effigies of Ba-al, but do not think to set yourself up on their empty altars. Do not make a cult of man, not even in fancy.

GIDEON
(Looking around)

My Lord? My Lord?

THE ANGEL

Attend me, Gideon, and mark my words.

GIDEON

My Lord?

THE ANGEL

Where are you looking, Gideon? I am here.

GIDEON

My Lord, where are you gone?

THE ANGEL

Here! I stand here! By the wine press here! I have not moved!

GIDEON

My Lord, please speak to me. We are not finished.

THE ANGEL

What is this game?

GIDEON

My Lord!

THE ANGEL

I stand right here!

GIDEON

Where are you, Lord? The matter is not finished!

THE ANGEL
(Crying out)

O Gideon, do not forsake me!

GIDEON

God! Where are you, God? I cannot see you, God! You have not answered what I asked you!

(At this point, ABIMELECH and HELEK come hurrying in from upstage left behind the tent.)

ABIMELECH

Ah! There he is! They said they saw him on the road!

HELEK

Oh, Gideon, how good to have you back.

(JOASH peremptorily admonishes the new arrivals to silence. Indeed, GIDEON's scene with THE ANGEL has been watched with mingled dread and confusion by his family. Now, GIDEON stands centerstage, as if transfixed, staring up to the heavens. THE ANGEL, who had turned exasperatedly away at the interruption, now moves intently to GIDEON, as angry as only a scorned god can be.)

THE ANGEL

Gideon, I pray you, do not scorn me! I will not be so cast off out of hand. You leave this house, return not to it ever. For I have had my fill of your betrayals, your sordid harlotries with other gods. And now there are new strumpets on the highway. Well, go then to those painted dialectics and libertine philosophies and logics that wait along the road for gulls like you, and, for a shekel, shrilly promise you the secret sensuality of time and space. You will be ravished, fleeced, and soon abandoned in some red-threaded hovel of despair. Then do not hope that God awaits at home when with ragged beard the penitent returns. Turn not your face from me! Beware my wrath! There is no divorce from God! Hear that! God gives no divorce, but just his curse!

(GIDEON, *to all effects and purposes, has not heard a word.*)

GIDEON

I do not see you, God, nor hear you now. What was between us now is done. And let the people say: "Amen."

(*A long silence fills the stage. After a moment,* JOASH *calls tentatively to his son.*)

JOASH

My son, the house of Abiezer waits to honor you on the threshing hill.

(*By the wine press,* THE ANGEL *looks sadly at his hands.*)

THE ANGEL

Gideon, I am the Lord your God who brought you out of the land of Egypt. I broke the bars of your yoke and made you stand erect. Will you spurn my statutes? Will you break my covenant?

GIDEON

(*His eyes closed against* THE ANGEL's *words*)

I must aspire, God.

THE ANGEL

(*Thundering*)

Then I shall do this to you and to all of Israel! I will make your heavens like iron and your earth like brass! I will scatter you among the nations!

(*With great effort,* GIDEON *forces his attention back to the others onstage.*)

GIDEON

(*To his family*)

Well, come, then, let us go to the festival.

THE ANGEL

I will unsheathe the sword after you! Your land shall be a desolation, and your cities shall be a waste!

GIDEON
(Forcing his attention on the ephod)
I shall put on this golden garment and wear it to the festival.
> (GIDEON, *with set jaw, starts upstage to the ephod.* THE ANGEL *raises his arm in lordly threat.*)

THE ANGEL
(Thundering)
Gideon! Do not touch it! This thing is mine!

GIDEON
(Whirls and cries out)
O God! I cannot believe in you! If you love me, let me believe at least in mine own self! If you love me, God!
> (THE ANGEL *stares at* GIDEON *with a face strained by deep emotion. Then his upraised arm falls to his side.*)

THE ANGEL
I love you, Gideon!
> (GIDEON *promptly turns and takes hold of the ephod.*)

GIDEON
Father, help me to put it on.
> (*With the apprehensive help of* JOASH *and of his son,* JETHER, GIDEON *contrives to get the weighty ephod over his head and down onto his body.*)

GIDEON
What a heavy thing it is.
> (THE ANGEL, *still deeply moved, looks up, smiles.*)

THE ANGEL
Oh, indeed it is.

ABIMELECH
(Staring in awe at the gold-clad GIDEON*)*
We all wait to hear you tell the miracle of God's victory over Midian.
> (GIDEON *turns slowly to the elders.*)

GIDEON
A miracle? Why do you call it that? *(Wrapping his arms around his uncles, he leads the small procession of his family off stage right)* Nay, my uncles, the war with Midian was not mysterious, but only the inevitable outgrowth of historico-economic, socio-psychological and cultural forces prevailing in these regions.
> (*They all exit off stage right to attend the festival of summer fruits on the hill.* THE ANGEL *has watched them go with amusement. Now, he cannot resist bursting into laughter.*)

THE ANGEL

Oh, it is amusing. *(He moves downstage, quite cheerful now, and regards the audience. Behind him, the stage is empty. After a moment he recites:)*

God no more believes it odd
That man cannot believe in God.
Man believes the best he can,
Which means, it seems, belief in man.
Then let him don my gold ephod
And let him be a proper god.
Well, let him try it anyway.
With this conceit, we end the play.

(THE ANGEL *bows. The lights black out.)*

Curtain

The Passion of Josef D.

For Susan

THE PASSION OF JOSEF D. *was first presented by Arthur Cantor, E.E. Fogelson and Mark Lawrence at the Ethel Barrymore Theatre, New York City, on February 11, 1964, with the following cast:*

(In Order of Appearance)

NADYA	Elizabeth Hubbard
CONSTABLE KENTINOV	Alvin Epstein
STALIN (JUGASHVILI)	Peter Falk
MURANOV	Gene Gross
KAMENEV	Milt Kamen
KAPINSKY	Michael McGuire
KLURMAN	Jon Silo
BRONSKY	Bruce Kimes
RUSIKOV	Mervyn Williams
BRUSTEIN	Rico Froehlich
ALLILUYEV	Ramon Bieri
OLGA EVGEYEVNA	Betty Walker
MOLOTOV	Simm Landres
CHEIDZE	Rico Froehlich
SUKHANOV	Nicholas Saunders
SKOBELOV	Mervyn Williams
LENIN	Luther Adler
KRUPSKAYA	Betty Walker
RYKOV	John A. Coe
ZINOVIEV	Michael Enserro
NIKITIN	Milt Kamen
LOMOV	Alvin Epstein
GENERAL KORNILOV	Jon Silo
ORJONIKIDZE	Nicholas Saunders
SVERDLOV	Gene Gross
TROTSKY	Alvin Epstein

SOLDIERS, PROCESSION, EXILES, WORKERS, PEASANTS, DELEGATES, MASSES — Sean Allen, Robert Berdeen, Frank Bouley, John Carver, John A. Coe, Carole Crook, Michael Enserro, Janet Frank, Richard Frisch, Bruce Kimes, Simm Landres, Penelope Laughton, Royce Lenelle, Michael McGuire, Sylvia O'Brien, Anthony Palmer, Gedda Petry, Richard Robbins, Nicholas Saunders, Peggy Steffans, Elaine Sulka, Carol Wilder, Mervyn Williams, Stafford Wing.

Directed by Paddy Chayefsky
Sets and Lighting by Will Steven Armstrong
Music Composed by David Amram
Costumes by Domingo A. Rodriguez

SYNOPSIS OF SCENES

ACT I—1917

SCENE 1: March 11
SCENE 2: March 22
SCENE 3: March 22
SCENE 4: March 25
SCENE 5: April 16

ACT II—1917

SCENE 1: July 19
SCENE 2: July 20
SCENE 3: October 23
SCENE 4: November 8

ACT III—1923-1924

SCENE 1: March 9, 1923
SCENE 2: January 26, 1924

ACT I

SCENE 1

Two soldiers nervously stand guard. The first is a boy; the second is an old man. They wear astrakhan hats and belted greatcoats but are having a chilly time of it nevertheless. A solemn procession of some thirty people enter upstage—shabby men, women, a cassocked priest. They carry crucifixes and banners with the Tsar's portrait on them.

PROCESSION
(Chanting solemnly)

Tsar Nikolai,
Dear Little Father,
Who is Our Father?
Our Father is Thee.
Father in the Flesh,
Father in the Body,
Witness Thy Children
On Supplicant Knee.
We Russians, on the whole, do not complain.
We take things as they come without a word.
We are tractable, submissive in the main.
Our capacity to suffer one can only call absurd.

FIRST WOMAN

Soldiers of the Ismailovsky Regiment!

OLD SOLDIER

Actually, darling, we are the Volinsky Regiment here. The Ismailovsky Regiment is quartered at the Admiralty Building.

FIRST WOMAN

Volinsky Regiment then. Soldiers, we are a delegation of pious souls from the Vyborg district who have come to petition our Holy Tsar.

OLD SOLDIER

The Tsar's not here, sweethearts. He's at the summer palace.

FIRST MAN

That shows you how much you know, you old mongrel. The Tsar left the summer palace Friday for the front lines.

OLD SOLDIER

In any event, dear ones, public demonstrations are forbidden, by order of General Hablakov, Commander of the Petrograd military district.

YOUNG SOLDIER

Go back to your districts! We are instructed to shoot!
(NADYA, *a girl of sixteen, crowds up to the front rank of the mob.*)

NADYA

Soldiers of the Preobrazhensky Guards!

OLD SOLDIER

Volinsky, darling. We are the Volinsky Regiment here.

NADYA

Soldiers, is the Russian Imperial Army instructed to shoot their fellow Russians now?

SECOND MAN

The bread ration's been cut again! Three ounces! How are we to live?

PREGNANT WOMAN

In the name of God, what a winter it's been!
(*A* THIRD SOLDIER *hurries on*)

THIRD SOLDIER
(*To the mob*)
What are you doing here? Workers are forbidden to leave their districts!

NADYA

We've already left our districts, comrade. There's a mob on the Nevsky now, three hundred thousand souls, packed shoulder to shoulder in front of the Parliament Building, shouting: "Down with the Government!" A sight to see, comrade!

THIRD SOLDIER

Push off, for Christ's sake, before you have us all in the pot. The Captain's making his rounds! Demonstrations are forbidden!

NADYA

Soldiers of the Semonovsky Regiment!

OLD SOLDIER

Girls, we are the Volinsky Regiment here. You must try to fix that in your minds. The Volinsky Regiment.

NADYA

Volinsky soldiers! Three hundred thousand people, standing in front of the Parliament Building and shouting: "Down with the Government!" is not a demonstration. The state of affairs in Petrograd, if we are to be precise, is open revolt. The Tsar's off in a sulk somewheres, who can find him? Not even his own ministers. Who, for that matter, can find his ministers? The palaces in Petrograd are all empty, soldiers. Who rules in Holy Russia? In the Parliament the deputies talk of revolution. The nobles whisper revolution over their teacups. Everyone in Russia plots revolution. But who shall do it? It seems we here in the streets shall have to set matters right ourselves. There's nothing left to do, eh?

OLD WOMEN

Eight million souls killed in this hopeless war! Who of us does not mourn? Yi! Yi! Yi!

NADYA

Soldiers, unarmed mobs do not make revolutions. It is the army, not the people, who must revolt. It lies with you, soldiers of the Petrograd garrison—the Semonovsky, the Pavlovsky, the Volinsky, the Preobrazhensky—the Revolution lies with you! We know your hearts are with us, soldiers. Come out into the streets with us. Together we shall make a revolution in Holy Russia. Without you we cannot win.

FIRST WOMAN

Come out with us, soldiers.

THIRD MAN

They say the Pavlovsky talk of nothing but mutiny in their squadroom.

FOURTH MAN

Even the Cossacks, they say.

NADYA

Come out with us, soldiers. It takes only one, and the whole Petrograd garrison will bolt their barracks.

(*A* FOURTH SOLDIER *dashes on*)

FOURTH SOLDIER

In the name of God, get out of here, you idiots! The Captain—
(*The other soldiers snap to attention as the* CAPTAIN, *followed by a* SERGEANT, *enters. He regards the mob at the gate.*)

OLD SOLDIER

They are just some pious souls, master, who've come to pray to our Tsar.
(*The* CAPTAIN *flicks his riding crop across the* OLD SOLDIER's *face. The mob slowly sinks to its knees, with the exception of* NADYA.)

FIRST WOMAN

Tsar Nikolai,

Dear Holy Father,
Who is Our Father?

PROCESSION

Our Father is Thee.

FIRST WOMEN

Our Father in Flesh,

PROCESSION

Our Father in the Body,

FIRST WOMAN

Witness Thy Children
On supplicant knee.

PROCESSION

We are not the sort to complain.
We take things as they come without a word.
We're tractable, submissive in the main.
Our capacity to suffer one can only call absurd.

CAPTAIN

Soldiers! Raise your rifles!

NADYA

Soldiers! Will you shoot your brothers?
   (*The soldiers hesitate.*)

PROCESSION

No fuss from us, we're docile, we're devout.
   The will of God is hard, but we endure.
We bow our brows beneath Thy Holy Knout.
   On the other hand, O Tsar, Thou mustn't be so goddam sure.
Tsar, Son of God!
Tsar of the Rich!
Art Thou really son of God?
Or more son of a bitch?

CAPTAIN

Fire!
   (*The soldiers fire into the kneeling mob. The people fling themselves flat.
   A woman screams.*)

NADYA
   (*Crying out*)

Soldiers of the Volinsky Regiment! I have it right this time, eh? We cannot win without you!
   (*The mob murmurs. Slowly, the people rise to their knees.*)

PROCESSION

Oh, we are not the sort to complain.
We take things as they come without a word.
(They slowly stand)
We are tractable, submissive in the main.
Our capacity to suffer one can only call absurd.
(The mob presses slowly downstage toward the soldiers)
No fuss from us, we're docile, we're devout.
The will of God is hard, but we endure.
We bow our brows beneath Thy Holy Knout.
On the other hand, O Tsar, Thou mustn't be so goddam sure.

CAPTAIN

Get back! Get back!

PROCESSION

The pious Russian brute now slowly stirs.
Enough's enough for even Russian clods.
O Christ! O Tsar! O Russian Lords and Sirs!
The devil take you all! We'll have to manage without gods.
(The mob sweeps over the soldiers. A soldier screams. There is a sudden burst of machine-gun fire from above. A few of the people fall. The rest press on.)

MOB

Tsar Nikolai!
Dear Little Father!
Who is Our Father!?
Not Thee! Not Thee!
(They exit. NADYA, who is about to follow, pauses to address the audience with an afterthought.)

NADYA

The next day, however, which was a Monday, the Volinsky Regiment did mutiny, and by nightfall, half the soldiers in the city were in the streets. The Russian Revolution was now a fact.
(She exits.)

Blackout

SCENE 2

Scene: A one-room shack in the outskirts of Krasnoyarsk, Siberia, ten days later.

At rise: JUGASHVILI *is asleep on some bedding on the floor. Enter* CONSTABLE KENTINOV, *a peasant sort in his forties, carrying a bundle of clothing, a bucket of water and a large brown bread. He sets the bucket down by the door.*

CONSTABLE KENTINOV

Jugashvili! Get up. You're a free man. There's been a revolution in Russia. The Tsar has abdicated. The country is in the hands of the Socialists. An amnesty for all political prisoners has been declared. You're a free man. Here are your boots. The cobbler was drunk and didn't get around to fixing them. *(Holds some brown bread aloft)* Not your usual ration, eh? I trust you'll make a good report on me when you get back to Petrograd. Constable Kentinov was a good fellow, you will say, as policemen go, didn't steal your packages from home, not that you got any, you blackguard. I've brought you a fresh bucket of water, by the way.

(Sits, crosses his legs. JUGASHVILI, *a dark, good-looking but glowering fellow in his late thirties, sits up, examines his boots. They gape with holes.)*

CONSTABLE KENTINOV

I looked you up, Jugashvili. You're quite a prominent revolutionary. I didn't know that. What a dossier we have on you, the fattest file in the lot. Good heavens, you're a hard customer. I dare say, you'll be an influential figure now that you Socialists are running the show.

JUGASHVILI
(Indicating the boots)
Kentinov, I can't go out in the snow in these boots.

CONSTABLE KENTINOV
I did my best, Jugashvili. The cobbler's drunk. I'll lash him properly for this. I say, Jugashvili, could I have a slice of your bread? Ah, you're a splendid chap! *(He takes out his knife and cuts off a chunk of bread)* Well, I ask you, Jugashvili. What do you make of this revolution?

JUGASHVILI
I don't make anything of it. It's the first I've heard of it.

CONSTABLE KENTINOV
Well, by Christ, Jugashvili, there's been a revolution in Russia!

JUGASHVILI

Yes. I'm on to that much.

CONSTABLE KENTINOV

The Tsar abdicated some six days ago. I'm not quite sure just who the government is right now. There seem to be two—an official Provisional Government which has been recognized by the British, French and Americans but by apparently nobody in Russia. Some sort of a Socialist committee called the Petrograd Soviet seems to be running everything. All my instructions are signed in the name of the Petrograd Soviet. Well, look here, I have a letter from my brother. Would you like to look at it? There's no need to read the first section there. That's all about my wife, who is a bit of a trollop and seems to be misbehaving herself. There, down the page a bit, where it says: "It's all bedlam here in Petrograd." I'm taking another piece of bread, old fellow. Well, what do you make of it, Jugashvili?

JUGASHVILI

(Studying the letter)

I would say your wife is a cheeky thing. Is she much of a looker?

CONSTABLE KENTINOV

Not much. What I mean is, you'll be getting a fine post in the new government, eh, Jugashvili?

JUGASHVILI

Not damned likely.

CONSTABLE KENTINOV

Well, the Socialists are running the show, eh? That's your lot, eh?

JUGASHVILI

I'm a Bolshevik, not a Socialist. For that matter, even among the Bolsheviks I don't count for very much. One of our party leaders—a fellow named Kamenev—once called me a gray mediocrity.

CONSTABLE KENTINOV

What a thing to say!

JUGASHVILI

I shall remember that.

CONSTABLE KENTINOV

I should think you would.

JUGASHVILI

He made that remark to Lenin on February twelfth, Nineteen Thirteen in Cracow.

CONSTABLE KENTINOV

Who's Lenin?

JUGASHVILI

Lenin is leader of the Bolsheviks. Do you know what Lenin answered him? "Stalin is my wonderful Georgian. A very capable fellow. I shouldn't underestimate him if I were you."

CONSTABLE KENTINOV

Who's Stalin?

JUGASHVILI

I'm Stalin. Stalin is my party name.

CONSTABLE KENTINOV

Ah, of course.

JUGASHVILI

His "wonderful Georgian." Those were his exact words. A singular man—Lenin. The first time I met him was in Nineteen Five. It was at a Bolshevik Congress in Finland. It was my first national congress. I was twenty-six years old, something of a lout. I stood in the back of the hall, kept my mouth shut. I speak poor Russian; I have this Georgian accent which embarrasses me. A fellow pointed out Lenin to me. He didn't seem much. A little bald-headed man with a doctor's beard. He looked like an auditor. I had expected a mandarin. Lenin's wife, an ugly woman, took me over to him. "Volodya," she said, "this is Ivanovich, delegate from Georgia." My party name was Ivanovich at that time. Lenin was sitting on a wooden chair, legs crossed, talking to two Lithuanians. "You look like a hard customer," he said. I said: "I am." He said: "Thank God for that. We have enough professors here. We want for hard customers." He has this gift, you see, of making one feel significant.

CONSTABLE KENTINOV

A good fellow!

JUGASHVILI

I only saw him a few times after that. I went back to Baku. We were organizing the oil workers in those years, Nineteen Six, Nineteen Seven. I did a year in Bialev prison—no, that time it was Batum. Bialev, Batum, Baku, Tiflis—out of one dungeon and into the other. I was doing a stretch in Solvychegodsk at the time of the Prague Congress. No, I was in Vologda. Nineteen Twelve, January. The coppers had transferred me to Vologda. Orjonikidze came to see me there. He said: "You're on the Central Committee of the party now. Lenin picked you himself." I couldn't believe my ears. Well, of course, I was boss of the Caucasian Bolsheviks by then, making a name for myself.

CONSTABLE KENTINOV

I'm sure you were well thought of, Jugashvili.

JUGASHVILI

There was a brief time when I was quite close with Lenin. That was in December, Nineteen Twelve. He was living in Cracow. Lenin sent for me. A peasant took me across the border in an oxcart. I stayed at Lenin's house for six weeks. We were quite close. Then he sent me to Petrograd to take charge of the Bolshevik delegation. I was picked up by the police. Somebody informed. I suspect Malinovsky. He's much too pious a Bolshevik for me. They packed me off to Yureika in Siberia—a desolation, snow nine months of the year. I lived in a cave like an anchorite. Two and a half years. There was a colony of exiles about ten hours away by dog sled. Kamenev, the fellow who had called me a gray mediocrity, was there. They held meetings and discussions. I went to one or two. How comical all that Marxist cant seemed in those wastes. Well—to put it plainly—that clever lot, the party Jesuits—Kamenev, Zinoviev—that lot think me a fool in matters of doctrine. The devil take them all. I lived alone in my cave, hunted a bit, fished. Two and a half years. I knew great despair. The post arrived every couple of months. A letter from an old comrade, Alliluyev, a package from his wife. They were the only ones. I never heard from Lenin in those two and a half years. He was in Switzerland. I wrote him several times; he didn't answer. I know for a fact he corresponded with Kamenev. I saw the letters myself. He mentioned me only once. "P.S. What is Stalin's last name—Jugash-something? If you see him, extend a greeting from me."

CONSTABLE KENTINOV

What a poignant story!

JUGASHVILI

By God, I know my Marx as well as any of those party priests. I come by it in the blood. What does Lenin say? "No man is born a Marxist." Not so; I was. My father was a serf, emancipated in Sixty-five, a brute let off his leash and left to raven for himself. A drunken cobbler who couldn't find one day's work in thirty. He hung about the shoe factories in Tiflis, fawning before the Armenian bosses. When he could find his way home, he reeled into our mud hutch, fell on my mother and studded her in a stupor, whimpering in his heat. A brute. We paid one ruble a month for our hut. That was all that divided us from the dogs that evacuated outside our door; they didn't pay rent. I don't have to cultivate my class hatred, by God. I came by it in the blood. Goddam, Kentinov! When are you going to get these boots mended? I can't go out in the snow with these damned boots!

CONSTABLE KENTINOV
(Leaping up)

I tell you, the cobbler's in an absolute stupor! I shall go shake him till his ears ring!

JUGASHVILI

Oh, sit down, you imbecile.
(A man's voice is heard off, shouting.)

MURANOV
(Off)

Stalin! Stalin! Hey! Where does one find Stalin here?

CONSTABLE KENTINOV

Who's Stalin?

JUGASHVILI

I'm Stalin. Haven't you heard a word I've said? Stalin is my party name.

CONSTABLE KENTINOV

Ah, yes.

MURANOV

Stalin! This is Muranov here!

JUGASHVILI

Muranov, one of our deputies in Parliament before the war. Well, it has begun—the ingathering of the exiles. They'll come pouring into Petrograd from every exile camp in Siberia. Bolsheviks, Social Democrats, Socialist Revolutionaries, Populists, Economists, Bundists, Trotskyites— the whole yammering throng of them. Oh, Christ! Petrograd will be choked with mendicant Marxists. There will be parliaments on every street corner, a caucus in every closet. The air will thunder with the thumping of gavels. What a clamor there will be in Petrograd! You can't imagine what a noise the splitting of hairs makes.

KAMENEV
(Off)

Stalin! This is Kamenev here! Can you hear me?

JUGASHVILI

Well! Kamenev himself.

KAMENEV
(Off)

Can you hear me, Stalin?

CONSTABLE KENTINOV

Long live the Revolution! There's a train to Tomsk in an hour. You'll have to stand on the tracks and flag it down.

(CONSTABLE KENTINOV *turns happily, comes back to the table, seizes the chunk of bread he had been chewing on and chews on it again, humming merrily as he does. Behind him,* JUGASHVILI, *who has retrieved his great-coat from the floor, where it had served as a blanket, is now buttoning it. He surveys* CONSTABLE KENTINOV *from behind.*)

JUGASHVILI
(Picking up the bread knife)

Well, Kentinov, you were a good fellow as policemen go.

(*He stabs the policeman in the back.* CONSTABLE KENTINOV *pitches onto the floor dead.* JUGASHVILI *pulls off the first of the dead man's boots, pauses to look at the audience.*)

JUGASHVILI

The moral of this episode is: When a barefoot fellow tells you he is revolting against tyranny, watch out: he's only after your boots. (*He pinches the second boot, stands*) There you have the class struggle in a nutshell.

(*With the boots in one hand, his carpetbag in the other, he heads for the door.*)

Blackout

SCENE 3

The interior of a cattle car heading west from Siberia. It is packed with revolutionaries, men and women, all in high spirits.

EXILES

Out of the prison camps
Of Verkholensk and Katka;
Down from the frozen wastes
Of Chutchki and Yakutsk;
Out through the stockade gates
Of Kunia and Kamchatka—
Fare thee well, Siberia.
Go to hell, Siberia.
From all Siberia
The exiles return!

KAPINSKY

What's the train stopping for?

AN EXILE

Somebody's on the tracks flagging the train down.
      (*Enter* STALIN—*as he will be known from now on*—KAMENEV *and*
      MURANOV, *carrying their various luggage. The first exile*, KLURMAN,
      throws up his arms in joyous welcome.)

KLURMAN

Kamenev! Bronsky, look who just got on the train! Kamenev!

BRONSKY

Kamenev! Come in! Make a place for Kamenev and his friends!

KAMENEV

I'm sure some of you know Stalin here.

WOMAN EXILE

He looks familiar.

KAMENEV

And this is Muranov, who is drunk.

KAPINSKY

Kamenev! You Bolshevik centrist!

KAMENEV

Kapinsky, you Menshevik compromiser!

KLURMAN
(*Embracing* KAMENEV)
How good to see you, Lev Borisovich!

KAMENEV
Just a moment, Klurman. The last time we met, in Prague in Nineteen Twelve, you called me a filthy Bolshevik factionalist and challenged me to a duel.

KLURMAN
(*Embracing* KAMENEV *again*)
Comrade! Comrade! Give me your hand!

ALL EXILES
Comrades! Comrades! Together we stand!

KLURMAN
For years we had an endless row
On what Marx said and why and how.
But all that is forgotten now.

ALL EXILES
The exiles return.
Brothers all in unity!
The exiles return.

(KAMENEV *pauses to contemplate the audience.*)

KAMENEV
It would be to the point here, I think, to give a brief history of the Marxist movement in Russia. Otherwise, our American comrades may find our ways curious, if not entirely grotesque.

YOUNG WOMAN
Capital idea!

KAMENEV
Here, in this one railroad coach, I see Klurman, who is a Left Menshevik conciliator; Rusikov there—

ELEVENTH EXILE
Kamenev, good fellow, do you remember Kherson prison in Poltava eight years ago?

KAMENEV
How are you, dear fellow? Rusikov there, as I say, is a Right Socialist revolutionary.

RUSIKOV
I'm a Left Trudovik now, Kamenev.

KAMENEV

A Left Trudovik, then. I, myself, am of the Bolshevik Right.

WOMAN EXILE

You occasionally waver to a Centrist position, Kamenev.

KAMENEV

Well, as you see, we have all cuts and stripes of Marxist thought here. The American mind, quite reasonably, expects one Socialist to be pretty much like any other, but nothing could be further from the fact. There are many species of Marxist, some still undiscovered, and each regards the others as the most reprehensible apostasy. So that you may understand our curious facility for fragmentation, and, with the editorial eye of my fellow revolutionaries here upon me—

THIRTEENTH EXILE

He's a good fellow, Kamenev!

KAMENEV

At any rate, a brief history of the Marxist movement in Russia. In the first half of the nineteenth century, Russian Socialism was agrarian in character. In the second half of the century, however, the introduction of heavy industry into Russia created the simulacrum of a proletariat.

BRONSKY

Simulacrum! What a splendid word!

KAMENEV

The doctrines of Karl Marx caught on, and, in Eighteen Eighty-three, the Russian Social Democratic Party was formed. How am I doing?

FOURTEENTH EXILE

Top-notch!

FIFTEENTH EXILE

First-rate!

BRUSTEIN

Hurrah for Kamenev!

KAMENEV

The Russian Social Democratic Party was formally begun in Eighteen Eighty-three by Vera Zasulich, for one, Axelrod, Plekhanov, and others who had gone off to Switzerland to escape the period of reaction that followed the assassination of Tsar Alexander Second. In the Eighties, Russian revolutionaries poured into Western Europe by the hundreds, amusing little figures in beards and astrakhan hats, standing on the steps of the State Library in Geneva, plotting a revolution they never for a moment took seriously. Being a revolutionary exile, in those days, was simply a

Russian way of life. But in Eighteen Ninety-five a young lawyer named
Ulyanov—

KLURMAN

Why is it you do not mention Bakunin?

KAPINSKY

Or the Workers' Union?

KAMENEV

My dear Kapinsky, the Workers' Union, although putatively a Marxist
organization, was actually anarcho-nationalistic in outlook, and Lenin
read them out of the Party at the Nineteen Twelve Congress in Prague—

BRUSTEIN

I do not recognize the Prague Congress!

KAMENEV

And I demand that these jackals of bourgeois autonomism be stricken
from the records of the Russian Marxist movement.

KAPINSKY

The Workers' Union takes a federalist position because—

KAMENEV

Smash their heads against the wall!

GRANDMA SILYONOVA

The Bolsheviks evidently intend to continue their schismatisms.

KAPINSKY

I demand the floor.

KLURMAN

Comrades! Comrades! Let us have an end to this incessant sectarianism.
We shall have enough to squabble over in the days to come. Let us at least
put aside old differences.

RUSIKOV

Well spoken, Feodor Feodorovich.

KAPINSKY

I do think, Kamenev, your reference to the Workers' Union as jackals of
bourgeois autonomism was gratuitous hyperbole.

KAMENEV

I retract the hyperbole.

ALL EXILES

Comrade! Comrade!
Give me your hand!
Comrades! Comrades!
Together we stand!

KAMENEV

At any rate— If we may pause for a moment in the singing of rousing songs—in Nineteen Three, all the Russian Marxist groups got together in Brussels to form one unified, national Social Democratic Party. It was at the Brussels Congress that Plekhanov, Martov and Ulyanov, now known by his party name, Lenin, and, of course, Pavel Borisovich Axelrod, drove the Economists from the Party. Economism, I must explain, was an early Marxist deviation and a betrayal of the working class in that it tended toward a syndicalist orientation of the proletariat. It derived its bourgeois conformism from the Bernstein fallacy—

RUSIKOV

If I may interrupt—

KAMENEV

—and indeed was to blossom out again—that hydra-headed monster— in Nineteen Seven at the plenary session of the Executive Committee, when Martov and Plekhanov and Pavel Borisovich Axelrod—

RUSIKOV

First of all, let us not confuse Economism with—

WOMAN EXILE

What has he got against Axelrod?

KAMENEV

—in open defiance of the London Congress Resolution of Nineteen Seven—

YOUNG WOMAN

What open defiance? The resolution in question—

RUSIKOV

What has Economism to do with Syndicalism?

YOUNG WOMAN

—was actually passed at the Stockholm Congress—

KAMENEV

The Mensheviks were invited to participate in the technical bureaus—

RUSIKOV

It is a characteristic Bolshevik trick—

KAMENEV

—but Martov, in open defiance—

KLURMAN

Comrades! Comrades!

FIFTEENTH EXILE

This is ideological diffusionism!

TENTH EXILE

Throw him out!

BRONSKY

It was Lenin and Bogdanov, who, in open defiance—

KAMENEV

In Nineteen Three, at the Brussels Congress—

KLURMAN

Comrades! Comrades!

BRONSKY

—of the majority resolution—

GRANDMA SILYONOVA

I demand the floor!

TENTH EXILE

Throw him out!

KAMENEV

—that the implications of the Menshevik position which at that time were merely seminal—

BRONSKY

Seminal! Dear me! What an elegance!

KLURMAN

Comrades! For God's sake!

KAMENEV

—was to blossom out again, that hydra-headed monster—

KLURMAN

Comrades!

FIFTEENTH EXILE

Factionalist!

SIXTEENTH EXILE

Opportunist!

NINTH EXILE

Schismatist!

KAMENEV

—in the liquidationist policies of Martov and Pavel Borisovich Axelrod!

KLURMAN

Comrades! Enough! Silence! *(The heated exchange sinks into silence)* First of all, Kamenev, hydra-headed monsters do not blossom out, at least, not twice in the same paragraph.

KAMENEV

Are you commenting on my oratorical style?

KLURMAN

I am merely suggesting, in the interest of unity, that we avoid the usual invective. Let us bury past recriminations. The Revolution has occurred. The will of the masses has spoken. In Petrograd, in Moscow, in Kiev, in Kharkov and Tver, the people have risen up against their oppressors. But even now, as I speak, the armies of counterrevolution are gathering. We Socialists must stand shoulder to shoulder against the forces of reaction that would undo the achievement of the Revolution. We must give our attention to—not the past—but what must be done now.

YOUNG WOMAN

Hurrah for Feodor Feodorovich!

NINTH EXILE

Well spoken, Klurman!

KLURMAN

I suggest that the principal issue confronting us is: What is to be the policy of the various Marxist parties with respect to the Provisional Government? Shall we support the Provisional Government or shall we oppose it? I say, we should do both.

KAMENEV

That is the usual Socialist position, ringing indecision.

RUSIKOV

Oh, sit down, Kamenev! Klurman is talking now.

KLURMAN

The Provisional Government is an out-and-out bourgeois government, a government of landlords and capitalists, and we Socialists, who control the Petrograd Soviet, could depose of the whole lot of them in a minute and take over the government if we wished.

ALL EXILES

Down with the Provisional Government!

KLURMAN

But, comrades, do we Socialists want to take over the government? Let us look at the situation realistically. Russia is bankrupt. The soldiers are deserting the trenches in brigades. The peasants are in revolt. The factories are idle. Famine stalks the land. And the German army stands poised in the marshes of Galicia waiting only for the first thaw of spring to launch their final offensive. They will sweep through us like Scythians. A matter of weeks at most. If we took over the government, our one act of state would be to sign a humiliating peace treaty. Then we would be faced with chaos at home and not even the Germans to blame for it. Now, who wants to take the rap for this desolate situation? Let the Provisional Government take the rap for it.

KAMENEV

You know, he's got a point there.

KLURMAN

The question facing us Socialists, it seems to me, is not how to take over the power, but, now that we've got it, how do we get rid of it?

FOURTEENTH EXILE

But if the Germans take over, what happens to the Revolution?

KLURMAN

We will insist on free elections and a representative Parliament.

RUSIKOV

But look here, Klurman, if that's to be the case, the net result of the Revolution would be a bourgeois-democratic republic, whereas I had assumed we Socialists prefer a Socialist state.

KLURMAN

Precisely! We are faced with a dialectical issue. Was this a bourgeois revolution or a socialist revolution? Since it is elemental Marxism that the bourgeois revolution must precede the proletariat revolution, then it is evident *prima facie* that the Revolution of March, Nineteen Seventeen, was a bourgeois revolution, and the historically proper government for Russia is a bourgeois government. I say, we must support the Provisional Government of Milyukov and Lvov.

ALL EXILES

Long live the Provisional Government!

KAPINSKY

Klurman, how can you say this was a bourgeois revolution? It was the Petrograd proletariat who made this revolution.

BRUSTEIN

Well said, Kapinsky.

KAPINSKY

The bourgeoisie had nothing to do with it. They were all hiding in their attics, peeking out from behind their curtains.

YOUNG WOMAN

I think we are forgetting here—

KAPINSKY

If the bourgeoisie want a revolution, let them make one themselves.

KAMENEV

I object to the totality of that statement.

BRUSTEIN

On the other hand, one might think of it as a continuing revolution—

KAPINSKY

That is Trotskyite doctrine—

RUSIKOV

You are all talking rubbish—

KLURMAN

Rusikov, what rot are you bringing up now?

BRONSKY

Liquidationist!

TENTH EXILE

Throw him out!

RUSIKOV
(To KLURMAN)

Where do you come to say I am talking rot?

KLURMAN

Because you are talking rot—

BRUSTEIN

Let us take the case of the French Revolution—

RUSIKOV

You are the one who is talking rot—

KAPINSKY

The French Revolution, which Brustein has dragged in by the tail—

VOICES

Compromiser! Trotskyite! Ultimatist!

BRUSTEIN

Listen, Kapinsky, how would you like a punch in the nose?

KAMENEV
(To KLURMAN and RUSIKOV)

As a matter of fact, you are both talking rot. It was neither a bourgeois revolution, nor a proletarian revolution—it was an agrarian revolution.

FOURTEENTH EXILE
(Sings with a high tenor voice)

It was a proletarian revolution.

ALL EXILES
(Sing)

A proletarian revolution.

SIXTEENTH EXILE
(Sings with a low baritone voice)

It was an agrarian revolution.

ALL EXILES

An agrarian-proletarian revolution.

SOPRANO EXILE
(Sings)

It was a bourgeois revolution.

ALL EXILES

It was an agrarian-proletarian-bourgeois revolution!
It was a feudal-agrarian, socialist-proletarian,
Capitalist-bourgeois revolution!
It was a feudal-agrarian-peasant,
Socialist-proletarian-working class,
Capitalist-bourgeois-democratic revolution!
Hallelujah!
Hallelujah!
Hallelujah!
Out of the prison camps, the exiles return.
Down from the arctic wastes, the exiles return.
Fare thee well, Siberia.
Go to hell, Siberia.
Brothers all united.
The exiles return.

(The EXILES *all exit with the exception of* KAMENEV *and* KLURMAN, *who remain standing staring belligerently at each other.)*

KAMENEV

When we get to Petrograd, Klurman, I challenge you to a duel, you filthy Bolshevik factionalist!

KLURMAN

Idiot! You are the filthy Bolshevik factionalist! I am the filthy Menshevik conciliator!

KAMENEV

That's right too. *(Wraps his arm around* KLURMAN's *shoulder as they exit)* Now, let's see if I have this straight. I'm the filthy Bolshevik factionalist, and you're the revolting Menshevik Conciliator. I must remember to get that right next time.

Blackout

SCENE 4

ALLILUYEV's *flat in a working-class district of Petrograd, two days later.*
ALLILUYEV, *a man of fifty, is reading* Pravda; *his wife,* OLGA EVGEYEVNA, *is
wearing her coat, trying to keep warm; his daughter,* NADYA, *is on her bed, dis-
consolate.*

STALIN'S VOICE
(Off)

Alliluyev! Hullo! Alliluyev!

ALLILUYEV

That must be Chugurin.
> (*He stands, slips into his overcoat.* OLGA EVGEYEVNA *hurries out to the
> stairway.*)

OLGA EVGEYEVNA
(Looking down the stairwell)

It is Josef Visaryonovich!
> (NADYA *stands bolt upright.* ALLILUYEV *strides to the doorway. Enter*
> STALIN, *carrying his bundle. The two men embrace. Tears stream down
> the faces of the two women.*)

ALLILUYEV

In the name of God, you hooligan, we've been expecting you every day.
Four years, you villain! You've been gone four years!

OLGA EVGEYEVNA
(Embraces STALIN)

It is good, Josef Visaryonovich, to have you back among us.

STALIN

It is good, Olga Evgeyevna, to be again with friends.

ALLILUYEV

You are staying with us, Stalin. Not a word now—Olinka, let the fellow
breathe. What have we got for the bravo to eat? Nadinka, embrace your
Uncle Soso. This is my Nadya, Stalin. Do you remember her at all? She's
grown into a handsome piece, eh? She idolizes you, talks of nothing but:
"Oh, if Comrade Stalin were only here!" By God, I've made her blush.
Here, here, give me your things, old fellow. Well, sit down, old fellow. In
the name of God, it's good to see you, Stalin.

STALIN

It's good to see you, Sergei Efimovich.

ALLILUYEV

That's a handsome pair of boots, I must say.

STALIN

Yes, I'm very fond of them. I took the tram down from the Visher Station. What a crush. Still, the city seems quiet enough, considering it's only ten days ago the Tsar abdicated.

ALLILUYEV

Well, all the shooting's over. The shops are open again. You can get tickets to the ballet, if you like. Kshesinskaya's at the Marinsky. Coffee is up to fifteen rubles a pound, and the bread ration's down to two ounces.

STALIN

You sound disenchanted, Sergei Efimovich.

ALLILUYEV

Well, the steam's gone out of it. My God, Stalin, all hallelujah broke out in this city just a week ago. Kerensky announced the Tsar's abdication from a balcony of the Parliament Building, and the city went insane with freedom. A soldier ran up to me, a peasant kid—"Grandpa," he said, "you shall see what it means to live in a free Russia!" Some peasant kid from Smolensk who never hoped for more than forty lashes. What shall I say? It was that sort of day, Stalin. I broke into sobs, and the two of us stood in the falling snow like idiots, embracing over and over again and weeping with joy. Free! Free! We were all free at last! Free elections, free press, free speech. Free, free, everyone is free. That is, of course, after the war. Let's not forget Germans, eh? We have to thrash them first. The day after the Tsar abdicated, Stalin, I awoke with the heavy heart of a man who's had his pocket picked by a whore. In one night of heavy snow, the Revolution was fleeced. In the morning, I looked out my window. The street was silent. There wasn't a footprint in the snow. The deed was done. The Petrograd Soviet had voted to support the Provisional Government. We workers had the power—the Petrograd Soviet had the power—and we handed it right back to Milyukov and the bosses, which means Russia will stay in the war. The Germans will be in Petrograd by July, and we Bolsheviks will go back underground.

NADYA

(In an absolute blaze of militancy)

Comrades! Tears will not grow flowers! We must consider what must be done! The government must sue for peace now! Immediate surrender! Nothing less! Since the Milyukov government will not do this, the Petrograd Soviet must take over the state. This will provoke civil war, you say. Well then, the issue is civil war! There is no other policy that can save the Revolution! If Russian blood is to be shed, let it be at least for a better Russia! What is our program? As clear as the nose on your face! Down with the Provisional Government! All power to the Petrograd Soviet! Immediate peace at any terms! Nothing less! And the devil take the waverers!

STALIN

By Christ, what a militant, Alliluyev.

ALLILUYEV

Well, she's right, eh? Peace now or the Tsar later.

NADYA

We lack for a strong leader, Comrade Stalin.

STALIN

I take it you are saying, "If Lenin were only here."

ALLILUYEV

If Lenin were here, we would have a revolution.

STALIN

And the British won't ship him back from Switzerland, eh?

ALLILUYEV

The British aren't fools. They're not going to ship an influential pacifist like Lenin back here when they're putting the screws on us to open the eastern front. They're taking special pains to keep him caulked up in Zurich.

STALIN

What a shambles!

MAN'S VOICE
(Off, shouting)

Alliluyev!

ALLILUYEV
(Shouting back)

We've got one foot out the door! (To STALIN) That's Chugurin. We have one of those interminable district meetings to go to. We shouldn't be more than an hour, two at the most. Olinka!

(OLGA EVGEYEVNA *hurries in from the kitchen with a bowl of soup and a plate of cheese which she sets down on the table. She hurries to the door, pausing to embrace* STALIN *with a fresh flow of tears.*)

OLGA EVGEYEVNA

It is good, Josef Visaryonovich, to have you back among us.

STALIN

It is good, Olga Evgeyevna, to be again with friends. Extend my fraternal greetings to the district committee, Sergei Efimovich.

> (ALLILUYEV *and his wife exit.* STALIN *promptly sits at the table and single-mindedly devours all the papers on the table. After a moment,* NADYA, *perched on her bed, speaks.*)

NADYA

Comrade Stalin, let us regard the Socialist position on the war in terms of its tenability as Marxism.

STALIN

(Now bolting away at his soup)

By all means.

NADYA

We shall accept as valid the Socialist contention that the Revolution was bourgeois in its historical purpose. But it is one thing to support a bourgeois government, and quite another to support a bourgeois-imperialist war whose only purpose is to take Constantinople from the Turks. To this, the Socialists reply: "We renounce all imperialist aims in this war, but we must defend the Revolution from German aggression." What trumpery!

STALIN

(Wolfing down some cheese)

Rascals!

NADYA

(Standing)

To this I answer: The new revolutionary Russia, by your own premise, is a bourgeois-capitalist state. Are Russian workers to bayonet German workers to preserve a capitalist state? That is deformed logic indeed!

STALIN

(Wiping his mouth along an elbow's length of his greatcoat sleeve)

Absolutely grotesque.

NADYA

The untenability of the Socialist position makes one shudder.

STALIN

(Pushes his food away and bursts into applause)

Very spirited, Nadezhda Sergeyevna. *(He reaches over and gives the girl's rump a good squeeze, which rather startles her)* By God, so you're sweet on your Uncle Soso, eh? *(He chucks her under the chin, lets his hand slip down over a breast, which he squeezes cruelly.* NADYA *cries out in pain.* STALIN *roars with laughter)* But, Comrade Alliluyeva, if you accept the validity of the bourgeois revolution, it follows you must support the emergence of the bourgeois state in Russia. War is an axiomatic manifestation of the bourgeois state. Hence, we should encourage the war as a confirmation of the dialectic. By God, you didn't think to hook an old fish like me with that seminary Marxism. Ho!

(He reaches again for her. She pushes him off.)

NADYA

Comrade Stalin, your interpretation of the role of imperialism in the bourgeois state can only be considered devious. I will cite you Comrade Lenin on this very point—in his book on emperio-criticism—

STALIN

Forget Lenin. Lenin's stuck in Zurich! That's amusing! I should give a lot to see Lenin at this moment. He's having a nervous collapse, I'm sure. The Revolution, which he considers his personal possession, is happening without him. He's missing the whole show. What a rage he must be in. Oh, that's amusing. He goes into these terrible rages, you know. That's amusing. Oh well, you don't know him, so you don't see how amusing it is.

NADYA

I find it hard to think of Comrade Lenin as amusing.

STALIN

He passes water like the rest of us. You're a party nun, by God. I must say, I didn't think to find a party nun in old Alliluyev's house—

NADYA

I have done good work for the party, Comrade Stalin.

STALIN

(Affably)

I'm sure you have. You Bolshevik nuns make good rank and filers. If you're highly principled enough, there's nothing too savage you won't do for the cause. You'll burgle, perjure, suborn your mother and burke your dear old granddad. We're lucky to have you. The party would be hard put to pay for all the brigands it would otherwise need for its chores. The only trouble with you dedicated oblates is you all wind up at forty, unfrocked Bolsheviks, tracking up everybody's kitchen with your dripping ideals. Mark my words, you'll turn out a police informer, Nadezhda. You'll turn in all your old comrades to the police, eh? As a matter of principle, of course.

NADYA

What a bitter outburst, Josef Visaryonovich.

STALIN

Did I sound bitter? I'm in splendid spirits, really.

NADYA

From my childhood I remember you as an austere zealot, with one suit of clothes as shabby as a hair shirt.

STALIN

I was poor, Nadezhda Sergeyevna, not ascetic.

NADYA

You had abandoned wife and child to work in the underground.

STALIN

I never abandoned my wife at all. I was damned fond of her. She died of cholera in Nineteen Five. I was at her bedside for three days. She left me with a two-year-old kid. Now, what was I to do with that? I donated him to my in-laws. Do you find this admirable? That's damned curious of you.

NADYA

You will tell me now that you took on the hounded life of a revolutionary as a lark.

STALIN

I'm a Georgian of the lower classes, Nadezhda Sergeyevna. Revolution is a common trade among us. In my time, a boy either cobbled or carpentered or apprenticed out to a terrorist society. We have hundreds of them.

NADYA

It pleases you to deprecate yourself, Josef Visaryonovich. This is a perverse modesty with many of you old Bolsheviks.

STALIN

You're determined to have me a lofty soul, eh? Well, the fact is I'm just a party tough. One of the brutes of the revolutionary movement, as Comrade Trotsky once called me.

NADYA

Josef Visaryonovich, I am on the verge of tears!

STALIN

"Lenin," Comrade Trotsky said, "is surrounding himself with the brutes of the movement." He meant me. He'll pay for that in good time.

NADYA

(Bursting into tears)

Trotsky is a political chameleon!

STALIN

As a matter of fact, you'd like Trotsky. He lacquers himself up every morning with noble sentiments. On a sunny day, his glister can be seen for miles. What are you keening about, you witless girl?

NADYA

I don't know what to make of you, Josef Visaryonovich!

STALIN

I'm a disappointment to you, eh? Ho! You had me worked out as something of a visionary, and I turned out a bully boy who tried to pull your knickers down. A hell of a hero, eh? By God, I fancy you! I don't usually get into a steam over your sort. You Marxist vestals have that emancipated look. That puts me off, that does. A man pokes up an interest in a girl, and it's a wilting sensation to look up and see that earnest, comradely eye. I've had a go at one or two of you lady revolutionaries. Oh, well, by God! It turns out such a militant affair. Hell, it's just meant to be a romp, not a defiance of bourgeois morality. Eh? Oh, well, as I say, I damn well like you, though, Nadezhda Sergeyevna. That's odd, eh? *(He regards her affably, his left hand, which is slightly deformed, tucked between two buttons of his shirt. Smiling and utterly sinister, he crosses slowly to* NADYA, *who sits on the edge of her bed, no longer crying. She stands, as alert as a deer)* Trotsky's right, eh? I'm a brute. I lack all purpose other than to preserve myself. Violent, cruel, greedy, and durable. *(With an abrupt movement of his right hand, he rips* NADYA's *blouse down to the belt, and, continuing the same movement, brings his hand back and forth across her face in two resonant swats.* NADYA *falls back onto her bed)* One of your masses, so to speak. An average ravening man.

NADYA
(Regarding him coldly)

Don't put your hand out to me again, or I shall kill you, Josef Visaryonovich. Twice this year I've had the dogs set on me by company coppers. Do you think to frighten me? *(She stands, angrily examines her torn blouse)* You shall make good this waist, Josef Visaryonovich. I have only one other.

STALIN
(Regards her respectfully)

You are a hard customer, Nadezhda Sergeyevna.
(She pulls the torn blouse off, flings it on the bed and rummages out another from a carton which is under the bed. STALIN *does not hide his admiration for* NADYA's *full young body, fairly bursting the light shift that now covers her.)*

NADYA

I am a Bolshevik, Comrade Stalin. I believe men are essentially decent fellows. I do not pretend there is virtue in revolution. A revolution, after all, is only a class seizing the power of state. But when that class contains the bulk of the people, the effect is a people's state, and that, Josef Visaryonovich, is virtuous. The Socialist state will be a truer democracy, without privilege or greed. It is an inevitable fact of man's advance. It is a desirable condition, and I will give my life in the struggle to achieve it. That is my purpose, Comrade Stalin. I shall live to see a better Russia. But, if not, I will have struggled, while you merely suffered. I will have aspired, while you merely endured.

STALIN

The Revolution doesn't seem to be faring as inevitably as it should, eh?

NADYA

The Revolution will persist. Its triumph is historically unavoidable. The Socialist state is imminent.

STALIN

But without Lenin there doesn't seem to be anyone around who could pull it off.

NADYA

Lenin will return. He is historically necessary for the success of the Revolution.

STALIN

He seems to be historically situated in Switzerland at the moment.

NADYA

He will return.

STALIN

I admire your conviction.

NADYA

Oh, is that what you've been admiring? You're a brazen fellow, you know?

STALIN

I find you handsome. Does that displease you?

(NADYA *is no longer angry. She buttons her new blouse, regarding* STALIN *with an amused smile.*)

NADYA

I've grown up in the slums of ten cities, Josef Visaryonovich. I'm not all that vestal as you think. (*For a long moment, they regard each other with evident approval*) Are you being wilted by my earnest and comradely eye?

STALIN

No.

NADYA

I think we make a good pair, eh?

STALIN

Yes.

NADYA

Don't think you shall get off buying me a new waist.

STALIN

I said I would make it good, eh?
> (*She is suddenly across the room into his arms. They embrace intensely.*)

NADYA

I have adored you since I can remember—since I can remember, Josef Visaryonovich!

ALLILUYEV'S VOICE
> (*Off, shouting*)

Stalin! Stalin!
> (*With a gloomy sigh*, STALIN *releases* NADYA.)

STALIN

My God, I don't have any luck at all today.
> (ALLILUYEV *and his wife burst into the room.*)

ALLILUYEV

Stalin! The Central Committee has received a telegram from Lenin! He is returning! Lenin and Zinoviev and forty other exiles are returning! Lenin shall be in Petrograd within a week!
> (STALIN *and* NADYA *exchange a look.*)

STALIN

Why would the British send Lenin back?

ALLILUYEV

The British aren't sending him. He has made arrangements with the Germans!

STALIN

The Germans? Of course, the Germans. They'd be delighted to ship Lenin back to Russia. What a sensible fellow he is!
> (ALLILUYEV *races to the open doorway and shouts down the stairwell.*)

ALLILUYEV

Lenin is returning! Do you hear? Lenin is returning!

OLGA EVGEYEVNA
> (*Crying out to the street below*)

Comrades! Workers! Lenin is returning!

ALLILUYEV

Lenin! Lenin! Lenin!

Blackout

SCENE 5

The Finland Station, April 16, at night. The upstage area is the street. It is thronged with workers, soldiers, sailors. An armored car, vintage 1917, extrudes from the left wing. On the roof of the armored car is a revolving spotlight going around and around on the dark stage. The center stage area is the waiting room, also thronged, but with officers and dignitaries. Three Socialist leaders sit disconsolately on a waiting-room bench. They are CHEIDZE, SUKHANOV *and* SKOBELOV. CHEIDZE *holds a wilted bouquet of flowers. Downstage is the station platform.* STALIN *and two Bolsheviks stand peering off into the right wing.*

CROWD
(Chanting)

Lenin! Lenin! Lenin!

STALIN
(To the Bolsheviks near him)

Ah! Rykov has finished his speech of welcome. Melnik, dash over to the band, like a good fellow, and tell them to strike up the "Marseillaise" again. (MELNIK *exits stage left. To* MOLOTOV) Molotov, go to the waiting room and tell the Socialist leaders that Lenin and his party are coming down the platform.

MOLOTOV
(Dashing into the waiting room)

Lenin is on his way down the platform!

(Everybody in the waiting room stirs to attention. CHEIDZE, SUKHANOV *and* SKOBELOV *rise from their bench with a melancholy sigh. A military band suddenly bursts into the "Marseillaise." Enter* LENIN, *striding in from downstage right. He is a short, intense, middle-aged man with a small beard and wearing a fur cap. He is carrying a bouquet of flowers. He is followed by his wife,* KRUPSKAYA, *a stout, little, middle-aged woman, and three Bolshevik Central Committee Members:* KAMENEV, ZINOVIEV *and* RYKOV.)

LENIN

Good God, Stalin, you're not going to make a speech, too.

STALIN

No, Vladimir Ilyich, but you'll have to endure three Socialist leaders who are in the waiting room to greet you in the name of the Petrograd Soviet.

(LENIN *strides into the waiting room, followed by his party*)

CROWD

Lenin! Lenin! Lenin!

(NADYA *enters in a state of exhilaration. She goes to* STALIN. *They watch the proceedings going on in the waiting room, where* CHEIDZE *steps forward offering his bouquet to* LENIN.)

CHEIDZE

Comrade Lenin, allow me to present myself. I am Comrade Cheidze, Chairman of the Petrograd Soviet. Comrade Lenin, you are one of the founders of the Party, a great name in the international Socialist movement, and we welcome you to Russia. On the other hand, Comrade Lenin, the Revolution is over. Russia is now a democratic republic. Our new democracy is threatened by war without and by reactionary forces within who already talk openly of restoring the Tsar. We Socialists consider our immediate task to be the defense of our new democracy against its enemies, from within and from without. Therefore, we support the present government. Will you join with us, Comrade Lenin, in defending our new democracy against its enemies?

(*He offers his hand.* LENIN *turns brusquely to the* CROWD.)

LENIN

Comrades! Workers! Soldiers! Sailors! Citizens of Petrograd! The leaders of the Socialist parties say the Revolution is over! I say it is not enough! So we shall make a new one!

CROWD

Lenin! Lenin! Lenin!

NADYA

Now, Josef Visaryonovich, we shall see a revolution in Russia.

STALIN

Yes, perhaps we shall.

Curtain

ACT II

SCENE 1

A street in Petrograd, July 29, 1917. A tacky vaudeville orchestra of four pieces, dressed in the period of 1917, is playing the music of "Nothing Has Changed." At center stage is a café table and chairs. A businessman named NIKITIN, *frock-coated and portly, enters furtively.*

NIKITIN

Two Russian capitalists meet on a street in Petrograd and will now pro-ceed—as advertised—to cut their own throats.

(A second businessman, LOMOV, *pokes his head out)*

LOMOV
(In a whisper)

Grisha—

NIKITIN

Lomov, dear fellow, how are you? You may come out. It's all quiet again. The shooting has stopped. The mobs have gone back across the river to their own parts of town. Looking about, I must say, things don't seem much different than before.

LOMOV
(Advancing gingerly to the café table)

The restaurants, I see, are open.

NIKITIN
(Also sitting at the table)

Oh, everything is open. Yes, everything seems *comme il faut.*

LOMOV

Comme il faut, you say.

NIKITIN

Nothing seems to have changed.

LOMOV
(Sings)

No, nothing seems changed.

NIKITIN
(Sings)

Well, the Empire, of course, is a bit disarranged.
In fact, it's dissolved. They've locked up the Tsar.

LOMOV
(Sings)

But the phones are still working.

NIKITIN
(Sings)

And the corner tram car.

LOMOV
(Sings)

The cinema's open just as before.

NIKITIN
(Sings)

And it's good to see we are still safely at war.
(GENERAL KORNILOV, *a dark, mustached man resplendent in a red uniform and followed by a Mongolian bodyguard—also in red—strides across
the stage and exits)*

LOMOV

Who was that?

NIKITIN

General Kornilov off to the front.

LOMOV
(Taking heart, singing)

No, nothing has changed.
Nothing has changed.

NIKITIN
(Sings)

Well, now,
An historic upheaval, of course, has occurred,
A new age is born, an old world interred.
To say: "Nothing has changed" is grossly absurd.

NIKITIN *and* LOMOV
(Singing)

Nothing has changed.
Nothing has changed.
We insist! Do you hear!

Nothing has changed.

LOMOV
(Snapping his fingers for a waiter)
Waiter!
> *(At this moment, an absolute horde of shabby women swarms over the stage, knocking over chairs, throwing rocks at offstage windows and shouting "Down with the Government!" Our two businessmen, needless to say, have slipped under the table, where, resolutely ignoring the tumult about them, they sing out between the shouts of the women)*

NIKITIN
(Sings)
Nothing has changed.

LOMOV
(Sings)
Nothing has changed.

NIKITIN
(Sings)
The gov'ment, of course,
Is completely deranged.

LOMOV
Oh, this Milyukov fellow's a good man, they say.

NIKITIN
(Sings)
Good God, man, Milyukov fell early last May.
We've had five ministries since—

LOMOV
Are you sure?

NIKITIN
(Sings)
—an appalling
Crashing of cabinets rising and falling.
Kerensky's premier now, at least for the week.

LOMOV
A Socialist premier!

NIKITIN
Grotesque!

LOMOV
What cheek!

NIKITIN *and* LOMOV
(Singing)

Nothing has changed.
Nothing has changed.

LOMOV
(Shouting to be heard over the women)

Are you game for the opera tonight?

NIKITIN
(Likewise shouting)

Well, who's on?

LOMOV
(Shouting)

Chaliapin! A triumph, I'm told, as Don Juan!

NIKITIN

No need to shout, Lomov. Those people have gone. *(He crawls out from under the table and shakes his fist after the departing women)*

Nothing has changed!
Nothing has changed!
Do you hear? Is that clear?
Nothing has changed!

(A shambling squad of soldiers, burdened beneath enormous fieldpacks and shouldering rifles, trudges across the stage to the rolling of drums. NIKITIN *stands stiffly to attention, his silk-banded hat held over his heart)* Good luck, boys! Brave lads! Sweet heroes! All Russia blesses you! Godspeed! Hurrah!

> *(The soldiers shamble off.* NIKITIN *produces a handkerchief and wipes a tear from his eye.)*

LOMOV
(Crawling out from under the table)

Come now, Grisha, you are carrying on unnecessarily.

NIKITIN

Lomov, dear fellow, those straggly recruits were all peasants from my estate in Samara. For years, I have share-cropped them unconscionably and reduced them to such hideous poverty, they now talk fondly of their days as praedial serfs. Must I say I feel as a father to them? Now, they are off to the front, perhaps to die, surely to be mutilated. You are fine lads, all! I weep for you!

> *(He weeps.)*

LOMOV
(Setting his chair aright)

Off to the front? What do they hope to do there?

NIKITIN
(Likewise setting a chair aright)

Good God, man, you must know Russia has launched a new offensive against the Germans.

LOMOV

I had no idea.

NIKITIN

We are attacking all along the Polish front.

LOMOV

What a curious thing to do.

NIKITIN

On the twenty-ninth of June, our artillery opened fire, and, on the first of July, two million of our men swept out of the trenches into the swamps of Galicia.

LOMOV

We shall be crushed within a week.

NIKITIN
(Sitting)

Utterly routed. It will be a debacle.

LOMOV
(Shouting off to the wing)

Fight on, boys! *(He suddenly starts for an upstage corner)* Bolt for it, Grisha! Here come those strikers again!

NIKITIN
(Scanning his newspaper)

Waiter! *(The mob of women shuffles sullenly back onstage and stands, a mute, smoldering group)*
Nothing has changed.
Nothing has changed.
Well, the peasants perhaps
Are the least bit estranged.
They're butchering bailiffs and burning the crops.
Dammit, the service is bad at the restaurants and shops.
Lomov, what are you doing over there?
    (LOMOV beckons nervously to NIKITIN, who crosses upstage to him)

LOMOV

I must ask you, Grigori Nikolayevich, not to let on I'm here. Those women there are all workers at my factory in the Vyborg district. For years I have wrung them out mercilessly, and I think it politic, considering their obvious temper, to—

FIRST WOMAN

By God, there's the boss!

LOMOV

There, they've seen me.

SECOND WOMAN

You old poltroon, we work ten hours a day six days a week for eight rubles four kopecks!

THIRD WOMAN

A pair of shoes costs three months' pay!

FOURTH WOMAN

All we ask is a living wage!

NIKITIN

Russians! For shame! Back to your benches! There's a war on!

FIRST WOMAN

Workers! Four months ago, we kicked the Tsar off his throne! We were going to have a democracy! Well, where is it? Where are those elections for a new Parliament they keep telling us abut? Instead of elections, they gave us war. Instead of reforms, they give us more war. Well, I say to hell with this war! Down with the Coalition Government, who wages this war!

(During this speech, our two capitalists have cautiously made their way back to the table, where they sit, a pensive pair.)

LOMOV

The lower classes are losing confidence in the government.

NIKITIN

Yes, that comes across quite clearly.

LOMOV

Waiter!

(The soldiers re-enter, bloodied, muddied, wounded and in an ugly frame of mind.)

LOMOV

(Studying his menu)

Nothing has changed.
Nothing has changed.

NIKITIN

(Studying his menu)

The food here is dreadful.
The chef is deranged.

LOMOV

Still short on milk—

NIKITIN

Ah! Persian caviar!

LOMOV

Prices are high, but, then, they always are.

NIKITIN

(Noting the soldiers, leaps up, beaming)
Well, my warriors, what's the word from the front?

FIRST SOLDIER

(To SECOND SOLDIER)
Look, Boris Isopovich, it's the master himself wanting news from the front.

SECOND SOLDIER

We beg your forgiveness, master, but we have no news from the front. You see, we all deserted on the first day of battle.
(The THIRD SOLDIER suddenly seizes NIKITIN by his lapels and shakes the startled fellow till his teeth rattle.)

THIRD SOLDIER

Listen, master, we're not fighting any more wars!
(The other soldiers also seize poor NIKITIN and handle him roughly. The women claw at him. LOMOV bolts for the wings again.)

FOURTH SOLDIER

All we want is our land back!

FIFTH SOLDIER

No more rent-gouging, you old villain!

SIXTH SOLDIER

No more working your fields for nothing!
(Hat knocked off, pince-nez dangling, shirt tails out, stunned and near tears, NIKITIN lurches across the stage. He sits on a step, holding his head in his hands, as GENERAL KORNILOV, followed by his bodyguard, re-enters, walking slowly, rapt in thought.)

LOMOV

Ah! General Kornilov, how do we fare at the front?

KORNILOV

Not very well, to be honest about it. The army of the north has been routed. The army of the south is in headlong retreat, and the Germans are marching on Riga.

LOMOV

Ah, a disastrous defeat. Do you hear that, Grisha?
(NIKITIN, quite shaken by his recent abuse, can only nod.)

KORNILOV

On July the first, I took command of the southern army, which was at half strength, some four hundred thousand of my troops having already deserted. I ordered the advance. We proceeded steadily through the Pripet Marshes for a few days, up to our medals in mud. At this point, however, we met up with the German army, a bad stroke of luck for us. Still, we put up a good show. Dreadful number of dead. My supply lines got a bit crossed, and the men were without food and ammunition for a day or two. At this point, the rest of the army deserted. They came sloshing past me by the brigade. That was the last I saw of those six divisions. Well, you see what's at the bottom of all this, of course.

LOMOV

Not quite, General.

KORNILOV

The Bolsheviks, man! This fellow Lenin and his damned Bolsheviks! Gentlemen, the Germans are marching on Riga. Russia is in her eleventh hour. All that can save us now is a strong leader who will rally the loyal troops, march on Petrograd and wrest the city away from these Bolsheviks.

LOMOV
(Delighted)

A coup d'état!

KORNILOV

Yes. We must find the right man for it.

LOMOV

Why not yourself?

KORNILOV

Why not indeed? I shall storm Petrograd at the head of a column of howling Cossacks.

(NIKITIN *suddenly springs erect and cries out.*)

NIKITIN

I cannot imagine a more suicidal idea! Kornilov, you could hang this fellow Lenin a hundred times over, and the state of affairs would remain the same. After all, what is it these insurgent masses ask for? They want peace, democracy, and reforms so that Russia might have a prosperous peasantry and a well-paid working class; in short, an abundant economy. Good God, Lomov, we're businessmen! Nothing could suit us better. What we upper classes must do—clearly enough—is collaborate with the moderate Socialists, make peace, establish a democracy, and make all the reforms necessary for a flourishing people.

LOMOV

What we lose in privilege, we shall more than make up for in profit.

NIKITIN

And nothing could be more stupid of us than to attribute the arrival of a glorious new age to Bolshevik spies.

LOMOV

Really, Kornilov, you and your Bolsheviks. What a crashing old fool you are.

NIKITIN

Russia has changed, Lomov, and we must change with it. Ah, God! What an insufferable thought!

> *(He takes out a knife and slashes his wrists and cuts his throat. Spouting blood by the bucketful, he clambers up onto the café table, produces a hangman's rope from his frock coat, throws the loose end up into the flies and ties the other end around his throat. Now, he brings out a dueling pistol which he sticks into his mouth and blows his brains out. Having done with that, he leaps off the table and dangles—a dead man at last—from the flies. LOMOV and KORNILOV are a little taken aback by all this but not uninterested. They stand, thoughtfully regarding the hanging man.)*

LOMOV

In July of Nineteen Seventeen, the Russian middle classes, having cut their own throats, slashed their own wrists, blown their own brains out, and hanged themselves from their own gibbet, announced they were being poisoned by the Bolsheviks.

> *(LOMOV and KORNILOV, suddenly beside themselves, now charge on the startled women and soldiers, laying about with walking stick and saber and screaming in a tantrum of fury.)*

LOMOV *and* KORNILOV

Assassins! Spies! Traitors! Kill the Bolsheviks! Padlock their newspapers! Issue writs of arrest! Lock them all up!

> *(The lights go abruptly out with the exception of one spotlight revealing NIKITIN swaying gently from his gibbet. He sings in a dead monotone.)*

NIKITIN
(Sings)

Nothing has changed.
Nothing has changed.
We insist. Do you hear?
Nothing has changed.

Blackout

SCENE 2

ALLILUYEV's *apartment, the night of Friday, July 20, 1917. The stage is dark.*
ALLILUYEV, OLGA EVGEYEVNA *and* NADYA *are seen asleep. The door is thrust
open. A shaft light shoots into the room from the landing.* STALIN, *silhouetted,
enters, crosses to the table, lights some candles.*

STALIN

Alliluyev, get up. They are bringing Lenin and Zinoviev here as I told
you they might. You'll have to hide them out for a few days. Kerensky has
issued writs of arrest for them. They've been denounced as German spies.

> (ALLILUYEV *puts on his trousers and boots, and exits out the door.* OLGA
> EVGEYEVNA *exits into the kitchen, dressing as she goes.* NADYA *slips into
> her skirt and blouse)*

NADYA

Lenin must demand an immediate trial. These spy charges must be
exposed as another of Kerensky's filthy tricks.

STALIN
(Trying to steal a kiss)

There won't be a trial.

NADYA
(Pushing him away)

What do you mean, there won't be a trial?

STALIN

Lenin offered to give himself up to the leaders of the Socialist parties if
they would guarantee his personal safety, but they refused to do that.

NADYA

Brutes.

STALIN

Well, Lenin wouldn't be their prisoner, eh? He will be the
Government's prisoner and in the custody of Government troops. Lenin
would be shot within five minutes by the first dragoon to pull his revolver
from its holster.

NADYA

Kerensky and his depraved ministers now seek to prop up their totter-
ing regime by political assassination.

STALIN

Oh, rubbish, Nadya. Three days ago, five hundred thousand Bolshevik soldiers, sailors and workers gathered in the streets of Petrograd to demonstrate against the war. Lenin came out on the balcony like a pope, commended this vast assembly for their revolutionary fervor and cautioned them against violence. You don't caution an armed mob against violence. You send them to fight or you send them back to their homes, but you don't caution a violent mob against violence. They were armed to the teeth and supported by machine guns, armored cars, gunboats—Kerensky called in troops to protect his government. What else should he have done? *(He lights another candle)* Well, we're finished. The Bolshevik party is back where it was ten years ago, an outlaw organization with its leaders hiding in exile.

NADYA

What a blunder this demonstration was. How could Lenin have allowed it?

STALIN

Apparently, he's an imperfect fellow like the rest of us.

NADYA

I had come to think of Lenin as less imperfect. When he spoke to the crowds from his balcony, how orderly this world seemed, how precision-made. He exalted one. I've never known such despair as I feel now.

STALIN

Oh, the first time one loses faith in God is always the most difficult, Nadinka. When I was a kid, my mother wanted me to be a priest. I even went several years to the seminary in Tiflis. By God, it turned out to be a hotbed of revolutionaries. Instead of becoming a priest, I became a Bolshevik. Not that there's much difference, except being a Bolshevik demands a nobler nature and doesn't pay half so well. The fact is, it was the abnegation of the Bolshevik's life that attracted me to it. All that poverty and penance must bring you closer to Christ, eh? Then, in the summer of Nineteen Five, my wife died. She died of the plague, poor old fish. She was twenty-two. The last three days, she never opened her eyes. Her face was wax yellow. She was dead but for a little bubble of breath on her lips. They said she felt no pain. Really? I wondered. I sat by the bed. Her leg twisted under the sheet. She wanted something. She mouthed a word. It had the look of a word; her lips moved, but it lacked a sound. I couldn't make it out. "Are you all right, Katka?" No answer. I thought to myself: "So this is death. Not a soft sleep, not the sudden smile of God, just a spongy weakness slowly suffocating her." She deserved better. She was a good woman, a good, good woman. I loved her. Then her mouth moved again, opened, shut, opened, shut. I bent my ear to her lips. I heard the word now. I heard it twice. Soft, almost silent, a shriek. She was saying: "Terrible. Terrible." I believed in Christ, so I asked him: "Tell me, Christ, is the end really terrible, even for the good ones? Is it so? Then, what is the purpose to anything? Or is there a God I so confidently ask this of?" I stood up beside the bed trembling. "We have made a mistake!" I cried out. "We have made a ghastly mistake! It has been Barabbas all along!" My wife died. I was plunged into terror. Beyond despair. A man can endure life if there is a reason for it, even an incomprehensible one. But to suffer for no reason at all is too hideous. One must deny the pain, and, without pain, how can life be detected? I stared into the cracked looking glass on the wall and saw merely mist. I had vanished, boiled out. I could not endure to live without a god. *(He stands, smiles at* NADYA*)* Ha! As you see, I'm here. Apparently, I've endured. What a persistent thing life is, eh? *(*NADYA, *who had listened to the story with tear-filled eyes, stands, presses herself against* STALIN *and bursts into sobs)* By God, I'm in a steam for you tonight, Nadinka. I simply must have a crack at you.

NADYA
(Terribly in love)
What an outlandish fellow you are.

STALIN
There's to be a Central Committee meeting here, but I'll be down directly it's over. It's a hot night. We'll go to the river. The Liteiny Bridge. There won't be a soul there at this hour. Agreed?

NADYA
Yes.
*(*RYKOV, *a goblin of a man, appears in the open doorway)*

RYKOV
Lenin is here.
*(*NADYA *detaches herself from* STALIN. OLGA EVGEYEVNA *enters from the kitchen bringing a samovar and some tin cups. Enter the Bolshevik Central Committee, a dispirited group. It consists of* KAMENEV; ZINOVIEV—*a fat fellow;* ORJONIKIDZE—*a burly Georgian;* SVERDLOV— a swarthy little man; and the gnomish* RYKOV. *They sink wearily down wherever they can find a place to sit.* ALLILUYEV *remains standing in the doorway. After a moment, enter* LENIN, *carrying a briefcase in one hand and holding his head with the other)*

LENIN
I have this frightful headache.

(OLGA EVGEYEVNA *sets the samovar and cups down and joins her husband in the doorway.* STALIN *escorts* NADYA *to the door. They exchange a nod, and she exits.* STALIN *closes the door.*)

STALIN
(To the audience)

Christ will now bid farewell to his disciples, eh?

(With a crash, LENIN *brings his briefcase down on the table)*

LENIN

We have blundered! Let us not underestimate our present adversity! All those troops that participated in the recent demonstrations will be disbanded or sent to the front. Our influence among the Petrograd garrison has been shattered. A revolutionary party without military support is a joke! We have been reduced to a joke! Very well! Very well! We start again! Put out your cigarettes! There will be no smoking. *(He thumps on the table for emphasis)* Important! Urgent! Exclamation point! First order of business! The First Machine Gun Company, the Second Machine Gun Company, the Pavlovsky Regiment, the Grenadier—Sverdlov! Urgent! A list of all military units in Petrograd sympathetic to our party. We must fight any move by Kerensky to withdraw these units from Petrograd. Rykov! Urgent! Immediate! A policy of incessant agitation among the Left Socialists. We must broaden our political base. Trotsky has made overtures to join our party. He is an influential figure. Pursue rapprochement with Trotsky and his group. Kamenev! I leave this matter of Trotsky in your hands. Above all, no demonstrations. Our policy is agitation! Agitation! Agitation! Let us erase this image of the Bolshevik as a political adventurer. We are revolutionaries, not conspirators. We do not make coup d'états. We wish to construct the Socialist Order in Russia. It must be with the will of the people. We must explain, explain, explain! The people will come to us. We are the minority party now. We shall be the majority. We shall be the will of the people.

(There is a knock on the door. STALIN *moves about the room snuffing out the candles. The room is plunged into darkness.)*

KAMENEV

You are being a little opéra bouffe, Stalin, don't you think?

STALIN

You've forgotten what it's like to be in the underground, Kamenev.

(He opens the door. ALLILUYEV *is revealed in the doorway)*

ALLILUYEV

We found a flat in the next building where we can hide Zinoviev.

ZINOVIEV

I should adore to sleep, Comrade Lenin.

LENIN

(Lighting a candle)

Of course. We're all exhausted. Some sleep. Then, back to work. Keep a good grip on your committees. The party apparatus must be kept disciplined. Good night. I may not see some of you for some weeks. Goodby. Stalin, stay a moment.

(The Central Committee exits. When STALIN *turns back to* LENIN, *he finds the bald little man quietly writing in a notebook.* STALIN *remains in the shadows by the door, waiting. The candle on the table, which is the only light in the room, flickers. A moment of utter stillness.)*

LENIN

Am I to stay here tonight?

STALIN

A day or two, till we find a way to smuggle you and Zinoviev into Finland.

LENIN

I'll require some books while I'm in hiding. They're in my sister's flat.

STALIN

Make a list. I'll get them for you.

LENIN

Set up a courier system. Daily communication.

STALIN

No problem.

LENIN

Will they arrest Kamenev?

STALIN

The moment he sets foot on the street tomorrow. Is Trotsky going to join us as he's announced?

LENIN

Yes. Why?

STALIN

He'll be clapped into jail along with Kamenev.

LENIN

What about you? Will they arrest you?

STALIN

Why should they? I'm not very important.

LENIN

Quatsch! You're important. You know it. If Kerensky wants to crush the Bolsheviks, you are the first of us he should clap into jail. Without you, the party apparatus would be fragmented in a month. Your organizational work has been significant. You'll be commended for it at the next Congress. It's time your name became known. Many of our own people have never heard of you. You'll be running the party while I'm in hiding.

STALIN

Very well.

(He starts involuntarily to cross himself.)

LENIN

What are you doing? You were going to cross yourself. Is that what you want to do?

STALIN

These childhood rituals crop up.

LENIN

I know.

STALIN

I was schooled by the priests when I was a kid.

LENIN

Yes. How badly damaged is the party?

STALIN

Tuesday was a blunder and it cost us dearly.

LENIN

Yes, a blunder, but we learned something. I'm delighted to find we could bring so many people out into the streets.

STALIN

(Insolent)

I submitted a report last week on the strength of the party. Apparently it did not reach your desk.

LENIN

(Annoyed by the younger man's insolence)

How badly damaged is the party?

STALIN

Not so bad, actually. We're still strong in Petrograd. The factory workers are solidly Bolshevik. We'll function through the unions and factory committees. You could probably put the same mob as Tuesday's on the street tomorrow.

LENIN

Good.

STALIN

The Moscow district committee has always been sluggish. That's Bubnov and his lot. I'll remedy that. We should lose altogether some fifty thousand, mostly in the rural provinces: Saratov, Kiev, Tambov, Tula, Kaluga. The hangers-on, no great loss. The party remains intact. It's our influence among the masses that's been badly damaged. The Bolshevik cause is at a low ebb, one might say.

LENIN

One might say? Are you being ironical?

STALIN

The national elections are now scheduled for September. I had hoped to surprise you with the size of the Bolshevik vote—six, perhaps seven million—eighty, ninety delegates, a sizable faction, eh? Good enough for a cabinet portfolio or two, eh?

LENIN

We are no longer concerned with minority factions and cabinet portfolios. We must, in fact, begin now to prepare for a seizure of power. But what is more important than taking power is, shall we be able to keep it. This is a nation of peasants. No party rules in Russia without the support of the peasants, seventy million of them.

STALIN

We don't count for a kopeck with the peasants.

LENIN

(Offering STALIN *his notebook)*

I've written on the peasant question. I'd appreciate your having a look at it.

STALIN

I shall be honored, Vladimir Ilyich. Of course, I'm not very much at theoretical doctrine, but—

LENIN

(In a rage)

Don't play the dullard with me! Your contempt for theory is a vanity! Correct it! You have a good mind! Don't restrict it to mere cunning! I contend the agrarian revolution has at last begun in Russia. The Russian peasantry—docile, illiterate, submissive—"the black horde," as Kerensky calls them in private—is on the verge of making an historic declaration. The peasant doesn't give a damn any more about this war. All he wants is his own little parcel of land.

STALIN

There's a war on. Are you going to make a land reform during a war?

LENIN

Then peace. The Bolsheviks are the only party whose program is peace. Therefore, the Bolsheviks are the only party who can offer the peasants land. In three months, perhaps four—November at the latest—when the crops fail, the peasants will turn to us! We may not count for a kopeck with them, but they will have no one else!

STALIN

(Regards the shrill little man for a moment)

My immediate concern is how I get you across the Finnish border. The guards have been doubled. They're scouring every bush. I'll use Shotman as courier. He's not as well known to the police as Sverdlov. We'll have to rig you up in some sort of disguise, I think. A bit opéra bouffe, as Kamenev might say, but we'll have to do it. It's not that I think you mad, Lenin. I no longer think you mad when you go off on these flights of fancy. In the end, it always turns out you were a sensible old peasant who knew where the crayfish hid in the winter. But the idea that we'll have the peasants in pocket in three months is a bit thick. A miracle. A handsome miracle. I'd like to see it. By Christ, you'll be raising the dead next.

LENIN

I detest irony in revolutionaries. It reveals a slovenly mind.

STALIN

Then talk sense. You underestimate Kerensky. Kerensky knows the peasants are boiling. Why do you think he's called national elections for September?

LENIN

There will be no elections in September. The propertied classes know just as well as you that any national elections will turn Russia Socialist. The only way the propertied classes can preserve themselves is to seize the government by force. Before September they will attempt to set up a military dictatorship, which in the curious lexicon of democracy is known as establishing law and order.

STALIN

Are you saying we may expect a Russian Bonaparte? General Kornilov?

LENIN

General Lavr Georgievich Kornilov. A mutton-headed Bonaparte, to say the least. He can't even get his soldiers to fight the Germans; does he expect them to storm Petrograd for him? The putsch will fail.

STALIN

By Christ, you may have something at that. All right, the putsch fails; the right-wing ministers must resign, leaving Kerensky and the Socialists holding the power all by themselves. But Kerensky and the Socialists have been avoiding the power from the first days of the Revolution.

LENIN

Yes! Why? They've merely to sue the Germans for peace and national-ize the land. But they're incapable of those simple acts. Why? Because peace means economic paralysis, famine, peasant violence, civil war. The prospect of peace is, in fact, more appalling than the state of war. One can almost sympathize with Kerensky for balking at the idea.

(He laughs.)

STALIN

All right. Let's say we seize the power. It can be done. It's still a putsch. All right, so we have the support of the peasants. It's still our power. We took it by force. It's still a putsch.

LENIN

We must have an organization. A national organization. A democrati-cally elected national organization.

STALIN

What organization?

LENIN

The Soviets.

STALIN

The Soviets are useless.

LENIN

Six hundred Soviets spread throughout Russia are not useless.

STALIN

They're useless. They're benevolent brotherhoods, fraternities.

LENIN

They represent the masses. The peasants, the workers—

STALIN

Peasants, workers—they're isolated benevolent fraternities.

LENIN

They are the masses! Organize them! We need a nationally organized congress of the six hundred Soviets!

STALIN

What for? They'll have no power.

LENIN

They will demand power! That will be the purpose of the congress, to demand power!

STALIN

The Soviets have no power. Who are they going to demand it from? Who's going to give it to them?

LENIN

We! We Bolsheviks! When we seize the government by military insurrection in November, it is essential that a people's congress be in session here at that time and we will give it the power! A democratically elected national congress of Soviets! You must create this congress!

STALIN

In three months?

LENIN

(Rising into a godlike rage)

Yes! It can be done. Peace! Land! All power to the Soviets! This is the tide of affairs! All the sweep of history points to this! History dictates the course of events! We have only to execute its will! You have a good mind, Stalin. Don't restrict it to mere cunning.

(STALIN *stares at the little man, towering before him in thundering majesty.*)

STALIN

You are either mad, or the shadow of God Himself.

LENIN

I heard your little joke before, about Christ saying goodby to his disciples. Who is it you suspect thinks of me as Christ? The Central Committee? Myself? The only one who's ever thought of me as Christ is you. Your articles in *Pravda* drip with obeisant references to me. "Our Great Leader—our Prophet, Lenin, who will lead us across the Jordan into the Promised Land." And all manner of clerical cant like that. How deep does it go? How primitive is this Byzantine Orthodoxy of yours? Is it incorrigible? Then resign from the Central Committee immediately. I consider the religious impulse the most frightful failing in a revolutionary. I broke with Badyaev in Nineteen Five—with Bogdanov, Lunacharsky and Gorki in Nineteen Eight—because of this incessant Russian mysticism they introduced into the revolutionary movement.

STALIN

I left the church in Eighteen Eighty-nine. I was expelled from the seminary for revolutionary activities.

LENIN

The renegade priest is often the most fanatic. Having abandoned one god, he is all the more famished for the next. I dislike these flashes of the Christian spirit in you, Stalin. The Christian spirit is cruel; it exults in the sufferings of society by attributing these sufferings to some occult force. We Bolsheviks do not require gods to explain the brutalities of men. Men manufacture their own sufferings; men can correct them. We are about to construct the Socialist order in Russia. Neither God nor His shadow will have anything to do with it. History proceeds as relentlessly as any other equation. We Bolsheviks do not require gods to make us meaningful; we are the historic facts of our time; that is our meaning. You, Stalin, are perhaps the most meaningful man in Russia today. It is urgent, underlined, exclamation point, that you recognize your significance. You, Stalin, and I—not Christ—will construct the Socialist order, and in this world. You will run the Party while I am in hiding. You shall run Russia after I am dead. The men in my family have a history of dying in their fifties. I am almost that now.

(*There is a knock at the door, but neither of the two men seems to have heard it.* STALIN *sits, a little frightened by* LENIN's *unblinking gray eyes, staring at him from across the table.*)

STALIN

I had supposed you were polishing up Trotsky as heir apparent. You've been very thick with him these last few weeks.

LENIN

Trotsky and I are bourgeois intellectuals. Our historic function was disaffection. Our historic task is revolution. You are the serf, Stalin. You are the oppressed masses, the inheritor of this century. You shall construct the Socialist order. There's someone knocking at the door.

(*Someone is indeed knocking.* STALIN *takes his revolver out again, blows out the candle. In the darkness, we can just see him moving quietly to the door. He opens it.* NADYA *is standing in the doorway's sudden rectangle of light. She smiles effulgently at him.*)

NADYA

I saw all the others leaving.

(STALIN *scowls*)

STALIN

Well, look here, I won't have any time for you tonight after all. (*He closes the door, crosses back to the table, lights the candle. He looks down at the seated* LENIN) You were telling me how significant I am. (*He sits, crosses his legs.*

LENIN *sips his tea.* STALIN *addresses the audience)* The moral of this episode is: a man would rather have a god than a woman any time.
(*He crosses himself*)

Blackout

SCENE 3

October 23, 1917. TROTSKY, *a great actor, enters. He is a small, pince-nezed man of thirty-seven with a little, pointed beard and a thin, malevolent face.*

TROTSKY

With Lenin in hiding, the principal Bolshevik role was taken over by Trotsky, a bravura actor in the grand style. A man of many parts—scholar, journalist, spellbinder—I'd played all sorts of bits and pieces in the revolutionary movement. Some very handsome roles really, but I came into my own when I took over for Lenin in August of Nineteen Seventeen. Lovely part that—high priest of the Bolshevik Party. I not only played the leading role, I also costumed and choreographed the entire Revolution, simply staged every minute of it really. And, I might add, with an incompetent company. But, as I say, a delicious part. Marvelous second act, absolutely bristling with ringing speeches. The curtain goes up— September, Nineteen Seventeen. General Kornilov has just made an unsuccessful attempt to set up a military junta. The Russian armies have been routed on every front. The Germans have taken Riga and are only a matter of miles from the gates of Petrograd. The cruel Russian winter can be heard howling in from across the steppes. Kerensky sits solitarily at his desk in the Parliament Building, shuffling and re-shuffling his cabinets. The vast Russian nation lay sprawled across one-sixth of the earth's surface, helpless, stupefied, without hope. A superb hush, the hush of futility.

(*Enter two of* TROTSKY's *supporting players, who put* TROTSKY *on their shoulders and bear him downstage.*)

Enter Trotsky, freshly released from prison, carried in on the shoulders of a sullen mob. He is promptly elected president of the Petrograd Soviet. (*He tries to leap gracefully from the backs of the players, but they have forgotten their routine. After a moment's patient explaining, they release him and exit*) As I say, my company is somewhat makeshift—(*Suddenly, the spellbinder*) The people want peace! Any kind of peace! Indecent! Obscene! Humiliating! But peace! An end to purgatory, one way or the other, heaven or hell, let's get on with it! Peace, no longer political, has become apocalyptic! (I play all this straight out in C-major and scored for trumpets, a sort of panache I'm damn good at.) Behind me, the masses of Russia—

(*Apparently, the* MASSES *of Russia are a bit late on their cue.* TROTSKY *snaps his fingers.*)

—masses—Russian masses—
    (The MASSES *now appear and take up their positions around the stage.)*
—the masses of Russia stir.
    (The comedian of TROTSKY's *supporting company beams coyly at the audience.* TROTSKY *scowls at this amateur behavior.)*
Don't beam. *(To the audience, once again the spellbinder)* The voice of Trotsky rings out across the land like an evangel! Habitually devout, the Russian people convert with the fervor of flagellants!

MASSES

All power to the Soviets.
All power to the Soviets.
All power to the Soviets.
    *(*TROTSKY *moves briskly about the stage as the masses sing; he puts them into various postures of prostration.)*

TROTSKY

Kneel! Lie prostrate! You are supposed to be the debauched masses of Russia. I don't expect you to grasp the complexities of expressionist theater, but I do expect you to hit the floor as you were told this afternoon. *(To the company comedian)* I don't much like that beaming. Yes, yes, I know you always get a laugh with it, but we'll not have it, nevertheless. *(He is suddenly the priest chanting a Gregorian chant)* On September Twelfth, the Petrograd Soviet went Bolshevik. The next day, the Northern Regional Conference went Bolshevik. The Moscow Soviet. The Central Siberian Soviet. The Soviets of Kiev, Yaroslav, Kazan, Samara—

MASSES

All power!

TROTSKY

The Tula Soviet.

MASSES

Tula!

TROTSKY

The Soviets of Novgorod, Tsarytsin, Poltava, Tambov, Saratov, Tomsk—During this I have a quick costume change. Off with cassock and cowl and into my shabby sackcloth as I come out the revolutionary conspirator. The Bolsheviks plot their insurrection. Secret meetings in cellars and garrets. A Congress of all the Soviets in Russia is called for the first week in November. But Lenin, needless to say, didn't intend for a moment to let the Congress decide whether or not to seize the power by military force. Lenin was a genius, to whom revolution was an art. He was not likely to entrust a majestic mural like the Russian Revolution to amateurs and dilettantes. From his hiding place in Finland, he bombards the Bolshevik Central Committee with bulky letters—underlined! Urgent! *(To the* MASSES*)* You're sagging! A daily fusillade of exclamation points, explaining the poetry of revolution. The job of preparing the military conquest of Petrograd is entrusted to Trotsky. I have a brilliant speech here entitled "Revolution As an Art."

> *(One of the* MASSES *is trying to get his attention.)*

Yes, yes, yes, I know. The masses have a few lines here.

MASSES

All power to the Soviets.
All power to the Soviets.
All power to the Soviets.
All other gods did fail us.
They were merely wine and wafers.
We asked for daily bread,
They let us starve.
What say the meek?
What say the meek?
The meek demand their inheritance.
They want their earth,
They want it now.
Hallelujah.
All power to the Soviets.
All power to the Soviets.
All power to the Soviets. Hallelujah.
Glory, Hallelujah.

> *(During this song,* TROTSKY *stages the* MASSES *into various Socialist Realism poses.)*

TROTSKY

At any rate—"Revolution As an Art." I stand. It is the October twenty-third meeting of the Bolshevik Central Committee. "Dabblers! Triflers! Why do you delay? Why must you wait for the Congress? The act of over-throwing a regime is not a matter for apprentices. We Bolsheviks are the artists here. We have been trained for thirty years. Insurrection demands calculation, economy, the precision of a poem. We must have a general, an army, weapons, a plan of attack— *(To the* MASSES, *who are finding their poses hard to hold)* You're sagging! With bold, vivid strokes, we will seize the rail-road stations, drawbridges, principal street-crossings, the telephone exchange, the telegraph agency, the post, the power stations. Now! The image is now! Don't you see it? It is blinding in its beauty! Poetasters!

Jongleurs! Versemongers! We have a great page of history to write! Are you content with jingles? And on and on in that vein. Very splashy. As I recall, the Masses have a few lines here.

MASSES

All other gods have failed us.
They were merely wine and wafers.
We asked for peace on earth,
They gave us war.
What say the meek?
What say the meek?
The meek will make their own damn peace.
The meek will take their own damn bread.
The meek will be
Their own damn gods.

TROTSKY

On November seventh, a Congress of all the Soviets in Russia was assembled in Smolny Institute—an elaborate building which had once been a finishing school for the daughters of the aristocracy.

(The set changes under TROTSKY's *stage-managership to the Smolny Institute.)*

The Congress had been assembled to discuss whether or not to demand Kerensky turn over his government. There was very little to discuss, actually. On November sixth, you see—the day before the Congress—we Bolsheviks had already seized the city of Petrograd. Kerensky fled in a limousine—borrowed, naturally, from the American Embassy. All that remained of his government was a handful of ministers who huddled in the winter palace and poignantly refused to capitulate. The palace was subjected to some six hours of inaccurate shelling.

(Cannon heard offstage. STALIN *enters on the upper landing.)*

At two in the morning, November eighth, the sound of the cannon suddenly stopped. (TROTSKY *races up the stairs to the balcony of the Smolny Institute set)* Comrades! The palace has been taken. The government has capitulated! The city is in our hands! Long live the Revolution!

*(*TROTSKY *and the* MASSES *exit.)*

Scene 4

Smolny, 2:00 A.M., *November 8, 1917. The set consists of a large ornate stairway. As* TROTSKY *and his* MASSES *exit,* STALIN *comes down the stairway.*

STALIN
(*To* SVERDLOV)
You'll see to the ovation for Lenin.

SVERDLOV
Yes, of course.

STALIN
An enormous one, eh? Stamping of feet, whistling, it should roll on for fifteen minutes at the least.

(SVERDLOV *nods and exits.* STALIN *suddenly becomes aware of* NADYA, *who had been part of the crowd onstage at the end of the previous scene.*)

STALIN
Why are you here?

NADYA
Have I become nothing but an intrusion to you?

STALIN
The winter palace has just fallen. Lenin's coming down to address the Congress of Soviets. Have you picked this moment to start another row?

NADYA
No, nothing so spirited. I really don't know why I came. It's all new to me, this role of discarded mistress. I suppose I thought that tonight—this night—I suppose I thought to effect some sort of reconciliation. Well, I'll stay for a moment to warm myself and then start back for the city. I saw some lorries in the courtyard. I should catch a ride easily enough. What a disjointed thing a great revolution seems at night. Everything's open—the casinos, the ballets, the shops. Huge crowds on the Nevsky, curiously gay, almost a carnival. Then shooting. Shouts. A squad of soldiers sloshes by in the mud. "Are you government troops or Bolsheviks?" Nobody quite knows. Oh, Soso, I love you helplessly. What have I done to disaffect you so?

(*A* WORKER *appears on the balcony.*)

WORKER
Stalin—

(STALIN looks up, nods. The WORKER exits.)

STALIN

Lenin's coming down.

(LENIN and TROTSKY appear at the top of the stairs.)

LENIN

What sort of reception will I receive at the Congress, Stalin?

STALIN

Enormous. A standing ovation. Sverdlov is arranging it. He's very clever at that sort of thing.

(LENIN and TROTSKY descend the steps.)

STALIN

The Socialists have all bolted the Congress. There's a handful of Mensheviki Internationalists left—Gorki and his lot. The Maximalists are still with us. You'll have no hoots or catcalls.

LENIN

I detest these big meetings.

(He exits.)

TROTSKY

(Utterly arrogant)

Keep yourself available, Stalin. I shall have some chores for you later.

(TROTSKY exits.)

STALIN

(Regarding TROTSKY's disappearing figure, mutters)

I shall kill that Jew some day.

(He turns and starts up the stairs.)

NADYA

Josef Visaryonovich!

STALIN

(In a sudden rage)

Go back to your district, comrade! They are surely dancing in the streets!

NADYA

Is it finished then with us?

STALIN

How many times must we have it out? Why do you persist? I made it plain last time!

NADYA

I implore you to be kind with me, Josef Visaryonovich.

STALIN

I have no more feeling for you!

NADYA

I demand to know who has usurped your love. I shall kill her.

STALIN

What a baroque demonstration. Well, there's no woman for you to con-
front in a jealous rage. It's quite another story altogether. How shall I say
it? I've been going through a religious experience these past few months.
I've found God again, so to speak. That's it, eh? I've found God again.

NADYA

What God?

STALIN

Lenin, of course. You're a smashing girl, Nadinka. But the best I could
get out of you would be pleasure. Lenin makes me meaningful, not so
transient a satisfaction, eh? He has this gift, eh, to make one feel significant. That's all any man needs a god for, I think.

(*A* WORKER *appears on the upper landing.*)

WORKER

Stalin, Molotov has rung up.

STALIN

What does the mutton want?

WORKER

They've taken the government printing plant.

STALIN

Well, let him print there then.

WORKER

They now have two rotary presses at their disposal.

STALIN

(*In another sudden rage*)

I said to print there then!

(*The* WORKER *exits. The excitement of the last few days begins to show
itself now through* STALIN'*s impassivity. He comes slowly back down the
stairs, his eyes glowing oddly.*)

NADYA

Josef Visaryonovich, I cannot give you up.

STALIN

Then let's get married. That's the proper thing for a man to do when
he's lost all feeling for his girl. Tomorrow, I shall ask your father for your
hand.

(A second WORKER *appears on the pit stairway)*

SECOND WORKER

Lenin has just entered the hall.

STALIN

Yes, I'm coming. We've done it. We've seized the power. In the Holy Name, we've done it. Three months, he said. November at the outside. It's all come to pass as Lenin prophesied. Singular man, Lenin, a singular man. He even exalts me. *(Stares disjointedly at* NADYA*)* You yourself said he has that facility. By Christ, I do everything but get down on my knees and commend my soul to that man. By Christ, if I could find my soul, I'd commend it to him fast enough.

(Suddenly, LENIN's *disembodied voice comes booming out from the pit.)*

LENIN's VOICE

Comrades! I am Comrade Lenin! We shall now begin to construct the Socialist order!

(For a moment, STALIN *stares off at the echoes of the disembodied voice.)*

STALIN

(Religioso)

Dear Comrade Lenin, I commend my soul to thee.

Curtain

ACT III

SCENE 1

The courtyard of the Kremlin in Moscow, March 9, 1923. The courtyard itself is an open cobblestoned expanse, but the surrounding set suggests the medievalism of the Kremlin—high, dark, enormously impregnable walls, blue and gold cupolas, glistening silver crucifixes, and even an interior quality of low arches dissolving into dark stone corridors thick with conspiratorial whispers. It is altogether a murky set, barbaric for all its piety; isolated, Russian. Enter from upstage, LENIN and his wife KRUPSKAYA. They are dressed in overcoats, shawls and mufflers. LENIN is ailing. As they walk slowly downstage, he needs the support of his wife. They find a bench downstage and sit wheezing—a sickly, middle-aged couple. LENIN, however, is in the best of spirits.

LENIN

Well, five years have passed since we Bolsheviks took over the government of Russia. We've been a disappointment, don't you agree?

KRUPSKAYA

Yes, I'm afraid that's so.

LENIN

What I find most dejecting is our banality. For all our posturing as social innovators, we've done nothing that hadn't been done many times by three centuries of incompetent tsars. We've waged incessant war, prorogued parliaments, imprisoned, exiled and shot anyone who disagreed with our policies, brutalized the peasants, betrayed the labor unions and are now terrorizing even ourselves with a secret police more insidious than the one that persecuted us. We've violated our treaties, conquered the defenseless Ukraine, invaded infant Poland, crushed the Republic of Georgia, annexed the Finns, imperialized the Baltic states. We have ruled by ukase, we have reigned in terror, and we have done all this in barely five years without introducing one original effect or one unfamiliar cause.

KRUPSKAYA

Well, I really don't see how we could have done otherwise.

LENIN

Oh, Lord knows we were justified in all our tyrannies; all tyrants are. We

339

did only what was necessary to defend our homeland and to restore order. We had good reasons for everything. What I find disenchanting is that they are the same reasons all governments have always given for their iniquities. We have been merely commonplace. Our one original act was to move the seat of government from Petrograd to Moscow, a city I detest. We have intruded our typewriters, telephones and electric lamps into this Kremlin, this medieval fortress where the barbarous princes of Moscow butchered their way to an empire. We have reverted, Krupskaya. I sit here four hundred years old like the great Prince Basil, contemplating my succession, while my boyars conspire under groined arches to seize the regency when I die. I wouldn't be in the least surprised if Ivan the Dreadful himself were to come walking out through that gate there— By the Holy Name, there he comes now.

(*Enter* STALIN. *He is wearing the simple military greatcoat he favored the rest of his life, and looks like the familiar Stalin of his later photographs. He carries a bulging briefcase and hunches his head against the cold March air. There is a brief, silent, but markedly hostile moment between him and* LENIN. *Then* STALIN *crosses past and exits. After a moment)*

LENIN

They say Stalin beats his wife.

KRUPSKAYA

Yes, I've heard that. There she is now, poor girl, watching us from behind her lattice. They say she is very disillusioned with our Communist state.

LENIN

Oh, well, who of us isn't? Have you talked with her lately?

KRUPSKAYA

Not since you broke with Stalin, of course. I did see her briefly some months ago, just after your second stroke. She asked me in for tea.

LENIN

Are they still living in those two tiny rooms in the servants' quarters?

KRUPSKAYA

Yes, very spare and Spartan. His wife told me they exist on no better rations than the meanest factory worker in Moscow gets.

LENIN

That's very earnest of them.

KRUPSKAYA

I spent about an hour with her. She kept breaking into tears. She wanted very much to have a talk with you, but, at that time, the doctors weren't allowing you visitors. Dear me, there she is now at the gate. I think she's coming over to talk to us.

LENIN

Oh, dear.

KRUPSKAYA

She's hesitating. Shall I smile encouragingly?

LENIN

Yes. I suppose you'd better.

(KRUPSKAYA *smiles toward the gate. After a moment,* NADYA *enters. She wears a babushka and a threadbare coat. She looks ghastly and seems to be avoiding an imminent nervous breakdown only by the greatest effort.*)

NADYA

Greetings, comrades. God grant you are in good health. I was told the doctor's report was exceptionally good this morning, Comrade Lenin.

LENIN

Yes. I shall be able to attend the Party Congress when it meets next month.

NADYA

May I sit?

LENIN

Yes, of course.

(NADYA *looks nervously at all the windows surrounding them, then sits.*)

NADYA

How very cold it is.

LENIN

You must arrange for a warmer coat than that one.

NADYA

We lack the coupons.

LENIN

Quatsch! Your husband is the General Secretary of the Central Committee. He is also a leading member of the Politburo, the Commissar of the Inspectorate, the Head of the Organizational Bureau, the Minister of Nationalities, the Chief of the Central Control Commission, and Lord knows what other departments, committees and councils he presides over. It is pure brass for the wife of the most powerful man in Russia to wear such a coat.

NADYA

You are determined to destroy Stalin.

LENIN

Oh, yes. Did you read my indictment of him in *Pravda* last week?

NADYA

Very scathing.

LENIN

I had the devil's own time getting it published. I had forgotten that among his other portfolios your husband was also editor of *Pravda*. The scoundrel simply stuck my article in his desk for three weeks. I had to call a meeting of the Politburo to force its publication.

NADYA

The article was not fair, Vladimir Ilyich.

LENIN

Oh, was it not?

NADYA

You accused my husband of turning the Bolshevik Party into his personal political machine.

LENIN

Surely you agree. He's packed the party with the Molotovs and Mikoyans and all his other pious gangsters.

NADYA

This submissive machine was made for your benefit, not Stalin's.

LENIN

Whatever the case, I shall smash him. He is too rude to hold such power. I shall finish him off at the Party Congress next month. My health, I may already have told you, will be adequate for that.

NADYA

You are his god, Comrade Lenin.

LENIN

Oh, yes, indeed, the villain's made a god out of me so that he can be a prophet. He's already murdered a thousand men for that illusory significance. He'll kill us all, destroy nations, corrupt the world, this obscene priest, in his impatience to be meaningful.

NADYA

It was you who gave him his significance! We have all paid a fearful price for that!

(She is suddenly seized by a spasm of shaking.)

KRUPSKAYA

Volodya, see how she trembles in that thin coat. Nadya darling, you must come into our flat, and we shall start the stove.

NADYA

You mustn't be solicitous of me. There are hundreds of eyes peering at us from the windows. They'll imagine all sorts of intrigue from our talking here.

LENIN
(A very kind man, really)

Quatsch! Krupskaya, go set a samovar. I shall bring her in directly. *(Stands)* Come, Nadya, we'll walk a bit. I must exercise, and it will help us to keep warm. I'm afraid you must take my arm.

(KRUPSKAYA *exits right.* NADYA *takes* LENIN's *arm, and they slowly circle the courtyard—a frail, shuffling, middle-aged man supported by a terrified young woman.*)

NADYA

I think I'm going insane, Vladimir Ilyich.

LENIN

Oh, dear me.

NADYA

I've lost some sense of substance. Things suddenly disappear even as I look at them—chairs, walls, stones. I sometimes stand shaking in the middle of my room as if it were a vast frozen waste. Then, in a few moments, this sensation passes, and I retain only a memory of some coldness so inconceivably painful I can't imagine how I lived through it.

LENIN
(Cheerfully)

You're having a nervous breakdown. It's occupational with revolutionaries. Not a day goes by but I hear of some old comrade who has blown his brains out.

NADYA

We very moral people shatter easily, I'm afraid.

LENIN

We're such humbugs, that's why. Our Russian Revolution was a revolution of humbugs. Lord, why do we insist on being meaningful creatures? Since there is no truth we know that bears that out, we assume there must be a truth we don't know that is more accommodating. That, I think, states the case for God. But you and I, Nadya, were even more corrupt than that. We know there is no God, so we reasoned ourselves to be ultimate. That, I think, states the case for humanitarianism. We looked back over our thousands of years of impotent constancy, and nevertheless insisted we'd been improving all that while. As if man was by nature a moral fellow impelled by an instinct to decency. That, I think, states the principle of progress, a deceit so transparent I can't imagine sensible people like you and I could have put any stock in it.

NADYA

But we did.

LENIN

Yes, we invested our lives in it, in the mystic belief that the lower classes naturally aspired to democracy, brotherhood, social justice and all those other passing compassions of the moment, when, of course, the lower classes have never aspired to be anything more than the upper classes. Dear me, Nadya, if we are to put faith into so fragile a pretense as man's morality, we must expect to be shattered regularly.

NADYA

I feel betrayed, violated.

LENIN

Yes, of course. But you mustn't enjoy it so. You make it sound pleasurable. Whatever's the matter, Nadya?
    (*This last in reference to the fact* NADYA *has begun to shake terribly again.*)

NADYA

I have these strange seizures.

LENIN

Do you shake like that often?

NADYA

Yes. I have found myself once or twice—perhaps more—I'm not sure, you see—on my hands and knees, whimpering—once in the street, I think. I'm not sure of that. In any event, it happened to me yesterday in my room—yes, yesterday, I think—perhaps last night—recently, at any rate—perhaps not. You see, it takes great effort for me to discern time now, even night from day. I've had very bad nightmares lately; but, you see, I'm no longer sure I wasn't awake when they happened. I'm not sure they happened at all.

LENIN

Is it you wish you were dead?

NADYA
(*In great distress*)

No! It's rather I wish I were alive! Do you see? I have no sensation of life! Do you understand?

LENIN

Nadya, you mustn't shout so.

NADYA

Nothing is real! Nothing is true! It is all fleeting, deformed! You must help me, Lenin! I cannot bear this transiency! You can't know what it's like!

LENIN

(*Cheerfully*)

Don't be vain. Of course, I know what it's like. Young people always think despair is their own shattering revelation. You're going to insist now I abandon all my illusions on the spot and face up to meaninglessness, insufferable as that may be. Well, you're right, of course. Nothing is real. Nothing is true. The human condition is relentlessly uncertain. That, it seems, is the primal terror. The human condition originates, it seems, in terror, total terror. It's appalling, of course, but now that you know that and have even experienced the anguish of it, you must stop carrying on like a mad woman. It's sentimental of you. Having discovered there is no truth, you are now making a truth out of that. You shall only end up disillusioned with despair, and that would be inefficient. Life is meaningless then, perhaps imperceptible, very well! That is hardly the final wisdom, merely the first commitment. We lack truth. Splendid! In terror, we flee everywhere for it. We are provoked to all sorts of adventures, wild fancies and sensations of beauty. We discover things—only knowledge, of course, never truth, but knowledge serves our purposes and discovery is delicious. There is adequate delight in despair. At any rate, it is sensual and we are capable of it. There you are. It is not all that disagreeable, is it? Have I comforted you? Apparently not. You seem even more desolate than before.

(*They have come full circle back to the bench.* NADYA *sinks on it totally spent.* LENIN *regards her, not unkindly. He sits beside her.*)

LENIN

It is what Trotsky would call an ineluctable axiom of history that when a young woman goes on at length about the meaninglessness of life, it means she's not getting along with her husband. Do you agree?

NADYA

Yes.

LENIN

Does he abuse you badly?

NADYA

Yes.

LENIN

You must leave him, Nadya.

NADYA

I should die without Stalin.

LENIN

Oh, what a silly thing to say.

NADYA

You're a poet, Vladimir Ilyich. To you, terror is passionate and credible. But for those of us not poets, life is too transient to be believed. It requires extraordinary faith—more, anyway, than I have. My love for Stalin, you see, is the only act of faith I'm capable of. It remains with me even now when walls and stones disappear; a great pain now, but I can feel that pain; it's substantial. I believe in my love for Stalin like he believes in God and you believe in terror. I must have something, you see.

LENIN

I'm going to destroy him, Nadya.

NADYA

Yes.

LENIN

I can do it, you know. I'm still Premier of Russia. I'm still boss among the Bolsheviks. I still hold majorities even in Stalin's own committees.

NADYA

I want him destroyed as much as you do, Lenin. *(She looks up, curiously hopeful and very much in love)* He loved me, you see, before you infatuated him. It's easiest of all to believe in gods, eh? That requires no faith at all. I want him back as he was, Lenin—a cutpurse, an assassin, a bully boy who'd end on the gallows in any sensible society—a terrified brute, you see, who couldn't endure life alone any better than I, and so he loved me. Love is a terrified act, eh? But, you know, I was inexplicably happy. I want that restored. I want his passion for the Socialist order destroyed. I want him back a brute. I can't continue much longer deprived of him.

(LENIN is quite affected by NADYA's declaration. He touches her face in an uncomfortable gesture of fondness.)

LENIN

I don't think you're being unreasonable.

(They are both suddenly aware of being observed from offstage left. They turn to see who it is. Enter STALIN, dressed as before and still pressing his bureaucrat's briefcase to his heart. He is in an ugly, dangerous temper)

STALIN

Lenin! Comrades Mdivani and Makharadze are in my office. They have just shown me a letter you sent them in which you say you intend to reverse all my policies in Georgia. What the hell do you think you're doing? Mdivani and Makharadze are for an independent Georgia. Are you supporting the national movement in Georgia now? We require the oil-fields of Georgia! We must have their oil! We cannot afford to let Georgia out of Russia! It took me two years to crush the separatist movement in Georgia!

(LENIN *stands, a towering little man in an enormous rage.*)

LENIN

Get out, you clumsy ward-heeler! Boodler! Intriguer!

STALIN

The Georgian Bolsheviks are my bureau!

LENIN

You have no bureaus! You are finished in this government!

STALIN

Don't meddle, Lenin!

LENIN

Carpetbagger! Jackleg!

STALIN

I'll bloody you as good as anyone else!

LENIN

Oh, come off it! Don't be bamboozler with me, Stalin! *(Slowly,* LENIN *shuffles across the stage to* STALIN*)* Trotsky says you're a master politician. That is your great talent, he says, your one talent. He's quite frightened of you now. You've petrified him, you cobra. Well, Trotsky is a brilliant clown, eh?, a classic comedian who sighs for a tragic death scene. You'll arrange that, I'm sure. But I'm not Trotsky, you cacique! I run this party, not you. Ward-boss! Jack-in-office! Did you really think to out-politic me? You make a tatty triumvir, Stalin. I had Kamenev and Zinoviev—both of them!—in my study this afternoon. Your triumvirate is over, Stalin. Zinoviev is packing for Petrograd now, and Kamenev, for all I know, is still crawling penance on my carpet, that's where I left him. We'll talk politics, eh, ward-boss? The Moscow Soviet's mine. So's Petrograd. You've got nothing but a handful of provincial delegates, and I even snatched your Caucasian deputies over the weekend. I'm going to drive you out at the Congress next month. I'll drive you off the Politburo. I'll drive you off the Central Committee. I'll read you out of the party altogether! You're a whipped dog, Stalin. You've got nothing to do but skulk off.

STALIN

You do me an injustice, Lenin.

LENIN

Yes, well, skulk off anyway. I never did like you, you know.

STALIN

I didn't intrigue against you, Lenin. You were on your deathbed for months. The question of your successor was imminent. It was between Trotsky and Zinoviev. They're both fools, but Zinoviev is at least harmless. He came to me and asked my support. He already had Kamenev. I control the provinces. Between us, we made a majority. Trotsky must be kept from power. He is a monumental idiot. He is still waiting for the world revolution, for the working class to rise up in the West. There is no working-class revolution in the West. It is suicide to wait for Socialism to be handed us by the British proletariat. Western capitalism has fifty years left in it. That is your own statement. *(His eyes take on a zealot's glow)* We must create Socialism alone! We must do it ourselves! We must do it here! We have perhaps fifteen years before the capitalist countries revive themselves for another war. Do you doubt that? It is your own statement. We are a century behind the capitalist countries. We must make up a century in fifteen years, or Socialist Russia will be the spoils of the next war. Socialist Russia will be dismembered into British, German and French colonies. That is your own prediction. Socialist Russia must be made impregnable against the capitalist countries. We have no time to wait for revolutions in the West. We must begin now. If Trotsky prevails, Socialism is doomed. So I gave my support to Zinoviev. That is the conspiracy you accuse me of.

LENIN

Do you seriously think to industrialize Russia in fifteen years?

STALIN

Yes!

LENIN

This is a country that still farms with wooden plows.

STALIN

We must electrify all the farms.

LENIN

Electrify some twenty million little farms?

STALIN

We shall have to collectivize the farms.

LENIN

Collectivize the Russian peasant? The only reason we Bolsheviks have stayed in power is that we gave every Russian peasant a parcel of land for himself. Do you think he's going to give it back to the state? He'll kill his cow first.

STALIN

Collectivization will not be a popular measure.

LENIN

Hardly. The peasants will revolt against us as they did against the Tsar.

STALIN

We'll have to execute thousands, tens of thousands, perhaps, certainly the prosperous peasants. But the prosperous peasants are an unstable political force anyway, potential counterrevolutionaries. They'll be no loss to the state. I shall electrify the farms, Lenin. I shall build dams and power stations to supply the electricity. I shall educate a generation of gawking peasants into engineers. I will industrialize Russia, Lenin. Heavy industry, eh? Iron. Steel. I shall manufacture, Lenin. Heavy machinery for heavy industry, for large-scale agriculture—guns, cannon, battleships, airships as well, eh? We talk now of heavy industry, Lenin. Heavy industry! Heavy industry requires oil! Eh? Oil! We're not rich in oil. We have a few riggings in Baku, Batu, Tiflis. The Georgian oilfields are life and death for us! We cannot allow the state of Georgia to separate from us! I had to crush the national movement in Georgia, so I crushed it! I crushed Mdivani and Makharadze! I had a hundred other Georgian leaders shot in their cells! I have Georgia in my grip now, Lenin! Don't meddle, Lenin! If you've lost your stomach for this kind of dirty business, then get back into your deathbed. By God, you're a long time dying. You mustn't hang on so, eh?

LENIN

You hideous monk, I shall have to keep you out of the kitchen. You'll be poisoning my dinners in your impatience to deify me with the proper rites. What sort of paganism have you planned for me, Stalin? Am I to die every year and be resurrected at Easter? I want you to resign your offices and return to the rank and file, Stalin. I told you that at our last meeting, but you went into a rage and insulted even my wife, who did nothing but poke her head in to see if you wanted tea.

STALIN

We must have Georgia's oil, Lenin.

LENIN

We'll trade for it, and we'll get more of it than now and at half the price. The state of Georgia depends on us entirely. We had to conquer them with the Red army. If we'd left them alone, they would have implored us to send troops to protect them from the Turks and from the British,

French and Americans, who will come ravening after their oil. We'll make very advantageous contracts for Georgia's oil. We're quite as predatory as the capitalists, Stalin. In God's name, let's at least be as efficient.

STALIN

Is that our aspiration, to be efficient?

LENIN

Yes. Efficiency wouldn't have killed a hundred of the best Bolsheviks in Georgia. You, you bungler, did.

STALIN

(Stubbornly)

It is my function to construct the Socialist order. Those were your words.

LENIN

You keep quoting me, Stalin.

STALIN

"We Bolsheviks are the Truth." Those were your words. "'We are the historic facts of our generation." Those were your words. "You, Stalin, shall construct the Socialist order." Those were your words.

LENIN

Well, I've changed my mind, you see.

STALIN

"You shall construct the Socialist order, Stalin." Those were your words.

LENIN

(In a rage)

They were not carved into a mountain with shafts of lightning! The Socialist order, I'm afraid, is sentimental. It's predicated on the idea that greed, cruelty and violence are unnecessary to man's condition. We consider democracy a moral improvement over empires, as if greed, cruelty and violence are less prevalent in America than they were in Babylon. Democracy, Stalin, is not any more decent than monarchy; it is merely more efficient in dealing with the greed, cruelties and violence of an industrialized world. Greed, cruelty and violence continue undiminished, now as before, and will continue undiminished until we put an end to ourselves by these very qualities we insist are not real. *(He stares at the sullen zealot in front of him)* We Socialists, it would seem, have only proclaimed another religion, and, like all religions, ours is just a contrivance to satisfy our presumption to be meaningful. Like all religions, Socialism will hound its heretics and massacre millions. Lord, the nations immolated to prove the truth of Christ! What will be left after our great truth? We're no longer concerned with establishing the Socialist order, Stalin. From now on, we don't offer our people salvation, only expedient relief from their disaffections and gratification for their momentary greeds. We'll feed the starving, knowing in a year they will complain about the chef as desperately as they did of their hunger. We shall then try to improve the cooking. You must do without gods and truth, Stalin! You must give them up! If there is a god, he'll have to manage for himself! We've got our own imperfect, impermanent and thoroughly satisfactory world to deal with! *(His innate good humor returns, and he almost reaches out to give* STALIN *a comradely poke in the shoulder)* Oh, come on, Stalin, I've got you licked. You used to have enough cunning to retreat gracefully. There's no need for a nasty party fight. You're a valuable man, a good trouble-shooter. You're a damned marvel at unraveling tie-ups in transportation and that sort of thing. I don't want to lose you altogether. I just want you out of power. Resign in tomorrow's edition of *Pravda*. I'll make a nice speech about you at the Congress, if it's a matter of face. I promise, you'll be pleased.

(STALIN *slowly lowers his face in a sullen gesture of defeat.)*

LENIN

That's a good fellow. Now, you must help me back to my bench, Stalin. I'm not entirely recovered yet, and my right leg in particular tends to buckle.

(STALIN *takes* LENIN's *elbow and slowly escorts the shuffling little man back to his bench.)*

STALIN
(As they go)
What will happen to Russia when the next war comes?

LENIN

I'm sure I don't know. Let's hope the capitalist countries will not exalt their current fashions in democracy into immutable truths as we exalted Socialism. Self-preservation is the principle of life. We have only to aspire to that, and it will be the saving of all of us. We are knowledgeable creatures. We are capable of self-preservation.

(He sits, exhausted by his scene with STALIN. NADYA, *who watched the exchange between the two men, regards her husband anxiously.* STALIN *seems suddenly aware of the chilly weather. He shivers.)*

STALIN
How very cold it is.

NADYA
You must arrange for a better coat than that.

STALIN
I must clean my office out.

(He starts offstage left, but, after a few steps, he suddenly stops.)

NADYA

I have strange seizures, Stalin.
(She crosses to her husband)

STALIN

I shall resign my portfolios, Lenin, but for me it's not a political defeat. It's a loss of faith, eh? *(He looks blankly at his wife)* I don't think I can endure that a second time.

NADYA

I have loved you for as long as I can remember, Josef Visaryonovich.

STALIN

It's turned out Barabbas again. It's no easier the second time, do you understand?

NADYA

Yes.

STALIN

(Stares at his wife, briefly revealing his pain. Then, with great effort)
By God, so you're still sweet on your Uncle Soso, eh?

NADYA

Yes.
(KRUPSKAYA enters from stage right.)

LENIN
(To his wife)

I need a few minutes more, and we shall all go in to tea. You'll join us, Stalin?

STALIN

If you wish.

LENIN
(Relaxing)

Yesterday I called in my secretaries and dictated notes for my last testament. It seemed only sensible. A man who's had two arteriosclerotic strokes in a year should consider the disposing of his effects. It was absurd, really, my three secretaries perched on their chairs and I propped up in bed, and I simply had no effects to dispose of. A vast empire, an apostolic succession, but no golden watches, no brooches, cameos, no family silver, no estates, no mortgages, no gambling debts—nothing, nothing real to bequeath at all. A few books (dear me, the libraries I've pawned during my life). Two old suits of clothes, worse for wear. Nothing, really, no legacy at all. For a long moment, we simply sat there, my secretaries and I. I suddenly felt totally devoid of identity. It gave me quite a chill. Perhaps, we should have had children, Krupskaya. It continues one, eh? I don't even leave behind a family name. My name is Ulyanov. I should like my name, Ulyanov, used more often, Stalin. Insert it into *Pravda* with increasing regularity, beginning tomorrow. I've come to dislike being called Lenin. It's a manufactured name. It lacks life. Krupskaya, we must— *(He seems to be having difficulty with the next word. He scowls, swallows, and begins again)* We must make a trip to my father's house in Simbirsk, Krupskaya.

KRUPSKAYA

They've made it a state shrine. We shall probably have to stand on line to get in.

LENIN

I'll arrange it. I have influence, you know, with the authorities. My father was superintendent of schools for the province of Simbirsk, Stalin, a dedicated official, a somber man, though. My sister Anna remembers our childhood as happy. I don't. I had three sisters, two brothers. I recall a grand piano in the living room. My mother occasionally sang Bellini's operas to us. Yet, for all the children, it was a silent house. My sister Anna says I was a noisy boy. I remember myself as morose. I spent much time on the docks. The Volga flows slowly by Simbirsk, slowly, almost unnoticeably. Dead dogwood branches drift helplessly—helplessly—hel—hel— *(He suddenly stands, crouched, his face swept with terror, his jaws working but unable to produce words until he forces out a shrill cry)* I am hemorrhaging!

KRUPSKAYA
(Racing to him in horror)

Lenin!

NADYA
(Sinking to her knees)

No—

KRUPSKAYA
(Holding her husband from collapse)

Stalin, you must help me!

(STALIN crosses slowly to where KRUPSKAYA struggles to hold her husband upright. LENIN's right arm and leg suddenly stiffen convulsively. He stares up at STALIN in total terror. His jaws continue to work uselessly, but, the right side of his face being paralyzed, his efforts to talk produce only grotesque twitches. Four men and two women run in from various directions. Two of the men hurry to help hold LENIN.)

STALIN
(To the third man)

Fetch Doctor Rosanov.
(The third man dashes off.)

KRUPSKAYA
(Wailing)

Lenin!

STALIN

Get him to his bed.
(Tenderly, the two men, now weeping unashamedly, carry LENIN's *frail body off right.* KRUPSKAYA *exits with them. A man and the two women still onstage take a few tentative steps to follow.)*

STALIN

Get back to your offices!
(A woman rushes in from offstage left.)

STALIN

Go back to your desk! You are to keep your mouths shut about this! *(To the man)* Antonov! Ring up Zinoviev and Kamenev and tell them to call me at my office. Tell Zinoviev there is no need to return to Petrograd.
(The man and the women exit, leaving the stage empty except for NADYA, *who is still on her knees, sorrowing, and* STALIN, *center stage, impassive, eyes slitted in thought.)*

STALIN

Well, I won't have to resign after all. By God, this is a stroke of luck for me. *(He turns to* NADYA*)* Ha! A stroke of luck, eh? A play on words, eh? Lenin's stroke—a stroke of luck! By God, that's amusing, eh? *(He picks up his briefcase from the stones and starts off left, then pauses)* You see the joke, don't you? Lenin's stroke is a stroke of luck for me. You see the joke, don't you?
(He doesn't wait for an answer. Clutching his briefcase, he exits left. NADYA *remains on her knees, unmoving, numb. Suddenly she is seized again with a spasm of shaking. After a moment, she drops down on all fours and whimpers piteously.)*

Blackout

SCENE 2

The House of the Trade Unions in Moscow, the evening of January 26, 1924. There is a speaker's lectern downstage center. Behind the lectern, there is a row of six wooden chairs. At stage right is a raised bier, draped in black cloth. Ten Red soldiers guard the bier, standing at stiff attention, their rifles at shoulder arms. Enter the pall-bearers from upstage. They are STALIN, KAMENEV, ZINOVIEV, BUKHARIN, TOMSKY *and* MOLOTOV. *On their shoulders they bear* LENIN's *catafalque. The embalmed body of* LENIN, *waxen and gleaming, lies on it. Grim-faced, the pallbearers march slowly downstage, bearing* LENIN *to his bier. When they have set the body down to lie in state, they march slowly to the row of chairs and seat themselves.*

Enter the funeral procession, which consists of the entire company of men and women, solemn, weeping, dressed in heavy coats. They fill the stage behind the six seated members of the Politburo. For a long moment, the stage remains in utter silence. Then STALIN *rises, goes to the lectern. He regards the audience.*

STALIN

Lenin died almost eleven months later, in January of Nineteen Twenty-four. During that time, he was, on the whole, incapacitated and did not take part in affairs of state. Here is the actual oath of allegiance which Stalin read to the Second Congress of Soviets while Lenin lay in state in the House of the Trade Unions in Moscow. It is in the fashion of a litany. *(He takes a scrap of paper from his pocket, flattens it on the lectern, intones)*

Comrades, we Communists are people of a special cut.

It is not given to everyone to be a member of such a party.

Sons of the working class, sons of misery and struggle, sons of privation and heroic endeavor, these are the members of the Communist Party. Comrades!

In leaving us, Comrade Lenin ordained us to hold high and keep pure the great calling of the Party member. We vow to thee, Comrade Lenin, that we shall fulfill this thy commandment.

ENTIRE COMPANY

Amen!

STALIN

In leaving us, Comrade Lenin ordained us to maintain the unity of the Party. We vow to thee, Comrade Lenin, we shall fulfill this thy commandment, too.

ENTIRE COMPANY

Amen!

STALIN

In leaving us, Comrade Lenin ordained us to maintain and strengthen the dictatorship of the proletariat. We vow to thee, Comrade Lenin, we shall fulfill this thy commandment, too.

ENTIRE COMPANY

Amen!

STALIN

In leaving us, Comrade Lenin ordained us to strengthen with all our might the alliance of workers and peasants. We vow to thee, Comrade Lenin, that we shall fulfill this thy commandment, too.

ENTIRE COMPANY

Amen!

STALIN

In leaving us, Comrade Lenin ordained us to strengthen and broaden the Union of Socialist Soviet Republics. We vow to thee, Comrade Lenin, that we shall fulfill this thy commandment, too.

ENTIRE COMPANY

Amen!

STALIN

In leaving us, Comrade Lenin ordained us to keep faith with the principles of the Communist International. We vow to thee, Comrade Lenin, that we shall not spare our lives in the endeavor to strengthen and broaden the alliance of the workers of the whole world—The Communist International!

ENTIRE COMPANY
(In roaring response)

Amen!

(The ENTIRE COMPANY, *the* POLITBURO *included but with the exception of* STALIN, *suddenly sink to their knees, bare their heads, lower their faces.)*

STALIN
(Chanting)

Dear Father Lenin!
Dear Little Father!
Who is our Father?

ENTIRE COMPANY

Our Father is Thee!

STALIN

Our Father in Flesh!

ENTIRE COMPANY

Our Father in Bone!
Dear Father Lenin!
Our Father is Thee!

(The ten soldiers raise their rifles preparing to fire a salute.)

STALIN

One night in November, Nineteen Thirty-two, Stalin's wife, Nadezhda Alliluyevna, returned from visiting friends and committed suicide. She was not quite thirty-one years old.

(The soldiers fire. It is deafening. The lights go out.)

Curtain

The Latent Heterosexual

To My Son Dan

THE LATENT HETEROSEXUAL *was presented by Paul Baker at the Dallas Theatre Center, Dallas, on March 18, 1968, with the following cast:*

(In Order of Appearance)

IRVING SPAATZ	Jules Munshin
HENRY JADD	Preston Jones
JOHN MORLEY	Zero Mostel
ARTHUR LANDAU	Randy Moore
SECRETARY	Betty June Lary
LESTER FREITAG	Barnett Shaw
CHRISTINE VAN DAM	Chris Richard
JIMMY CHURCHILL	Maurice Harrel
MEL DELANEY	Fritz Lennon
LANDAU'S SECRETARY	Roberta Rude
NURSE	Margaret Webb
ATTENDANT	Harry Porter
HANDYMAN	Tim Green
DR. KLUNE	Ken Latimer

Directed by Burgess Meredith
Settings by Virgil Beavers
Lighting by Matt Tracy
Costumes by Ryland Merkey

SCENE 1

The office of IRVING SPAATZ, *a tax consultant: October 11, 1960, in the after-noon. At curtain rise,* SPAATZ *(short, in his fifties, bespectacled, necktied, as serene as a Buddha) ushers in* HENRY JADD, *a middle-aged intellectual, and* JOHN MORLEY, *an enormous Bodenheim of a man in his forties, the hero of our play. He wears an ill-fitting suit and is on the verge of tears.* JADD *and* MORLEY *carry coats which* SPAATZ *takes and drops on the upstage couch.* MORLEY *sinks down onto the couch and stares piteously off.* JADD *hands* SPAATZ *a large envelope and sits in the client's chair facing* SPAATZ *across the desk.*

JADD
(A man under strain)

We appreciate your seeing us, Irving. We won't take up much of your time. Here's Mr. Morley's royalty statements and the notices the government sent him. Mr. Morley's the author of *A Corporation of Cadis*, which we published on our spring list last year. It's sold over forty thousand in hard cover to date. The paperback version, as of October one—Dell works on the calendar year—at any rate, Lamarchina, the man at Dell, says it should do a million, even a million five—well, you've got all the figures there. Anyway, this grotesque man here has made a potful...

SPAATZ
(Studying the papers JADD *gave him)*

Some seventy-two thousand last year.

JADD

Yes, and Stanley Kramer bought the book for the movies, though what he hopes to do with it I can't imagine. The point is, the government's attached Kramer's check, which is in the amount of sixty-seven thousand five hundred, that's less our commission for negotiating the sale. Apparently, Dell's been put on notice as well, attaching all Morley's money there too, you see (MORLEY *breaks into a sob*) because the stupid son of a bitch didn't pay his taxes last year.

SPAATZ
(Still studying the papers)

He's apparently not paid his taxes for any year.

(ARTHUR LANDAU, *a lawyer in his forties, bespectacled, likewise serene, likewise necktied and in shirt sleeves—obviously the canonicals of this priestly caste—enters. He smiles benignly at* JADD *who waves freely back.*

363

LANDAU *pulls a chair up to the desk, takes the papers which* SPAATZ *holds out to him and silently examines them.)*

JADD

Irving, Mr. Morley here's one of our disenfranchised aesthetes. Such *bürgerlich* rituals as paying taxes are entirely alien to him. I've known him since he was a reedy boy of eighteen, if you can imagine him reedy. I was editing a little magazine in Chicago in those days. He came swishing in with a sheaf of short stories, spinsterly things about sensitive Cincinnati schoolboys whose English teachers turn out to be faggots. His style has changed since then, of course. He is currently one of the leaders of the panic-stricken participle school of writing, and his subject is less maiden-ly. *The New York Review* described his last book as fetid...

MORLEY

(Muttering)

Fecaloid. Norman Mailer wrote the review.

JADD

In that case, it was probably fecaloid. At any rate, Morley's book is about the homosexual community in Tangiers. Hot sperm spurting and smooth-skinned Arab boys on every page, some instant Upanishad here and there and what is perhaps meant to be Swiftian satire on American middle-class-ness. This fecaloid pile of prose is presented to us as man's search for serenity, a search presumably conducted with a proctoscope...

MORLEY

(Erupting from the couch)

You old fruit! An hour ago you were comparing me to Proust.

JADD

(Just as shrilly)

I said you had a Proustian tendency to the agglutinization of detail!

MORLEY

I never agglutinized a detail in my life!

JADD

(In a state)

Irving, I can't tell you what I've been through today! This fruitcake has been trying to slash his wrists with a letter opener all morning. I must explain to you, Irving—this man's a miser. I mean miser in the total cari-cature of the word. I mean, he actually has a little room on the fourth floor of his house where he keeps two brass-bound coffers—so help me, God!— two little pirate's chests filled with antique gold pieces—doubloons, napoleons, Russian imperials, half-neds and louis d'or; and he sits up there in that little room—I'm not making this up, I've seen it with my own eyes!—he sits up there counting and cackling over these gold pieces. For hours! It's absolutely elemental, Irving, that you grasp this fact about this grotesque man! Well, I called the nut this morning, and I said: "John, Random House has received a note from the government telling us to hold any money we've received for you, because of nonpayment of taxes." There was this long pause. Then Richard, that little flit he has living with him, got on the phone hysterically. In the background, I hear inhuman shrieks. "What the hell's going on, Richard?" I said. "He's lamenting," said Richard, "He's rending his caftan and lamenting." "Rending his caftan?" I said. "Is he wearing a caftan?" "Yes," said Richard, "He's wearing a caftan, a green-striped izar and a fringed cashmere girdle." Which gives you some idea of what I mean by grotesque. On top of everything else, this nut's a junkie and, by the time I got to his place, he was floating around in a narcotic trance. Irving, if you've never seen a faggot junkie poet caparisoned in a yellow caftan, green-striped izar and a fringed cashmere girdle, slashing at his wrists with a letter opener—well, now you know what I've been through all morning. I don't like to trouble you with this kind of nonsense, Irving...

SPAATZ

It's no trouble, Henry.

MORLEY
(*Screaming at* JADD)
You also compared me to Joyce! You said I had revivified poetry in the novel form, not as Wilde and Pater did, by lacquered ornamentation—

JADD

I never said any such thing. It sounds like Alfred Kazin.

MORLEY

Kazin detested my book. He told me so personally.

JADD

Nonsense, he resolutely compared you to Hawthorne.

MORLEY

He compares everyone to Hawthorne! And I wasn't trying to slash my wrists with that letter opener. I was doing with that letter opener what you're supposed to do with letter openers—I was trying to open a goddam letter. That very letter Mr. Spaatz is looking at right now, as a matter of fact, that announcement from my bank that the government has put a lien on my house! Well, goddam! What kind of depraved despotism is this! I'm not going to pay a penny, Spaatz! I finally hit with one lousy book which took me twenty-five years to write! What about all those years I waited on tables and scrubbed floors and scraped for tips guiding tourists in Marrakesh—

JADD

Oh, for God's sakes!

MORLEY

And you clam up, you papist!

JADD

Papist?

LANDAU

Mr. Morley, do you have any records that go to prove you worked twenty-five years on your novel?

MORLEY

Crates of it.

JADD

As a matter of fact, Random House is considering publishing his journals.

MORLEY

What I try to do, you understand, is capture stylistically the fragments of terror which is the human condition. Kazin thought the whole thing gibberish. You son of a bitch, I said, forty thousand in hardback alone isn't gibberish. Kazin, you understand, has come out strongly for the lyric poetry of William Blake, a reasonably safe predilection in the middle of the twentieth century. Oh, would all our lyricism be so orderly. Am I right? Eh? Today, we deal with the plummeting hysteria of prose. Hyphen. The hell with it. Pussy on the table. Listen, Spaatz, boobie, for God's sakes, help me. This is the first money I've ever made. Don't let them take it away! Please, don't let them take it away! For God's sakes, don't make me crawl! Leave me a shred of dignity!

JADD

My God, will you go back and sit down!

> (MORLEY, *who had fallen to his knees in a posture of supplication, returns to the couch, where he sits, moaning softly and occasionally beating his breast.* JADD *leans back in his leather chair, closes his eyes and sighs long-sufferingly.* SPAATZ *and* LANDAU *study the papers of* MORLEY's *case. A long moment of silence is interrupted by* MORLEY *muttering more or less to* JADD.)

MORLEY

Agglutinization of detail. Jesus Christ! Surrealist association, you fat-assed pimp. I pinched the whole style from Eliot. "Rocks, moss, stonecrop,

iron, merds/Rat's coat, crow-skin, crossed staves in field." Eliot, Eliot, you
dim, old *fadaise*. Jesus Christ—agglutinization of detail—Jesus Christ—
>   (As MORLEY *drifts off into sullen inaudibility, there is another long silence.*
>   *Then* SPAATZ *and* LANDAU *begin a traditional murmured liturgy.*)

SPAATZ

Consistent violator?

LANDAU

Yes, if they want to get nasty about it?

SPAATZ

What are they calling it now, felony or misdemeanor?

LANDAU

They've been leaning toward felony.

SPAATZ

I think we'd better ask for sixty days. On the fifty-nine, can we throw the
spread back thirty-six months?

LANDAU

There's probably a limitation on the year.

SPAATZ

Mel just got a favorable ruling on Victor Loew.

LANDAU

And there's interest charges on the prior twenty-three years.

SPAATZ

No, this is income-splitting.

LANDAU

Maybe you're right at that.

SPAATZ

What'll we throw into sixty-one? Entertainment?

LANDAU

In my opinion, the government would resist the purchase of narcotics as
entertainment.

SPAATZ

Development and Research?

LANDAU

Yes.

SPAATZ

Not dissimilar from the Kurnitz thing.

LANDAU

They're getting rough on joint-ventures, Irving. The government was disagreeable about Kurnitz's leaseholds. We have a holding corporation threat here.

SPAATZ
I think for sixty though.

LANDAU
It's fragile. I was thinking of a foundation. By the way, we'll need a deposition from Leverett.

SPAATZ
Yes. (*To* MORLEY, *who has come out of his despair to stare fascinated through tear-filled eyes at* SPAATZ) Well, Mr. Morley, you're in one of those technical binds that come up in tax matters now and then, more frequently than you might think, as a matter of fact. Willful failure to file a tax return is punishable by a ten-thousand-dollar fine and a year's imprisonment. In the government's eyes, you've willfully failed to file tax returns since your majority, which was twenty-two years ago. Since the government has no figures on your income other than last year's, they'll assess your delinquencies on a like basis. There are interest charges of six percent on all those years. There's also a twelve-percent assessment on your willful failure to pay your quarterly installments for all those years. With all the fines, penalties and assessments, applicable to your case, you're technically liable for—how much do you make it, Arthur?

LANDAU
About five hundred thousand.

SPAATZ
That's what I have. About five hundred thousand dollars, Mr. Morley, and, of course, twenty-two years in a federal prison.

MORLEY
My God, what are you saying?

SPAATZ
The practice in cases like this is to have the client declared incompetent by a reputable psychiatrist, which takes everybody off the hook. The government would just as soon not open that can of beans, as you can readily see—

MORLEY
What can of beans? What the hell is he talking about?

SPAATZ
—and they readily accept these psychiatric depositions. We've had similar cases over the years. We generally refer our clients to a psychiatrist named Leverett, a first-rate man, associated with the Karen Horney

Institute. If you'd like, we'll arrange an interview with him.

(*He regards* MORLEY *agreeably;* MORLEY *stares back, at first incredulously and then sullenly.*)

SPAATZ

Are you offended by this, Mr. Morley?

MORLEY

No, I'm not offended. It's just such a tacky gambit, that's all. The old psychiatrist wheeze. Third-rate farce. I mean, after that black mass you and your apprentice just intoned, I'd expected something more occult. Henry said you were a sorcerer in financial matters. The arch-image of tax consultants, he said. Conjures up loopholes before your very eyes. I had expected something of a show frankly, all sorts of sinuously complex structures rising in wisps out of inkwells. Hardly this scenario psychiatrist. I don't think it's very clever. I want my money back.

SPAATZ

Well, we're going to turn you into a corporation, how's that?

MORLEY

(*Considering it, then smiling*)

Oh, I'd like that.

SPAATZ

Also a familiar tax device, I'm afraid, lacking in creative invention. The first thing any accountant does with a client of irregular income is incorporate him. So, in a few days, Mr. Morley, you'll sign papers inaugurating your career as a publishing house. Random House will actually publish your next book, your scandalous journals, but only as your agent. You'll reimburse Random House for printing, advertising, and distributing costs, for which your company will receive ten percent of the publisher's profits. You as the author will contract with yourself as the publisher for this book. How's that for sinuous complexity?

MORLEY

The most voluptuous thing I've ever heard.

JADD

There will be some compensation in royalties, of course.

SPAATZ

Of course, Henry. We're not going to do Random House dirty. We represent them too, you know. Now, Mr. Morley, we're also planning on making a charitable foundation out of you as well.

MORLEY

A charitable foundation! My God, may I call you Irving?

SPAATZ

Of course. You endow universities with scholarship funds, that sort of thing.

MORLEY

Oh, my God! Will that save me money?

SPAATZ

Well, if you were a charitable foundation right now, you could save fifteen to twenty thousand dollars on this year alone. What we would do is assign the residual rights of your already published book to your corporation, the publishing house, in exchange for twenty thousand dollars' worth of preferred stock which your corporation would issue for the purpose; which stock you then denote to your charitable foundation—is he all right, Henry?

(This last is in reference to the fact MORLEY *seems to be going through some sort of lubricious experience. He is lying sprawled on the Swedish modern couch, eyes closed and murmuring in a way that can only be described as sensual.)*

JADD

He's trying to make the point, I think, that he finds all this talk about money stimulating.

SPAATZ

I see. Well, all this doesn't help us out much for this year's taxes, of course, Mr. Morley. It will take us about a year to get a ruling on your foundation. This year, I'm afraid there's very little we can do. It may please you to know, Mr. Morley, the fee of the psychiatrist who will declare you incompetent is deductible. As is, of course, our fee here. How much do you spend a year on narcotics, Mr. Morley? We can't very well deduct them as medical expenses or entertainment, at least not in the government's appreciation of the word. But let me ask you, Mr. Morley—

MORLEY

(Opening his eyes)

For God's sakes, call me John.

SPAATZ

John, then, is there anything about dope addiction in your new book?

MORLEY

Curious you should ask. I'm beginning a book on dope addiction this very evening.

SPAATZ

In that case, we can deduct whatever you paid for narcotics last year as Development and Research.

MORLEY

Development and Research?

SPAATZ

Yes.

MORLEY

I tell you, I'm going to come any minute.

LANDAU

By the way, you won't be able to keep all those antique gold pieces, Mr. Morley. It's against the law to have private gold hoards.

MORLEY

I'll do anything you say. I'm hopelessly in love with both of you.
(*He flutters his eyes at the two tax men in shameless flirtation. He bounds happily around the room.*)

SPAATZ

I'm also going to suggest, John, that you get married to take advantage of the joint tax declaration.

MORLEY

(*Whose critical eye had been caught by an Impressionist print on the wall, now turns back to* SPAATZ, *smiling again.*)
What do you mean?

SPAATZ

You'd have to get married before the end of this calendar year if we're to derive any immediate benefit out of it.

MORLEY

(*Frowning*)
Do you mean to a woman?

SPAATZ

Well, of course to a woman. The marriage must be recognized by law. Do you have some woman friend who would go through the formality of a marriage for you? We might be able to work out something advantageous for the lady as well.

MORLEY

I don't have any women friends. (*He crosses the room to* SPAATZ's *desk where he stands, a large unkempt man, his right arm akimbo in the traditional posture of effeminacy. He smiles sweetly*) I'm a flaming faggot, Irving. I was sure you were on to that. I don't go around waving the flag, of course, and I definitely do not proselytize. Homosexuality is, to me, an inner satisfaction, a pride in a heritage of greatness. To marry a woman would be an inadmissible rejection of my identity.

SPAATZ

It'll save you about fifteen thousand dollars on your 1960 taxes.

MORLEY

Oh, well, in that case, dig someone up for me.

(*The phone on* SPAATZ's *desk rings.* SPAATZ *answers, murmurs, hangs up.*)

JADD

(*As he stands up*)

Well, Irving, we won't take up any more of your time. Set up an appointment with the psychiatrist. I'll see that this lunatic gets there. I'm sorry I had to bother you with this.

SPAATZ

(*As he too stands*)

Not at all, Henry. It was a very welcome break in the dusty routine.

JADD

Well, let's just be grateful he didn't put on his cosmetics today. He frequently does, you know.

MORLEY

(*Who has been flouncing about in a growing manic state, suddenly erupts*)

My God, this experience has been chilling! I came into this office a shattered soul, and, in a matter of minutes, you people have incarnated me into a publishing house, a charitable foundation and even a married man. It's the most goddam transcendental thing that's ever happened to me. And let me tell you, boobie, I've spent my whole life hunting down transcendental things. Back in 1940, when I was twenty-one, I went off into the Sudanese desert in search of patristic passion. Saint Anthony of Padua sort of thing. I lived entirely alone, subsisting on berries and insects, and abusing myself with the usual practices of mortification. I liked being an anchorite, and I might still be there, Christian as hell, a haggard bag of bones, but, of course, the war started. Battalions of Germans came *ein-zwei-drei*-ing down with their goddam tanks, and the British North African Army came rumbling in from El Alamein. Bang, bang, boom. Well, I'd like to see Saint Anthony operate under those conditions. I hauled my ass back to Cairo, turned myself in to the American Consulate, still wearing my tattered rags and streaming putrescence from hundreds of self-inflicted wounds. Didn't faze anyone in the American Consulate. That sort of thing's a common sight in Cairo. Well, I've spent my life trying to retrieve that serenity in the desert. Not until now have I felt so transfigured!

> **JADD**
> *(Handing* MORLEY *his overcoat)*

Yeah, well, let's go, guru.

> *(*JADD *herds* MORLEY *out of the office.* SPAATZ *closes the door after them, goes silently back to his desk.* LANDAU, *who had stood, sits again. The curtain begins slowly to descend as the two tax men begin another murmured priestly liturgy.)*

> **LANDAU**

Who've you got outside, Willie Nicholson?

> **SPAATZ**

Yes. Has Mel been keeping you up on that business?

> **LANDAU**

Yes. Who's the lending agency?

> **SPAATZ**

Hanover. I think it's premature.

> **LANDAU**

Yes, so do I.

> **SPAATZ**
> *(Picking up phone, murmuring into it)*

Send Mr. Nicholson in.

> *Curtain*

SCENE 2

SPAATZ's *office, two weeks later. At curtain rise,* SPAATZ *enters, wearing a winter coat and hat from which he brushes the snow as he hangs them on the coat-tree. He crosses to his desk.*

SPAATZ
(Picking up the phone and murmuring into it)

Lillian, is Mr. Landau in his office? *(He returns the phone to its cradle, crosses to the coat-tree, slips out of his jacket, hangs that up, and is once again restored to his familiar sacerdotal costume of short-sleeved white shirt and necktie. The phone rings. He crosses to his desk to answer it)* Arthur, that nut's here again...Well, did you see him today? He's wearing makeup. He's wearing orange lipstick and little spots of rouge on his cheeks like a kewpie doll. Please send him home.

(A SECRETARY *enters with sheaves of filing folders, correspondence and messages which she piles on the desk, already awash with documents. She sits, stenographic pad and pencil poised.)*

SPAATZ

Arthur, I have a note here from you that Lester Freitag's coming up. Is that the nonsense he spoke to me about yesterday?...Oh, dear, when's he coming up?...No, never mind, I'll call Marty Halloran right now. *(He flashes his phone)* Lillian, see if Marty Halloran at the Manhattan Regional Office is in, thank you. *(Hangs up, dictates to his secretary in the same breath)* By hand, attention of Mr. Harry Pfeiffer, re Loan Agreement between Hanover Trust Company and Nicholson and Mayer comma Inc parenthesis nineteen sixty close parenthesis underline dear Harry I enclose for your comments copies of a correspondence between the Food and Drug capital F capital D commissioners and myself. Until the F.D.A. rules on the product comma the Loan Committee capital L capital C at the Hanover Trust Company advises me Hanover will insist on an quote uncomfortable clause close quote to the effect that the Hanover Trust Company parenthesis quote the Bank capital B close quote close parenthesis shall have the right comma at any time thereafter and in their sole discretion—*(The phone rings)*—comma to demand—*(He answers the phone, fishing out a paper from his desk)* Marty, Irving Spaatz here. Listen, Marty, I've got one of those sometime things again. Do you know Lester Freitag?...Well, he's a tax lawyer, handles mostly show-business accounts.

He also handles most of the call girls in the city…Yes, one of those things. He's having a little run-in with your department right now…

(MORLEY *appears in the doorway, quite the same as he was last time we saw him except that he is indeed wearing orange lipstick, black circles of Arabian kohl around his eyes and has spots of rouge on his cheeks like a kewpie doll. Carrying his shabby coat, he shuffles in, an enormous, frightened, painted schoolboy of a man, and sits apprehensively on the edge of the upstage couch.*)

SPAATZ

Well, the girl's name is Christine Van Dam…Van Dam, V-a-n capital D-a-m. Apparently, a rug manufacturer in Detroit deducted this tart as an entertainment expense, deducted her eleven times, in fact; and some zealot in your department named Hirschkorn—

(*The second phone on his desk rings; the* SECRETARY *answers in a murmur.*)

SPAATZ

—couldn't help but stub his toe over Miss Van Dam, and this defender of the faith decided to look up Miss Van Dam's Ten-forty; and there she was, a television actress and/or model (which is how Freitag lists these tarts on their returns) who claimed to have earned two thousand three hundred dollars in fifty-nine, an improbable figure since she had earned something over six thousand dollars from the rug manufacturer alone. Jimmie, I've reflected on the matter, and the answer is still no, and, as a friend, I want to say again I think it improper for a law firm of your repute to handle this kind of client…I'm sure of that, and thank you for having considered me. Anyway, this Hirschkorn has called the girl for a hearing next Thursday, and Freitag phoned me yesterday to see if I could help nip the silly business. He's coming up in a few minutes. Can I tell him it's nipped?…Thank you, Marty. (*He hangs up and in the same breath dictates*)— from the undersigned comma and forthwith upon such demand comma assign and hypothecate to them as collateral security for the repayment of the Loan Capital L comma marketable securities having a readily ascertainable market value and acceptable to them comma equal to at least one hundred thirty percent of the then—(*The phone rings*)—unpaid principal amount of the Loan capital L and—(*He answers the phone, grunts and hangs up*)—shall deliver to them said securities comma together with blank stock powers relating thereto. Helen, tell Mr. Landau Mr. Freitag is here, would he take care of that? I've spoken to Marty Halloran, and the matter is dropped.

(*The* SECRETARY *nods, stands, exits.* SPAATZ *turns his attention to* MORLEY, *who is anxiously wringing his hands.*)

MORLEY

Arthur says you're cross with me.

SPAATZ

What'd you expect, coming down here wearing orange lipstick?

MORLEY

It's the current fashion.

SPAATZ

It's calculated mischief to attract my attention.

MORLEY

Well, you've been icy the last few days, Irving.

SPAATZ

You've been making a nuisance of yourself. I told you last week there was no reason to hang around here every day. And now the clerks complain you've taken over the library.

MORLEY

That happened only once, and I apologized the moment...

SPAATZ

John, go home. There's at least another week before they'll finish filing your corporate charter in Delaware. We've asked for and received a sixty-day extension from the Westchester Board, so we have till December sixteenth to prepare your returns. That's six weeks away, so, for heaven's sakes...

MORLEY
(Standing, frantically contrite)

You're right, of course. Please forgive me. It's just I've never had a corporation before. I know I'm hovering over it like a new mother—

SPAATZ

Yes, exactly.

MORLEY
(With growing panic)

—but I've come to it late in life, a child of my middle years, so to speak, and it's so delicate. It has this holding corporation threat. The joint venture with Random House is an utterly transparent dodge—

SPAATZ

It's entirely supportable.

MORLEY

Can't you give it some net-leaseholds, something like that?

SPAATZ

The government's been getting sticky about these syndication deals.

MORLEY

Some real estate titles—

SPAATZ

And, if Kennedy gets elected, they'll be even stickier.

MORLEY

—apartment houses, that sort of thing, for a ten-percent return. I've been reading up, you see, the management corporation retaining of course—

SPAATZ

John, for the past year the government has tended to treat title-buying as an investment and not ownership.

MORLEY

(In near hysteria)

How about mortgaging my house and investing the money in cattle-raising? I don't know how you put up with me, Irving. *(He slips into the client's chair by the desk, smiling the most enchanting smile; it's impossible not to like the man)* I went for my psychiatric examination with Dr. Leverett yesterday, Irving. I arrived promptly and behaved well throughout. His report will be entirely supportive of our case. I'm an instance of character corrosion, unable to sustain any meaningful relationships with other human beings. I relate only to inanimate things. I think of my own writings, for example, in much the same way other men think of women. This poem is a slattern, that story a bitch, this one a silly little thing but fun for a weekend.

SPAATZ

I don't see anything unusual in that. Artists have been falling in love with their own creations since Pygmalion.

MORLEY

Well, I think the doctor's point is it's one thing to fondle a statue you've sculpted; you're nuts, however, if you expect it to bear children. Dr. Leverett doesn't think I've quite reached that point yet, but I bear watching. *(Stands, moves about with gathering agitation, spasmodic in his speech and manner)* He says I'm on the verge of a breakdown. I expect he's right. I have a constant and familiar sensation of hysteria. I've gone mad before, you know. Oh, yes, I've done that turn. Eight months at Rockland State, shock treatments and all. *(Suddenly shrill and thoroughly hysterical)* I defend myself, you see, by all these theatrical excesses! I play mad so even my madness will seem a deceit! But I'm terrified it may be my only incontrovertible fragment of reality! Dr. Leverett thinks a breakdown is imminent!

He wants me to start therapy tomorrow! For God's sake, Irving, what do you think?

SPAATZ
(With sober consideration)

Well, I'd rather you didn't incur large medical expenses like that until next year when we can possibly derive some tax benefit from it.

MORLEY
(Deprived of his hysteria, goes back to his chair and regards SPAATZ *for a long moment)*

In that case, of course, I'll put my breakdown off till January.

SPAATZ

Why have it at all?

MORLEY

Good God, you mean it's not even deductible next year?

SPAATZ

Well, only those medical expenses that go beyond three percent of your adjusted gross income. It's not really worth it.

MORLEY

The hell with it, then. I won't have a breakdown at all. *(He flicks a Kleenex from its container on* SPAATZ's *desk and sets about wiping his makeup off)* You have healing powers, Irving.

(The SECRETARY *looks in inquiringly.* SPAATZ *nods to her. She enters and stands in the back, note pad in hand.)*

MORLEY

I'm going home and write that book on dope addiction you suggested so we can deduct all last year's heroin as Development and Research.

SPAATZ

Very sensible.

MORLEY
(Murmuring)

Development and Research. How goddam purposeful can you get? *(He finishes wiping off his makeup and offers his face for* SPAATZ's *approval)* All off?

SPAATZ

There's a smudge of black around your eye, but you'll need a mirror for that.

*(*MORLEY *stands, looks around for his coat, which is on the couch, as the door opens and* LANDAU, *shirt-sleeved and necktied, pokes his head in.)*

LANDAU

Irving, I've got Lester Freitag in my office. Do you have a minute?

SPAATZ

Yes. (*The phone rings.* SPAATZ *answers*) I'll be with him in few moments.
(*He hangs up.*)

LANDAU

Who's that? Willie Nicholson?

SPAATZ

Yes. (*To the* SECRETARY) Get me the rest of the Loan Agreement between
Nicholson and Mayer and Hanover.
(*The* SECRETARY *exits.*)

LANDAU

How's it going with Hanover?

SPAATZ

They're sticking to their collateral security clause.

LANDAU

Mel says you refused to buy the interim-demand.

SPAATZ

Yes, much too risky.
(*Forgotten,* MORLEY, *clutching his overcoat, slips out the door.*)

SPAATZ

I'm sorry I had to saddle you with Lester.

LANDAU

Not at all. Lester tells me this particular girl made upward of fifty thousand dollars last year. I had no idea prostitutes made that kind of money.
She can't declare any of it, of course, without getting arrested. She lives
pretty high, charges at all the good shops, and she just bought herself a
four-room co-op in Murray Hill. Lester doesn't know where he can possibly hide all that.
(*The door is thrust open, and* MORLEY, *overcoated now, roars back in.*)

MORLEY

Irving, you haven't forgotten about marrying me off, have you?

LANDAU

As a matter of fact, Irving, that's really why I dropped in just now. Do
you think we could sell Lester this curious contract?

SPAATZ

(*Taking a moment to sort this thought out*)
You're being arch, Arthur.

LANDAU

It makes a good mutual shelter. The girl could throw all her posh charge
accounts into the joint declaration, and Morley's company would pick up

that expensive co-op she just bought as a business expense.

SPAATZ

You're presuming a purely technical arrangement.

LANDAU

The statute doesn't stipulate a single marital domicile.

SPAATZ

Still, if Morley's company's picking up her flat as a business expense, I'd feel a lot better if the girl took up actual residence in Morley's home. We're vulnerable as it is on that income-splitting. I wouldn't want to throw in a totally transparent marriage as well. The examiner may lack the necessary sense of drollery.

LANDAU

Very well. Let the girl move into Morley's place. If the arrangement doesn't work out, they can get divorced January first. Technically, the government still has to recognize the marriage.

SPAATZ

I'd like to hold off on that. I've a hunch we could use the divorce better in sixty-two or sixty-three. Have you tried this out on Lester yet?

LANDAU

Yes, he's not unreceptive.

SPAATZ

(Turning to MORLEY, who hasn't quite caught up yet)

Well, John, Arthur here, usually cautious to a fault, has hit on the abandoned idea of marrying you off to a high-priced client of one of our colleagues. While the law itself does not insist you and the girl have to live together, anything less, in my opinion, would be patently evasive, and I will not recommend it. The marriage, of course, remains a purely technical one, and I understand the girl makes fifty thousand a year; which means she won't be hanging around the house very much anyway. On the plus side, marriage has many tax advantages, principally the possibility of divorce. And, of course, if you marry, you get the immediate and continuing benefit of the joint declaration which, this year alone, I think, comes to fifteen thousand.

LANDAU

It actually works out to about thirteen four.

SPAATZ

A not insubstantial saving. At any rate. I'd like you to consider this idea of Arthur's—

MORLEY

There's nothing to consider. The idea's radiant. I'd marry a mad dog for thirteen thousand four hundred dollars.

SPAATZ

I don't want you to be headlong about this, John. Marriage is a sacrament—

MORLEY

My God, you boys are on to something ultimate here, don't you know it? I tell you, I felt it the first moment I came in here—a sensation of beatitude, of illuminated innocence. One avoids nervous breakdowns because they are not deductible; one writes books because they are; one marries for the joint tax declaration; one divorces for the property settlement. My God! Don't you recognize the apocalyptic clarity of all that? Of course marry the wretched whore! You'd better find out if she'll marry me. You must make clear to her the totally technical nature of the marriage.

LANDAU

Oh, she understands all that, John.

SPAATZ

Is she here?

LANDAU

Yes, Lester brought her up. She's in my office. A stunning baggage.

SPAATZ

If she made fifty thousand last year, I would certainly think so. Why don't you bring her in? The two of them might as well meet and see what they think of each other.

MORLEY

(Petrified at the information the girl is down the hall, now bolts in terror for the door)

I'm getting the hell out of here!

SPAATZ

Take it easy, John.

MORLEY

(Panic-stricken)

She won't like me, don't you understand? I mean, look at me, for God's sakes!

LANDAU

(Standing)

Maybe we ought to put the meeting off at that, Irving. You've got Willie Nicholson waiting outside.

SPAATZ

Willie's fifteen minutes early as usual. Arthur, go fetch Lester and the girl, and, John, sit down and compose yourself.

(LANDAU *exits.*)

MORLEY
(In a state)

Look, Irving, let's be sensible about this. It was a wonderfully funny idea, of course—ha-ha-ha—but I can't insert some silly slut into my house. It'll be a circus, for Christ's sake. I have to consider Richard. He's such a dim thing. When I mentioned the idea to him last week, he burst into tears. An operating whore, for Christ's sake! Some big-titted bawd who'll flap around in the kitchen all day reading *The Daily News*! Look, I don't want her in the kitchen, is that clear? She's to stay out of my kitchen! You make that clear to her! First thing!

SPAATZ
(With some asperity)

John, you're only going to meet the girl. There's no commitment involved. If it's impracticable, of course we'll drop the idea. But if you are to get married, it'll have to be an arrangement similar to this. So sit down (MORLEY *sits*) and behave yourself. For all you know, you might like the girl.

MORLEY
(Erupting from the couch again)

Oh, my God! Here they come! Tell her to go home!

SPAATZ

Sit down, John!

(MORLEY, *who had started for and whirled away from the now opening door and who for a moment seemed to be about to hurl himself through the twelfth-floor window, jerks to a rigid halt at the penetrating sound of* SPAATZ's *voice and abruptly sinks into a sitting position on the couch. He stands again as* LANDAU *ushers in* LESTER FREITAG, *a coarser breed of tax lawyer, and* CHRISTINE VAN DAM, *an utterly beautiful girl of twenty-three. They carry their coats over their arms.* MISS VAN DAM *wears a black shantung suit, obviously expensive. A brief flurry of hellos and introductions ensues. Despite her shyness, there is something predatory in* MISS VAN DAM's *beauty. She looks at* SPAATZ *when introduced the way a man looks at a woman, seeing him naked on the first glance and considering an affair as she shakes his hand. Throughout this,* MORLEY *has braced himself with his back to the windows, staring down in petrified panic at the floor.)*

LANDAU

John, this is Miss Van Dam, Mr. Freitag—

(MORLEY *manages to nod his head a few abrupt bobs but keeps his gaze resolutely on the floor.*)

FREITAG

(*Sitting, to* SPAATZ)

Listen, Irving, you really serious about this?

SPAATZ

Of course.

(*Slowly,* MORLEY *forces his eyes up from the floor to literally boggle at* MISS VAN DAM, *who is waiting for* LANDAU *to drag a chair up for her.*)

FREITAG

(*To* SPAATZ)

Because the funny thing is I've been advising Christine here for months to marry one of these big swingers of hers from out of town—

(MISS VAN DAM, *aware of* MORLEY's *attention, turns to look at him across the room.*)

FREITAG

One guy, in particular, from Cleveland, he's ready to leave his wife and kids for her. But she's a compulsive whore—

(*Suddenly,* MORLEY *sweeps across the room to* MISS VAN DAM *and stands staring at her as he would at a painting, backing off a pace to get better light on her. The girl seems pleased by his intense scrutiny, and she smiles boldly back at him; her eyes rake him up and down with the most shamelessly wayward interest.*)

FREITAG

I could get her a studio contract tomorrow, but do you know how much legitimate income she'd have to make as an actress to come out with an adjusted gross of fifty grand a year? She's better off whoring.

MORLEY

(*Suddenly back to the couch where he sits down, crosses his legs and pats the hair over his ears in a caricature of effeminacy*)

I don't like the suit at all, dear.

CHRISTINE

(*Turning slowly around as if modeling, pinching in the skirt at the thigh*)

It's too loose here, don't you think?

MORLEY

Oh, that too. I mean, you've got a sweet ass, dear, you ought to show it. But the whole thing's much too stark for you. Where'd you get it?

MORLEY

Saks.

MORLEY

Oh, they're so contrasty at Saks. I mean, you've got this gorgeous pale face, dear, utterly dramatic in itself, you don't want simple blacks.

CHRISTINE

I think they've tailored the jacket too tight, don't you? It makes my bust bigger than I really am.

MORLEY

They've got you bulging on top like a mother, and the skirt's much too long. You need to be taken in from all directions. If I had some pins here, I could do the whole thing for you in twenty minutes. Now, sit down. I want to talk to you.

CHRISTINE
(Sitting)

I told her she was making it too tight on top and too loose on the bottom.

FREITAG

Irving, there's a couple of things—

MORLEY

Shut up. Miss Van Dam, you're to stay out of the kitchen. That's paramount. The kitchen is my province. Stay out of it. And I don't want you wandering around the house in tatty kimonos. I'm going to give you one of the guest bedrooms on the third floor. It has a view of the river if you crane your neck a bit. You will keep both room and bath impeccably clean. We have no one in to help. You know what it's like getting decent help nowadays. And I don't want stockings, brassieres and garter belts dangling from the shower rods and dripping on the tiles.

(FREITAG *chuckles, shakes his head, winks at* SPAATZ.)

MORLEY

Shut up. *(To* MISS VAN DAM, *who nods at everything* MORLEY *says like a maid applying for a position)* During your lunar indisposition, Miss Van Dam, you will simply stay out of the house altogether. I don't want to find half filled boxes of objets d'art behind the plumbing in the can. When I have friends in, stay in your room. If, by hazard, you bump into my friends, just stride rudely off without a word. You will not show your transparent tolerance of us poor deviates. Above all, stay away from the boy who lives with me. He's mine. Resist that vanity common to all women that makes each think she alone can straighten out a homosexual. If I catch you near Richard, I'll tear your eyes out—they're lovely, by the way—where do you get that delicious gray eye shadow? No visitors. I assume you will want a television set. Very well, but you will not have the use of the family car. If you have your own car, you may use the garage, but if you scratch up my Chrysler, three lawful cuts of the ground ash, my dear. You may use the telephone, the one in the front hall, not the one in the kitchen, and no more than three times in one day and for no longer than three minutes at any one time. Neither Richard nor I expect cheerful hellos in the morning. We prefer you do not join us at meals. If you have to go into the town of Ardsley, see to it you conduct yourself with decorum. I am well liked in Ardsley. No soliciting in the streets. I occasionally have the neighbors in for dinner. Mr. Spaatz thinks you should play the mistress on these occasions. Just pass the food around and keep your mouth shut. And, of course, this above all, to thine own self be true, neither a lender nor a borrower be, and he who steals your purse steals trash, Miss Van Dam.

(He smiles his enchanting smile at her. She looks a look of utter longing at him.)

CHRISTINE

Are you really a poet, Mr. Morley? I never met a living poet.

MORLEY

Oh, there are no living poets, Miss Van Dam. We're not entirely sure there ever were. They've found some shreds of sonnets in England and, embedded in a chalk wall of a cave in France, some yet undetermined thing which might be the legendary inward eye. But all evidence, such as it is, suggests that, if there ever were poets, they were all burned into extinction during the interglacial period of despair.

(They stare at each other, enchanted.)

FREITAG

Irving, if she's going to maintain residence in Ardsley, why can't we throw off an allocable share of her New York apartment as her studio?

SPAATZ

We're writing it off as Morley's company, Lester. That's a hundred percent write-off. We can't deduct it twice.

(MISS VAN DAM leans to FREITAG and whispers. FREITAG nods.)

FREITAG

Miss Van Dam says the deal is okay with her, Irving. She'd like to get married.

CHRISTINE

(To MORLEY)

I'd like a simple ceremony, wouldn't you?

MORLEY

Yes, a small intimate affair, just a few close accountants and lawyers.

FREITAG

Well, how are we going to work this out? I understand you need this for the calendar year.

SPAATZ

The sooner the better.

MORLEY

(*Leaning toward* MISS VAN DAM)

Did you know Proust never dated his letters? What an affectation!

Curtain

SCENE 3

SPAATZ's *office, six months later. At curtain rise,* SPAATZ, JIMMY CHURCHILL, *a gray-haired corporate lawyer in his sixties, and* MEL DELANEY, *another lawyer-acolyte in the* SPAATZ *office (and consequently also shirt-sleeved, necktied, and benign), are having an impromptu conference lunch (wax-paper sandwich wrappings and plastic coffee containers all over the desk).* CHURCHILL *wears a spring suit. The phone rings.* SPAATZ *answers.*

SPAATZ

I said, no calls.
(*He hangs up.*)

DELANEY

Well, we can't expose your people in this transaction, Jimmy.

CHURCHILL

Christ no. Have you any idea of the punitive action they'd face? (*Scans the front page of* The New York Times *lying on the desk; to* SPAATZ) Boy, your people are in a lot of trouble!
(*There is a knock on the door and* LANDAU, *shirt-sleeved, necktied, bespectacled, benign, pokes his head in. He smiles to* DELANEY, *waves cheerfully to* CHURCHILL—"*Hi, Jimmie*"—*and calls softly to* SPAATZ, *who is now in deep speculation.*)

LANDAU

Irving, I've got John Morley coming up in a few minutes.

SPAATZ

Who?

LANDAU

Morley. The novelist Henry Jadd brought up last October. You said yesterday you'd like to say hello.

SPAATZ

I'm all jammed up, Arthur. Give him my best.
(LANDAU *smiles, exits, closes the door softly after himself.*)

CHURCHILL
(*Standing*)

Why don't I call my people, see how it sits with them so far?

DELANEY
(*Rising*)

Use my office, Jimmie. I have a direct line outside.

CHURCHILL
(To SPAATZ*)*

There's no trouble amending the certificate?

SPAATZ
(Deep in meditation, murmurs)

It's a family corporation.

DELANEY

I'll be right back, Irving.

*(*SPAATZ *merely nods.* DELANEY *ushers* CHURCHILL *out. The door closes.* SPAATZ *is alone onstage. He sits, a Buddha-like man, his hands folded in his lap, his face a mask of meditation. Then he reaches over for* The New York Times *on the desk and rereads a front-page item which apparently concerns a client of his. He picks up his phone.)*

SPAATZ

Ask Arthur if he'd come in, please.

(He hangs up. The door opens, and MEL DELANEY *returns.)*

DELANEY

They're going to insist on a proprietary interest in any intermediate agency—

SPAATZ

Mel, do you remember this fellow Morley that Arthur was last talking about? He was that nutty novelist who used to hang around here about six months ago. He used to wear lipstick. I think we introduced you once.

DELANEY

Oh, yes.

(The door opens and ARTHUR LANDAU *slips silently into the room, closing the door softly behind him. He sinks back on the couch upstage, crossing his legs.* DELANEY *stretches out on one of the client chairs.* SPAATZ *leans back in his swivel chair behind the desk, folds his hands on his belly; and the three shirt-sleeved monks engage in an interchange.)*

SPAATZ

Arthur, let me try something on you. Has Mel been keeping you up on this Nicholson and Mayer business?

LANDAU

I've been reading the papers, of course.

DELANEY

Hanover just blew the whistle on them.

LANDAU

Surely, that's not unexpected.

SPAATZ

They're in the hole for four million dollars plus contracts and commitments for construction and merchandising in the amount of nearly twenty millions. Now, Jimmie Churchill, who's in Mel's office now, approached me some months ago to handle the accounts of a foreign investment syndicate with a lot of accumulated cash in Switzerland.

LANDAU

How foreign is this syndicate?

DELANEY

Let's just say it can't be a principal in the loan.

SPAATZ

It's Mafia money, Arthur. Specifically, it's Frank Tosca's money.

LANDAU

Frank Tosca? Presumably, Irving, this loan would be in the form of convertible debentures. Surely, a reputable drug company like Nicholson and Mayer...

SPAATZ

As Mel says, the syndicate can't be a principal to the loan.

LANDAU

You're suggesting Morley's corporation as intermediary?

DELANEY

It'll throw a hell of a lot of dividend income into it.

LANDAU

They'll want a proprietary interest.

SPAATZ

Fifty percent for, say, fifty thousand.

DELANEY

You'll have to throw in something better than that, Irving, maybe a hundred percent of the Class B.

LANDAU

That'd have to be issued.

DELANEY

You'll need a Swiss subsidiary.

SPAATZ

I think we ought to form in Liechtenstein first.

LANDAU

To hold foreign distribution rights?

SPAATZ

Something like that. Has this publishing company of Morley's published anything yet?

LANDAU

As a matter of fact, we've got a small unreasonable accumulation of capital. They've put out two books of his in conjunction with Random House, and they're both doing well.

SPAATZ

I think we're on firm ground here, don't you, Mel?

DELANEY

Hell, yes.

LANDAU

Let me throw it at Morley when he comes up.

DELANEY

Isn't he the guy you married off?

SPAATZ

Yes. How's that working out, Arthur?

LANDAU

Very well, it seems. Irving, I know I told you about the time with the man from White Plains.

SPAATZ

(Reflecting a moment and then beginning to wheeze out a rusty chuckle)
Oh, dear me, yes, oh yes, that curious library—

DELANEY

What's so funny?

LANDAU

Well, apparently, Mr. and Mrs. Morley have fallen dementedly in love with each other.

DELANEY

You've got to be kidding, Arthur. He was a howling faggot, wasn't he?

LANDAU

Well, perhaps not. *(To* SPAATZ*)* Did you ever get a chance to read that psychiatric report Dr. Leverett sent in. *(*SPAATZ's SECRETARY *enters to clear away the lunch things on* SPAATZ's *desk)* Frances, ask Louise to bring in Mr. Morley's files; they're on my desk.
(The SECRETARY *exits bearing paper plates, wrappers and containers.)*

DELANEY

Look at Irving, will you? He's going to bust a binding in a minute.
(Indeed, SPAATZ *is chortling, grunting and chuckling away.)*

LANDAU
(*Chuckling just a bit himself*)

Well, I had to go up to Morley's house last December. By this time, Morley had been turned over to the Collection Division, and I was dealing with a man named Gutman.

DELANEY

Don't know him.

LANDAU

We were claiming income-splitting, and Morley had trunks and crates of journals and diaries which went to our case; so we decided to hold the examination at his house. Accordingly, I picked up this Gutman at the Ardsley depot at ten o'clock in the morning, and we drove out to Morley's house, which is one of those shambling, gray, turn-of-the-century, four-story clapboard buildings with dormers and filigreed balconies; you can see it from the river. Both Mr. and Mrs. Morley were in the driveway waiting to greet us. Morley was wearing a red-checked lumberman's mackinaw and smoking a cigar. Mrs. Morley had her arm linked through his; they were smiling; it seemed strange. I asked Mrs. Morley how long she'd been living up here. She said three weeks. I asked how it was going, and she said, "Great!" She kept hanging on her husband's arm with what I thought a questionable excess of affection. Gutman asked me if they were newly married. I said yes. Then we went into the house, which, I must say, gave Gutman and me quite a start. You walk into almost total darkness and the smell of incense. That incense takes a little getting used to. Morley, who had been under a Turkish influence at the time he bought the house, had achieved a plausible look of Levantine voluptuousness by having knocked out the walls of what had been an entrance foyer, parlor, living room and dining room to make one large inner room, a sort of inner courtyard. There were divans, yataghans, cushions and rugs everywhere. The walls and windows were covered with hangings and rich baldaquin tapestries on which were hand-painted blue and gold cypress trees and incarnadine peacocks. I had to take Morley's word for that since, as I say, the room was almost black. About now, Gutman was beginning to see this wasn't going to be a run-of-the-mill examination, especially when, as we were going up the dark stairway, Mrs. Morley apparently reached over and fondled him briefly.

(SPAATZ, *whose chortling jag had momentarily subsided begins to wheeze and chuckle even more rustily than before.*)

DELANEY

What do you mean?

> LANDAU

I mean, she stuck her hand inside his overcoat and gave him a quick tug.

> DELANEY

The examining agent?

> LANDAU

Yes.

> DELANEY

You've got to be kidding, Arthur.

> LANDAU

I'm only telling you what Gutman told me. I heard this gasp, and then Gutman grabbed me by the arm in the darkness and said: "What the hell is this?" I said: "What?" He said: "She just give me a feel." Well, we continued up the stairs, but Gutman was clearly put off by the experience. He kept muttering: "What kind of nuthouse is this?" Well, then, Morley took us into his library, which was on the second floor and—

> DELANEY
> *(Chortling)*

You mean she just grabbed his pintle, just like that?

> LANDAU

Yes.

> *(The three tax men are now all cackling and hissing laughter. Indeed, tears stream from* DELANEY's *eyes, and he has to stand and stomp around a bit, clutching his sides.)*

> LANDAU

Well, Morley ushered us into his library, which he warned us was, quote, cluttered. Mel, it was stupefying. It has to be seen to be believed. It took up the whole of the second floor. Here again, Morley had knocked out all the walls of what must have been three bedrooms, and the enormous room that resulted had been turned into one impenetrable jungle of books. Rank, fetid, streaming with books, the floor a matted tangle of them. Stacks, piles of them, some neatly bound, others growing to terrifying heights. Books ramified from the walls and dangled from the ceiling, at least fifty thousand of them, hard cover, soft cover, dust-jacketed, leather bound, vellum, folios, manuscripts, codices, incunabula, tomes and directories, first editions, texts, manuals, lexicons, thesauri, novels, romances, quartos, octavos, duodecimos, grammars, primers, Bibles, Korans, sutras, scrolls, parchments, megillah, gray, green, brown, blue, red, yellowed with age, black with grime, spotted with coffee and food stains and smelling eternally of what Morley announced to be that most civilized of all smells, the primordial musk of doubt. Morley obviously was a very bad case of book hoarding. He still had primers bearing the imprimatur of the Cincinnati Public School system.

SECRETARY
(Entering with a small pile of manila file folders which she puts on the desk)
Mr. Morley's here.

SPAATZ
(Standing)
I'll fetch him. You tell Mel the rest of the story.
(SPAATZ *exits with* LANDAU's SECRETARY.)

LANDAU
(Leafing through one of the files just brought in)
There's not much more to tell really. Ah, here— *(He has found the page in the file he was looking for)* This is the psychiatrist's deposition we had to get on Morley. Standard boiler plate, and then, suddenly, at the end, the doctor says he doubts Morley's a homosexual. *(Reads)* "His primary background suggests impotence rather. The patient seems to have had a few shattering adolescent experiences and took for granted he was homosexual. I suggest he had mistaken his terror of sexual impotence for a terror of women, his inability to fulfill the male role for a desire to play the female role."

DELANEY

How about that?

LANDAU
(Continuing reading)
"In America, a country whose national lunacy is virility, where a man's measure is the multiplicity of his erections—and where a high officer of our government is said to have interrupted councils of state to unzipper his pants, unleash his beef and flop it on the conference table, saying: "Has Mao Tse-Tung got anything like that?"—in such a society, impotence is far more of a stigma than homosexuality, and the patient might well have fancied himself a homosexual all these years just to maintain his self-respect."

DELANEY
(Standing)
Or his sanity.

LANDAU
Yes, the doctor makes that point too. *(Reads)* "The patient's theatrical posture of effeminacy seems to be the only recognizable identity he can find for himself. In all probability, the patient's ego structure would collapse without this pretense to homosexuality."

(The door opens, and SPAATZ *ushers in* MORLEY. LANDAU *closes the file and stands. There is a smiling flurry of hellos.)*

SPAATZ

You remember Mel Delaney of our office, I'm sure, John.

MORLEY

Yes, of course, how are you, Mr. Delaney?
(Handshakes, etc. The MORLEY *we are looking at now is a noticeably different man from the* MORLEY *we last saw. He is neatly groomed in a dark-blue suit and carries his cashmere overcoat neatly folded over his arm. Most striking perhaps is the ten-gallon Stetson hat he's wearing. All traces of effeminacy have disappeared. He seems in excellent spirits.)*

DELANEY

I'd better go see to Jimmie Churchill.

LANDAU

How's Mrs. Morley, John?

MORLEY
(Smiling)

She's pregnant.
(This information raises eyebrows on SPAATZ *and* LANDAU *and causes* DELANEY *to pause.)*

MORLEY

Fourth month. It's beginning to show. How do you like them apples, Charlie?
(He extracts a cigar from his jacket pocket, nips off the end.)

LANDAU
(Reaching over to pump Morley's hand)

That's wonderful, John.

SPAATZ

Mrs. Morley must be very pleased.

MORLEY

Exuberant. I'm picking her up at the gynecologist's in half an hour, so whatever you got for me to sign, let's get at them.

LANDAU

Actually, John, the only thing that needs any discussion is we'll have to siphon off some of our unreasonable accumulation of surplus in the form of salary to you as president.

DELANEY

Congratulations, Mr. Morley.

MORLEY

Thank you, son.
(DELANEY *exits.*)

LANDAU

However, if we add a large salary to your royalty earnings, it's going to throw you into a hell of a tax bracket.

MORLEY

(Suddenly standing, beaming with enthusiasm)
I tell you, men, I'm pretty damned excited about this baby!
(He thumps LANDAU *a manly thump on the shoulder.)*

SPAATZ

For heaven's sake, John, are you speaking with a drawl?

MORLEY

A reversion to the Midwestern twang of my youth. Well, boy, what you gone do about the tax bracket you just threw me into?

LANDAU

What I want to do, John, is to have that library appraised.

MORLEY

(Pauses in the act of lighting his cigar to frown)
My library?

LANDAU

We should take advantage of your charitable foundation. We'll have a ruling on that before the end of the year.

MORLEY

Do you mean to use my library as a charitable donation?

LANDAU

Yes, you donate the library for equivalent shares of non-voting preferred stock—

MORLEY

The answer's no, thumbs down, *verso pollice*, absolutely not. I'm not likely to give away my library.

LANDAU

You only give it away in title, John. The library stays in your house on loan. Not a book leaves your house.

MORLEY

Forget it, Charlie. That library's my one incorruptible vanity. Goddam, you two boys are the blandest bastards I ever like to see. I come walking in here after six months and announce my wife's pregnant, and you boys act like you got queers walking in here all day telling you their wives are pregnant. I tell you, in your most fevered fancies, you ain't never gone conceive the improbable events of the past half year. *(Glances at his watch, takes off his Stetson, sits down, lights his cigar)* Men, I would like to think of my marriage as an enchanted state and of my wife as a water sprite who resurrected me with a kiss. But I see you have a copy of Dr. Leverett's report here, and so you already know clinically that I'm not the accomplished faggot I thought I was. Lord knows, all that crumbled the first moment my wife unzippered my corduroy trousers. She was the aggressor, of course. I just stood there, mute and trembling like a fawn throughout the whole experience. My wife is a predatory lady. Like so many women who are constantly told how desirable they are, my wife distrusts her beauty and can affirm herself only with the love of incompetent men. She has all sorts of merry ways. She likes to make covert love in public places, the men's room at Idlewild Airport. She's a Dutch girl, by the way, a bit of irrelevance that pleases me. At any rate, twenty minutes after she arrived at my home for her first visit last Thanksgiving, she ravished me ruthlessly in my library; and we've been maniacally in love with each other ever since. And I mean love. I mean, bug-eyed, unbridled, carnivorous love. Well, goddam, do you know what it's like to find out after forty years the damn thing works? Men, you're talking with the hottest pistol down to the docks! *(Puffs futilely on his cigar, which has gone out)* Well, this outlandish state of affairs would have quickly degenerated into an utterly conventional marriage except for the note of distortion brought in by the Babcock boy living in the house. Poor Richard found himself in the role of my betrayed wife, while my actual wife was thrust into the posture of my mistress. In this curiously miscast manner, the rest of the wretched drama played itself out. Christine and I now conducted our marriage as if it were a clandestine affair. She maintained the pretense of her own bedroom on the third floor, and we met only in trysts. Christine took to brazenly clumping down the stairs on her way to our midnight meetings in the library, for, like all illicit lovers, it was necessary we be caught. We kissed and fondled whenever Babcock briefly left the room, darting away from each other at the sound of his returning footsteps, and sometimes carefully not in time. He must've seen us several times, but he refused to understand. Then—one day in February, when the snow was thick on the ground, Richard was in the kitchen, and I came in from shoveling snow, wearing my red-checked mackinaw, sweating bullets and looking for all the world like something out of Jack London. I slumped onto a chair and said: "Man, I'm bushed." Christine came in at that moment, and I whacked her affectionately across the ass. Richard broke into a sweat and ran out of the room. I turned to my wife. "He knows," I said. "What shall we do?" she said. "For God's sakes," I cried, "let's deal with this like adults!" I embraced her. We kissed hotly. I simply can't tell you how futilely banal we had all become. I followed Richard up to his room for the confrontation scene. He had already shot some heroin into the deflated vein of his left arm and was beyond understanding anything I said. I plunged inexorably on regardless. "I love her!" I shouted. "I can't live without her! I'm helpless in the grip of this passion," I shouted. "If there ever was anything between us, it's over, Richard! For God's sakes, let's behave like intelligent people!" The poor hopped-up son of a bitch, utterly confused, began to cry. "For God's sakes, don't cry!" I caterwauled and stormed out of the room. (MORLEY *relights his cigar*) Well, I won't go through the whole farce. We spent the rest of the night in a series of familiar emotional scenes until I had convinced Richard grand passions were called for. We were back in the kitchen by then. He was coming off his jag. He was on a twelve-hour cycle. It was nearly midnight. We were all slumped around, drained and drawn. He got up to leave the room. He was only going to the john, but my wife and I both leaped from our chairs and seized the startled boy. "You're not going to do anything foolish?" I hissed. He realized at last something foolish was in fact expected of him, some act that would put an end to this insane play-acting, that would make credible the incredible feelings Christine and I felt for each other. Somebody had to be hurt. Love, like everything else in the human condition, is perceptible only through pain, do you agree? (*The cigar, which had gone out again, dangles from his limp fingers.* MORLEY, *suddenly saddened, stares at the floor*) About five minutes later, we heard the front door slam, and a few minutes after that we heard the grind of the Chrysler's motor disappearing into the distance of the still winter night.

SPAATZ

He drove the car over the highway embankment.

MORLEY

Yes. At the emergency parking area near the Washington Bridge. He died suspecting his heart had been broken. The homosexual community still regards his gesture with awe.

SPAATZ

You've made the whole thing up.

MORLEY

No, it happened exactly as I told it to you. It was even in the papers. (*Stands, returns the Stetson to his head*) Well, I got to get going, men. I got to pick up Maw.

(He starts for the door but is restrained by SPAATZ's *voice, barely more than a murmur, but nevertheless compelling.)*

SPAATZ

One of our corporate clients, John, is Nicholson and Mayer, the well-known pharmaceutical company, specializing in women's medications. The name might mean something to you. They've been all over the papers the last two days. They're the manufacturers of Formalex, the prenatal pill which has caused the deformed birth of seventy-odd babies. Perhaps you've read about it.

MORLEY
(Turning)

Yes, I have.

SPAATZ

Well, Nicholson and Mayer embarked on an ambitious expansion program last year, based on the prospects of being the first drug company on the market with an oral contraceptive pill, Contrex. And so they went to the banks for a four-million-dollar loan with which to begin construction. Two days ago, the roof fell in on Nicholson and Mayer. The Formalex business. Seventy-three babies, if they lived, would mature into withered, armless or legless creatures, and four young mothers had died of puerperal fever. Lawsuits totaling nearly a billion dollars in damage claims have already been filed against them, and the banks blew the whistle on them. The note, which falls due in ten days' time, is being called up by Hanover Trust. They are also committed to over eighteen million dollars in construction and purchase contracts. They're a financially sound company, and they can weather this storm if only they can get Contrex on the market. But for that they need twenty-two million dollars, and they have no place to get it. All this clear so far?

MORLEY
(Takes off his Stetson, sets it on the desk)

Yes.

SPAATZ

I know where I can get twenty-two million dollars in a hurry.

MORLEY

I never doubted that for a moment, Irving.

SPAATZ

Some months ago, I was approached by a reputable corporation counsel, Jimmie Churchill of Watts, Fitzgerald, Churchill and Whitcomb, to handle the accounts of an investment syndicate in Switzerland. What

Jimmie Churchill was in fact saying was that his client was Frank Tosca, a *capo mafioso*, who is, at this moment, facing deportation proceedings. Needless to say, I wouldn't touch the account with a ten-foot pole. However, I don't see why Tosca's investment syndicate can't lend Nicholson and Mayer twenty-two million dollars. Neither principal would want to expose this deal, of course. So we need an intermediary company by which to effect the transfer of the money. So. John, how would you like to be a *Gesellschaft?*

MORLEY

A *Gesellschaft*—

SPAATZ

The loan would be made in the following way: the foreign investment syndicate would form a Swiss corporation with a numbered Swiss bank account. You, John, in your corporate form, will reincarnate in the shape of a Swiss company, the John Morley Gesellschaft A.G. First, however, we will have incorporated you in Liechtenstein as the John Morley Société Anonyme, so that you can take advantage of the fixed tax they have in Liechtenstein. The foreign investment Swiss corporation transfers the twenty-two million dollars to John Morley Gesellschaft A.G. which turns it over to John Morley Société Anonyme, and the John Morley Société Anonyme promptly shoots the money to its parent corporation, the well-known publishing company, Morley House, Inc. in New York. Morley House, Inc. lends the money to Nicholson and Mayer at five percent with a stock option. Morley House, Inc. will immediately exercise its option because you don't want to get stuck with debenture income.

MORLEY

Good God, no.

SPAATZ

The first eighty-five percent of dividend income is not taxed, you see, while debenture income is taxed from the first dollar. The foreign invest-ment syndicate will want some control over their money, of course, so you'll have to sell them, let's say, fifty percent of your company's common stock and a hundred percent of your Class B nonvoting stock.

MORLEY

I don't remember having any Class B nonvoting stock.

SPAATZ

You'll amend your Certificate of Incorporation to issue ten thousand shares of Class B nonvoting stock which you'll sell to the syndicate for the twenty-two million dollars you'll lend Nicholson and Mayer at five percent with an option to buy their Class B nonvoting stock which they will have issued after amending their Certificate of Incorporation; in this manner, the foreign investment syndicate will have gotten the legitimate outlet for investment they want, Nicholson and Mayer will be redeemed from bankruptcy, and Morley House, Inc. will be a multimillion-dollar corporation with extensive holdings in drugs and pharmaceuticals and with two international subsidiaries.

MORLEY
(Staring at SPAATZ *as a tear slowly tracks down his cheek; in awe)*
I have seen the face of God.
*(*SPAATZ *exits.* MORLEY *and* LANDAU *are alone onstage.* LANDAU *begins to gather up the files he had brought in.* MORLEY *remains sitting rigidly and blank for a moment.)*

MORLEY
(Fluttering)
It's the most frightening sensation. I feel quite faint.

LANDAU
I'm sorry, John, I didn't hear you.

MORLEY
I said I've just felt the strangest mythopoeic feeling. Do you know how, in Greek myths, heroes are forever being turned into trees and nymphs into waterfalls? Well, I swear to you, Arthur, I have the feeling as I sit here that some sort of physical reconstruction is going on in me. I'm changing into a *Gesellschaft.* (LANDAU *smiles, turns his attention again to his files and papers.* MORLEY *stands, rather shakily; he has to hold on to the edge of the desk)* Goddamnedest thing. *(He snickers nervously, carefully puts his Stetson back on, gathers his light top-coat off the back of the chair)* If my wife calls, tell her I'm on my way. *(He exits, still shaky, knocking his elbow against the jamb as if he didn't have complete control of his faculties. His voice sounds from off)* Goodbye, Arthur.
*(*LANDAU *is now alone onstage. He experiences an odd sensation of imbalance himself. He sits in* SPAATZ's *swivel chair and frowns.)*

LANDAU
(Calls back)
Good-bye, John.
(The door opens, and SPAATZ, CHURCHILL, *and* DELANEY *come back in.)*

SPAATZ
Arthur, Jimmie's unhappy about using a publishing house. It doesn't give his principal enough leverage for future investment. They suggest form

ing a new parent corporation—Morley Associates, let's say—which would operate Morley House, Inc. as a division.

LANDAU

You've got a holding corporation.

SPAATZ

Jimmie suggests liquidating a couple of their own companies into the parent organization.

LANDAU

How are you going to split it, Jimmie?

CHURCHILL

Right down the middle.

LANDAU

I'm going to insist on a mutual buy-out clause.

CHURCHILL

That's okay with us.

LANDAU

Morley just left. I can probably still catch him at the elevators.

SPAATZ

No, let's get this thing worked out first. We can throw it at Morley later. What sort of gross do these companies have, Jimmie?

CHURCHILL

Four, five hundred thousand. As a matter of fact, I have figures on the construction company back in Mel's office.

SPAATZ

Let's have a look at them.

(*He exits, followed by* CHURCHILL *and* DELANEY. LANDAU *busies himself with his papers again. He suddenly looks up to the doorway and is startled to find* MORLEY's *head, seemingly suspended there, staring at him from the corridor.*)

LANDAU

I think you should know, John, that at this moment, you are a holding corporation called Morley Associates with three operating divisions in publishing, construction, and in interstate trucking.

MORLEY

(*Reflecting on this for a moment*)

Listen, Arthur, how much did you say donating my library will save me in taxes?

LANDAU

About twenty-five thousand dollars.

MORLEY

Go ahead with it then. Send over the appraisers.

(His head disappears. LANDAU *is again left alone onstage, frowning, troubled, somehow surely aware that extraordinary things are to happen.)*

Curtain

SCENE 4

The conference room at Morley Associates, Inc., seven months later. There is a large modern conference table with large modern conference chairs distributed around it. At curtain's rise a SECRETARY *is placing pads, pencils, pens and ashtrays in front of each chair. The door opens and* LANDAU *enters, carrying two briefcases and wearing a light coat and hat. The* SECRETARY *smiles at* LANDAU, *takes his coat and hat.*

LANDAU

Thank you. (*The* SECRETARY *exits.* LANDAU *begins to empty his briefcases of files and documents. There is a knock on the door.* MRS. MORLEY *enters hesitatingly. She wears a fur stole and looks ravishing.* LANDAU *smiles benignly at her; she smiles shyly back. They nod at each other.* MRS. MORLEY *looks around the room.* LANDAU *turns back to his files and documents*) Does your husband know you're here, Mrs. Morley? (*He reaches for the phone on the table*)

CHRISTINE

His secretary says he's with Mr. Churchill, but they're both coming down here. (LANDAU *smiles, nods, turns back to his unpacking.* CHRISTINE *smiles, nods, finds a chair in the back of the room, sits and looks around*) Well, they're very nice offices. Do they have the ninth floor too?

LANDAU
(*Unpacking away*)
Yes. Haven't you been here before, Mrs. Morley?

CHRISTINE

No.

LANDAU

My dear Mrs. Morley, I've just realized you're no longer pregnant. May I offer congratulations? Is it a boy or a girl?

CHRISTINE

It was a boy, Mr. Landau, but it was stillborn. Five weeks ago tomorrow.

LANDAU

Oh, I am sorry. I didn't know. I've spoken to your husband a number of times, but he never said anything.

CHRISTINE

He doesn't like to talk about it.

LANDAU

Of course.

CHRISTINE

Has he seemed strange to you lately, Mr. Landau?

LANDAU

No. Subdued, but I wouldn't say strange. I haven't really seen him all that much. My business with him is usually over the phone. Is something wrong?

CHRISTINE

(Muttering)

He hasn't been home in eight days.

LANDAU

I'm sorry, I didn't hear you, Mrs. Morley.

CHRISTINE

I said, he hasn't been home in eight days. He stays here in the office all the time. He sleeps here.

LANDAU

What do you mean he sleeps here?

CHRISTINE

He sleeps in his office. He must have a couch there or something. He has clothes down here, shaving equipment. He lives here, he never goes out. He hasn't even been to his analyst. I know because his analyst called this morning to find out why he's missed his last three sessions. I don't know what he does for food. I suppose he sends out for it. He sounds all right. I talk to him on the phone every day. I said to him last night: "What do you do down there, John?" He said: "Nothing. Reading. Sitting." Maybe he has a TV set in his office. I don't know.

LANDAU

I'm not sure I understand you, Mrs. Morley. Do you mean he literally lives here in his office?

CHRISTINE

His analyst says it's a hysterical reaction to the baby's stillbirth.

LANDAU

I didn't even know he was going to an analyst.

CHRISTINE

Oh, yes. About three months ago he stopped taking dope, just like that, and he started going to an analyst. He says he can't deduct the dope, but he can the analyst. Mr. Landau, I've known a few junkies in my time. I've even known one or two who kicked it. But this is the first junkie I've ever known who kicked it for tax purposes. Don't you think that's strange?

LANDAU

Well, if you need a reason for going off dope, a tax savings is as good as any.

CHRISTINE
(With urgency)

He also gave up writing. He hasn't written a word since last spring. He says it jeopardizes his company's tax position. Let me put it this way, Mr. Landau. When I first met my husband, he was a faggot, junkie, poet. Well, he stopped being a faggot, he kicked the junk, and he hasn't written a word since last spring. He's the husband of a whore, the father of a dead son. I mean, the only thing that's real to him any more is this corporation of his. He talks about it like it was alive.

LANDAU

I don't think you could call that strange, Mrs. Morley. To any good businessman, a corporation is a living thing. All of us are very fond of Morley Associates, not just your husband. As a corporation, it even has a sense of humor, having been born in ludicrous circumstances and having matured as something very close to a travesty on the American business structure. Its growth rate is phenomenal. We have to keep reducing the ratio of dividend income to gross income, you see. Your husband's partner has already liquidated three of his own companies into the corporation. One of these, a construction company in California, is building a senior citizens' development near the city of Riverside: so, not five months after Morley Associates was incorporated, it added to its corporate family a real estate development subsidiary and a real estate management subsidiary; and I don't know if your husband told you, but his own publishing company, Morley House, Inc., which has also been liquidated into Morley Associates and is being operated as a separate division, aside from its two foreign subsidiaries in Switzerland and Liechtenstein, has begun negotiations for the purchase of a local television station in Amarillo, Texas; and we are just now completing the purchase and sale of a luggage company in Saarbrücken, West Germany. You must admit your husband's corporation is a vigorous young lady. She takes up two floors of this building, a healthy, ruddy-complected, air-conditioned goddess with two hundred people on her various payrolls, her own finance department and this very well-appointed conference room. I don't find it hard to understand your husband's infatuation for his corporation. She's a raving beauty.

CHRISTINE
(*Near tears*)

He lives here, don't you understand? He's wrapping himself up inside this corporation. He's closing out the rest of the world, Mr. Landau.

LANDAU

Do you think he's going mad? Is that what you mean?

CHRISTINE

Yes, Mr. Landau, I think he's going mad.

LANDAU

What does his analyst say?

CHRISTINE

His analyst says this is a familiar withdrawal syndrome. John'll come out of it, and I just have to be patient.

LANDAU

Well—

CHRISTINE
(*Crying now*)

I love him, Mr. Landau.

LANDAU

You mustn't cry, Mrs. Morley.

CHRISTINE
(*Standing*)

I told him on the phone last night I was coming down to bring him home today. He said: "Don't intrude." I don't care what he says. I've got the Chrysler downstairs, double-parked, probably got a ticket by now, I'm going to take him home with me. I just can't watch him go mad, Mr. Landau.

> (*The door opens, and* JIMMIE CHURCHILL *enters, followed by* MORLEY. *They are both dressed as corporate executives are expected to be dressed.* MORLEY *doesn't seem at all as strange as his wife had indicated. His left leg seems a bit game, and he's affecting the use of a gnarled walking stick, but on the whole he seems less eccentric than ever. He crosses past his wife as if he didn't see her and makes for the chair at the upstage end of the conference table.* CHURCHILL, *on the other hand, turns to* MRS. MORLEY *and beams at her.*)

CHURCHILL

Well, this is nice. We don't see half enough of you, Mrs. M. Listen, why don't you and John have dinner with us tonight? (*Reaches for the phone*) I'll give Florence a ring. She's very fond of both of you.

MORLEY
(To CHRISTINE, *in glacial rage)*

I told you to stay the hell away from here. I want to be left alone! Totally, arctically alone! Get out!

(CHRISTINE darts a brief, humiliated look at each of the other men; then turns, goes to the door and exits. MORLEY promptly sits at the head of the conference table, as expressionless as a statue. CHURCHILL, in the embarrassed silence, takes another chair, reaches for the phone.)

CHURCHILL
How long's this going to take, Arthur?

LANDAU
(Arranging the enormous piles of documents he's extracted from his briefcases)

Ten, fifteen minutes at the most.

CHURCHILL
(On the phone)

This is Mr. Churchill. Get me my law office. *(Regards* MORLEY, *who is sitting stiffly, staring at the shimmering table top)* John, I think I know you well enough to say you treat your wife brutishly. She's a damned nice woman and utterly devoted to you, aside from the fact she's one of the most beautiful sights in Christendom. Florence is nuts about her. When we were up to see you that last time— *(To* LANDAU*)* Their kid, you know—

LANDAU
Yes, I know.

CHURCHILL
Damn it, John, your wife's a woman, and it doesn't demand much sensitivity to know an experience like the one she's gone through is a shocking blow to any woman's sense of femininity. And you kept asking her to tell funny stories about the men she used to know when she was on the town. I thought Florence was going to belt you over the head with that Egyptian samovar you've got in the middle of the kitchen. *(On the phone)* Janet, this is Mr. Churchill. I'm still at Morley Associates. I'll be here another ten, fifteen minutes…Yes. I know. Ask Mr. Whitcomb to hold the fort. I'm coming directly after I finish here. *(He hangs up)* My law partners are getting sore as hell. I spend more time here than I do at my own practice.

(MORLEY is now sitting in a formal executive posture at the head of the conference table, pen poised, waiting for LANDAU *to lay the first document before him.)*

CHURCHILL
I don't know why you make such a ritual out of this contract signing.

MORLEY

Because it's a ritual.

LANDAU

(*Leaning over and putting a document in front of* CHURCHILL)
As a matter of fact, you first, Jimmie.

(CHURCHILL *scrawls his signature.* LANDAU *retrieves the document, goes
to* MORLEY's *side, lays the document in front of the rigid* MORLEY.)

LANDAU

This, John, is the Secretary's Certificate, signed by Jimmie here as
Secretary, which establishes the authority of the meeting of the Board of
Directors of Morley Associates at which the motion to acquire the shares
in the Steuben Leder Aktiengesellschaft of Saarbrücken was approved.
You sign here as Chairman certifying the accuracy of Jimmie's signature.

(MORLEY *signs.* LANDAU *takes that paper away, deposits a sheaf of onion
skin in its place.*)

LANDAU

Now, these are the minutes of that Board of Directors meeting I just
spoke of, at which the acquisition of the stock was approved. Three copies,
I'm afraid. Just sign here—as Chairman, John—(*Leafs through to the next
copy*)—and here—(*Leafs through to the third copy*) and again here—
(*Transfers the sheafs to* CHURCHILL) Three copies, Jimmie—

(CHURCHILL *sets about signing.* LANDAU *places more papers in front of*
MORLEY.)

LANDAU

This is the Waiver of Notice, John, in which you, as Chairman of the
Board, waive the formal ten-day notice of the Board meeting you just
signed the minutes of. Thank you, Jimmie.

(MORLEY *signs. With one hand,* LANDAU *moves the Waiver of Notice over
to* CHURCHILL; *with the other he selects a thick wad of contracts and sets
them before* MORLEY.)

LANDAU

Now, this, John, is the Contract of Purchase and Sale between Morley
Associates and the Steuben Leder Aktiengesellschaft. Initial here, please—
and here. (MORLEY *initials.* LANDAU *flips a page*) And again here. (MORLEY
initials. LANDAU *hands* CHURCHILL *a document*) Opinion letter from the
German lawyers, you might want to see that. (*Flips another page for* MOR-
LEY. MORLEY *initials.* LANDAU *hands* CHURCHILL *another document*)
Financial reports and representations and their accountants' opinion letter. (*To* MORLEY) And here. (MORLEY *initials*) The reason we're buying this
company, John, as I think Jimmie's explained to you—(*Flips a page.* MOR-

LEY *initials)*—is because Nicholson and Mayer are marketing their contraceptive pill in March of next year, and they—yes, here—*(*MORLEY *initials.* LANDAU *flips a page.* MORLEY *initials)*—and they could conceivably declare a dividend this December on the strength of that.

CHURCHILL
(Studying the documents handed to him)

They almost went bankrupt six months ago. If they declare anything, it will more likely be next June.

LANDAU
(Flipping another page)

And your full signature as Chairman of the Board there.
*(*MORLEY *pens his signature. The process of signing has by now developed into a rhythmic ritual, in which* MORLEY'*s arm dips, he initials, the arm goes up, pauses, dips, initials, up, down, scrawl, up, down, scrawl, piston-like, mechanical.)*

CHURCHILL
(Now scanning The New York Times*)*

You going ahead with that television station in Amarillo?

LANDAU

It provides us with offsets against profits. *(He removes the signed contract from before* MORLEY, *sets another in its place)* Five copies, I'm afraid, John. Just initial wherever marked in the margins.

CHURCHILL
(Stands, stretches)

My people in Texas tell me Vice-President Johnson has a hammerlock on the whole television business down there.

LANDAU
(Examining other contracts)

Even if we run it at a loss, there'll be such appreciation we can still unload it as a capital gain at disposal. *(He flips the page for* MORLEY, *up, down, scrawl)* These contracts conclude only the first stage of the negotiations, John. The actual closing—*(Flips a page. Up, down, scrawl)*—that is to say, the passing of title—*(Flips a page, up, down scrawl)*—the transference of the German company's stock to Morley Associates—*(Flips a page, up, down, scrawl)*—will take place in about ten days; at which time, we will hold a Board of Directors meeting—*(Flips a page, up, down, scrawl)*—in which Morley Associates, as principal stockholders in the German corporation, will vote out the old Board of Directors—*(Flips page, up, down, scrawl)*— and vote in their own Board. At that same meeting, we'll conclude an ancillary bit of business—*(Flips a page)*—and your full signature as Chairman here. *(Up, down, signature.* LANDAU *sets new contract before* MOR-LEY, *up, down, scrawl)* You may recall, we set up a Liechtenstein Corporation to take care of the foreign distribution of the publications of Morley House, Inc.—*(Flips a page, up, down, scrawl)*—on which we pay a fixed tax to the Liechtenstein government of two hundred dollars a year for the next seventeen years. *(Flips a page, up, down, scrawl)* What we want to do now is to engage your Liechtenstein Corporation—*(Flips a page, up, down, scrawl)*—as the selling agents of the Steuben Leder Aktiengesellschaft—*(Flips a page, up, down, scrawl)*—so that the bulk of the Steuben company's gross—*(Flips a page, up, down, scrawl)*—which comes to nearly two million Deutsche Marks—*(Flips a page, up, down, scrawl)*—will be taxed on the fixed rate of the Liechtenstein subsidiary—*(Flips a page, up, down, scrawl)*—which, you recall, is only two hundred dollars a year—*(Flips a page, up, down, scrawl)*—providing an annual savings in taxes—*(Flips a page, up, down, scrawl)*—of some three hundred thousand dollars—*(Flips a page, up, down, scrawl)*—and your full signature there, as Chairman of the Board.

CHURCHILL
(Looking out the window now)

Is Irving still down in Washington?

LANDAU
(Setting another contract before MORLEY*)*

Yes. I just spoke to him. He says the Kennedy Administration is going to crack down on foreign corporations, but it'll be at least a year before they can push that through. In my opinion, it's well worth it. *(Flips the page for* MORLEY*)* As marked in the margins, John. *(Comes down to* CHURCHILL *at the downstage end of the table, bearing a handful of documents)* The minutes of the Board Meeting and the Waiver, Jimmie, and I think that's all for you.

> *(*CHURCHILL *sits, extracts his fountain pen, and quickly scrawls three copies of this and three copies of that. Behind them,* MORLEY'S *piston-like ritual has now been enhanced to go up, flip page, down, scrawl, up, flip page, down, scrawl.* LANDAU *begins to stack the already signed material back into a briefcase. He glances at* MORLEY *mechanically signing away, then at* CHURCHILL *also scrawling his signature, then to* CHURCHILL.*)*

LANDAU

Mrs. Morley tells me Morley hasn't been home in eight days. He hasn't left this building. He sleeps in his office.

CHURCHILL
(*Signing away*)

Maybe he's got a broad.

LANDAU

That would be too orthodox for Morley. No, this seems to be some form of agoraphobia, a terror of the outside world. According to Mrs. Morley, his analyst says it's only temporary. She's nevertheless worried about it.

CHURCHILL
(*Frowning, looking back to* MORLEY, *who initials metronomically away*)

John, have you been staying over in the office nights?

MORLEY
(*Without pausing—up, down, scrawl, flip*)

Yes. I'm withdrawing into the sanctuary of my corporate identity which I find superior to my human identity. (*He pauses in his signing; his eyes are aglow with fervor*) It is my belief that beyond the frayed little terror of life, on the far side of despair, there is a perfect and permanent identity of each of us, a consummate essence. I've caught momentary refractions of this before in my life, induced by rigorous religious practices or psychedelic drugs, but I've never felt it so strongly as I do now. I am convinced that inside this corporate identity of mine, there is serenity.

CHURCHILL
(*Muttering to* LANDAU)

He's putting us on, isn't he?

MORLEY

You've often asked me, Jimmie, what I do in my office all day. Well, I sit at my desk, hunched over the corporate accounts like a medieval sorcerer—the invoices, remittances, petty-cash receipts, manifests, bills of lading, ledgers, passbooks, balance sheets—balance sheets—it's in the balance sheets, you see. Somewhere in that infinite innocence of numbers lies the formula for ultimate unity.

(CHURCHILL *looks to* LANDAU *to see what he makes of this.* LANDAU, *who has been organizing all his papers and documents, merely smiles.*)

LANDAU
(*To* CHURCHILL)

I've drafted a letter to the Amarillo lawyers requesting additional financial information on the television station for fifty-eight and fifty-nine, Jimmie, and I've got the F.C.C. application with supporting documents and schedules with me, if you'd like to see those.

CHURCHILL

Hell, there's no hurry on that, is there?

LANDAU

None at all.

CHURCHILL
(Muttering to LANDAU*)*
So what do you think we ought to do?

LANDAU
(Shrugging)
I suppose we ought to let it ride, as long as his analyst is in touch with the situation.

CHURCHILL

He just can't live here, Arthur.

LANDAU

I'm sure he's tidy. Of course, the lease for these premises has no allocation for residential purposes, but I'm not sure he's actually violating that.

CHURCHILL
(To MORLEY*)*
For Christ's sake, John, what is it, the baby? Is that what this is all about? For God's sake, a blue baby isn't the end of the world. My niece had two. She didn't go into a morbid retreat like this. Go on home and give your wife a good bang in the sack and have another one, for Chrissakes. (MORLEY *doesn't seem to hear. Up, down, scrawl, flip page, up, down, scrawl, flip page.* CHURCHILL *mutters to* LANDAU*)* Well, look, I've got a law practice to take care of. Am I finished here? *(He crosses to the door, pauses)* Good-bye, John.

MORLEY
(Up, down, scrawl, flip page)
Good-bye, Jimmie. See you in the morning.

CHURCHILL

I'll see you, Arthur.
*(*LANDAU *smiles, nods.* CHURCHILL *exits.* LANDAU *is already at* MOR-LEY's *elbow with a new batch of documents, the first of which he sets down before* MORLEY.*)*

LANDAU

Now, John, we're setting up a pension plan for the executives and non-union personnel of the corporation. *(Up, down, scrawl.* LANDAU *flips page)* This is a copy of the first agreement. *(Up, down, scrawl)* Contributions to the pension fund are of course deductible—*(Up, down, scrawl)*—so you get an annual deduction in your personal tax—*(Up, down, scrawl)*—of twenty-five thousand dollars—*(Up, down, scrawl)*—and at age sixty-five—*(Up, down, scrawl)*—If you choose to collect your pension in a lump—*(Up, down, scrawl)* you are taxed at the minimal capital-gains rate. *(Up, down, scrawl)* This one you also have to sign as one of the trustees. *(MORLEY scrawls his signature)* And that, John, is that for today. *(He gathers the remaining documents and returns them to his briefcases. Behind him, MOR-LEY remains sitting rigidly, arm still stiffly poised, pen in hand)* Did she take my hat and coat outside, do you know?

MORLEY
(Expressionless, rigid)
Is it cold enough to need a coat, Arthur?

LANDAU
(Clamping the briefcases shut)
Not really. It's warm for September, but I'm one of those people who put on their coats the day after Labor Day and keep them on till the summer solstice. What's wrong with your leg, by the way?

MORLEY
(Rigid, expressionless)
I think it's a muscular weakness of hysterical origin, part of this agora-phobia I seem to be caught up in. It just suddenly stiffened last night.

LANDAU
(Moving to the door)
Well, take care of it.

MORLEY
I'm being very careful.

LANDAU
(At the door)
I'll see you, John.

MORLEY
Good-bye, Arthur. My best to Irving when you see him.
(LANDAU smiles, nods his priestly little nod, and exits. MORLEY is alone onstage, sitting in his frozen posture at the head of the conference table, arm rigidly up, pen poised like a dart. For a long moment, he simply sits this way. Then suddenly, despite the fact the polished table before him is desolate of any paper, MORLEY's arm comes down, he scrawls with his pen, the arm goes up, a fractional pause, then down, scrawl, up, down, scrawl, up. Then as the whole mechanical ritual continues, tears begin to track down MORLEY's cheeks and, in a moment, his shoulders shake with sobs. Grunts of anguish escape from the distraught man. And all the while he sobs and weeps, his right arm goes up, down, scrawl, up, down, scrawl. The door to the room opens, and MRS. MORLEY slips back into the room. She closes the door softly behind her and stands for a moment silently regard-

ing the singular spectacle of her husband at the table. Then she moves to a chair to the side of her husband, who, to all appearances, is not aware she is there or that her eyes are as filled with tears as his. Then, suddenly, the hysterogenic signature-signing ritual ends. MORLEY's arm sinks slackly to his lap. The pen slips from his fingers and clinks on the vinyl floor. MRS. MORLEY rises, goes to her husband, and, with some effort, manages to get him standing. She wraps his arm around her shoulder and they manage a step together toward the door.)

MORLEY
(Muttering)

My stick. Don't forget my stick. It cost seventeen bucks.

CHRISTINE
(Reaching back for the stick)

What's happened to your leg, John?

MORLEY

I don't know what the hell it is. It just stiffened on me. *(They make their way across the room to the door, MORLEY muttering)* Seventeen dollars for a walking stick I told the girl not to spend more than ten....

(MRS. MORLEY opens the door, and they exit. MRS. MORLEY reaches back with her free hand and quietly closes the door behind them.)

Curtain

SCENE 5

MORLEY's *house in Ardsley, nine months later, the afternoon of Monday, June 11, 1962. The sun shines down mercilessly on the old Hudson Valley mansion, its four floors of peeling gray paint, its rusty ironwork. The general vegetative effect is one of rankness. The trees are heavy with leaf, and the weeds and yellow wild flowers grow everywhere, even in the driveway and between the slate in the footpath. At curtain's rise,* SPAATZ, *squat, indestructible, wearing a seersucker suit, is regarding the ramshackle house and its surroundings with worry.* LANDAU, *bland, bespectacled, also in a seersucker suit, enters. He carries his inevitable attaché case.*

LANDAU
I thought I'd better bring the figures on the property arrangement.

SPAATZ
I'm not sure we should thrust everything at him at one time.

LANDAU
Jimmie insists he's lucid, and he seemed competent enough to me the last time I was here.

SPAATZ
Well, let's wait and see how it goes. What are those odd growths there?

LANDAU
I suspect they're familiar local weeds and wild flowers, marguerites and daisies and the like.

SPAATZ
I don't mind telling you I have a feeling of foreboding about this afternoon.

CHURCHILL
(Entering, wearing a summer suit)
She's gone up to tell Morley we're here.

LANDAU
Irving's worried about throwing the Liechtenstein business at him.

CHURCHILL
Stop fretting, Irving. You're not going to find a lunatic. He's simply an invalid. You've always found him all right, Arthur, haven't you?

LANDAU
Oh, yes.

CHURCHILL

By all means, tell him about the Liechtenstein ruling. He tends to drift occasionally if you just chat with him, but in matters of business he's as penetrating as ever, and the son of a bitch can be pretty penetrating, as you know. He's become reclusive, of course. He has that trouble with his leg, so he stays in his library mostly.

SPAATZ

I must say I'm looking forward to seeing that library.

LANDAU

It's been appraised and catalogued, Irving. It's no longer that jungle of literature he used to have. It looks like a public library now.

CHURCHILL

No mean sight, regardless.

LANDAU

No, indeed, still pretty impressive.

CHURCHILL

Ah!

> *(This last in reference to* MRS. MORLEY *entering. She is wearing Levis a gray V-neck sweater but somehow manages to seem totally naked)*

CHURCHILL

Chris, you remember Mr. Spaatz.

CHRISTINE

Oh, yes.

> *(The fact is,* MRS. MORLEY *gives the impression* SPAATZ *has never left her thoughts. She takes his hand, refuses to let it go, and trains a look of barely repressed rapture on him.)*

SPAATZ

Actually, Mrs. Morley, I don't think we've seen each other since you and your husband first met in my office, and that would be a year and a half ago.

CHRISTINE
(Breathlessly)

Yes.

> (SPAATZ, *a little startled to find* MRS. MORLEY *has no intention of unclasping his hand, looks questioningly at her. She quickly releases his hand and looks guiltily away, as if she had been indiscreetly exposing their secret intimacy.)*

LANDAU

You look very well indeed, Mrs. Morley.

CHRISTINE

Thank you. You look very well too, Mr. Landau.

(SPAATZ now finds she has taken his arm and is pressing against him.)

CHURCHILL

You said John was edgy today.

CHRISTINE

Well, he hasn't been good all week really. *(She darts a quick ecstatic look at SPAATZ and lets her hand fall from his arm to take possession of his hand again)* His hearing, which has been erratic for months now, faded out almost completely yesterday, and he complained that his eyes hurt this morning.

(SPAATZ looks at the other two men to see if they're aware of the flagrant pass being made at him. Neither LANDAU nor CHURCHILL seems especially concerned.)

CHURCHILL

It's very important we see him today, Chris. We wouldn't have driven all the way up here if it weren't.

CHRISTINE

Oh, listen, this visit's the best thing in the world for him. The one thing that perks him up is talking business. He's expecting you. Why don't we go up? I'll bring the coffee later. I brought some chairs from the kitchen so you can all sit.

(As she turns smiling to lead the way, she slips her hand under the flap of SPAATZ's seersucker jacket and shamelessly if briefly fondles him. SPAATZ startles and leaps back.)

LANDAU

Did you say something, Irving? *(SPAATZ can only shake his head)* She's an interesting woman, don't you agree? Jimmie tells me she takes tireless care of Morley. She dresses, bathes and feeds him as if he were a baby.

SPAATZ
(Musing)

I think this will be an afternoon I will not readily forget.

(They exit after MRS. MORLEY and CHURCHILL. The scrim rises on MORLEY's library, which indeed looks like a room in a public library. There are countless enfiladed rows of ten-foot-high wooden bookshelves, marked by category: Anthology, Biography, Fiction, History, Manuscripts, etc. Fiction is ticketed off alphabetically by little wooden markers reading H-L and so on. There are even wooden index cabinets, precisely like these in public libraries. The entire stage is filled with these racks of books, arranged in sections, except for downstage right, MORLEY's work area—where MORLEY sits in a checked shirt and rumpled corduroy trousers, barefoot. He sits

stiffly, his arms rigid on the armrests, his thin shanks shooting straight out, knee by knee. He is quite mad. This area of the enormous library room is the only one which isn't darkish; it is in fact over-illuminated by a blast of white summer sunshine bursting in through a window on the right wall. MORLEY, *staring stiffly, blankly ahead, seems unaware that his wife, followed by* CHURCHILL *and* LANDAU *and, lastly,* SPAATZ, *have entered from upstage and are coming down the central aisle toward him.)*

CHRISTINE
(Shouting from about five feet)

John! Mr. Spaatz and Mr. Landau and Jimmie Churchill are here!
*(*MORLEY *slowly turns his head just enough to acknowledge the three men standing in silhouette halfway down the aisle.)*

CHURCHILL
(Booming out)

How are you, John?
*(*MORLEY *doesn't answer; he seems sullen, rebellious. The three men come further down the aisle.* MRS. MORLEY *has started back up.)*

CHRISTINE
(To SPAATZ, *with a soft smile, suggesting an assignation is being made)*

I'm going down for the coffee and cakes now.
*(*SPAATZ *nods, smiles, and, protecting his crotch with his right hand, moves aside to let her pass.)*

LANDAU
(Seating himself at the work table)

Well, how are you, John?
*(*MORLEY *doesn't seem to have heard.)*

CHURCHILL
(Booming out)

I don't know whether Christine told you or not, John, but Frank Tosca was shot last night—

MORLEY

What are you yelling about?

CHURCHILL

I'm sorry. I thought you were having one of your deaf spells.

MORLEY

I'm not.
*(*SPAATZ *joins the men in the work area, slips onto a white kitchen chair.)*

SPAATZ
(Smiling his serene smile)

Well, John, are you up to a conference? Or would you rather we came back another time? You seem to be in a temper. (MORLEY *says nothing.* SPAATZ *takes the silence to mean he should go on)* John, Frank Tosca was shot at around nine o'clock last night by three unidentified assailants in the lobby of his apartment house on Central Park West. He was taken to Roosevelt Hospital where he died less than an hour later without ever regaining consciousness. Jimmie was notified, and he called me at home, and this morning we conferred on what to do about Morley Associates. You know, of course, that in your original contract with Tosca, you had a mutual buy-out clause providing for the cross purchase of the stock of the deceased stockholder by the survivor, and we here all recommend strongly you exercise your repurchase option and buy Tosca's stock from his estate.

MORLEY
(Murmuring)

Very well.

SPAATZ

The repurchase will be made at book value. I haven't determined that yet, but it will easily come to a couple of million dollars. However, it's the corporation that exercises the repurchase option; the money will come out of the corporation; it won't cost you anything personally.

MORLEY

Very well.

SPAATZ

Jimmie, here, who's executor, says Tosca's estate goes to his estranged wife and his two sisters who live in Naples. That's going to delay matters a little, but not very much. Jimmie'll have to draw up waivers of citation for the heirs to sign, and the waivers for the two sisters will have to be executed through the U.S. Consulate in Rome. But Jimmie says he should have all that done by the end of July.

CHURCHILL

First week in August at the latest.

MORLEY

Very well.

SPAATZ

At that point—is it sixty days, Arthur?

LANDAU

Yes.

SPAATZ

At that point, Morley Associates has sixty days to give notice to the estate of the deceased stockholder of its intention to exercise its repurchase option. That means that either at a stockholders' or a Board of Directors meeting—

(MRS. MORLEY *returns bearing a large tray of coffee, cups, plates and cakes.* LANDAU *leaps up to help her with it.*)

SPAATZ

—you, John, as the surviving stockholder, vote your shares or cause the Board to purchase back Tosca's shares, which will make you the single stockholder in Morley Associates. In effect, you are now Morley Associates, John, and Morley Associates, Inc. is you.

(MRS. MORLEY *brings a plate with a piece of cake on it to her husband.*)

CHRISTINE
(In that admonitory tone one uses with children)

I want you to have some cake. You hardly ate breakfast and very little lunch. I've taken all the raisins out, so don't tell me you don't want it.

(MORLEY *sets the plate on his lap.*)

SPAATZ

At any rate, Jimmie has already started drawing up the petition to submit Tosca's will to probate, which will take a day or two. Thank you, Arthur.

(*This last in reference to a cup of coffee poured and passed to him by* LANDAU.)

CHURCHILL

Let me call my office and push them on that.

(*He exits back up the aisle.*)

CHRISTINE
(To her husband, with motherly tut-tutting)

Now, just don't sit there with the plate on your knee. Eat it.

(MORLEY *nibbles at the cake. His wife strokes his hair affectionately, smiles at* LANDAU.)

LANDAU

Shall I pour you a cup, Mrs. Morley?

CHRISTINE

Thank you, no. I'm going to leave you to talk.

(*She smiles at* SPAATZ *with the extravagant shyness of a fawn and then at* LANDAU *and exits off up the aisle.*)

LANDAU

You're very lucky in your wife, John.

(MORLEY *stares down at his cake on his knee.*)

SPAATZ

Yes, a lovely woman, John. Obviously devoted to you. Arthur and I are now going to suggest you get a divorce.

(MORLEY looks up to regard SPAATZ briefly. SPAATZ smiles to reassure him the suggestion was not merely an idle remark. MORLEY pinches off a piece of cake, nibbles at it, makes a wry face and returns the piece to the plate on his lap.)

SPAATZ

You remember we converted your Liechtenstein subsidiary, John Morley S.A., into the selling agent for that German luggage company to get the benefit of the fixed tax rate; it saved us several hundred thousand dollars this year. Unfortunately, the Kennedy Administration is cracking down on foreign corporations. A new statute will be in effect within a few months. It'll require American corporations to report their foreign earnings and pay regular American taxes, which is at least a fifty-two-percent bite. The situation isn't totally irremediable however. This ruling applies only to foreign subsidiaries entirely owned by American companies. If the subsidiary is at least fifty percent owned by a non-American shareholder, the old tax situation continues to prevail. Mrs. Morley, we understand, still retains her Dutch citizenship. If you give her fifty percent of the stock of your Liechtenstein subsidiary, we can retain all the original tax benefits, which comes—let me repeat—to a few hundred thousand dollars every year, no mean consideration. However—*(SPAATZ uncrosses his legs and recrosses them the other way)*—however, we are now faced with another sticky business. If you make a gift to your wife of fifty percent of the Liechtenstein stock, she'll have to pay an enormous gift tax, vitiating most of the tax savings effected by the transfer. However—*(SPAATZ switches legs around again)*—Arthur informs me that if husband and wife enter a separation arrangement pursuant to a divorce, any such property arrangements are exempt from the gift tax. You get the point, I'm sure. If you were to settle fifty percent of your Liechtenstein stock on Mrs. Morley as part of the property arrangement in a divorce, you would not have to pay the government their tax on foreign subsidiaries, and Mrs. Morley would not have to pay a gift tax.

LANDAU

The divorce itself is entirely technical, you understand, John. There is no actual separation.

SPAATZ

She continues to live right here with you, John. The whole thing is done overnight. Mrs. Morley simply flies down to El Paso.

LANDAU

As a matter of fact, American Airlines has a special divorce flight, which takes off daily at four in the afternoon, I think.

SPAATZ

Mrs. Morley simply crosses the border to Juárez, and the next morning she goes to the courthouse, picks up her decree, grabs the next flight back to Idlewild, and she's back home that day. The two of you can remarry the next morning, if you want to.

LANDAU

I think that would be pushing things, Irving.

SPAATZ

The government has to recognize the divorce, Arthur.

LANDAU

Yes, but I'm afraid they might disallow the settlement, which is, after all, the purpose of the divorce.

SPAATZ

What's the time on that sort of thing, anyway, three years?

LANDAU

From date of filing.

SPAATZ

When would that be?

LANDAU

April.

SPAATZ

Sixty-six then.

LANDAU

Yes.

SPAATZ

(*Turning back to* MORLEY *and smiling*)

Arthur prefers you wait three years before remarrying. But that's only a technicality. Mrs. Morley will continue to live here all that while, and your lives will go on as they do now.

(MORLEY *lifts his right arm and with a backhand sweep sends the plate he has been holding crashing against the window on the wall, shattering it, the piece of raisinless cake crumbling to the floor.*)

MORLEY

No! (*He forces himself to stand on obviously incapable legs, clutches one of the chair's armrests for support*) I will not separate from her!

SPAATZ

I'm not sure you understand, John. The only actual separation will be for the one night Mrs. Morley flies down to Mexico.

(The strain of standing has spent MORLEY, *and he's breathing heavily)*

MORLEY

(Gasping)

No! Not one night! Not one minute! She's my last sensation of sanity!

SPAATZ

Please, John, don't take on so. It was only a suggestion. We had no idea you'd feel so strongly about it.

MORLEY

(In a hoarse, hissing whisper)

Listen to me! I'm going insane—hideous! I am literally taking leave of my senses! I no longer hear—see—taste—smell—I no longer feel pain! I no longer feel hunger or desire—I can hardly walk, I can hardly stand! I'm being stripped of all my creature functions! I'm losing all those faculties that identify me as a human entity! I am hardening! I am literally hardening into some abstract reality!

SPAATZ

I hope you've been seeing a doctor about this, John.

*(*MORLEY *exsufflates more air out of his constricted body and sits.)*

MORLEY

(Himself again)

As a matter of fact, I have.

SPAATZ

Who?

MORLEY

Your Dr. Leverett. He's been my psychiatrist, off and on, for a year now.

SPAATZ

What'd he say?

MORLEY

He told my wife I suffer from psychogenic hysteria, not violent, but I should be institutionalized. He's been here several times. He has, needless to say, been making a pass at my wife, and I told him the last time he was here that, if he patted my wife's ass one more time, he'd find me a good deal more violent than he had diagnosed. She's all I've got. If I lose her, the game's up with me. She's the only link with reality I retain. As you see, when I talk about her, I manage to be reasonably contained.

SPAATZ

Did Dr. Leverett say what he thought was wrong with you?

MORLEY

Irving, I know what's wrong with me. It's metaphysical, not medical. I'm being reified, disincarnated and converted into an abstract. I'm surrendering my human identity to take on the disembodied identity of my corporate identity. Everything human about me is atrophying. *(He leans toward* SPAATZ, *eyes glinting dementedly)* Something's being done to me. There's juju afoot. I'm being stripped of my senses—and, my God, when I think of all those Encratic practices I've pursued, the hours I've squatted under carob trees in Oriental meditation, chanting anagogic formulas—the books of Ba, the fetal cauls and fern seeds I've incanted over at midnight, the madstones, periapts and pentacles I've hung about my neck—and all for the single purpose of surpassing the senses! Well, I'm surpassing them! It's happening! Hideous! I hear you now through yards of static! I see only boneless shades of you. I can't determine day from night or whether I'm asleep or awake. The hours pass in formless, shifting terrors. All sensation of substance—walls, chairs, tables, this floor—dissolve, exfoliate into deformed chemical complexities, dazzling, colorless, horribly incomprehensible images, screaming stones—I can't breathe! I can't breathe! *(He is standing again, gasping desperately for air, and at last succeeds. He cries out into the suddenly airless room)* Oh, God Almighty, I don't want to go mad! *(His face is suddenly illuminated with terror as if by a flash of lightning. His jaw slumps slack. He strains to say something, and, after a moment forces some lifeless words from the primeval rictus of his mouth)* I—can't talk—*(Then he suddenly flings up an arm to protect himself against some invisible swooping thing and cries out a piteous and primitive moan)* Hideous! Hideous!

(Abruptly he sits again, his arms riveted to the armrests, his long lean legs straight out, knees locked together, his sizable bare feet as rigid as stone.)

LANDAU

(Understandably disconcerted by all this, stands and addresses MORLEY*)*

Shall I get your wife? *(When* MORLEY, *immobilized, doesn't answer,* LANDAU *turns to* SPAATZ*)* What do you think we ought to do?

SPAATZ

(Frowns a moment, studying MORLEY's *rigid form, and suddenly speaks)*

There's a very strong possibility N & M may decide to make a public offering of their shares and be listed on the Exchange.

MORLEY

(Crossing his long legs and saying in a normal voice, smiling even)

The New York Exchange?

SPAATZ

Yes.

MORLEY

I didn't think the governors allowed corporations on the Exchange which have nonvoting stockholders.

SPAATZ

That's just the point. They'll have to recapitalize and eliminate their nonvoting shares by converting them.

MORLEY

Nevertheless, I want you to destroy my corporate identity, Irving. I want Morley Associates liquidated.

SPAATZ

Well, it isn't all that easy, you know.

MORLEY

I want it liquidated and its assets strewn to the winds. I want it impaled at midnight through its heart. This monstrous deformity is devouring me and will devour us all in its maniacal maw. (SPAATZ *frowns.* MORLEY *stands, shouts*) I want Morley Associates liquidated! I'm the sole stockholder, and I want the thing liquidated!

SPAATZ

It's a sizable corporation with various and complex interests! It has a life of its own! It's not so easily destroyed! *(Stands)* My God, what am I arguing for? Frankly, John, I think Arthur and I ought to leave you now. We obviously overexcite you. We'll send Mrs. Morley up. It'd be better if we go, Arthur.

(*He hunches up the aisle,* LANDAU *following. When they get about halfway to the rear,* MORLEY *roars out, bringing them to a sudden halt.*)

MORLEY

My God, it's you, isn't it, Irving? You're the one who's doing this to me! All that numerological jabber, all those phylacteric incantations. You're a goddam son-of-a-bitching cabalist, aren't you?

SPAATZ
(*Murmuring to* LANDAU)

You better get his wife.

MORLEY
(*Shouting*)

The pair of you! The sorcerer and his apprentice!

LANDAU

John, please don't work yourself up into another state!

MORLEY

A year and a half ago I stumbled into your gingerbread office, a lost, frightened soul in terrified flight across the great yawning terror of doubt—a human being, in short!—and you chanted some hag-ridden formulas and dangled some fylfots and made the sign of the gammadion and turned me into a corporation!

> (LANDAU's *attention has been riveted by something in the upstage left corner of the room, obscured to us by all those racks of books. So aghast is he that he is at first unaware of the fact* MORLEY *has run amok. The raging poet has lunged against one of the book-packed ten-foot shelves and sent it crashing to the floor, toppling another rack of shelves in the process, books scattering in every direction.*)

MORLEY

My love triumphs over your sinister sacraments! I love her, and she loves me! The spell is broken, you wretched wizards!

> (*Crash! as he thrusts over a second rack, causing a small avalanche of books to pour in a spuming tumult onto the floor.*)

SPAATZ
(*To* LANDAU)

Get his wife.

> (LANDAU, *however, while stepping back to avoid still another thundering torrent of books which* MORLEY, *raging with release, has sent crashing down, remains staring in mute astonishment at offstage left. Crash! and another swash of books comes tumbling down.* MORLEY, *standing knee-deep in surging books, suddenly calms.*)

MORLEY

There—I feel much better. Don't look so frightened, Irving. I'm not going berserk. I'm only restoring some disorder to my life. There were a few months just after my marriage when I think I was happy. I'm going to restore the conditions of those days. I'm going back to my heroin, my library and my wife. You liquidate that corporation of mine, Irving. I don't care how complicated it will be—you liquidate it. Watch out to the right!

> (*He pushes mightily against another long shelf of books, sending Fiction A–D cascading to the floor in a new tidal wave of crashing bindings and pages and exposing to* SPAATZ *what* LANDAU, *shocked into muteness, has been and is still staring at. Indeed,* SPAATZ *joins him in staring, mouth agape, at offstage left. Whatever cause for astonishment is going on offstage remains obscured to* MORLEY *as well as to the audience by those racks of books still standing.* JIMMIE CHURCHILL's *voice rises suddenly from that direction.*)

CHURCHILL's VOICE
(Offstage left)

Oh, Christ, don't stop now—

MORLEY
(Heading upstage, wading ankle-deep through the books, shouting happily)
Christine! Christine!

SPAATZ
(Staring off)

Holy cow!

(Now MORLEY is also staring aghast offstage left. The happy smile has been wiped from his face.)

CHURCHILL's VOICE
(offstage left)

Goddam, what the hell—

(MORLEY suddenly stiffens like an epileptic and pitches forward onto the floor in a dead swoon.)

SPAATZ
(Calling to offstage left)

For God's sakes, Jimmie, are you out of your mind? With eleven rooms in this house, did you have to pick this one?

CHRISTINE
(Entering on her knees from offstage left, staring at her husband's body)
Did he see?

LANDAU
(Kneeling to examine Morley)

Of course he saw.

CHRISTINE

Is he dead?

LANDAU

No.

CHRISTINE

I have this compulsive attraction to impotent men, Mr. Spaatz. It's the only way I can affirm my femininity.

SPAATZ
(Squatting beside LANDAU)

That seems a curiously unnecessary thing to say at this moment, Mrs. Morley.

CHURCHILL
(Entering from offstage left, tucking his shirttail in)
I'm in love with this woman, Irving! She's the only woman I've respond-
ed to in fifteen years!

SPAATZ
(As they all struggle to raise Morley's limp body)
Yeah, well, zipper your damn pants.

CHURCHILL
(Staring at the book-strewn nightmare all around him)
What happened to all the books?

LANDAU
Maybe we better get a doctor.
*(SPAATZ and LANDAU, bearing MORLEY's limp body between them, lum-
ber back through the piles of books and manage to get MORLEY back on his
chair. Petrifaction promptly sets in. No sooner are his arms restored to the
armrests than MORLEY's head, which has been lolling on his chest, slowly
comes up, and his eyes open to stare as vacuously as a statue's.)*

CHRISTINE
John, can you hear me? *(She raises her voice)* John! Can you hear me?
(She turns away, on the verge of tears) Oh, boy—
*(LANDAU shakes MORLEY by the shoulder, tentatively at first and then
more vigorously. MORLEY sits stonily, his body renitent to the touch.)*

LANDAU
He's in a catatonic condition.

CHURCHILL
(Zippering his pants)
We better get a doctor.

CHRISTINE
(Erupting into tears)
I can't take it any more! You don't know what it's been like here. He's
going crazy, and I'm going crazy with him. I've got to get away from him.
But he'll never divorce me, never! Especially now. He's insanely jealous.
He locked me in a room on the fourth floor because he thought I was flirting with that psychiatrist, which, God knows, I was. And now, I mean, now
he's caught me, oh, my God, what's going to happen to me? And I just
can't leave him! I have to take care of him, you see! Shall I call that psychiatrist, Mr. Spaatz?
(SPAATZ frowns, then he cocks his head and regards MORLEY carefully.)

SPAATZ

(To MORLEY *suddenly)*

Well, you know, John, the government's position on these Liechtenstein corporations is understandable. They're upset by all that money being accumulated abroad by American corporations which is eventually brought back as a capital gain.

(The effect of this remark on MORLEY *is extraordinary. He suddenly sighs, leans back comfortably in his chair, sets one long leg akimbo across the knee of the other, smiles.)*

MORLEY

About how much money will this divorce save me, Irving?

SPAATZ

About two hundred thousand a year.

MORLEY

Well, what the hell are you waiting for? Take the lousy whore away.

(Saying this, he abruptly reverts to petrified state, his legs uncrossing themselves like pistons and relocking themselves into the position SPAATZ *first saw him in this afternoon, knee to knee, the arms concreting on the armrests, his eyes resuming the emmarbled vacuity of a statue.* MORLEY *has finally, for all general purposes, gone mad.)*

Curtain

SCENE 6

MORLEY's *home, a year and a half later.* MORLEY's *library, now stripped of all its books, is shatteringly empty. The only articles of furniture are a large bed with a golden coverlet and a wooden armchair of ancient elegance, a sort of curule with armrests. The general effect is one of cavernousness. Drawn Venetian blinds cover the windows, and the floor, clinically dustless, seems glazed in the subdued light. It is as bare as a madhouse. At curtain's rise* MORLEY *is propped up in bed; he wears pale-blue pajamas; he is almost unrecognizable. He seems tiny, a fragile, porcelain old man with large, blue, blinded eyes, shocking in their expression of helplessness. His hair is entirely white. He sits absolutely motionless, emmarbled. A starchily white middle-aged matron of a* NURSE *enters, carrying a red bathrobe and a hypodermic needle. She lays the bathrobe on the bed and efficiently administers the injection, to which* MORLEY *reacts no more than would stone. She sets the hypodermic down and begins the business of getting* MORLEY's *lifeless arms into the sleeves of the bathrobe; it's like dressing a doll.*

NURSE
All right, let's get the robe on now. Your visitors have just come.
(A hulking ATTENDANT *enters carrying a chair.)*

ATTENDANT
Where do you want this?
(The NURSE *indicates by a motion of her head that she wants the chair set down beside the curule.)*

ATTENDANT
Eddie's digging up some bushes. He said he'd be right up.
(A hulking HANDYMAN *appears in the doorway. He wears a mackinaw and holds a pair of pruning shears.)*

HANDYMAN
I'm here. What do you want?

NURSE
I want you to put him on the chair.
(Putting down his shears, the HANDYMAN *and the* ATTENDANT *pick up the now bathrobed* MORLEY *and carefully carry the huge doll of a man to the curule, where they set him carefully down.)*

NURSE
I think we're going to need another chair.

DR. KLUNE

No, that'll be fine, Mary, thank you.

(SPAATZ *and a psychiatrist,* DR. KLUNE, *have entered.* SPAATZ *still has his winter coat on and carries an attaché case.* DR. KLUNE *carries his coat.* SPAATZ *stares at the change in* MORLEY.)

NURSE

(To the doctor)

I just gave him a shot, but he hasn't been responding to the shots lately.

(The ATTENDANT *and the* HANDYMAN *exit.)*

SPAATZ

(To the doctor, in lowered voice)

Landau told me I'd be appalled at the deterioration, and indeed I am.

DR. KLUNE

You don't need to whisper. He can't hear you.

SPAATZ

Listen, is he capable of signing his name?

DR. KLUNE

I honestly don't know. He functions a little bit. I've been treating him with these new tranquilizers, but not very successfully. He has moments of rational behavior, but they're becoming more occasional.

SPAATZ

Are you sure he can't hear?

DR. KLUNE

He responds, as I've explained, only to stimuli affecting his corporation. He has totally identified with his corporation. I'm sure if you talk to him about his corporation, he'll hear and understand you and might even talk to you. Otherwise he has no sensory faculties at all.

SPAATZ

(Staring at MORLEY)

He's only forty-six years old, you know.

DR. KLUNE

Yes. Now, I'm a little anxious about this, Mr. Spaatz. As I understand it, you want to dissolve his corporation.

(A strange little sound escapes from MORLEY, *causing everyone to turn to him.* DR. KLUNE *moves* SPAATZ *a few paces off.)*

DR. KLUNE

As you see, he responds to anything dealing with his corporation, which is just what concerns me—the possible pain your talk with him might cause him. If whatever you're going to say is painful to his corporation, he physically suffers in response. Do you understand what I'm saying?

SPAATZ

Yes.

DR. KLUNE

Is what you're going to say to him painful?

SPAATZ

Not necessarily. There are enormous tax benefits to be derived from a liquidation, the total tax bite in such an instance being only twenty-five percent.

DR. KLUNE

Presumably, that's good.

SPAATZ

Well, he's paying fifty-two percent on his separate corporations now, and a twenty-five percent tax is obviously more attractive than a fifty-two percent bite. The point is, something has to be done. Nicholson and Mayer decided last month to make a public offering, and we've got to decide whether to accept conversion on a one-to-one basis or sell our holdings at face value. Now, Morley's company, an indefatigable monster, has been expanding at a formidable rate. At the same time, Mr. Churchill, the de-facto executive, has decided to return to his own law practice, and so there's no one left to actually administer the company. We voted yesterday to liquidate; but we require Mr. Morley's signature, he being the single stockholder, on this document I told you about over the phone, called Stockholders' Consent to Corporate Action. So, in one sense, what I'm going to say to Mr. Morley will be agreeable in that he stands to make a number of millions out of it. On the other hand, let's not kid ourselves. I'm about to persuade Mr. Morley to liquidate his corporation, and, from what you say, that would seem to mean the liquidation of Morley's physical self as well.

DR. KLUNE

No, I don't think that would happen. It might even be therapeutic to strip him of his corporate identity. At least then we'll be able to deal with him and not his delusions.

SPAATZ

Does that nurse have to stand there like that?

DR. KLUNE

Well, he might topple over otherwise. He has absolutely no control of his faculties.

SPAATZ

I regard this whole business with considerable misgivings.

DR. KLUNE

You can only try, Mr. Spaatz. It's understood, of course, that if I ask you to stop, you must.

SPAATZ

Of course.

> (SPAATZ *frowns, slips out of his coat, drops it on the bed. He comes down-stage to where* MORLEY *has been sitting stonily throughout all the preceding matters.* DR. KLUNE *remains watchfully upstage by the bed. The* NURSE *retains her tutelary position at* MORLEY's *elbow.* SPAATZ *pulls the other chair up with a scrape and sits. He unlatches the attaché case, looks up, tries a smile.*)

SPAATZ

Hello, John. (MORLEY, *of course, doesn't respond.* SPAATZ *extracts the necessary papers from his attaché case. He darts a look at* MORLEY *and erupts into his report*) I have here, John, a financial statement, both consolidated and by individual divisions and subsidiaries, wholly or substantially owned, and statements also for our affiliated companies. I have a copy for you if you want to follow along. (*Obviously not*) The significant figure on this consolidated statement is Earnings, Net, which, as you see, as of December thirty-first, 1963, came to just short of forty-seven million dollars.

DR. KLUNE
(*Moving a step closer*)

Ah—

> (SPAATZ *looks up from his papers to see* MORLEY's *blind blue eyes slowly blinking.*)

NURSE

His eyes blinked.

DR. KLUNE

Yes, I know.

SPAATZ

Shall I go on?

DR. KLUNE

Yes.

SPAATZ

Our scope in operations has expanded considerably in the past year, mostly in the field of real estate, and, as you know, we have established a separate subsidiary, the Union Safety Security Title and Guaranty Company whose gross earnings—(*He holds a paper up for* MORLEY's *steadily blinking eyes to see*)—marked Comparative Statement down near the bottom—passed over the six million mark in sixty-three, a rise of four hundred thirty-two thousand and nine dollars over the previous year. We had that nonrecurring title loss there, as you see, but net earnings rose to two hundred seventy-six thousand, four hundred and thirteen dollars, and we are, of course, optimistic about the financing of quality high-rise residential units located in several Western states.

(A low, rusty, creaking sound escapes MORLEY, *and* SPAATZ *looks up startled to find that* MORLEY *is now smiling—that is to say, the expression of a smile is now chiseled on* MORLEY's *face.)*

SPAATZ

This item here—Mortgages Receivable and Construction Loan Advances—represents first and junior liens, principally on apartment houses and commercial properties in Santa Barbara, Anaheim and Carmel, all in California. In line with our basic long-term investment policies, our major effort has been in the acquisition of properties through sale-leaseback arrangements with builders, usually our own wholly or substantially owned subsidiaries and affiliates; and, if I may call your attention now to the balance sheet for Bello Construction Company of Pasadena, California, sixty-two percent of the capital stock of which was purchased in sixty-two by our Tri-State Division, Trucking and Construction—

(Here, SPAATZ's *words drift away into inaudibility, for he can only stare speechless at the transformation going on in* MORLEY. *The hunched-over little puppet of a man to whom* SPAATZ *had first begun his report is now expanding visibly on the chair as if someone were pumping air into him. He is sitting erect and is once again recognizable as the six-foot man* SPAATZ *had known before. The vacuity in* MORLEY's *eyes has been replaced by an intense concentration which he directs at* SPAATZ *and which makes* SPAATZ *squint as if he had been caught in a bright shaft of light.)*

NURSE

Well, is that something, or isn't it?

SPAATZ

(To MORLEY*)*

Shall I go on?

*(*MORLEY's *granite-like head nods.* SPAATZ *continues, unable to take his eyes from* MORLEY, *as fascinated as a mongoose by a cobra.)*

SPAATZ

I would like, John, to take each of the divisions, subsidiaries and affiliates separately with a view toward placing a marketable value on them in the event of a most profitable opportunity for a spin-off. We have every reason to expect I.G. Farben to pick up the bulk of our foreign companies;

their German attorneys have twice made us offers. And we could readily spin off the Bello Construction Company, for example, to a syndicate representing the minority stockholders at book value which would—if you will examine the attached memorandum—come to a capital-gains profit of just short of six hundred thousand dollars. This money could then be invested in trusts and tax-exempt bonds.

(*Again* SPAATZ *finds himself sinking into silence as* MORLEY *slowly, agonizingly rises from his seat, like man emerging from the primordial slime, to stand in terrifying height directly in front of* SPAATZ, *who, perched on the edge of his chair with papers spread out on his lap, goes nervously on.*)

SPAATZ

Generally speaking, just about all your divisions and subdivisions are prospering, and, if you were to spin off just the affiliates and partially owned subsidiaries, you could effect a profit in excess of seven million dollars.

(*Suddenly,* MORLEY's *right arm shoots up to form a posture of rigid triumph, rather like the Statue of Liberty in pose, and at the same time there roars out of his grotesquely grinning mouth a grotesque cheer-like sound, as if he were trying to create the effect of a Nuremberg rally.*)

MORLEY

Aaaaaaaahhhhhh ! ! ! ! ! !

(*Poor* SPAATZ *is startled into half-standing, sending the papers and his attaché case splashing to the floor.*)

SPAATZ

(*Muttering to the doctor*)

Maybe I ought to quit. I'm frankly unnerved by this whole business.

DR. KLUNE

I'll be damned if I know what to advise you. (*He reaches up to the statue of* MORLEY *towering over him and probes* MORLEY's *upraised arm; it is rigid*) Can you give him some mildly negative news so we can at least get him back on the bed? Right now, he's in a cataleptic state, and he'll hold that arm up there forever if we don't get it down for him.

(SPAATZ, *squatting to gather the fallen papers, nods nervously, leafs through the disordered papers, finally finds the one he wants, stands.*)

SPAATZ

Of course, John, that's the rosy end of the spectrum. We have one or two unhappy accounts to report.

(*A grunt of pain escapes* MORLEY *but he retains his monstrous posture of grinning, forward-thrusting triumph.*)

SPAATZ

The fact is, your publishing division, Morley House, is very, very sick indeed. We've dumped over half a million dollars into that wretched television station in Amarillo, and we've been unable to get F.C.C. licensing. President Johnson seems to have all of Texas television tied up. Last year's winter list of books was a disaster, and we've got a four-hundred-thousand-dollar obligation held by West Texas Guaranty and Trust due in February. They might very well proceed against our other companies the guaranteed that loan.

(The effect of this news on MORLEY *is horrifying. A moan of anguish wrenches itself loose from him, and his posture of statuesque strength crumbles into one of contorted pain. The stiffly upraised arm comes plunging down to grasp at his stomach as if he had been struck there, and the grinning mask of elation is replaced in a staggering flash with an expression of excruciating agony. The* NURSE *and* DR. KLUNE *get him slowly back onto a chair where, before* SPAATZ'S *astonished eyes, he slowly deflates, dissolves, collapses back into the tiny, mute mummy of a man* SPAATZ *had found waiting for him when he first came into the room.)*

DR. KLUNE
(To the NURSE*)*

You'd better administer a sedative.

(The NURSE *heads for the door.* DR. KLUNE *hurries after her with further instructions.* SPAATZ, *left alone onstage with* MORLEY, *and upset and eager to get away, crushes all the papers back into his attaché case, grabs his coat from the bed, and makes for the door.)*

MORLEY
(In an intense whisper)

Irving—*(*SPAATZ, *at the door, looks quickly to the hallway for help, but there's no one immediately there.* MORLEY *slowly turns his head to stare at him with pitifully moist blue eyes)* Irving—

SPAATZ
(Coming slowly back into the room)

Yes, John, what is it?

*(*MORLEY'S *white face contorts with the effort to talk.)*

MORLEY
(In an intense whisper)

I want to die. I would like very much to die. Please.

(A stinging sensation of compassion shivers through SPAATZ. *Tears well in his eyes.* DR. KLUNE *reappears in the doorway, comes downstage to* SPAATZ.*)*

DR. KLUNE

Did he say anything?

SPAATZ

Yes. He said he wanted to die. Is he in such great pain?

DR. KLUNE

Yes. I think he is. It's commonly thought insanity is a refuge from the pain of life, but it isn't really. If I had to describe Mr. Morley's condition, I would say he lives constantly exposed to the ultimate terror of life which is the existential state of all men. It must be insufferable.

SPAATZ

Why doesn't he kill himself?

DR. KLUNE

He lacks the locomotor faculty, don't you see? He's utterly helpless to do anything for or to himself.

(SPAATZ *nods. The two men make for the door.* SPAATZ *pauses.*)

SPAATZ

Could I talk to him for a moment?

DR. KLUNE

Yes, of course.

(SPAATZ *frowns in thought, then comes back downstage into the echoing room.* MORLEY *hasn't moved a muscle since his last words. He seems unaware of* SPAATZ's *return.* SPAATZ *pulls the other chair up, sits, folds overcoat on his lap.*)

SPAATZ

The situation with Morley House is not unredeemable by any means, John. Our obligation to West Texas Guaranty and Trust is secured by your company's pension plan. West Texas Guaranty and Trust has been designated beneficiary. Your pension is, of course, covered by insurance, at the proportion of one hundred times your monthly pension, which, in this instance, is fifty thousand a year or four thousand a month, so you are carrying four hundred thousand dollars' worth of insurance for your pension. That's only good, of course, if you're dead, John. Do you understand what I'm saying? You could make a hell of a tax savings if you were to die, John. Can you hear me, John? It would be of great benefit to your corporation if you were to die.

(*There is no response from* MORLEY. *Indeed, he seems not to have heard a word. After a moment,* SPAATZ *stands and, feeling unbearably sad, goes back to the upstage door.*)

MORLEY
(In an intense whisper)

Irving—*(SPAATZ turns)* Thank you, Irving.

(SPAATZ nods and exits. For a long moment, MORLEY remains stony and silent. Then, slowly, he rises from his chair, turns stiffly and slowly makes his way to the bed where he finds the pruning shears left by the HANDY-MAN. MORLEY sinks slowly to his knees.)

MORLEY

Did you ever hear the story of the man who got married to get the benefit of the joint declaration, got divorced to maintain his Liechtenstein tax status, and finally killed himself on the advice of his accountant? Well, there was once this poet—not a very good one, I'm sure—but possibly the very last of his kind—

(So saying, MORLEY plunges the shears into his stomach, twisting it about with such a sureness of hand you would have thought he had committed ritual suicide many times before, his face adamantine, innocent of the pain of his disemboweling himself. With one last sigh, he sinks to the floor, just about dead, certainly beyond saving.)

Curtain